Missio Dei:

Joining God on the Adventure of a Lifetime

missio Dei

joining God on the adventure of a lifetime

Elizabeth Renicks and JuLee Davis

purposeful design®
p u b l i c a t i o n s

Colorado Springs, Colorado

Purposeful Design Publications is the publishing division of the Association of Christian Schools International (ACSI) and is committed to the ministry of Christian school education, to enable Christian educators and schools worldwide to effectively prepare students for life. As the publisher of textbooks, trade books, and other educational resources within ACSI, Purposeful Design Publications strives to produce biblically sound materials that reflect Christian scholarship and stewardship and that address the identified needs of Christian schools around the world.

References to books, computer software, and other ancillary resources in this series are not endorsements by ACSI. These materials were selected to provide teachers with additional resources appropriate to the concepts being taught and to promote student understanding and enjoyment.

Unless otherwise identified, all Scripture quotations are taken from the Holy Bible, New International Version® (NIV®), © 1973, 1978, 1984 by International Bible Society. Used by permission of Zondervan Publishing House. All rights reserved.

Scriptures marked (GNB) are taken from the Good News Bible: Today's English Version, © 1993 by Thomas Nelson. All rights reserved.

Scriptures marked (KJV) are taken from the King James Version.

Scriptures marked (The Message) are taken from *THE MESSAGE*. © 1993, 1994, 1995, 1996, 2000, 2001, 2002. Used by permission of NavPress Publishing Group.

Scriptures marked (NKJV) are taken from the Holy Bible, New King James Version, © 1982 by Thomas Nelson, Inc. Used by permission. All rights reserved.

A Walk Through the Bible by Lesslie Newbigin is reproduced by special permission of Regent College Publishing.

Because this page cannot legibly accommodate all the copyright notices, credits immediately follow the index and constitute an extension of the copyright page.

Printed in the United States of America
17 16 15 14 13 12 11 10 09   1 2 3 4 5 6 7

Renicks, Elizabeth, and JuLee Davis
  Missio Dei: Joining God on the adventure of a lifetime
  ISBN 978-1-58331-249-0   Student edition   Catalog #7078

Design team: Bethany Kerstetter, Daron Short
Managing editor: JuLee Davis
Editorial team: Karen Friesen, Cheryl Chiapperino

Purposeful Design Publications
A Division of ACSI
PO Box 65130 • Colorado Springs, CO 80962-5130
Customer Service: 800-367-0798 • www.acsi.org

Table of Contents

121468

Practices Unit

We can be overjoyed every time someone creates a window into the basic theme of the Bible and transforms it from a book about our personal salvation into a divine revelation of God's concern to reach out to all peoples and to restore all creation.
—*Ralph D. Winter, PhD, U.S. Center for World Mission, Pasadena, CA*

Preface

Divine interruptions. They are all around us. If only we have eyes to see what God is doing and ears to hear what He is saying to us.

Sometimes a particular event, a set of circumstances, or a person comes into our lives—a "divine" interruption—at just the right time to move us in a different direction. I had recently joined ACSI and was developing a curricular product on unreached people groups of the 10/40 Window. We were partnering with another organization on the project, and someone there recommended that I take the Perspectives on the World Christian Movement course. I knew that adding *one more thing to my plate* would make life more difficult—after all, I was starting a new job in a new city—but I decided to go ahead and enroll in the course. Little did I know that God would use the first speaker on the first night to turn my world upside down.

That speaker, Dr. Don McCurry, talked about the Bible as being "one story," and he (and of course, the Holy Spirit!) throughout his talk proceeded to unravel every underlying assumption I had held about the Bible and its message. Pieces that hadn't made sense in the past fell away, and new insight started to form. I had been maneuvering through life with a skewed view—like trying to drive a car that has wheels out of alignment. God was beginning to bring my focus back into alignment. I started seeing the world differently. A new passion formed.

A missional hermeneutic for interpreting the Bible provides much more than a lens through which to understand the Bible. It provides meaning and purpose for our lives. And when Jesus said, "Come, follow me," He wasn't inviting His followers to have an intellectual discussion; He was showing them *a way of life*. God wants us to fully experience life with Him, and our participation in missio Dei provides a window into the kingdom of God here on earth and the opportunity we have to influence the world around us.

Near the end of the fifteen-week Perspectives course, the speaker asked the "what" question: "What are you going to do with what you have learned from this course?" The answer came quickly, for the Lord had been preparing me for what would come next. His answer was to introduce concepts I had learned in the Perspectives on the World Christian Movement course to a new generation, and that is our purpose for writing this book. The *Missio Dei* materials were developed from the framework and some of the overarching concepts of the original course. They are designed to set you on a path of discovery, a journey worth exploring and investigating. Life is not always easy, and there are no easy answers. In this book we encourage you to ask the hard questions, such as, Why am I here? Is there a purpose for my existence? Ultimately our goal is to help you recognize that you have been placed on this earth for a purpose, for something much larger than yourself.

God formed a fabulous team of people to carry this project forward. While there were bumps in the road along this journey, God continued to reveal and reconfirm His call in the midst of challenges and setbacks. I'll never forget one of our first meetings as a writing team. At the time the task seemed enormous and impossible, but the Lord impressed Zechariah 4:10 upon my heart, and He reminded us *to not despise the day of small things*. Here we are, eight years later, with a finished book! My encouragement to you is to remember that there are no "small things" in God's economy. God takes our lives and connects us to something significant. We are a part of an epic story that has been going on from the beginning of time until this very day. I am reminded each day that we are just vessels, jars of clay. The power comes from Him (2 Corinthians 4:7).

On earth we are living "between two trees"—a tree at the beginning of God's story (the tree of the knowledge of good and evil described in Genesis 2) and a tree for the healing of the nations (found in Revelation 22:2).* May you fully experience God's presence and power as you set your feet on this path of discovery and join Him on the adventure of a lifetime!

JuLee Davis

*Concept from Rob Bell's *Nooma: Trees* (2005).

Acknowledgments

We are grateful to our families for their support and encouragement throughout the development of this book:

- To my husband, Marshall: Your support, understanding, prayers, and love are reflected throughout this book. The words *thank you* are not enough. To my sons, Will and Jackson: May God bless you through this work when you get old enough to read what Mommy was writing when you were little boys. You both brought much to bear on what is here. (ER)

- To my children and grandchildren—Gabrielle, Brenton, Jamie, Kiara, and Brooke: You are my inspiration! Your presence and encouragement were a "cup of cold water" during many stages of this journey. To my parents, LeRoy and Joyce: Your love and support are a precious gift, something I will always be thankful for. (JD)

It is impossible for a project of this scale to be completed without the diligent and faithful prayers of God's people. We are thankful for the quiet "warriors" behind the scenes who lifted our hands in the midst of battle (similar to what Aaron and Hur did for Moses in Exodus 17:10–12): Thank you for faithfully praying during each step of the process.

We are indebted to Jim Sawyer at Jim Elliot Christian School in Colorado for his involvement in the project during the early days of research for the book: Jim, your passion for inspiring high school students to live missionally is contagious, and we appreciate your insight and expertise.

We are extremely thankful that the Newbigin family and Regent Publishers allowed us to reprint Lesslie Newbigin's amazing book *A Walk Through the Bible*. May a new generation of people be exposed to the *story* of the Bible.

We are blessed to work with Pete Gannon in producing the music video *Carrier*: Pete, thank you for your passion in revealing God's heart through visual tools. We are also grateful for the ministry of Jared Anderson and for the permission we received from the team at Integrity Music to use Jared's song "Carrier."

We want to thank the church bodies at Grace Church in Alabama and at New Life Church in Colorado: Thank you for your prayers, support, and encouragement during the development of this book. Your provision of opportunities to discuss, pray through, and teach the contents of this book was a tool God used to shape and refine much of what is here. What wonderful environments to be immersed in during the writing process!

We are privileged to work with like-minded organizations that share the same vision and desire to see God's kingdom reign here on earth:

- We are deeply grateful to Dr. Ralph Winter, Greg Parsons, and others at the U.S. Center for World Mission: Thank you for your encouragement through the years of "testing the idea" to actually developing the book. Thank you for allowing us to adapt the original material for a new generation. We appreciate the work you do to inspire people to join God in His mission.

- We want to thank the staff from Caleb Resources (formerly Caleb Project): We are thankful for your partnership and encouragement while the book was being developed. We are also thankful for your beautiful images of people around the world, which we used in the music video *Carrier*.

- We are thankful for Bryan Nicholson and others at Global Mapping International: Thank you for your work in developing the maps for the History Unit. We also want to thank Patrick Johnstone at WEC International: Thank you for allowing us to use, in the creation of our maps, concepts and statistics from your upcoming publication, *The Future of the Worldwide Church: Possibilities for 21st Century Ministry*.

We are so grateful for the "collective voices" (and their publishers) that contributed to the content of *Missio Dei*. One of the exciting things we discovered while writing the book was how other authors shared a similar message. Isn't that just like God to drop a pebble and let us see the ripples!

We are blessed to have such a dedicated team of editors, designers, and support personnel who worked together to make this book a reality. It was truly a joy to see the hands, feet, eyes, and ears working together in unity for the glory of God (1 Corinthians 12:12–27).

We dedicate this work to our Lord and Savior, Jesus Christ: Thank You for inviting us to participate in Your mission here on earth. We are humbled to be a part of the work You are doing. "We have this treasure in jars of clay to show that this all-surpassing power is from God and not from us" (2 Corinthians 4:7).

Welcome to the Journey

Faith is nothing less than the consuming experience of God. It is not a set of beliefs or even a lifestyle, but breath and pulse and life itself. It is the opposite of hype; it is heartbeat. —*Leonard I. Sweet*

The gospel is not just a message to be proclaimed; it is the form of our participation in what God is doing in and for the world. —*James V. Brownson, Inagrace T. Dietterich, Barry A. Harvey, and Charles C. West*

Welcome to the journey. "What?" you may be thinking. "Did I miss boarding a plane somewhere?" Well actually, no. It isn't that kind of journey. It may at some point involve an airplane, but the journey under discussion at the moment is the journey of your life. There are basically two options: One is to take the road intended for you. The other is to head off in a direction that wasn't intended. You have a choice of which path to take. But the thing is, none of us know exactly what the intended path looks like in advance. This may sound like bad news to you, especially since you are in a stage of your life during which a lot of decisions about your future are being discussed. You may be asking yourself, "Should I go to college? Where? What should I study? What do I even want to do with my life?"

What is a person to do? If you had God's idea of the intended route for your life, it would sure be a relief, wouldn't it?

Well, there is good news and bad news.

The good news is, this book is designed to point you toward the journey intended for your life. And the bad news (or at least the not-so-definitive news): it isn't an A + B + C = "Your Specific Path" kind of book. You won't find cookie-cutter answers here. What

??

How do you feel about journeys or adventures? Does the idea of a new adventure thrill you or make you nervous? Why is that?

you will find is a lot of encouragement to embrace the absolutely essential component of a life on its intended path—an intimate relationship with God that is the foundation of joining Him on the adventure of a lifetime.

You may be wondering about the book's title, *Missio Dei*. What in the world does that mean anyway? The term *missio Dei* means literally "the mission of God." Though the phrase itself has a long history in circles of people who study the theology of mission, it is not as widely known by most Christians. But it is a phrase that perfectly sums up the perspective of the Bible. As writer Christopher J. H. Wright says, "There is one God at work in the universe and in human history, and … this God has a goal, a purpose, a mission that will ultimately be accomplished by the power of God's Word and for the glory of God's name. This is the mission of the biblical God" (2006, 64). And that is the truth that we will examine in this book. We want to look not only at how the mission of God is the centerpiece of all of history, but also at how we are invited to participate with God on that mission. Thus, the subtitle of this text is *Joining God on the Adventure of a Lifetime.*

> *"There is one God at work in the universe and in human history, and … this God has a goal, a purpose, a mission that will ultimately be accomplished by the power of God's Word and for the glory of God's name. This is the mission of the biblical God."*

We are invited to be a part of God's mission. This book and this course are intended to offer perspective on both the mission of God and how to join Him in it.

So why do we need another book about how to live for God?

It has to do with the landscape …

We are living in postmodern territory. People are beginning to think differently about all spheres of life. Christians are recognizing that the changing landscape means we have to listen very closely to how God is leading us to respond to the world around us. In his book *The Gospel According to Starbucks*, Leonard I. Sweet says it this way: "Christians have much to learn about faith as a lived experience, not a thought experiment. Rational faith—the form of Christianity that relies on argument, logic, and apologetics to establish and defend its rightness—has failed miserably in meeting people where they live. Intellectual arguments over doctrine and theology are fine for divinity school, but they lose impact at the level of daily life experience.… Life at its very best is a passionate experience, not a doctoral dissertation" (2007, 5).

Experience, not explanation, is the crux of relationship—any relationship, including relationship with God. God wants us to experience life *with* Him. One of the foundational concepts of the Bible (and also of this course) is that God is on mission all around us, and we are invited to participate in what He is up to. He invites us to join Him, to join in an adventure that along the way embraces each of our specific gifts, talents, contexts, desires, and personalities. This is an adventure you don't want to miss! "Today, too many Christians line up to follow God out of duty or guilt, or even hoping to win a ticket to heaven. They completely miss the warmth and richness of the experience of living with God. They fail to pick up the aroma of what God is doing in their part of town" (Sweet 2007, 9).

Missio Dei: Joining God on the Adventure of a Lifetime is a collection of things to think about and practices to embrace as you move down the path of your life. The contents of this book are like the items you might put together in preparation for a hiking trip or some other sort of cross-country sojourn. So, what can you expect?

Well, don't expect this book to be a guide to life with one-size-fits-all answers for you. Only God can give you the answers you need to navigate the terrain of your own life. And only in close relationship with Him can you discover what He has in store for your particular journey with Him. What you will find in this book are some tools to help you along your journey. These tools fall into four categories—Bible, culture, history, and practice—so there are four units within this book. They can be thought of as four different lenses through which to view the mission of God.

The first unit focuses specifically on the Bible, the compass part of your travel kit. It is the tool that points you in the right direction for meeting God and joining Him in His mission. You cannot participate with Him without knowing what the Bible says. So, naturally, that is our starting point. And if you think you already know what the Bible has to say about your life with God, you might be in for a surprise!

The second unit looks through the lens of culture. You can think of this section as the binoculars in your travel kit—the lenses that give you an opportunity to see beyond your immediate surroundings to the bigger, wondrous world around you. Doing this is important because we tend to be consumed by our own surroundings and our own culture. But God is not limited to one culture or one context to work through. He is at work all around the world, in ways that might amaze you. In the chapters on culture, we are going to pick

up the binoculars and take a wide-angle look around to see what God's thoughts are on these matters.

The third section of the course focuses on the narrative of history. You can think of this section of the course as a travelogue, a collection of stories from those who have come before you on this journey. Many, many people have participated with God on His mission throughout history. Checking out their perspectives, successes, and failures is instructive to us as we consider our world today. If you were planning a trip to a city that is new to you, you might consult someone who had been there before to find out the best places to stay and eat, and to learn about the best activities there. The History Unit lets you read about the varied experiences of those in the past as you prepare to journey with God in the future. Henri J. M. Nouwen says, "I have to keep my eyes fixed on Jesus and on those who followed him and trust that I will know how to live out my mission to be a sign of hope in this world" (1994). We focus on mission in the past as a way of affirming that God has always been at work and that He continues to invite us to join Him in that work to the present moment.

Finally, *Missio Dei* concludes with a unit called "Practices." Think of this section as a backpack full of essentials. On a hiking trip, you would want to make sure you have some food and water in your pack as well as other items to make your hike more manageable. In the same way, the final chapters of this book will help you explore some basic and essential practices that will nourish and assist you on your journey with God. From intimacy with God, to spiritual passion, to embracing community, we will explore some things you'll want to have as you move through life. Just as you wouldn't leave town without a few basic necessities, you won't want to go too far down the road with God without understanding some of the things you need to make that journey the best it can be.

Throughout the coming chapters, you can expect to be challenged not only in your thinking but in how you live your day-to-day experience with God and others. You will be asked to consider new ideas and to take steps into new experiences in your relationship with Jesus. Perhaps some of this thinking and action will take you outside your comfort zone. But stretching our muscles is the only way we can hike farther and longer than we have before. You are invited to stretch yourself, to participate, and to enter into a deeper understanding of the adventure of a lifetime that God invites you to join Him on.

We close with another quote from Sweet: "Imagine how different the Christian life would be if it was understood not as something to ponder or to observe in others—but as the one thing in life that has to be fully experienced" (2007, 29). Furthermore, imagine how different life would be if we as believers in Christ understood that the experience of life with God isn't simply to make our own lives richer—in other words, to fulfill *our* individual needs—but it is to fulfill a much-larger purpose. What if we recognized that God is calling us to something grand, larger than ourselves, and best lived not individually but in community, in a *kingdom*? These are some of the terrains we will be covering during the course of this book.

??

What expectations or desires do you have in relation to this course? Are you dreading it? looking forward to it? Why do you think you have those feelings?

Bible Unit

unit one

UNIT INTRODUCTION

How do you evaluate decisions you have to make on the path of your life? Do you rely on the opinion and advice of friends? Do you pray? Or do you try to muddle through and figure things out for yourself, hoping you are making the right choices and not taking wrong turns? In the following chapters, a large part of our focus will be on the Bible—a compass that can really guide your journey through life.

In this unit, we will take a look at the story of the Bible. Be prepared for it not to sound as familiar as you might expect. You see, most of us come at reading the Bible in ways that may not give us the true picture. Maybe you think you know the story of the Bible. But this may be your chance to hear it from a new perspective, as though for the first time. As we unpack it, we'll take a look at the dynamic adventure of a lifetime that God invites you to be a part of. So, let's pick up the compass and see what it reveals to us about where we are.

In this unit we'll explore the following Big Ideas:

- The Bible, from Genesis to Revelation, tells the story of God's purpose.
- God's purpose is relationship, redemption, and reconciliation.
- God invites us to participate in His purpose; He blesses us so that we can bless others.
- God's story is unfolding as we see and participate in God's kingdom throughout the earth.
- The spread of God's kingdom takes place in the context of warfare with Satan.

1

The Bible, God's Story

Truth, naked and cold, had been turned away from every door in
the village. Her nakedness frightened the people. When Parable
found her, she was huddled in a corner, shivering and hungry. Taking
pity on her, Parable gathered her up and took her home. There, she
dressed Truth in story, warmed her and sent her out again. Clothed
in story, Truth knocked again at the villagers' doors and was readily
welcomed into the people's houses. They invited her to eat at their
table and warm herself by their fire. —*Jewish teaching story*

"Tell me a story!" This request has been made by many a child. You
probably uttered these words once or twice yourself before you were
even three years old. From childhood into old age, human beings
are big fans of stories. We swap them with our friends, we watch
them on television, we even read them in books.

Part of what makes a good story is the ability of the storyteller,
whether an author, a filmmaker, or someone telling a story in person. A storyteller conveys the details of an experience or a story, and
a good storyteller invites the listener to experience the story with
him—to enter into the world of the story. Think
about the last time you got wrapped up in a good
story. Didn't it have something to do with the
telling itself?

*Some of the best
stories are ones that
communicate something
real and important to us.*

Something to know about stories is that they
aren't always fiction. Some of the best stories are
ones that communicate something real and important to us. The
Jewish teaching story above emphasizes how important a story can
be in communicating truth. We wrap truth in story all the time.
For instance, instead of telling friends the simple, truthful fact that
we were embarrassed by our recent fall in the lunchroom, we will
give all the gory details—the water we didn't see on the floor, the

fact that we were in the front of the line, the french fries that were flying all over the place, the humiliation of wearing ketchup for the rest of the day. A storyteller re-creates the experience so that the hearers feel as if they were in it.

Another factor in the success of storytelling is the hearer. If you as the hearer aren't tuned in—focusing and looking for the next turn of events—the most energetic and dynamic storyteller in the universe may not get your attention. Sometimes we bring expectations to a story that keep us from really hearing it. Maybe we think we already know how it ends or what it is really about, or we are just too distracted to hear a story at all. So how we listen affects the story.

> *Given how much we enjoy stories, it should come as no surprise that God chose story as one of the prime means by which He would reveal Himself to us.*

Given how much we enjoy stories, it should come as no surprise that God chose story as one of the prime means by which He would reveal Himself to us. And that's what the Bible is: God's story. There are plenty of people who want to identify the Bible using titles such as *God's Little Instruction Book, God's Deep Book of Theology,* or *God's Big Book of Boring Sermon Material.* But the reality is, the Bible is a story. It is truth as story.

And it is not just a set of little stories that happened to end up in one book together. True, the Bible was written over a period of many years by a variety of authors. But it is more than a collection of stories. It is *a* story. One story. That's right, from Genesis to Revelation, the Bible tells one big story of God's purpose. And what an exciting story it is—one that contains more elements of suspense and adventure than all of Hollywood put together! It is a story of creativity and imagination; of rebellion and bloodshed; of quests, adventure, discovery, and exploration. And it is a love story—from beginning to end.

But also throughout this story, you see a main character acting with purpose and for specific reasons. That character is God Himself. He is both the storyteller and the main character of this story. What you are about to read is a wonderful version of God's story, the Bible—starting with Genesis and ending with Revelation, and having lots of stops in between. In 1999, the Newbigin family had the following story, entitled *A Walk Through the Bible,* published from a series of talks that the late Anglican bishop Lesslie Newbigin (2005) broadcast and produced for Premier Radio in Great Britain. Notice the British variation in the spelling of some words, such as *neigh-*

bour instead of *neighbor*. Think of this story as a highlight reel that captures the one story that weaves its way through all the books of the Bible. As you read, you'll recognize a lot of the familiar little stories of the Bible. But listen carefully to the one big story you will hear in this telling:

A Walk Through the Bible
by Lesslie Newbigin

A Unique Account

For at least a thousand years, the Bible was, for practical purposes, the only book known to people in Europe. They didn't have it in their hands before the days of printing, of course. They knew it through the teaching of the Church: through its readings, its preaching, its liturgy and sacraments; through the cycles of the seasons of the Christian year; through art, music and architecture.

The story told by the Bible was *the* story by which people understood the meaning of their lives, and for several centuries, even after the invention of printing in Europe in the mid-fifteenth century, it was the only book most households had. Most households today have a Bible. But do people read it in the way they read other books? Do they read it as a whole, as a story from beginning to end? I think not. Most of us treat the Bible as an anthology of helpful thoughts to which we may occasionally turn, and from which we can obtain comfort, guidance, direction. And even in our readings of the Bible in church, we tend to look at only very short passages which reinforces the impression that the Bible is a collection of nuggets of wisdom from which we can choose what we find helpful. But in that case, of course, it is not the Bible itself that decides what is worth reading: we decide in advance. The Bible is not our authority.

Many years ago a Hindu friend of mine, a very learned man, said to me something I have never forgotten:

> I can't understand why you missionaries present the Bible to us in India as a book of religion. It is not a book of religion—and anyway

we have plenty of books of religion in India. We don't need any more! I find in your Bible a unique interpretation of universal history, the history of the whole of creation and the history of the human race. And therefore a unique interpretation of the human person as a responsible actor in history. That is unique. There is nothing else in the whole religious literature of the world to put alongside it.

He was right. And when he said the Bible is not a book of religion, what he meant was that it is not a book which encourages us to turn away from the down-to-earth business of ordinary life, from our responsibilities as actors in history. It does not encourage us to turn away from the world of our daily newspapers to a so-called spiritual world beyond. It is rather an interpretation of the whole of history from creation to its end, and of the human story within that creation. And that is the story I want to tell.

Before we begin, let me say three things about this story. The first thing is that every good story has a hero or heroine. The Bible has a hero and that hero is God, because the Bible interprets the whole of reality and the whole of history in terms of the actions, the doings, the speakings, the promises of God. And therefore the Bible is the way in which we come to know God, because we don't know a person except by knowing his or her story.

The second point is that the Bible tells the story of the whole human race in terms of a particular story of one race—that of Israel—and of one person within that race—Jesus of Nazareth. It doesn't directly tell us the story of China or Mexico. The story of all the nations is the background of the biblical story, as we shall see—but it is not at the centre.

God makes himself known to us in the context of our shared life as human beings.

The story is told from the point of view of the people whom God chose to be the bearers of his purpose, because God does not wish to make himself known to us in the isolation of our own individual souls. He doesn't communicate with us on a one-to-one basis as if by telephone. God makes himself known to us in the context of our shared life as human beings because that is what our human life is. We therefore come to know God through one another—and specifically through the people whom he chose to be the bearers of his purpose.

Thirdly, to be those chosen people, to be the place where God is made known in history, is to be chosen for suffering, for agony, for conflict—and that is the story that the Bible tells.

In the beginning …

And now let us turn to look at this book, and let us look at those majestic words with which the Bible opens: "In the beginning God created the heavens and the earth."…

And so we have in Genesis a picture of the creation of light to be distinguished from darkness, of the dry land to be distinguished from the chaos of the sea, of a home in which living creatures could grow and thrive, of the creation of the animals and of human beings among them, and of the special responsibility given to human beings of being in the image of God. And to this human family he has given the specific responsibility of cherishing his creation, of bringing it to that perfection for which God intended it, so that it, with the whole human race, should truly reflect his glory.

And finally, as the climax of the story we have this wonderful picture of God resting on the Sabbath day to enjoy his works, to look at his creation and enjoy it, and his gift to us human beings of that same rest, so that our life is not a ceaseless struggle but at the heart of it there is this invitation simply to rest and enjoy God. Joy is that for which the world was made. In the great words of the Scottish Catechism: "The purpose for which we were made is to glorify God and enjoy him for ever."

But as we know it is not like that now. What has gone wrong? Here we come to the Bible's unique insight. The thing we don't like to talk about. The thing that New Age spirituality tries to hide. The thing theologians call "the Fall." What has happened? We have been given freedom. And we have been given knowledge of the goodness of God. God did not want us to know evil; he wanted us to know only good. But there creeps in that little snake of suspicion: "Should we not find out for ourselves the other side of the picture? There must be another side. Why should it be hidden from us? We are free, we are responsible; is it not our duty to find out all the facts? Let us find out for ourselves what is good and what is evil. Surely we can't simply trust God for that!"

And so the fatal step is taken, the bond of trust is broken, and we are lost. We know that we are naked, vulnerable, easily hurt. We hide ourselves from God. We compete with each other. The neighbour given to us to be a neighbour becomes our rival. The world given to us to be our garden becomes a wilderness with which we have to fight.

Read about the Creation and the Fall in Genesis 1–3.

And so there comes that terrible cry echoing throughout the garden: "Adam, where are you?"

It is the cry of a mother whose child has run away in a crowded supermarket, a cry of anguish, a mixture of wrath and love; it's a cry that echoes right through the Bible as this loving and holy God seeks the children, the foolish stupid unbelieving children, who have run away because they thought they could find out for themselves better than God could tell them.

And right through the Bible runs the anguish of God as he seeks his foolish people. And it finally is echoed in that terrible cry from the cross when the son of God puts himself in the place of the rebellious Adam, in our place who have run away from God, and he cries out in anguish: "My God, my God, why hast thou forsaken me?"

God will not leave us until he has won us back to be his children.

Chosen by God

We have come to the point where Adam and Eve decided that they could not trust God but must find out for themselves what is good and what is evil. That act of mistrust brought to an end the innocent relationship with God, with one another and with the natural world.

Because now we have to depend upon ourselves to decide what is good and what is wrong, and because we know we are not capable of this, we are anxious, and because we are anxious, we become aggressive. Our neighbour becomes our rival, the natural world is no longer our home but a hostile environment to be tamed. There is a descent into violence. And the story is told with terrible clarity in the following chapters of Genesis. The first two brothers, Cain and Abel, become respectively murderer and victim. Murder, jealousy, strife become the order of the day, and the whole human world degenerates into chaos in a spiral of violence.

Noah is chosen

And so the point comes when God is sorry that he started the experiment. He decides to wipe the earth clean of this evil race, keeping only one family to make a fresh start—the family of Noah. And when that family comes out of the ark on to land which is once again dry, God makes a gracious covenant with Noah—and not only with Noah but with the whole creation—promising that never again will he destroy the earth, promising that Noah's descendants

Read about Noah's story in Genesis 6–9.

will fill the world and replenish it with happy people, and providing in the rainbow a sign of his promise.

And so in the next chapter (Genesis 10) we have the beginning of the fulfilment of that promise: the seventy nations into which the Hebrew people divided the human world are described as the descendants of Noah. They are what in the rest of the Bible are called the Gentiles or the heathen; they are the background of the whole story. They are introduced to us here as the result of God's promise to Noah, and throughout the Bible they are the ultimate recipients of God's blessing. But once again the same sad story is repeated. The nations who are spread over the earth are no longer content to have what one might call a human's eye view of the world. Once again they want a God's eye view. "Let us build a tower with its top in heaven so that we can really see the whole scene from above and not just from below."

And so there is the tower of Babel, or Babylon—symbol of all the great imperial powers that have sought to unify people on the basis of a human programme.

ABRAHAM IS CHOSEN

But once again the end is disaster. The human race is scattered in mutual incomprehension around the world. And once again the patient God makes another fresh start. From among these heathen nations he chooses one man, a wealthy man, with many flocks and herds and servants, living in one of the great centres of power and civilization of the ancient world—Ur of the Chaldeans. And God calls this man to leave his home, his wealth, his security, and to go to a land which he does not know, trusting only in the promise of God.

Here is the beginning of a new kind of human living, one that does not depend on the securities we have accumulated over the past, but depends wholly on what God has promised for the future. A new kind of life—living by faith. And so Abraham makes his journey into the land of Canaan, and with his son Isaac and his grandson Jacob they live there as strangers in a foreign land—a land which has been promised to them and yet in which they possess nothing except a grave in which to bury their dead.

But even here, these people called to the life of faith are once again subject to grave trial. Famine drives them into Egypt where they become first of all refugees and then slaves, oppressed, downtrodden by the most powerful military regime in the known world.

The tower of Babel is described in Genesis 11:1–9.

The lives of Abraham, Isaac, and Jacob and his sons are described in Genesis 12–50.

Exodus 1 describes these events.

Eventually they become so numerous that their oppressors call for population control. The male Israelites are to be slaughtered. One of them escapes: Moses is rescued by a daughter of Pharaoh, and brought up in the imperial court.

MOSES IS CHOSEN

As a young man Moses becomes an heir to the riches, the learning, the culture, the science, the technology of the greatest civilizing power in the world at that time. And yet he knows at the same time that these slaves are his kinsmen. One day in a fit of fury, seeing an Egyptian beating one of his fellow Israelites, he loses his temper and kills the Egyptian, and then when his sin is discovered, flees, and takes refuge as a double refugee among the tribe of Canaanites in the Sinai peninsula.

There he marries his employer's daughter and settles down to the life of a shepherd. But God has not forgotten his promise. One day as Moses is out with his flocks in the shimmering heat of the desert he sees a bush burning and yet not being consumed. And coming near to see what is going on he hears himself addressed: "Moses, Moses."

"Yes?"

"I am sending you to rescue my people from Egypt."

"Who me? You must be joking! A fleeing rebel? Who am I to rescue your people?"

"But I will be with you."

"But who are you? If I go to the Israelites and say, 'Someone, I don't know who, has sent me to rescue you,' won't they ask me who he is? What is his name? What is your name?"

" 'I will be who I will be.' That is my name. 'Yahweh.' 'Jehovah.' 'The Lord.' Your ancestors knew me by the name that all Semites know for God, 'Allah,' 'El,' but they did not know my personal name. This is my name. I will be with you."

THE PEOPLE ARE CHOSEN

And so Moses goes, and there is that mighty struggle with the power of Egypt which the book of Exodus tells, and finally Moses leads his people out of Egypt across the Red Sea and into the desert

Moses' story begins in Exodus 2 and continues throughout the books of Exodus, Leviticus, Numbers, and Deuteronomy.

of Sinai. A rabble of slaves. And what a rabble. At every sign of trouble their hearts melt. When they have no water they want to kill Moses. When they have no food they want to turn back again to Egypt where at least they had something to eat. But Moses, endlessly patient with them, struggles with their follies and finally brings them as God had commanded to that same mountain where God had promised to meet them. And there God makes a covenant with them to be a royal priesthood and a holy nation.

See Exodus 19:1–6.

Note first of all that it is a covenant not a contract, it is not something mutually agreed [upon] as the result of bargaining. It is a unilateral action on the part of the sovereign Lord who has taken this rabble of slaves to be his people and committed himself absolutely to them, to be faithful to them even when they are unfaithful to him. And they are to be a priesthood to all the nations; through them the righteousness of God is to be revealed. And so God gives to them those famous ten words—what we call the ten commandments.

Read about the commandments in Exodus 20:1–17.

And it is very important to recognize two things about these ten commandments. People often criticize them for being negative, but the first great statement is not negative but positive: "I am the Lord your God who brought you out of the land of Egypt. I am the one who rescued you, so don't go after other gods."

We are tempted to follow all kinds of gods who promise all kinds of good things: prosperity, pleasure, happiness and everything: "But they don't really love you. I am the God who loves you, and who rescued you and who brought you out of the land of Egypt. So don't go after other gods."

That is a tremendously positive statement. And then there are some negatives: don't commit adultery, don't murder, don't steal, don't covet, etc. But you see the great point about a negative command is that it leaves you free. Positive commandments telling you exactly what to do in every situation don't leave you any freedom. A negative commandment leaves you freedom within limits. It's like the fence around the school playground. It leaves the children inside absolutely free to develop their own games, to do their own thing, but they know that outside the fence there is danger. And Israel through all its generations never ceased to thank God for the fact that they had been given that fence. As compared with the other nations of the world, who did not have that protection, and who were constantly tempted to stray away into all kinds of follies, leading to lying and adultery and murder and corruptions of all kinds, the people of Israel were grateful that they had been given this protection. All through their history there is a continual thanksgiving to God for this wonderful gift.

And so God calls Israel to be a holy priesthood for all the nations, to be the nation through whom the rest of the world would come to know the living God. But as the story progresses we shall see what a costly thing it is to be a priesthood for all the nations.

Judges, Kings and Prophets

Moses is on Mount Sinai and Israel is at the foot of the mountain, already forgetting their covenant and falling into paganism and idolatry. Moses has to wrestle with a disobedient and unbelieving Israel all through their journey across the desert. They must learn to depend on daily manna for food and miraculous springs from the rock for drink, and for their guidance a pillar of cloud by day and fire by night. Later generations would look back on those years as a time when Israel was taught to live by faith and not to seek any other kind of security.

Read the story of the spies in Numbers 13–14 and Deuteronomy 1:19–46.

But when Israel finally comes to the borders of the Promised Land, once again their faith fails them. The spies they sent out, with two exceptions, report that the inhabitants were too strong for them and the Israelites lose their courage and want to turn back again to Egypt. Once again God's patience seems to be exhausted, but Moses, the good priest of the priestly people, pleads with God for his people and God relents to the extent that their children at least shall come into the Promised Land.

REACHING THE PROMISED LAND

Read about this in the book of Joshua.

And so it was that a generation later, under Joshua, they crossed the Jordan, took possession of the land and expelled or slaughtered its native inhabitants. When we read this and compare it, for example, with the teaching of Jesus we are horrified by what we would now call ethnic cleansing. We have to remember that we are here dealing with the long, long story of the training of a people to understand the nature and purpose of God, and we are at an early stage in this training. We have to understand all of this in the light of the later teaching of Jesus.

The point here is that there was needed the "experiment" of a people possessing a land in which the will of God could be expressed in a stable political, economic and social order—the kind of order indicated in the law books of the Pentateuch (Genesis to Deuteronomy). We can still learn from these what it would mean to have a society governed by the law of God. And although this was not to be in the case of Israel it nevertheless represents an essential part in the story of God's training of a people to be the priests for all the nations.

The book of Joshua gives us a picture of a complete settlement of the land, but when we move to the book of Judges we have a very different picture. All is not settled; there is chaos. Over and over again the people lapse into idolatry, are overrun by neighbouring nations, plead for help and are rescued by some kind of charismatic leader. There is mayhem, murder, gang rape and all kinds of horror. Over and over again there is the refrain: "At that time there was no king in Israel; everyone did what was right in his own eyes."

A picture of anarchy. And so the point comes at which the people begin to say, "We want a king like the other nations."

Prophecy—the nation's conscience

And here we come to the beginning of the story of the prophets, who from Samuel to John the Baptist were to be the guides, warning, teaching, directing the people of Israel through the ensuing centuries. In this situation of chaos, when Israel is at the mercy of her neighbouring nations, when the priesthood is discredited and there is no stable rule, the people come to Samuel and say, "Give us a king." And God tells Samuel to tell the people what it will be like to have a king: he will take their lands to be his gardens; he will take their women to be his concubines; he will take their men to be his soldiers and his forced labourers and his slaves; he will take their money in taxes. That is what a king will be like. But nevertheless the people say, "We want a king, we want to be like the other nations." They are tired of chaos. And God says to Samuel, "Give them a king." And Samuel anoints the young man Saul as king.

And so we have set out for the first time a theme which will appear throughout the Bible: the ambivalence of the political order. If we were all obedient to God's law we would not need a king, we would do from our hearts what is right. If we need kings, law courts, police and prisons it is because we have forsaken God. And therefore God gives us a political order, and yet he warns us that it is itself a source of profound corruption. That warning is sadly and swiftly realized. The kingship of Saul begins with such promise but ends in tragedy. Saul, tempted to insane jealousy of his ablest military leader, finally ends in the tragic suicide on Mount Gilboa and the defeat of Israel's armies.

For more details of this time, see 1 Samuel 1–10.

We first meet David in 1 Samuel 16. His story runs through 1 and 2 Samuel. Also see 1 Chronicles 11–22 and 28–29.

Read about Solomon in 1 Kings 1–11 and 2 Chronicles 1–9.

First Kings 12–22, 2 Kings, and 2 Chronicles 10–36 record these events.

There follows a period of confusion until David emerges as the leader of the whole nation of twelve tribes. And subsequent generations will look back on David's reign as an ideal time when true kingship was exercised in the maintenance of justice and the protection of the poor. And yet the Bible is quite frank in recording not only David's personal sin but also the confusion in his family life which was to lead to civil war and the sad ending of his kingdom.

David is followed by Solomon in whom the prophecies of Samuel are amply fulfilled. Solomon becomes a typical oriental potentate gathering to himself power, riches, women, gold, engaging in huge building projects and centralizing power in Jerusalem. It is not long, indeed Solomon is hardly in his grave, before the whole thing has broken up and his ablest labour leader, Jeroboam, has carried away ten of the twelve tribes to found a separate kingdom with Samaria as its capital, and to form a separate centre of worship to replace the temple in Jerusalem.

The centuries which follow tell us a miserable story of wars between these two kingdoms—the northern kingdom of Israel and the smaller southern kingdom of Judah—and between these kingdoms and their neighbours—Philistia, Moab, Edom, Syria—while gradually the imperial power of Assyria dominates the eastern sky. The time comes when Assyria, after gobbling up all these small kingdoms, finally moves in to besiege and destroy Israel, take away its king, destroy the city of Samaria, remove its inhabitants to be slaves in the imperial estates of Assyria. In their place, pagan peoples from the east are moved in to colonize the land. The northern kingdom of Israel is ended.

Meanwhile the southern kingdom of Judah with its capital in Jerusalem was to hold out for some time longer. It had good kings and bad ones. The good king Hezekiah sought to restore the people to obedience to the law; the very bad king Manasseh did his best to destroy everything that Hezekiah had achieved. The good king Josiah sought (sadly too late) to bring Judah back to its true allegiance. In his time the version of the law which we find in the book of Deuteronomy was republished. And yet Judah too was doomed. The Assyrian empire had been replaced by Babylon as the superpower of the east, and in due course the Babylonian power was to reach into Judah. At first the city of Jerusalem was besieged and captured, its leaders removed and a puppet king installed and then, twelve years later, the city was finally destroyed, along with the temple, and all but a miserable remnant were taken into exile to be slaves and refugees in Babylon.

It looks as if this is the end of the story, as if God's promises to Abraham and to Moses have come to nothing. That it is not the end is due to the ministry of the great line of prophets from both the northern and the southern kingdoms: Elijah, Elisha, Amos, Hosea and others in the north; Isaiah, Micah and others in the south. These were raised up by God in generation after generation to warn Israel and Judah of the consequences of their folly; to remind the people of God's covenant of mercy and justice; to make clear to them that the God of Abraham, Isaac and Jacob is not like the gods of the nations, existing merely to sponsor the interests of that nation and satisfied as long as the necessary sacrifices and offerings are made. "The living God is a God of justice and mercy and he will be satisfied with nothing less than a people in whom his justice and his mercy are alive."

That message in generation after generation meant that the prophets had to speak against the spirit of their times, against popular opinion, against all the political powers—and to bear the consequences. Those who were faithful to this prophetic tradition were able to interpret the disasters which befall God's people not as a defeat for God but as the manifestation of God's righteous judgement. They were able to learn the hard lesson that to be God's chosen people meant to bear the sin of the world. They were able to point the way forward to that final consummation of the whole story in which the very son of God himself should suffer for the sin of the world.

Return and Renewal

We have reached what looks like a dead end. The two Israelite kingdoms of Israel and Judah have been destroyed. Their cities are in ruins, their people have been carried away captive and their temple has been burned to the ground. It looks as if the end of the line has come.

What has become of the great promises to Abraham, Isaac and Jacob? What has become of the covenant with Moses? Of the promise that Israel is to be a royal priesthood, a holy nation on behalf of all the nations of the world? Can't we hear the mocking voice of the Gentiles as we listen to it in the psalms: "Where is that God of yours now?" And is it not remarkable that in the same psalms we still hear, out of the depths of humiliation and suffering, this triumphant cry: "Our God reigns and shall reign over all the nations."

See, for example, Psalm 9:7–8 or Psalm 47:7–8.

On any ordinary expectation one would have thought that this story would have been forgotten, buried in the rubble of history, unless perhaps it was dug up by modern archaeologists. How is it that this was not the end? The answer is in the work of those prophets to whom I have already referred—and very specially to two prophets living at the same time, one in Jerusalem and the other among the captive slaves in Babylon.

JEREMIAH AND EZEKIEL

The first of these, Jeremiah of Jerusalem, is one who perhaps more than any other mirrors in his life the ministry of Jesus. Jeremiah speaks of himself as a child who does not know how to speak and yet in the power of God he becomes a mighty fortress, standing for the truth amid all the storms and the violent and swirling currents of history in his time. He is absolutely clear that God's judgement is pronounced against his people. The reforms of Josiah have come too late. The people are too deeply corrupted. They still imagine that God is like one of the so-called gods of the nations, one whose only business is to protect them and look after their interests provided they offer all the necessary sacrifices and worship.

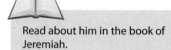

Read about him in the book of Jeremiah.

And so Jeremiah stands in the gate of the temple while the crowds of worshippers stream in and says to them: "It's no use. It's no use. It's no good saying, 'The temple of the Lord, the temple of the Lord, the temple of the Lord' (Jeremiah 7:4), and thinking that because you worship in this temple that God is going to protect you. He is not. He is going to punish you for all your sins."

No wonder they put him in prison. And even when the armies of Babylon had captured the city and carried away its king and all its leading people and put a puppet king in his place, and Jeremiah was in prison, he still continued to affirm both God's judgement on the city and his absolutely unshakeable faith that in the end God would fulfil his promises and that he would rule again over his beloved land.

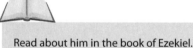

Read about him in the book of Ezekiel.

Meanwhile at the same time, another great prophet, Ezekiel, was giving to his fellow exiles in Babylon a matchless picture of the transcendent glory of God. Ezekiel convinced the people that God was still the Lord of all history, promising them a day when the mighty spirit of God would visit them afresh so that even a valley of dry bones could be turned into a mighty army, and assuring them that the glory of God would one day fill the temple in Jerusalem once again—and fill the whole world.

It was through the ministry of these great God-inspired prophets that the defeat and exile of Israel was to be interpreted: not as a defeat for God but as a manifestation of God's faithfulness to his covenant.…

It was through this experience that Israel was able to understand in a new way what it meant to be a holy nation. And it is from this time that we have the vision of Israel as the suffering servant of the Lord, who fulfils the Lord's will not by winning military victories but by bearing the sin of the world—the servant who will be numbered among the transgressors, upon whom the iniquity of us all will be laid. It was to these pictures that Jesus would turn for the interpretation of his own ministry and the true interpretation of Israel's calling.

POLITICS, POWER AND GOD'S PEOPLE

But meanwhile with the ever-changing ebb and flow of national politics, the power of Babylon is now replaced by that of Persia. And the newly reigning emperor Cyrus issues a decree that priests, Levites and other leaders may return to Jerusalem and rebuild the temple. God has been faithful: Cyrus is the instrument of God's gracious purpose to fulfil his promise to his covenant people. They have learnt that their exile and defeat is God's punishment for their sins. But now they have been punished enough. God's word to them is a word of comfort. They are to be forgiven, and they will return with joy and singing to Zion.

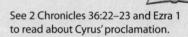

See 2 Chronicles 36:22–23 and Ezra 1 to read about Cyrus' proclamation.

And so the Jewish leaders are able once again to re-establish a visible community even though it is not an autonomous state. The temple is rebuilt. The walls of Jerusalem are reconstructed under Nehemiah and the covenant renewed under the leadership of Ezra. And now there is yet another turn in the wheel of fortune. The empire of Persia is overrun by a still mightier empire, that of Greece. Alexander the Great sweeps through all the lands of the Middle East as far as India and establishes a new empire in which Greek language and Greek civilization are to replace the native cultures and religions of the area.

Greece prided itself on its unique civilization, its art, its philosophy, its religion—and the consequence of Alexander's victory was that the sacred places of Israel were desecrated. Greek culture was introduced: such phenomena as the Greek games with their naked athletics and Greek customs abhorrent to the Jews, such as the encouragement of homosexual practice, threatened this new kingdom with destruction.

Under the leadership of the family of the Maccabees a military revolt took place and in the ensuing wars thousands of faithful Israelites died rather than break God's commandments by fighting on the Sabbath. Jerusalem was besieged and captured, and the leadership had to flee to the mountains in order to regroup and find a new base for their national life, an action which was to be echoed in later words of Jesus.

And from this time we have the great prophecy of Daniel with his vision of the brutal beast-like empires of Assyria and Babylon, Persia and Greece, each trampling the earth with their mighty powers. But there comes to the Ancient of Days one not like a beast but like a son of man and to him is given the power to reign and of his kingdom there shall be no end. And the question always was, "When will this son of man appear?"

But always there was a faithful remnant in Israel. It now had a new source of strength … Certainly the sacrificial worship of the temple in Jerusalem still continued. But a new and vital centre of religious life was developed in the synagogue where God was worshipped in the singing of the psalms, in the reading of the law and the prophets, and in prayer for the coming of God's kingdom.

Israel was again a visible community. And yet how small, how feeble! What a puny thing the temple was compared to the mighty temple of Solomon. In the psalms we hear the voice of this faithful remnant. On the one hand there is the mocking word of the Gentiles who had lordship over them: "Where is now this God of yours who rescued you out of Egypt?" But on the other hand there is both the triumphant cry—"God reigns over all the nations"— and that cry from the depths of humiliation and darkness: "O Lord, how long, how long?"

And we come to the last three books of the Old Testament, Zechariah, Haggai and Malachi, which hold out the promise that the messenger of the Lord will come and establish his reign. It is to these three books that Jesus most frequently appeals in his later teaching. But meanwhile, in one more turn of the political wheel, the power of Greece was to be overcome by the still greater power of Rome. Israel becomes a province of the Roman Empire. The Holy Land is trampled by the feet of Roman soldiers and the people of Israel have to acknowledge another lordship than that of God by paying taxes to the emperor in Rome. And still the cry goes up, "How long?"

It is into this world that Jesus will be born.

God's Kingdom and Jesus

In our journey through the story told in the Bible we have come to the time when Jesus is to be born.

The children of Israel no longer inhabit their own kingdom. They are scattered right across the Mediterranean world and far into what we now call the Middle East. They are without their own king or their own kingdom. Assyria, Babylon, Persia and Greece have all gone, but the mighty power of Rome still dominates the world, and Israel still longs for the day when they will see the fulfilment of God's promise that he will reign over all the nations. And there is a faithful remnant in the land which continues to cry out in the words of the psalms: "Lord, how long?"

The faithful remnant is centred in the worship of the synagogue with its reading of the law and the prophets and its singing of the psalms, always looking towards that day when God's reign will be manifest. The puppet king Herod, installed by the Roman power, has rebuilt the temple on a magnificent scale, hoping thereby to ingratiate himself with the people, and the temple worship is carried on. But the synagogues are the main centre of devout hope and faith. One may say that there were four different ways in which this hope for the kingdom was expressed.

1. Political Revolt

There were in the first place those who thought that the Maccabees had given the right example—that Israel must rise in revolt and throw out the pagan power. And so there was always an eager expectation of some leader who would arise and rally Israel to the cause as the Maccabees had done. And there was a continual succession of such freedom fighters, all of whose revolts were ruthlessly crushed by the Roman power so that the sight of a crucified terrorist hanging from a cross by the wayside had become terribly familiar to the people of Israel.

2. Cooperation

At the other end of the spectrum were the priests and the Sadducees who administered Herod's temple and who had made a kind of accommodation with the ruling power. They too looked for the coming of the kingdom of God, but for the time being they were content to work alongside the ruling powers and to continue the worship of the temple as laid down in the law.

3. Keeping the Law

And then there were the Pharisees, whose worship and life were centred in the synagogues, with their regular reading of the law and the prophets. It was their faith that if Israel could perfectly keep God's law, then God would in his own way and time intervene to establish his kingdom. And they therefore sought to ensure the meticulous and absolute obedience of all true Israelites to the law in all its detail.

4. Withdrawal

Finally there were those who had withdrawn from public life, those about whom we know through the recently discovered Dead Sea scrolls. They had established monastic communities in the desert, withdrawing from the conflicts of public life, believing that by a regime of prayer and fasting they could hasten the day when God would intervene to save his people and establish his reign.

THE WAY OF JESUS

It is into this world that Jesus was born. We know very little about the first thirty years of his life except for that fascinating glimpse of him as a child of twelve in the temple, discussing the interpretation of Scripture with the teachers of the law. But there are two things I think we can confidently say on the basis of what we know from his later teaching.

First we can be confident that he was a master of the Scriptures, as already suggested by that story of his childhood visit to the temple. We can affirm this because of the fact that even his enemies addressed him as "rabbi." The word *rabbi* did not denote, as it does now, a professional teacher. It was given to anyone who showed himself to be a true master of the interpretation of Scripture. The fact that Jesus was consistently addressed as rabbi even by his opponents shows that he was indeed acknowledged to be such a master, and we must take it that in those hidden years before his public ministry he was deeply engaged in the search to hear his father's word in the Scriptures.

The second thing that we can confidently say is that from the beginning Jesus knew God as his father. We can say this because of the word that he consistently used in addressing God, the word *abba*. This is an Aramaic word expressing the deepest possible intimacy between a child and its father. The Gospels, as we know, were written in Greek, the public language of the time. Why then do the writers go out of their way to keep this Aramaic word? Surely it was because they could never forget the actual sound of this word on the lips of Jesus. It was the word that characteristically expressed his relationship to his father. And we can affirm, I think confidently, that in those hidden years, Jesus was both engaged in the profound study of the Scriptures and that he knew God as his father in the most intimate possible way.

But meanwhile Israel waited for God to act. It seemed that there was a long, long silence. It was centuries since the authentic voice of prophecy had been heard in the land. But there came a day when the rumour reached the streets and bazaars of Nazareth of a new prophet, John, Jesus' kinsman, who had appeared in the desert and who seemed to represent once again the authentic figure and voice of a prophet like Elijah. And his was a radical call to the whole of Israel to repent.

Read the following chapters about John's life and ministry: Matthew 3 and 14; Mark 1 and 6; Luke 1, 3, and 7; and John 1 and 3.

Israel had entered the Promised Land by going through the waters of Jordan. John calls Israel to go back to the starting point, to make a radically fresh beginning, to go through the waters of Jordan in a baptism of repentance for the forgiveness of sins and to make a new start. And multitudes were responding to this call. To Jesus this came as a call from his father. He knew that his hour had come, and a day came when he laid down the carpenter's tools for the last time and took the long road down from the hills of Galilee to the banks of the Jordan. We see him in public for the first time, standing among a crowd of repentant sinners asking for the baptism of repentance for the forgiveness of sins. He makes no distinction between himself and them. He is part of Israel. He is identified with Israel in its sin. He is numbered with the transgressors. John, as we know, resisted, but Jesus insisted and so went down into the waters of the Jordan and received from John the baptism of repentance for the forgiveness of sins.

And then that event happened which was to launch Jesus on his public ministry. He heard a voice from heaven: "This is my beloved son in whom I am well pleased."

See Matthew 3:17, Luke 3:22, or Mark 1:11.

And he received from heaven that anointing of the Holy Spirit which Ezekiel and the prophets had promised: the Holy Spirit of power to bring in the kingly reign of God. And that is why from the time of Jesus onwards we have to rethink the very concept of God in terms of Father, Son and Holy Spirit.

Immediately, in the power of the spirit, Jesus is driven out into the desert to face the awesome question, "What does it mean to be

Read about this time of tempting in Matthew 4:1–11 and Luke 4:1–13.

the son of God? What does it mean to be anointed by the Spirit to usher in God's kingdom?" And for those forty days Jesus wrestled in the wilderness, facing one after another of the choices which the world offers for winning leadership among men and women. There is first of all the economic route: satisfy their immediate needs, feed the hungry, give them what they need. Give them the feel-good factor and they will follow you. Jesus rejects that.

And there is the religious way: do something spectacular, something which cannot be explained except as a miraculous act of God and the people will follow you. Jesus rejects that.

And there is the political route: mobilize the political forces of the world in order to gain control over the world. Jesus could have taken that route, but he rejected it and in rejecting it we can say that he chose the way of the cross. And so he comes back from the desert, back to his native Galilee and makes this great ringing announcement: "The time has come. The kingdom of God is at hand. Repent and believe and follow me."

"Well, what is new? Every devout Jew knows that God reigns! It's what he sings in the temple every Sabbath. So what's new?"

"What is new is that the kingdom of God is here now, facing you."

"But where is it? We don't see it!"

"You don't see it because you are looking the wrong way. You are expecting something different. Turn round, repent and come with me. Believe me and come with me and you will discover what the kingdom of God is."

Because the truth is that Jesus himself is the presence of the kingdom. The kingdom is not a new political regime. It is not a new programme. It is not a new ideology. It is not a new philosophy. It is the person of Jesus. And to know what God's kingly rule is, one must believe in Jesus and come with him.

Well this sets the whole of Galilee tingling with excitement. People follow him, but people are also perplexed: "What is this kingdom? Where is the kingdom?" They follow but they question, and they are puzzled.

And in the next chapter we will try to show how Jesus taught and manifested the reign of God in his own ministry.

Sacrifice

We have arrived at the point where Jesus has come into Galilee announcing that the kingdom of God has come.

Most of Jesus' hearers thought it was quite clear: God is the rightful king of all the earth and all these rulers—Assyria, Babylon, Persia, Greece, Rome—are all usurpers. To say that the kingdom of God is at hand must mean that the Roman power is about to be thrown out and that Israel is going to be once again under the direct rule of God, who from Zion will rule all the nations. So naturally when Jesus announces that the kingdom of God is at hand it creates immense excitement. There are crowds who come to listen but there is also skepticism, there is puzzlement. What exactly does this kingdom mean?

Naturally also the authorities in Jerusalem are worried, and so they send scouts to find out what is going on, to listen to Jesus and discover whether in fact he is really a trouble maker. And so Jesus has to use coded language in his teaching, he speaks in parables so that the scouts from Jerusalem cannot pick up his words and use them as a basis for an arrest. But on the other hand those with ears to hear will be able to understand.

But it is not only words. Jesus has an extraordinary authority. With a word he heals the sick; he gives sight to the blind; he cleanses the lepers. And what is even more serious, he announces the forgiveness of sins. The law provides a proper procedure for the forgiveness of sins: one goes to the temple and offers the necessary sacrifices and through the mediation of the priest one receives forgiveness. Jesus has come to set people free. His words have an extraordinary authority. They have power. And yet they are words of grace and kindness. But at the same time they are words as sharp as a razor.

Out of the crowds who followed, some friendly, some curious and some hostile, Jesus had chosen twelve to be his special companions so that by living with him, sharing in all his wanderings, in his teachings, in his meals, they would learn to know him in his own full reality as the presence of the kingdom of God. They were of course also exposed to all the ideas that were floating around among the general public about who Jesus was.

A NEW KIND OF KINGDOM

Jesus takes his close companions to a place away from the crowds and puts to them a question: "Who do you believe that I am?"

Read Peter's words in Matthew 16: 13–17, Mark 8:27–30, and Luke 9:18–21.

And God puts it into the heart of Simon Peter to give that decisive answer: "You are the Christ, you are the one whom God has sent to reign, to establish his kingdom."

And immediately Jesus begins to teach them what kind of a kingship this will be. In line with all that he had learned from the Scriptures he taught them that the one who reigns in God's name must be one who suffers, who is rejected, who is humiliated but who will finally be vindicated. And in order that this might be strengthened in the minds of his disciples, God gave to him and to them that marvellous experience on the Mount of Transfiguration when Jesus was filled with the glory of God and the disciples had a vision of Moses and Elijah—representing the law and the prophets—bearing witness to Jesus and encouraging him on his way to the cross. And from that moment Jesus sets his face to go to Jerusalem for the final showdown.

He chooses for his final entry the season of the Passover, that season of maximum excitement, maximum expectation that God would deliver his people once again as he had delivered them from Egypt in those events which are commemorated at Passover time. And he chooses as the manner of his final showdown a prophecy from Zechariah which spoke of a king who would come riding on a donkey to claim his kingship.

Read about this entry into Jerusalem in Matthew 21, Mark 11, Luke 19, or John 12.

So Jesus, accompanied by his disciples and his followers, rode on a donkey right into Jerusalem and right into the heart of the temple. And there he threw out those who were doing the necessary business of the temple—namely providing the animals for sacrifice and the special coinage for the official offerings, thus for one symbolic day bringing to a halt the regular worship of the temple. Why did he do this? As his teaching made clear it was to demonstrate that God's judgement had been pronounced upon this temple, that it would be destroyed and that in its place there would be a new temple, a new place where God dwells, a new place where sacrifice can be offered and where men and women can know that they are in the home of God. That temple would be built not with the gigantic stones of Herod's temple but with the living stones of men and women reconciled to God through Jesus Christ.

It was the most open possible challenge to the leadership of Israel and it could not go unanswered. For obvious reasons Jesus did not stay in Jerusalem during those days leading up to the Passover but spent the nights in a nearby village. But each day of the following week he sat in the temple openly teaching, with no further need for concealment. And among the parables of that week was one of which the meaning could not possibly be doubted. Jesus took the old parable from Isaiah, which spoke of Israel as God's vineyard in which he hoped to grow the fruit of justice and mercy but in which he had failed to find fruit. Jesus retells that story with the owner of the vineyard sending his messengers one after another, all of them to be rejected by the tenants, until finally the owner of the vineyard plays his last card and sends his beloved son. And him they cast out and kill.

No one could possibly doubt the meaning of that parable: the authorities must either surrender to the teaching of Jesus or destroy him. And the decision is taken to destroy him. But it was necessary that his disciples should be prepared to face what was to come. And so on the last day before the Passover he gathered his disciples together for one of their familiar meals and demonstrated in an action something that words alone could never show. He took the bread of their meal, broke it, gave it to them and said: "This is my body broken for you."

Read this parable in Matthew 21: 33–44, Mark 12:1–11, or Luke 20:9–18.

He took a cup, shared it with them, and said: "This is the new covenant in my blood shed for you and for many. Drink it all of you."

What do these actions mean? Their meaning is surely plain. He is saying to them, "What I now have to do I must do alone." No one else can do what Jesus has to do at that moment. But he is doing it not in order that they may be left behind, but in order that they may follow, that they may be with him, that they may be actual partakers in his act of final sacrifice. This cup will be the new covenant which Jeremiah had promised, in which the law of God will be written not on tablets of stone but in the hearts of men and women. And he commands them to do this so that when everything else seems to have been shattered beyond repair, they will have this action to bind them forever to him and make them partakers of his dying and of his victory.

DEATH AND VICTORY

And so he leads them down that long flight of steps—which is still there today—into the garden of Gethsemane. There is that final agony of doubt, "Is this indeed the father's will?" And Jesus in that final agony masters all the doubts and temptations that could assail him and surrenders himself to his father's will. And when he goes up those steps again it is without the disciples for they have panicked and fled. It is as a prisoner to be tried and condemned.

The story of Jesus' arrest and crucifixion is in Matthew 26–27, Mark 14–15, Luke 22–23, and John 18–19.

So he comes face to face with those who have become unwittingly the agents of the enemy—Caiaphas and Pilate. And when challenged he bears witness to the fact that he is indeed that son of man whose coming had been promised. And so he is condemned, humiliated, flogged, taken out to die. One more crucified fighter for the kingdom. But unlike all who had gone before, Jesus' words are not curses for those who torture him, but words of forgiveness. As each nail is hammered in he repeats the words, "Father, forgive them," and his final words are of peace and forgiveness to a terrorist crucified beside him, and for his heartbroken mother and disciple.

Then come those terrible hours of darkness, followed by the cry: "My God, why hast thou forsaken me?"

At the very beginning of this book I referred to the cry of God in the Garden of Eden: "Adam, where are you?"

The agonized father seeking for the son who has been lost. Now the beloved son of the father has shared the fate of the lost children, and with them, for them, on their behalf, as one of them, he cries out to the father: "My God, why hast thou forsaken me?"

He goes down into the very depths of dereliction so that there could be no depths of despair into which we could ever fall in which the son of God would not be there beside us. And then all things achieved he cries out: "It is finished."

The work is done. The prince of this world is cast out. And Jesus bows his head and gives up his spirit. This is the victory that overcomes the world—how it is, and how it has been seen to be, will be the subject of our next chapter.

New Life, New Communities

So Jesus has been crucified, is dead and has been buried. To his contemporaries it must have seemed that this was just one more failed revolution, one more nail in the coffin of Jewish hopes for the kingdom of God.

How has it happened that today, among all the world's faith communities, much the largest and still rapidly growing is that community which looks to the cross as the sign of victory? The one way in which it can be explained is the story told in the Bible itself, namely that on the third day the tomb in which Jesus had been laid was empty and that he was rallying his disciples and sending them out as his witnesses into all the world.

Life after death

Here we come to the crunch issue. It is not difficult to believe in a good man who was condemned and put to death. But that three days later he was alive and radiant and inspiring his disciples to a new worldwide mission? That runs against everything in our experience. If it is true it requires a radical rethinking of everything we have understood hitherto about the fundamental nature of the world. And this is not a new problem. It is rather silly to suggest that it arises because of our modern scientific knowledge. The fact that people who have been dead for three days don't rise again on the third day was well known long before the invention of computers. No! The Church has always recognized that this is something utterly unique, something which cannot be explained in terms of the ordinary laws of physics and chemistry.

But there is one analogy for it, one other fact which cannot be explained by the laws of physics and chemistry and biology—and that is the fact of creation, the fact that a world has come into existence. And the Christian Church has always maintained that what happened on that Easter day was a kind of new creation, the beginning of a new era for the world. The first fruit of God's intention to recreate the whole cosmos according to his glorious purpose. That I believe is the truth. I do not believe that on any other basis one can make sense of the subsequent history. And so we now continue the story on the basis of this biblical record.

How marvellously this astounding news is broken. How gently this explosion of new reality breaks on the world. The women who alone seem not to have been totally shattered by the events of Good Friday come to the tomb, they have a vision, they are told he is alive but they don't believe it. Mary Magdalene, the first to whom the risen Lord appears, runs to tell the disciples—but they do not believe. And yet slowly bit by bit there are more and more evidences, more and more stories that make it impossible to doubt that he is indeed alive. And finally Jesus rallies his disciples, sends them out to proclaim what the world must know: that death, sin, the devil have been finally conquered and that Jesus is the Lord of all. Because the world must know who is in charge, to whom all men and women are ultimately responsible. Everyone must know—we have no right to keep that secret to ourselves. And so the news spreads. First of all among Jews, because the ministry of Jesus was first of all to Israel.

Read about the Resurrection in Matthew 28, Mark 16, Luke 24, and John 20.

Jesus has told his disciples that they are to wait in Jerusalem because they will receive that full anointing by the Holy Spirit which had been promised in the prophets and which he had received at his baptism. And so with joy and expectation they wait in Jerusalem until the day comes when they do indeed receive that anointing of power which sets them alight and drives them out into the streets tingling with the joy of this new message.

Conflict and unity

There is rejection but there is also acceptance, and so there is inevitably conflict. The news spreads first among the Jews and then among the Gentiles. We come to the remarkable ministry of Saul (later known as Paul) who had been a leader in the persecution of the early Church, but who was confronted on the road to Damascus by the living Lord Jesus and turned into a blazing apostle of the new faith. He and his colleague Barnabas worked in Antioch helping to develop a great new community of people—both Jews and Gentiles—who knew that Jesus was Lord. This was a new phenomenon. Every Jew knows that the world is divided into Jews and Gentiles. But if Gentiles accept Jesus as Lord and are baptized into the family of Jesus, what are they? They are no longer heathen. They are not Jews by race—but they are not Gentiles either. There had to be a new name to give to this new reality. I imagine in India that we might have called them "Messiahwallas." The name they gave them in Antioch was "Christians." And Christians became a community that spread throughout the world, especially as the apostles went from city to city throughout the whole of what we now call the Middle and Near East. Remember that in all the great cities of the Mediterranean world there were synagogues where the scattered Jewish community met on the Sabbath to read the law and the prophets and to pray for the coming of the kingdom. And around these synagogues there was always a company of Gentiles who were attracted by the purity of the Jewish faith and were spoken of as "godfearers."

When Paul and the other apostles went around the synagogues and were invited as visiting scholars to give whatever message they had, they stood up to announce that what had been read in the law and the prophets in the earlier part of the service had now been fulfilled in the coming of Jesus. Those wonderful pictures of the suffering servant, the servant of the Lord upon whom the sin of the world is laid and who bears all our transgressions—they have been fulfilled in the life and ministry and death and resurrection of Jesus.

Inevitably this again created conflict. There were those who accepted this news with joy. But there were those who could not accept it. And so the division arose between the two groups, and more and more Christians separated themselves from those who could not accept this message and who must therefore continue to hope that God's promises would finally be fulfilled in a new age in which Zion would become the capital of the world and Jehovah would rule all the nations.

New and old

In the book of the Acts of the Apostles we get a picture of the Church moving westwards until finally it is established in the centre of the empire in Rome, in the person of Paul who is there as an apostle but also as a prisoner, awaiting death in the footsteps of his master. And in the great epistles which form the next part of the New Testament we have windows into the inner life of that young Church and the problems it had to face.

The great problem was how to relate the new message of the gospel to the old law. Were all the laws of Moses binding upon the Gentiles? Could Gentiles who became Christians continue to behave in the way that Gentiles had done in the past? Ways which were an abomination in the eyes of Israel? Crucial was the question of circumcision which had always been foundational in Jewish practice. Paul's answer to this problem was that circumcision had been given to Abraham and his successors as a sign and not as a precondition of the grace of God, that the promises of God came before the law of God and that what was a sign must not be turned into a condition.

See Romans 4.

In the greatest of his letters—the letter to the Romans—Paul is looking forward to the time when, having finished his ministry in the eastern part of the Mediterranean, he hopes to move to the west and make Rome the centre of a new mission to the whole western Mediterranean. There is already in Rome a church consisting of Jewish and Gentile converts and he wants them to understand his message and to grasp the way in which he sees the relation between the old and the new. There are also letters—for example to the Corinthians—which deal with quite different problems. How are Gentiles to act under their new lordship of Jesus Christ? How are Gentiles, born and brought up as Gentiles and living still in a wholly Gentile environment—how are they to obey the law of God as it is set forth in Jesus?

See Hebrews 7:11–10:39.

And in the epistle to the Hebrews, there is a parallel to Paul's argument about how Jesus fulfils the moral law. The writer of this letter shows that Jesus also fulfils all that is written in the Old Testament concerning the priestly ministry of the temple and the priesthood—that in Jesus, all that was prescribed in the Old Testament by way of offering, sacrifice and priesthood has been fulfilled so that the Christian Church is itself now in Christ a holy priesthood.

The New Testament continues with the pastoral letters of Peter, James, and John, which give us a picture of how these new communities of Christians are to order their lives so that they can become centres of new life in the midst of that dying Roman world. And finally we come to the book of the Revelation of St. John in which the final consummation of all things is prefigured—and that will be the theme of the last chapter in this book.

Future Revelation

We are coming to the end of this story of the Bible as a whole—a story which focuses on the particular history of one nation, Israel, and focuses on one man, Jesus. And so the story is told because God has chosen Israel and Jesus to be bearers of his purpose for the whole of creation and of the human race.

At the beginning of the Bible, before we begin to have the story of Israel beginning with Abraham, we have those first eleven chapters of Genesis which speak of the creation of the world. And now at the end of the Bible we have the book called the Revelation of St. John, a picture of the end of the world. We ended the last chapter with St. Paul in Rome, the centre of the civilized world as it knew itself—Paul as a missionary but also as a martyr, facing death for his master's sake.

In the story told in the Gospels Rome is in the background. Now Rome moves to the centre. Rome, that mighty power which dominated the known world with its awesome military strength, its vast commercial networks stretching right across the known world, its propaganda machine constantly saturating the world with its own ideology of power and glory; Rome which in its own eyes was the apex of human civilization, but which in the eyes of Israel was the great harlot seducing the world with false claims to glory. And in this final book of the Bible we see the ultimate resolution of the conflict between God and this centre of power—a conflict in which all that is opposed to God has its most concentrated expression. And the conflict will be fought out between this power on the one hand and the one who is described in this book as the "Lion of Judah" and the "Lamb slain from the foundation of the world." From one side it will be fought with all the weapons of military, commercial and ideological power. On the other side it will be fought with the weapons of faith, hope and patient suffering and sacrifice.

On the one side there is the power of the lie—untruths which are multiplied many times through all the machinery of propaganda. On the other side there is the word of truth, spoken and acted in Jesus, the word which is like a sharp two-edged sword, cutting through all the subterfuges, confusions and lies that fill the world. And this means that in the end there must be a day of judgement. As Jesus had said: "There is nothing hidden that will not be revealed."

In the end there will be no space for delusion. Everything will be seen as it is. That is the meaning of Jesus being the light of the world: it means that in his presence there can be no lies. Everything must be seen as it truly is.

Rome represents, from the point of view of the Bible, the supreme example of what had been exemplified in Babylon, Assyria, Persia and Greece—the pride of humankind seeking to establish in our own power the final authority over the human race. God's response to this is the gift of the holy city which is not the achievement of human power but the gift of God's grace, perfect in beauty, embodying all the perfection to which human culture in all its forms aspires—its politics, its culture, its art and everything that we summarize in the word "civilization." Into that city we are told that the kings of the earth shall bring their treasures. In that sense it is the consummation of the whole human struggle to create a truly good and beautiful world. But it will not be the product of human pride; it will be the gift of God.

HISTORY AND OUR STORY

At the beginning of this book I said that the Bible gives us the whole story of creation and of the human race and therefore enables us to understand our own lives as part of that story. But every human attempt to see the story as a whole runs into an insuperable difficulty. If the meaning of my life is its contribution to some historical project of civilization which in the end will lead to a perfect society in the future, then from my point of view the problem is that I shall not be there to share in it. I shall be dead before it arrives. And that means that I am essentially expendable. I am not part of God's ultimate purpose. The logic of this has been developed with terrible precision in some of the movements of the twentieth century in which millions of men and women have been sacrificed for the sake of some ideology, some vision of a perfect society in the future.

If I cannot accept this, if I cannot believe that my human life and the lives of those whom I know and love are simply raw material like the shavings left on a workshop floor after the job is done, then the alternative seems to be that I seek for meaning in personal fulfilment. And that inevitably takes me away in the end from total involvement in the human project of civilization. It means that I am led to put my hope in some personal future for myself which must necessarily be beyond this world because I shall not be present when this world comes to its goal. And so there is a kind of spirituality that leads us away from our active involvement in the business of this world. That is what my Indian friend meant (as quoted in chapter 1) when he said that the Bible was not a book of religion but was a unique interpretation of universal history and therefore an interpretation of the human person as a responsible actor in history.

So the alternatives seem to be either finding meaning for history as a whole at the cost of no meaning for my personal life; or else finding meaning for my personal life at the cost of no meaning for the story as a whole. To discover the third option—which I believe to be the answer—we have to recognize that the core of the problem is death. It is death that removes me from the story before it reaches its end. And death, as the Bible tells us, is the wages of sin. We die because nothing that we have done or been is good enough for God's perfect kingdom. I know that before my obituary is written. We are not fit for God's eternal kingdom. What the gospel does is to show us that Jesus' life from a purely earthly point of view ended in failure—and yet, because he committed himself in total obedience and love to his father, he was raised by the father to glory as the first fruits of a new creation.

So in so far as I commit all that I do, imperfect as it is, to God in Jesus Christ, knowing that much of it is utterly unfit to survive and yet trusting that what has been committed in faith will find its place in God's final kingdom, that gives me something to look forward to in which both my hopes for the world and my hopes for myself are brought together. The book of Revelation offers us the vision of a city which is on the one hand the perfection of all human striving towards beauty, civilization and good order, and on the other hand is the place where every tear is dried and where every one of us knows God face to face, and knows that we are his and he is ours. That is the vision with which the Bible ends, and it is a vision that enables us to see the whole human story and each of our lives within that story as meaningful, and which therefore invites us through Jesus Christ to become responsible actors in history, not to seek to run away from the responsibilities and the agonies of human life in its public dimension. Each of us must be ready to take our share in all the struggles and the anguish of human history and yet with the confidence that what is committed to Christ will in the end find its place in his final kingdom.

That means that as I look forward I don't see just an empty void, I don't see just my own death, I don't see just some future utopia in which I shall have no share. The horizon to which I look forward is that day when Jesus shall come, and his holy city will come down as a bride from heaven adorned for her husband.

の

Thus ends Newbigin's book—an interpretation of the whole of history from beginning to end. And now that we've read Newbigin's account, we have to ask, What is God up to? What is this story God is telling through the Bible and onward, forward in time into our lives? That's what the next chapter is going to help us find out.

The Mission of God

2

Imagine yourself as a living house. God comes in to rebuild that house. At first, perhaps, you can understand what He is doing. He is getting the drains right and stopping the leaks in the roof and so on: you knew that those jobs needed doing and so you are not surprised. But presently He starts knocking the house about in a way that hurts abominably and does not seem to make sense. What on earth is He up to? The explanation is that He is building quite a different house from the one you thought of—throwing out a new wing here, putting on an extra floor there, running up towers, making courtyards. You thought you were going to be made into a decent little cottage: but He is building a palace. He intends to come and live in it Himself.

—*C. S. Lewis*

So, what is God up to? What is this story He is telling through the Bible and onward, forward in time into our lives? What can this story tell us about God and His plans and purpose?

Because our culture is so filled with stories, we know a great deal about the way they should be told, whether or not we could explain that structure to another person. We have a sense of what should go on in a good story. For example, we know that stories have a main character, or a protagonist, who is the focus of the main action in a story. If there isn't a clear protagonist, we sense that something is not quite right about the story that we are hearing. Without a clear main character, we don't know where to focus our attention as hearers of the story.

We also know that the main character of a story has an objective—an overall purpose that he or she is pursuing. This objective is what drives or motivates all actions by the main character. In theater, one of the first things an actor does in preparing to play a character is examine the script to find information that explains what the character's main goal or super-objective is. An actor desires to understand what a character wants more than anything else, and this understanding helps the actor know how to create a better picture of the character for the audience. Human beings are like characters in a play. We are motivated by objectives and purposes, even if we can't always identify them. If we are thirsty, we try to find something to drink. If we are afraid of failing a class, we try to study hard and do assignments on time. Well-written stories have main characters that are consistent in the objectives and purposes they pursue. As readers or hearers of a story, we sometimes get confused and lose interest in the story if we can't figure out what the character is after.

So, keeping the idea of character and objective in mind, let's look at the story of the Bible. It should have been clear to you after reading the previous chapter that the main character of the Bible is God. Sometimes we get confused about this and think that maybe we as individuals are the main character. But it is important to understand that the Bible is the story of God acting to achieve a particular purpose, or objective, throughout history and eternity. We are characters in this story, to be sure, but we are not the protagonist. God is. Without Him, the story doesn't exist. As Colossians 1:17 says of God the Son, "He is before all things, and in him all things hold together."

The main character of the Bible is God.

Students of literature and theater are adept at studying and unpacking the characters in a story. In English class you may have learned about the difference between a flat, two-dimensional character and a round, fully developed character. The most interesting characters in literature are complex, well developed, and worth coming back to again and again for the ways in which they can surprise us, teach us, and inspire us. God is most certainly a fully developed, multidimensional character. He is worth studying intently, not just because He is an interesting character in a story, but because His story is truth. The Bible is truth cloaked in story so that we can better hear and understand it.

Let's take a look at God as He is revealed in the Bible. What do we find as we study this protagonist, this main character of the greatest story ever told? At the beginning of the Bible, the first thing we see is an all-present, all-knowing, all-powerful Creator God: "In the beginning God created …" (Genesis 1:1). What did He create? The world—a beautiful and lavish setting for humankind, His most treasured and spectacular creation. This creation of human beings didn't just happen; it was intentionally crafted by God, who gave attention to every detail. When it came time on day six to bring humans onto the stage of the newly created world, God said, "Let us make man in our image, in our likeness" (Genesis 1:26).

All those other things that God created were certainly nice—perfect, in fact. Who could deny the grandeur of a majestic mountain range, the terrifying power of a lion's roar, or the inky infinity of the night sky? But as wondrous as they are, none had the distinguishing feature of being made in God's image. Because we are made in the image of God, we can reason. We have self-awareness. We are relational beings who enjoy and desire community and fellowship with others. The role of relationship and community is a part of the story of God and the Bible from the very beginning—literally.

Let's return to Genesis 1:1: "In the beginning God created the heavens and the earth." The Hebrew word for God used here is the plural word *Elohim*. Bible teacher Kay Arthur notes that etymologically *El* means "mighty" or "strong." She also calls attention to the ending syllable of Elohim: "The 'him' ending of Elohim is very significant, for it is a plural ending in the Hebrew that indicates three or more" (1992, 19). Three or more? Doesn't that sound like the Trinity? The very first mention we have of God is with a name that describes the Trinitarian nature of His being. Though much about the nature of the Trinity is mysterious, clearly the three-in-one nature of God indicates that there is a relational dimension to God Himself. There is an ongoing relationship between Father, Son, and Holy Spirit. It isn't unrealistic to say that in His very nature, God is relationship. He is, in and of Himself, a community.

And we were made in His image. It isn't very far into the story of the Bible that we see that one of the results of being made in the image of God is man's own need for relationship and community. Just a few paragraphs farther into Genesis, God declares the following: "It is not good for the man to be alone. I will make a helper suitable for him" (2:18). God made for the man, Adam, a companion named Eve (see vv. 21–23). This first relationship between humans was pure and true and fulfilling, as indicated by the fact that Adam and Eve were naked together and felt no shame. Humankind had embarked on relationship—both relationship with other humans and relationship with God. The importance of these relationships cannot be understated, for relationship is at the very heart of God, both in His Triune being and in the fruit of His labor described in Genesis and culminating with the creation of humankind. Relationship is, you could say, His objective.

Some people spend a lot of time trying to figure out why God made us. They speculate that perhaps He was bored or lonely or just felt like making something. But certain things are evident from the Bible. First of all, you don't see in Genesis a story of God

---

The Trinity

While much has been written about the Trinity, at best it is a mystery not fully comprehended by finite minds. We have nothing concrete to adequately compare it to in our world, but many analogies exist that describe various aspects of this mystery of the Godhead. Theologian Henry C. Thiessen (1979, 90) outlines the basics of the doctrine of the Trinity:

> Though the term "trinity" does not occur in the Bible, it had very early usage in the church. Its Greek form, trias, seems to have been first used by Theophilus of Antioch (d. A.D. 181), and its Latin form, trinitas, by Tertullian (d. ca. A.D. 220). In Christian theology, the term "trinity" means that there are three eternal distinctions in the one divine essence, known respectively as Father, Son, and Holy Spirit. These three distinctions are three persons, and one may speak of the tripersonality of God. We worship the triune God. The Athanasian Creed expresses the trinitarian belief thus, "We worship one God in the Trinity, and the Trinity in unity; we distinguish among the persons, but we do not divide the substance." It goes on to say, "The entire three persons are coeternal and coequal with one another, so that … we worship complete unity in Trinity and Trinity in unity."

The Athanasian Creed mentioned above is one of several creeds of the Church, the most widely known today being the Apostles' Creed and the Nicene Creed. While all the major creeds affirm the Trinity, the Athanasian Creed goes into the most depth and detail and, though not widely used in contemporary liturgy, is still considered to be a classic statement of Trinitarian theology. You may wish to investigate the texts of these creeds to explore more about the Trinity. Other resources include Bible dictionaries and Bible commentaries.

making a fabulous universe and then going off and leaving it. He intended to be in relationship with His creation. Remember the interest God showed in Adam's work of naming the animals in Genesis 2:19? We also catch a glimpse of this relational aspect of God from the passage in Genesis 3, in which Adam and Eve had just finished making coverings to hide their nakedness: "Then the man and his wife heard the sound of the Lord God as he was walking in the garden in the cool of the day, and they hid from the Lord God among the trees of the garden" (v. 8). The fact that God was walking in the Garden shows that He was in close relationship with His creation. (We see another manifestation of this through the Incarnation, which we will discuss later in the book.) Even though Adam and Eve tried to hide from God, verse 9 says that "the Lord God called to the man, 'Where are you?' " Here we see a beautiful picture of God as He seeks those He created and reaches out to them despite their sinful actions.

Second, God created us in His image, and part of His nature is relational, as we've already seen earlier in the chapter. Third, the Bible tells us that what God created brings Him pleasure: "God saw all that he had made, and it was very good" (Genesis 1:31). We, created in His image, can bring Him pleasure. Parents can tell you how much joy and pleasure come from the relationship they have with their child. But parents have to have a relationship with the child for that pleasure to occur. And the same is true of God with us. Our God is a relational God, and He desires an intimate relationship with us.

Let's get back to the idea of what God's objective, or purpose, is. If the Bible stopped at the end of Genesis 2, we could say that God's creation of pure and intimate relationship with us was fulfilled and complete. But you know what happened next. Adam and Eve messed up, big-time. As a result, the rest of us were born messed up (at least in the sense that we inherited Adam's sin nature), and our intended relationship with Holy God was broken. Romans 5:12 explains that through Adam, sin and death came to all people. As Adam's children, we have inherited a brokenness that distorts and twists our relationship with God. We are still created in His image, but our reflection of His image is now fractured and splintered by sin.

The purpose of God is still relationship with us, as it was from the very beginning. But because of our sin, there is a more complex path required for achieving that purpose. It involves fixing what is broken. That pursuit of relationship now requires redemption and reconciliation because of sin.

??
Who was the first "missionary" in the Bible?

(Read about it in Genesis 3:9 where God reaches out to Adam and Eve after they try to hide from Him.)

Let's look a little more fully at what each of the three elements of His purpose means for us. First, notice that redemption and reconciliation are needed in order to have relationship. The fall of man described in Genesis 3 makes it necessary for something to occur to restore our broken relationship with God. Despite our fallen state, we do have a relationship to God in the sense that we are His creation and He is our Creator. No matter how hard or how far one might try to run from God, it is impossible to evade the truth that we are by our very nature His creation (see Psalm 139). Even feuding neighbors have a relationship with one another; it is just a negative, nonproductive one. But whether this relationship is between feuding neighbors or between sinful humans and God, it is not intimate, fulfilling, or intended by God. It is just a twisted, corrupted, fractured correspondence between two parties. What God seeks with us is the restored, right relationship of fellowship unbroken by rebellion and sin—that "dwelling with," or community, which He intended from the beginning. Fallen man's fractured relationship to God is the stage upon which redemption and reconciliation must occur for true relationship with God to be possible. It is to these two important elements of God's objective that we now turn.

Outside of a sermon or a Bible class, perhaps the most frequent use of the word *redeem* we hear these days is in reference to airline frequent flier miles, credit card perks, or grocery store coupons. These contemporary uses of *redeem* are very similar in nature to the redeeming that we see in the Bible. To redeem frequent flier miles, a person exchanges a credit of miles flown for something like a free ticket or an upgrade to a better seat on the airplane. At the grocery store, redeeming a coupon basically turns the piece of paper the coupon is printed on into cash toward buying an item. In each case, something new is obtained or some sort of exchange occurs.

According to the *Merriam-Webster Online Dictionary*,[1] the word *redeem* has six different but related definitions (see sidebar). Implied in the first definition, "to buy back: repurchase" or "to get or win back," is the idea of ownership or restoring something to its rightful owner, even if there is a cost involved. The second definition includes the idea of freedom and release and makes use of the familiar term *ransom*. When a ransom is paid for a kidnap victim, usually money is exchanged for the victim's safe release. To free the captured one, there is an exchange that costs something. Farther down the list of definitions you see ideas such as repair, reform, exchange, and atone. The list concludes with the synonym *rescue*. All these ideas are present in the biblical presentation of God's purpose of redemption.

Redeem

Main Entry: **re·deem**

Pronunciation: \ri-ˈdem\

Function: *transitive verb*

Etymology: Middle English *redemen*, from Anglo-French *redemer*, modification of Latin *redimere*, from *re-, red-* re- + *emere* to take, buy; akin to Lithuanian *imti* to take

1 a : to buy back : REPURCHASE **b :** to get or win back

2 : to free from what distresses or harms: as **a :** to free from captivity by payment of ransom **b :** to extricate from or help to overcome something detrimental **c :** to release from blame or debt : CLEAR **d :** to free from the consequences of sin

3 : to change for the better : REFORM

4 : REPAIR, RESTORE

5 a : to free from a lien by payment of an amount secured thereby **b** (1) **:** to remove the obligation of by payment <the United States Treasury *redeems* savings bonds on demand> (2) **:** to exchange for something of value <*redeem* trading stamps> **c :** to make good : FULFILL

6 a : to atone for : EXPIATE <*redeem* an error> **b** (1) **:** to offset the bad effect of (2) **:** to make worthwhile : RETRIEVE

synonym see RESCUE

By permission. From the *Merriam-Webster Online Dictionary* ©2008 by Merriam-Webster, Incorporated (www.Merriam-Webster.com).

In our fallen state, we are not able to be fully who we were intended or created to be. This is true in the sense that we have a broken relationship with God, our fellow human beings, and even ourselves. We stand in need of redemption, as does the entire world since the Fall. We see this need in the violence of humankind; in our anger with ourselves and with others; in scandal and shame, lying and corruption; and in every strip of darkness that surrounds us. It is no accident that newscasts are filled with crime, violence, corruption, and a poisoned environment. We live in a fallen world. At some level, we all long for things to be different, healed, repaired. Whether or not we articulate this longing as a need for redemption, in the depths of our beings we desire rescue and restoration.

Read more about this story in the book of Ruth.

Ruth the Moabitess knew of the need for redemption. While she probably wouldn't have used the term either, she knew that she needed help. A young widow and a foreigner in a new land, Ruth clung to the protection and livelihood that her mother-in-law, Naomi, could offer through family ties in Naomi's native Judah. In a culture in which women were not granted legal status, Ruth and Naomi lived hand-to-mouth, depending on the kindness of kinsmen and strangers to meet their needs. In this context, God provided Ruth a literal redemption through Boaz, who acted as her kinsman-redeemer. The concept of kinsman-redeemer is articulated several times in the Pentateuch. The rights and responsibilities of nearest relatives included marrying a widow to ensure the continuance of the family line and to secure the opportunity to purchase back property that may have been sold, thus restoring the fortunes of an impoverished relative (see Genesis 38:8; Leviticus 25:25, 47–48; Deuteronomy 25:5–10). Though Boaz was not the nearest relative, he respectfully negotiated with Ruth's rightful kinsman-redeemer to secure the right to purchase Naomi's land and to marry Ruth. Both Naomi and Ruth were rescued from financial uncertainty in this transaction, and Ruth received a new identity. No longer Ruth the Moabitess, she is known ever after as part of the lineage of King David and, ultimately, Jesus. The author of the book of Ruth paints a picture of Ruth's new identity as a member of Boaz's family and as David's grandmother in the closing verses of the book.

Bible scholars often identify the Old Testament concept of kinsman-redeemer as it is demonstrated in the story of Boaz and Ruth as a preview of the work Christ would do as the Redeemer of the world. The *Holman Bible Dictionary* notes that the Old Testament terms and ideas of redemption "are frequently used symbolically to emphasize dramatically the redemptive or saving activity of

God. The basic Old Testament reference is the Exodus. At the sea God redeemed His people from slavery in Egypt." [2] God also later redeemed, or rescued, Israel from Babylonian captivity, and the Psalms are filled with cries for redemption from difficult times and situations. Even the book of Job, believed by many scholars to be the oldest book in the Bible, affirms God's redeeming work and purpose in history: "I know that my Redeemer lives, and that in the end he will stand upon the earth," cried Job in the midst of his distress (Job 19:25).

Christ is indeed the Redeemer of the world. In Jesus' sacrificial death on the cross, the ultimate price was paid for the redemption of fallen man. And it was a permanent, costly price. "For you know that it was not with perishable things such as silver or gold that you were redeemed from the empty way of life handed down to you from your forefathers, but with the precious blood of Christ, a lamb without blemish or defect," proclaims 1 Peter 1:18–19. The Greek word for *redeemed* as it is used here is the verb *lutroo*, which means "liberate by payment of ransom."[3] Notice that in this verse written to believers, Peter draws out the costly nature of redemption for them. The redemption of humankind through Christ's work on the cross required the spilling of blood. Bloodshed is a long-established price for biblical salvation, beginning with the first blood that was shed on earth: that of the animal whose skin was used to cover Adam and Eve's nakedness—a covering that was both a literal and metaphorical saving from shame.

Christ, a sinless man and thus a lamb without blemish or spot, is the perfect kinsman-redeemer.

Christ, a sinless man and thus a lamb without blemish or spot, is the perfect kinsman-redeemer. He was both willing and able to make the transaction that exchanged sinful lives for new ones. Just as a coupon is handed over in exchange for a product or service, in the redemption process we exchange our old "empty way of life" (1 Peter 1:18) for a new, true life. Romans 8 and Ephesians 2, among other passages, articulate this redemption from one way of life to another. Paul sums it up in a letter to the Corinthians: "Therefore, if anyone is in Christ, he is a new creation; the old has gone, the new has come!" (2 Corinthians 5:17).

Throughout the Bible we see God at work to accomplish the purpose of redeeming—from Noah, who was saved from the flooding of the world by means of an ark; to the people of Israel, who were led out of slavery in Egypt; to Christ, who is the ultimate revealing of God's long-planned work through Christ's life. And 1 Peter 1:20–21 finishes out the picture: "He [Christ] was chosen before the creation of the world, but was revealed in these last times for your sake. Through him you believe in God, who raised him from the dead and glorified him, and so your faith and hope are in God." God's purposeful plan of redemption has been in place for a long, long time.

Another aspect of God's work revealed in the story of the Bible is reconciliation. According to the *Merriam-Webster Online Dictionary*, *reconciliation* simply means "to restore to friendship or harmony."[4] God is in the reconciliation business, and His ultimate goal is the reconciliation of all things under the headship of Christ. Ephesians 1:9–10 describes it this way: "And he made known to us the mystery of his will according to his good pleasure, which he purposed in Christ, to be put into effect when the times will have reached their fulfillment—to bring all things in heaven and on earth together under one head, even Christ."

Reconciliation—the restoring of harmony or of friendship—is causally related to God's purpose of redemption and relationship. Because of sin, our relationship with God is out of harmony; true friendship with Him is impossible in our fallen, sinful nature. We stand in need of reconciliation. But how can we who are so tainted by sin be in harmonious relationship with a God who is holy—who, by His very nature, is the antithesis of sin? It is only through the redemptive act of Christ. Here is the redemptive act: "But because of his great love for us, God, who is rich in mercy, made us alive with Christ even when we were dead in transgressions—it is by grace you have been saved" (Ephesians 2:4–5). In the words of the old hymn "There Is Power in the Blood," written by Lewis E. Jones in 1899, "there is … wonder-working power in the blood of the Lamb." And that wonder-working power is the power of Christ's blood to redeem us from our sinful nature and reconcile us with God. When we are redeemed, we can be in harmony with God because the imbalance between our sin and His holiness has been cancelled by the redemption process. So, by the nature of accepting the redemptive work of Christ, we are in fact reconciled to God. But there is more to it than that.

Reconciliation requires a certain measure of living out our restored friendship or harmony with God. Just as in any relationship, there has to be mutual activity or communication in order for the relationship to be functional. Let's say you had a fight with your best

---

By permission. From the *Merriam-Webster Online Dictionary* ©2008 by Merriam-Webster, Incorporated (www.Merriam-Webster.com).

friend and in the process both of you were hurt by the other's words and actions. Maybe another friend acted as a negotiator to broker a "peace treaty" of sorts between you, relaying explanations of actions and messages of forgiveness. Let's say that, technically speaking, through the negotiations of your go-between, your friendship has been restored. But if you don't speak to each another or spend time together, or if you secretly fear that your friend really hasn't forgiven you, are you really living in a state of reconciliation? Could people who observe your relationship detect whether you are reconciled if you don't talk to each other or if you are constantly asking people whether they think your friend is still mad at you?

It's the same way in our relationship with God. He desires to fellowship with us, to dwell richly in and through us. That is real reconciliation. That is the story of God that the Bible tells. Look at Ephesians 2:22 and at the C. S. Lewis quotation at the beginning of this chapter—God is making Himself a palace of a dwelling place in you.

> *Reconciliation requires a certain measure of living out our restored friendship or harmony with God.*

We started this chapter with an exploration of the relational nature of God and His purpose—His pursuit of a relationship with us. Redemption and reconciliation result in a restored relationship with God. But what does that relationship look like, and what are the implications of such a relationship? Through the Bible, God reveals what His intentions are for community and fellowship with His creation. In Exodus 25:8, God instructs Moses to have the people of Israel make a sanctuary for Him, and then He would dwell among them. This instruction to create the tabernacle expresses the desire of God to be in close communion with His people. But Hebrews 9:24 describes that earthly tabernacle as a mere copy of the perfect and permanent dwelling place of God in heaven. The relationship of community we shall ultimately have in heaven with God is described in the portrait of a new heaven and a new earth found in Revelation 21. Verses 2 through 4 paint the picture of that perfected union:

> I saw the Holy City, the new Jerusalem, coming down out of heaven from God, prepared as a bride beautifully dressed for her husband. And I heard a loud voice from the throne saying, "Now the dwelling of God is with men, and he will live with them. They will be his people, and God himself will be with them and be their God. He will wipe every tear from their eyes. There will be no more death or mourning or crying or pain, for the old order of things has passed away."

The promised perfected picture continues in Revelation 22:4: "They will see his face, and his name will be on their foreheads." We will then know Him fully, just as we have been fully known (1 Corinthians 13:12).

Until that time, however, by the redemptive power of the blood of Christ, we are able to be in a relationship with God in which He comes and makes His home within us. Jesus told His disciples, "If anyone loves me, he will obey my teaching. My Father will love him, and we will come to him and make our home with him" (John 14:23). This relationship, marked by love, reveals Him to the world around us. John 13:34 records the instruction Jesus gave to His followers: "A new command I give you: Love one another. As I

Experiencing God in True Worship

The Bible has a great deal to say about the desire of God that worship and glory be given to Him. This aspect of the Bible—that God desires to receive glory—troubles some people in that it can make God out to be in need of an ego boost. When we speak of God's purpose as being relational, it is not without an understanding of how God's desire to be given worship and glory ties into that relationship. In the excerpt below from the book *Perspectives on the World Christian Movement*, Steven C. Hawthorne examines the intertwined nature of worship, love, and relationship with God:

Since God is supreme, every creature should bow down in subjection. But can this really be the logic at the center of the universe? Our hearts won't buy it. There is something more. The Scriptures are loud about the truth that God is love. God calls people to love Him with all that they are. Where is God's love, and ours, in response?

A God who demands worship just because He's supreme doesn't seem like a very loving God. In fact, such a God might not seem like He is worthy to even be admired. God's penchant for praise might make Him appear to be struggling with a low self-image problem. It's foolish to speak of God's jealousy for worship as if He were a petulant tribal deity threatened by rival gods. God is not threatened; rather He is immeasurably saddened by false worship. When people worship anyone or anything besides Him, they become like it. God has better intentions for people.

What is true worship anyway? Worship takes place when people recognize who God is and offer public acknowledgment and freely approach God, personally offering face-to-face gratitude and day-to-day allegiance. Worship is genuine relational interaction with God. That's why God always welcomes us to worship with a gift. He never needs the worship gifts. But the gift brings the giver. That is why the nations are urged to come bringing a gift, offering God tokens of their finest worth (Psalm 96:8 and many others). By their sacrifices and gifts, they offer themselves….

Why is God so desirous of worship? Two reasons: He is delighted by the sincere love that comes to Him in true worship. But there is more: By wooing people into true worship, God is able to fully bestow His love upon them. You can see it in Psalm 96:6.

Splendor and majesty are before Him,
Strength and beauty are in His sanctuary.

"Splendor and majesty" do not refer to God's self-experience. Rather, along with "strength and beauty" (the parallel passage says "joy" in 1 Chronicles 16:27), they are features of God's presence that are to be the experience of people who approach Him in true worship. There can be nothing more splendid or majestic for humans than to be elevated and placed in the gorgeous, heart-stopping grandeur of God's regal presence.

Worship is the way that people glorify God. When looked at from God's point of view, we can see that worship is also God's way of glorifying people—in all the best sense of bringing people into their highest honor. Worship fulfills God's love. He loves people so vastly that He wills to exalt them to something better than greatness; He wants to bring them into an honored nearness to Him. Stretch your mind and your heart as far as you can, but you'll never perceive the extent of what God has prepared for those who love Him (1 Corinthians 2:9). (1999, 36–37) have loved you, so you must love one another. By this all men will know that you are my disciples, if you love one another." Again and again, the Bible tells us that the hallmark of a relationship with God is love—love that springs from God Himself. In 1 John 4:19, we read that "we love because he first loved us."

The purity of an unfractured relationship between God and humankind is an expression of His original plan. In such a restored relationship, the perfection of God's glory can be revealed and displayed. If God were merely a character in a play, we could break down the script and confidently identify His objective as relationship. But He is no imaginary character in a story. He is Yahweh—the great "I AM"—the all-powerful, all-sufficient Creator-God of the universe. How humbling it is to think of His pursuit to redeem and reconcile each of us so that we might have a restored relationship with Him. What priceless gifts are relationship with God, redemption, and reconciliation! And what a world they open up to us as His children. When we receive these gifts, we are charged with the mission and joy of working for reconciled relationships in the world around us. We have both an intake and an outflow capacity when it comes to God's gifts to us—a topic we'll explore in more depth in the next chapter.

The Bible tells us that the hallmark of a relationship with God is love—love that springs from God Himself.

❧

NOTES

1. *Merriam-Webster Online Dictionary*, s.v. "redeem," http://www.m-w.com/dictionary/ (accessed April 17, 2008).
2. *Holman Bible Dictionary*, ed. Trent C. Butler, s.vv. "redeem, redemption, redeemer," http://www.studylight.org/dic/hbd/ (accessed July 17, 2007).
3. *The New Testament Greek Lexicon*, s.v. "lutroo" (by Joseph Henry Thayer and William Smith), http://www.studylight.org/lex/grk (accessed April 27, 2007).
4. *Merriam-Webster Online Dictionary*, s.v. "reconciliation," http://www.m-w.com/dictionary/ (accessed April 17, 2008).

3

The Invitation:
Blessed to Be a Blessing

What the gospel offers … is the opportunity to be drawn into something larger than ourselves—into God's overflowing love that moves out in ever-widening circles, embracing the whole of creation. The gospel sees our humanity not in terms of needs to be met, but in terms of capacities and gifts to be offered in God's gracious service. We are created not to consume but to know God, not merely to meet our own needs but to participate in God's life and mission. —*James V. Brownson, Inagrace T. Dietterich, Barry A. Harvey, and Charles C. West*

By now it should be very clear to you that when we look into the Bible, we see what God is doing. In the previous chapters, we've established that the Bible is a story about God. As the main character, God is working to bring about His purpose—a pure, unblemished relationship with humankind, the pinnacle of His creation.

As we read the story of the Bible, we see God as He reaches out in relationship to us. Because of this, we sometimes get confused and believe the story of the Bible is about *us*. It is true that God desires to be in relationship with us; He desires it so much that He went to great expense to lavish His love on us through Christ. As we examined previously, God pursues relationship with us through redeeming us from our fallen state and reconciling us to Himself. What a blessing this is!

God invites us to participate in His purpose; He "blesses us so that we can bless others."

But if we stop there, we have missed the point. If we focus only on the relationship we can have with God and the blessings we receive from Him, then we are hearing only half of the message. If we come to the Bible with eyes only toward what we can get from God in terms of comfort, ease, and blessing, then we have misread the story, because the story is larger than that. God invites us to participate in His purpose; He "blesses us so that we can bless others." But what does this mean? It means, quite simply, that He is giving us an invitation to join Him. God is asking us to go along with Him on mission, and His mission is far-reaching—to the peoples of the world and to the depths of people's hearts. This has been His plan for us throughout His story in the Bible, and it is a very exciting plan! Let's take a look.

The Bible begins with a beautiful setting and a very significant tree—the Garden of Eden and the tree of the knowledge of good and evil described in Genesis 1–3. The Bible concludes with another beautiful setting and another significant tree—the new Jerusalem of heaven and the tree of life whose leaves "are for the healing of the nations" (Revelation 22:2)—nations that have been cursed by inheriting Adam's sin nature. What happens in the time between these two beautiful settings is the story of God's purpose being carried out to completion. As author and pastor Rob Bell says, "We live between the trees" (2005a).

The Bible continues with a narrative of humankind's ongoing sinful rebellion against God in Genesis 3–11, resulting in men and women being alienated both from God and from each other. These chapters culminate with the people's prideful attempt to construct the monument known as the tower of Babel, which resulted in the confusion of communication and the scattering of the nations "over all the earth" (Genesis 11:8). Christopher J. H. Wright says the following in *The Mission of God*:

> Genesis 1–11 poses a cosmic question to which God must provide a cosmic answer. The problems so graphically spread before the reader in Genesis 1–11 *will not be solved just by finding a way to get human beings to heaven* when they die. Death itself must be destroyed if the curse is to be removed and the way opened to the tree of life. The love and power of God must address not only the sin of individuals but also the strife and strivings of nations; not only the need of human beings but also the suffering of animals and the curse on the ground. (2006, 199)

So what does God do next, according to Wright? "He sees an elderly, childless couple in the land of Babel and decides to make them the fountainhead, the launch pad of his whole mission of cosmic redemption.... The call of Abram is the beginning of God's answer to the evil of human hearts, the strife of nations and the groaning brokenness of his whole creation" (2006, 199). This event, which propels us into the heart of the story of the Bible, begins in Genesis 12 with Abraham, as you will recall from chapter 1.

A Word About the Nations

Did you know that the Bible words translated as "nation" or "nations" mean something different than what we typically think of when we hear those words? Usually we think the word *nation* is synonymous with the word *country*, which brings to mind places such as India, Kenya, China, or the United States. According to *Merriam-Webster Online Dictionary*, the geopolitical definition of *nation* is "a community of people composed of one or more nationalities and possessing a more or less defined territory and government."[1] But when you see *nation* or *nations* in the Bible, the term generally has a different meaning, one related more to ideas of ethnicity, common language, and culture than to a particular country.

This distinction is important because a nation (as we tend to think of it) can have many cultural and ethnic groups within its geopolitical borders. In fact, today in our world there are more than six billion individuals living in over 230 geopolitical nations, but these nations are divided into more than sixteen thousand specific groups of people, or people groups.[2] This concept of a biblical nation as more than our idea of a geopolitical nation has great implications for the scope of mission that God invites us to join.

NOTES

1. *Merriam-Webster Online Dictionary*, s.v. "nation," http://www.m-w.com/dictionary/ (accessed April 17, 2008).
2. Joshua Project, "Ethne Overview," http://www.joshuaproject.net/ethne.php (accessed April 14, 2008).

From the *Merriam-Webster Online Dictionary* ©2008 by Merriam-Webster, Incorporated (www.Merriam-Webster.com).

The story of Abraham marks a very important and pivotal point in the Bible. Paul, in his writings to the churches in Galatia, refers to the opening lines of Genesis 12 as nothing less than the "gospel in advance" (Galatians 3:8). It is here that we see the beginning of the great narrative story of the Bible—a God who is pursuing relationship with people in all nations of the earth. With the introduction of this particular story, God begins revealing His mission to redeem and reconcile us to Himself so that we might enjoy things the way He intended them to be in the Garden of Eden before the Fall. Wright says that "God's mission is what fills the gap between the scattering of the nations in Genesis 11 and the healing of the nations in Revelation 22" (2006, 455).

John R. W. Stott sums up the significance of the call of Abraham and the opening lines of Genesis 12: "God made a promise … to Abraham. And an understanding of that promise is indispensable to an understanding of the Bible and of the Christian mission. These are perhaps the most unifying verses in the Bible" (1979). So, how does Genesis 12 begin?

> The Lord had said to Abram, "Leave your country, your people and your father's household and go to the land I will show you. I will make you into a great nation and I will bless you; I will make your name great, and you will be a blessing. I will bless those who bless you, and whoever curses you I will curse; and all peoples on earth will be blessed through you." So Abram left, as the Lord had told him; and Lot went with him. Abram was seventy-five years old when he set out from Haran. (Genesis 12:1–4)

"The whole of God's purpose is encapsulated here," says Stott (1979). That's worth examining more closely. First, it is almost impossible to overlook the word *bless* in this passage. Either alone or as a root word, *bless* occurs five times in the space of two verses. So, it is clear that God intends here to announce His desire to offer blessing. But there is more here than just a blessing for Abraham. What Stott calls the encapsulation of "the whole of God's purpose" is God's clearly stated intention to bless "all peoples on earth" through Abraham. Of course, from our vantage point in history and in the completed narrative of the Bible, we can see that God's intention to bless all nations has indeed come (and is coming) to fruition through Christ, the direct descendant of Abraham. We will examine this connection between Abraham and Jesus more closely later. As the name of Jesus is proclaimed throughout all the earth,

As the name of Jesus is proclaimed throughout all the earth, the missional purpose of God to bless all nations with the opportunity for relationship with Him is marching forward through time.

the missional purpose of God to bless all nations with the opportunity for relationship with Him is marching forward through time.

So, there is a long-range plan announced in this passage. And just in case Abraham—or anyone else—might have missed it, God returned to Abraham and extended and reaffirmed this promise several times. First, He extended the promise to include a covenant gift of land to Abraham's descendants (Genesis 15:1–21). Next, God declared that the covenant between Him and Abraham would be marked by the sign of circumcision (Genesis 17:1–22). Finally, at the end of the moving passage describing Abraham's unquestioning obedience to God's command to sacrifice Isaac, Abraham's son, God restates His initial promise to Abraham and reiterates His intention to bless all the nations of the earth through Abraham's offspring (Genesis 22:15–18).

Not only did God make this purpose clear to Abraham several times, but He reaffirmed His intentions to Abraham's son Isaac when He told him, "I will make your descendants as numerous as the stars in the sky and will give them all these lands, and through your offspring all nations on earth will be blessed" (Genesis 26:4). Finally, Abraham's grandson Jacob also receives a restatement of this promise of blessing during a dream recorded in Genesis 28:12–15. Again God promises, "All peoples on earth will be blessed through you and your offspring" (Genesis 28:14). Repeatedly God states His intention to bless not just Abraham and his family, but all nations.

Despite the prominence of the idea of blessing in Genesis 12:1–4, it is not the only important thing to notice in this passage. Abraham didn't just get to sit back and receive a lot of blessing. Something else was at work also. If you look again at the passage, you'll notice that it has an interesting structure. Yes, five different references to *bless* or *blessing* are made in verses 2 and 3. But these verses are sandwiched between two verses that involve a specific command and a specific act of obedience. The command came in Genesis 12:1: "The Lord had said to Abram, 'Leave your country, your people and your father's household and go to the land I will show you.' " In other words, without a lot of explanation or detail, God commanded him to go. God desired for Abraham to be set apart from his former identity, to be re-created into the man God intended him to be. In the same way that we become a new creation in Christ (2 Corinthians 5:17), God called Abraham to be set apart in a very literal way—by leaving behind just about everything that was familiar to him.

Genesis 12:1 is the first part of a type of "If …, then …" statement by God—"If you go, then I will bless." Abraham was offered an invitation to obey. And in Genesis 12:4, we see that he chose to do just that: "So Abram left, as the Lord had told him." By faith, Abraham followed God's command. If the relationship between obedience and blessing is not clear in Genesis 12, it is set out very definitely in the Genesis 22 reaffirmation of this covenant. Here God plainly states the relationship between Abraham's obedience and the blessing: "And through your offspring all nations on earth will be blessed, because you have obeyed me" (Genesis 22:18). Through obedience to God, Abraham embraced another facet of the promise of blessing—that he was blessed in order that he might be a blessing to others. Obedience on Abraham's part led to blessing not only for himself but also for those around him and for those who came after him. This is blessing with a purpose. The intention God had for calling Abraham, and therefore Israel, into a special covenantal relationship with Him was with a view toward His ultimate plan of blessing all the nations through Israel. Walter C. Kaiser Jr. observes the following about Abraham: "This man and his descendants were to be missionaries and channels of the truth from the very beginning" (1999, 12).

God called Abraham to be set apart in a very literal way—by leaving behind just about everything that was familiar to him.

We cannot overlook an extremely important component of Abraham's act of obedience: faith. Without faith, Abraham could not have gone to an undisclosed location, leaving behind all that was familiar. Abraham had to have faith to believe God even when he was not able to see with his own eyes the fulfillment of God's promise. To aid in this walk of faith, God gave Abraham a vision of the promise to hold on to. In Genesis 15, when Abraham questioned God about this faith to believe even though he had no children, God promised Abraham that he would have "a son coming from [his] own body" (v. 4). Then God took Abraham outside and showed him the sky: "Look up at the heavens and count the stars—if indeed you can count them … So shall your offspring be" (v. 5). Can you imagine being childless and looking into the night sky at the millions of stars and being told that your descendants would be as numerous as them? This mental image would be something that Abraham would remember the rest of his life and ponder on those days when things didn't look so good. It took faith to believe God and that vision, but "Abram believed the Lord, and he credited it to him as righteousness" (v. 6). It takes faith to obey—faith in the living God, Creator of the universe, who desires

??

Can you imagine being childless, looking into the night sky at the millions of stars, and being told that your descendants would be as numerous as the stars?

relationship with each of us. That is the faith of Abraham, and it is the same faith we are invited to have today.

Let's return to the idea of blessing with a purpose. In Genesis 12:1–4, we see an invitation from God for Abraham to be blessed, but it is a blessing with a specific purpose. A mission to all the nations is embedded in the lines of promise found in Genesis 12:2–3. This promise of purpose and mission is held before Abraham, but it required a response on His part. That response enabled Abraham's part in the mission to go forward. This pattern is modeled again and again in the Bible.

In his book *Unveiled at Last*, Bob Sjogren talks about the concept of reading the Bible in a way that looks for what he calls "top lines" and "bottom lines" in a particular passage. A top-line verse concerns a blessing that is promised or offered, and a bottom-line verse is one that concerns a responsibility or a response that is required. Top-line verses are often accompanied by bottom-line verses somewhere nearby. The fact is that some of us read the Bible looking only for those top-line blessings we can receive without taking a look at the bottom-line response or responsibility that comes alongside the blessing. This is the difference between reading the Bible as a story about us and our plans and reading it as a story about God and His plans. For example, Sjogren applies this pattern to Genesis 12:1–4: "The top line refers to God's blessing of Israel. He wants to bless His people. The bottom-line responsibility reveals that He wants His people not only to enjoy that blessing, but then to turn around and be a blessing to all families on the face of the earth" (1992, 29).

When we read the Bible with an eye on God's plan rather than our own, we can see beyond our own desires to a picture of a purpose: a purpose that is much bigger than ourselves, a purpose that God invites us to participate in. The ultimate fulfillment of God's purpose of relationship, redemption, and reconciliation is described in Revelation 7:9, which says, "After this I looked and there before me was a great multitude that no one could count, from every nation, tribe, people and language, standing before the throne and in front of the Lamb. They were wearing white robes and were holding palm branches in their hands." This picture of a diverse throng of worshippers around God's throne is the fulfillment of God's desires expressed to Abraham. Throughout the Bible we see God using Israel to reveal Himself to the nations in different ways. Among the examples is the blessing of Gentiles such as Rahab of Jericho (Joshua 2:1–21) and Jethro, Moses' father-in-law (Exodus 18:1–12). Later, David's faith gave bold testimony of

??

What is the difference between a top-line verse and a bottom-line verse in the Bible?

God's greatness to the Philistines who were gathered en masse to witness the defeat of Goliath (1 Samuel 17). Consider the temple of Solomon, completed during his reign, which contained an outer court dedicated to the Gentiles (1 Kings 8:41–43). During Israel's captivity, the faithfulness of servants such as Daniel brought blessing and faith in God to the Babylonian king Nebuchadnezzar and a later ruler of Babylon, King Darius the Mede (Daniel 2:46–49, 3:28–30, 6:19–28). Old Testament prophets often spoke of many nations worshipping God, not to mention God's commissioning of the reluctant prophet Jonah as a missionary to the entire Gentile nation of Ninevah. The Bible reveals a continuation of this theme of God's heart for people of all nations through the earthly ministry of Jesus.

When we read the Bible with an eye on God's plan rather than our own, we can see beyond our own desires to a picture of a purpose: … a purpose that God invites us to participate in.

Speaking of Jesus, what about the phrase "the gospel in advance" that we referred to earlier? Galatians 3:7–8 says, "Understand, then, that those who believe are children of Abraham. The Scripture foresaw that God would justify the Gentiles by faith, and announced the gospel in advance to Abraham: 'All nations will be blessed through you.' " What does the gospel have to do with Israel and the Old Testament? According to Christopher Wright, "the ingathering of the nations was the very thing Israel existed for in the purpose of God; it was the fulfillment of the bottom line of God's promise to Abraham" (2006, 194). The "ingathering of the nations" Wright refers to is that which the New Testament shows the beginnings of in Acts 1:8—Jesus' commission to believers to be witnesses to the ends of the earth. It is the mission that continues to this day, the mission that will be completed so that the worship around the throne of God pictured in Revelation 7:9 will come to fruition.

Paul brings clarity to the direct link between Abraham and Jesus: "The promises were spoken to Abraham and to his seed" (Galatians 3:16). The Scripture does not say "to his seeds," meaning many people, but "to his seed," meaning one person, who is Christ. Here we see the connection between the promise given to Abraham and the ultimate fulfillment of these promises that came through Abraham's descendant, Jesus Christ. And it doesn't stop there. The promise reaches out to you and me. According to Paul, "there is neither Jew nor Greek, slave nor free, male nor female, for you are all one in Christ Jesus. If you belong to Christ, then you are Abraham's seed, and heirs according to the promise" (Galatians 3:28–29). Thus, the faith of Abraham paved the way for the birth of the nation of Israel and ultimately the birth of Jesus Christ. Today, our faith in Christ brings us into this line of God's covenant people, which extends to all nations. Through Christ we become part of what N. T. Wright, the bishop of Durham, calls "the single, true, worldwide covenant family promised to Abraham."[1] So the story of our faith begins with the story of Abraham's faith, just as God promised thousands of years ago.

Reading the whole Bible as one story of God gives a richness and depth to our understanding of not only His mission but also our place in it. Perhaps the idea of joining God in a purposeful mission is a new concept to you. It is for many people. For some people, though, the idea of faith in God, or salvation, is the idea of being saved from hell—a type of fire insurance, so to speak, protecting us from an eternity in hell but having little bearing on life here and now. But this isn't the fullness of what the Bible teaches about God's desire for relationship with us. Have you ever wondered why God doesn't just take us to heaven after we are saved? The reason He doesn't is exactly what we have been talking about. We have a purpose, beyond redemption, right here on the earth. God has established a kingdom right here, and we have the privilege of being a part of it. The work of Christ enables us to enter not only into a future life with God in heaven, but also into our current life with God as we go on mission with Him to people of all nations on earth. There are millions of hurting people who need God's blessing, and we have an amazing opportunity to be vessels that God can use to bless others.

In their book *Adventures in Missing the Point*, Brian D. McLaren and Tony Campolo clarify through the following story the important idea that not only are we saved *from* something—eternity in hell—but we are saved *for* something—an amazing adventure on mission with God.

The Parable of the Race
by Brian D. McLaren and Tony Campolo
Excerpt from *Adventures in Missing the Point*

Consider the Parable of the Race. Once upon a time, in a land of boredom and drudgery, exciting news spread: "There is going to be a race! And all who run this race will grow strong and they'll never be bored again!" Exciting news like this had not been heard for many a year, for people experienced little adventure in this ho-hum land, beyond attending committee meetings, waiting in lines, sorting socks, and watching sitcom reruns.

Excitement grew as the day of the race drew near. Thousands gathered in the appointed town, at the appointed place. Most came to observe, skeptical about the news. "It's too good to be true," they said. "It's just a silly rumor started by some teenaged troublemakers. But let's stick around and see what happens anyway."

Others could not resist the invitation, arriving in their running shorts and shoes. As they waited for the appointed time, they stretched and jogged in place and chattered among themselves with nervous excitement. At the appointed time they gathered at the starting line, heard the gun go off, and knew that it was time to run.

Then something very curious happened. The runners took a step or two or three across the starting line, and then abruptly stopped. One man fell to his knees, crying, "I have crossed the starting line! This is the happiest day of my life!" He repeated this again and again, and even began singing a song about how happy this day was for him.

Another woman started jumping for joy. "Yes!" she shouted, raising her fist in the air. "I am a race-runner! I am finally a race-runner!" She ran around jumping and dancing, getting and giving high fives to others who shared her joy at being in the race.

Several people formed a circle and prayed, quietly thanking God for the privilege of crossing the starting line, and thanking God that they were not like the skeptics who didn't come dressed for the race.

An hour passed, and two. Spectators began muttering; some laughed. "So what do they think this race is?" they said. "Two or three strides, then a celebration? And why do they feel superior to us? They're treating the starting line as if it were a finish line. They've completely missed the point."

A few more minutes of this silliness passed. "You know," a spectator said to the person next to her, "if they're not going to run the race, maybe we should."

"Why not? It's getting boring watching them hang around just beyond the starting line. I've had enough boredom for one life."

Others heard them, and soon many were kicking off their dress shoes, slipping out of their jackets, throwing all this unneeded clothing on the grass. And they ran—past the praying huddles and past the crying individuals and past the jumping high-fivers. And they found hope and joy in every step, and they grew stronger with every mile and hill. To their surprise, the path never ended—because in this race, there was no finish line. So they were never bored again. (2003, 26–27)

The racers who were so delighted just to have entered the race are much like those who miss the important Bible truth that we are blessed to be a blessing. We are invited by God Himself to participate in the most important and exciting work we could possibly ever be a part of—in fact, what we were created for: blessing others out of the blessing we have received from Him. Think again of God's invitation to Abraham. God didn't say, "Sit back, Abraham, and watch me bless you." He asked Abraham to follow Him, to trust His leading even when it didn't make sense. By being willing to follow God, Abraham entered into a life of blessing that continues to have ramifications to this very moment in history. The gospel, the good news that Jesus Christ offers redemption and reconciliation with God, offers more than "fire insurance," a protection from eternity without God. James Brownson and others write the following in *StormFront: The Good News of God*: "The biblical understanding of salvation is that our lives become swept up into something larger and greater than ourselves, into God's purposes

> *"The biblical understanding of salvation is that our lives become swept up into something larger and greater than ourselves, into God's purposes for the world."*

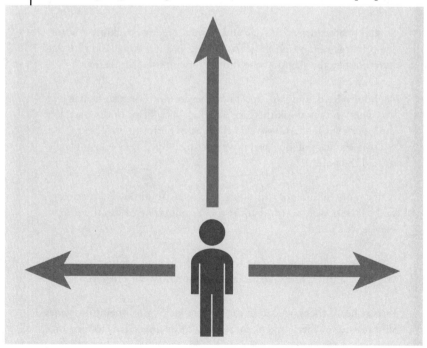

for the world" (2003, 34). We can choose not to fully join in, but then we are a lot like racers who dance around simply because they have crossed the starting line.

In the previous chapter, we looked at the relational heart of God and His purpose to redeem and reconcile us to a restored relationship with Him. But the Bible reveals that we are not invited solely into a "vertical" relationship with God. Through that vertical relationship with God, we are invited, enabled, and compelled to engage in a new level of "horizontal" relationship with people around us.

Our restored relationship with God is the means by which we can restore relationship with others around us. This is a weighty matter that is very different from what the world around us teaches and celebrates. Both the vertical and horizontal aspects of relationship demand time and effort to be cultivated. Consequently, relationship with God is something to be invested in with our whole being. This is clearly the heart of Jesus' teaching, and it is particularly evident in Jesus' response to a Pharisee's question about the greatest commandment:

> Jesus replied, " 'Love the Lord your God with all your heart and with all your soul and with all your mind.' This is the first and greatest commandment. And the second is like it: 'Love your neighbor as yourself.' All the Law and the Prophets hang on these two commandments." (Matthew 22:37–40)

First, observe that Jesus describes a full commitment to loving God—with our whole being, as it turns out. This command is a restatement of a command initially given to Israel thousands of years ago (Deuteronomy 6:5). Just as the Israelites lived in lands that were surrounded by pagan cultures in which the people worshipped many gods other than the one true God Yahweh, we too are surrounded by a culture whose people idolize other gods—wealth, celebrity, power, and a host of others—that are neither worthy of worship nor able to fulfill our needs. When this command was originally given, it was accompanied by instructions to surround oneself with discussion and reminders of God's commands (Deuteronomy 6:6–9). This is an indication that God is fully aware of the many other things that compete for our time and energies, the things we are likely to worship and pursue besides Him.

Let's look at the second part of Matthew 22:37–40. It is only through a love relationship with God in Christ that we can find the ability to truly meet the second command Jesus mentions—to love our neighbors as ourselves. In establishing the nation of Israel, God never forgot other nations, nor did He intend for Israel to. Similarly, the New Testament parable of the good Samaritan (Luke 10:25–37) clearly shows Jesus' teaching that mercy is to be freely distributed, regardless of nationality or other status. Although Jesus did focus a great deal of His attention on restoring the "lost sheep of Israel" (Matthew 10:6), He didn't overlook the opportunity to minister to those outside Israel as well, such as the Roman centurion who requested healing for his servant (Matthew 8:5–13), the Canaanite woman who had a demon-possessed daughter (Matthew 15:21–28), and the Samaritan woman who found Living Water at the well (John 4:1–42). Of course, the death and resurrection of Jesus mark a turning point in the story of God's mission to the nations, as God's redemptive work erased lines of division between Gentile and Jew (Ephesians 2:14–22).

The death and resurrection of Jesus mark a turning point in the story of God's mission to the nations, as God's redemptive work erased lines of division between Gentile and Jew (Ephesians 2:14–22).

This kind of love—the kind that reaches across cultural, racial, economic, political, religious, and all other lines—is the love that flows from the heart of God, the love that enables redemption and reconciliation in our relationships with one another. Jesus spoke of this in John 13:34–35: "A new command I give you: Love one another. As I have loved you, so you must love one another. By this all men will know that you are my disciples, if you love one another." While this "new command" may not sound all that different from Jesus' earlier command to "love your neighbor as yourself," this one *is* different because in it Jesus includes Himself as a model for our love. In identifying His love as the standard—a kind of love that makes one willing to lay down his life for the benefit of others—Jesus expands our definition of loving others so that it is centered on the idea of sacrifice and mission. Verse 35 leaves no doubt that our love for one another is a testimony of Christ to those around us.

Another noteworthy facet to biblical teaching about our relationship with each other is the inclusion of information about the treatment of our enemies. Jesus' Sermon on the Mount includes the instruction to "love your enemies and pray for those who persecute you" (Matthew 5:44; see also Luke 6:27–36). Paul notes in Romans 5:10 that God reconciled us to Himself while we were His enemies, indicating that even "enemy status" cannot stand in the way of our extending love to another person. We, having been blessed by God with the opportunity for redemption and reconciliation through Christ, must surely do no less than participate in blessing others. Just as was Abraham, we are blessed to be a blessing. Paul's take on it is this: "All this is from God, who reconciled us to himself through Christ and gave us the ministry of reconciliation" (2 Corinthians 5:18).

So, this is the type of race we are invited to run—not a celebration over simply crossing the starting line, but a full-on, unending adventure of following God and participating in His mission of reconciling the world to Himself. You are cordially invited on mission with the King of kings, Creator of the universe, to help lavish His goodness and gifts freely on a hurting and needy world. Along the way there will be more blessing than you can dream of.

Could there be a more exciting invitation?

ᴄᴐ

NOTE

1. N. T. Wright, "New Perspectives on Paul" (paper presented at the 10th Edinburgh Dogmatics Conference, Rutherford House, Edinburgh, 2003), http://www.ntwrightpage.com/Wright_New_Perspectives.pdf (accessed July 17, 2007).

The Kingdom of God

Because the truth is that Jesus himself is the presence of the kingdom. The kingdom is not a new political regime. It is not a new programme. It is not a new ideology. It is not a new philosophy. It is the person of Jesus. And to know what God's kingly rule is, one must believe in Jesus and come with him.
                                                              —*Lesslie Newbigin*

Remember McLaren and Campolo's story, "The Parable of the Race," from the last chapter? In that story, some of the entrants were completely clueless about how to be in a race—they crossed the starting line and that was it. Others in the parable saw this bizarre behavior and, realizing there is more to a race than just starting, took up the challenge of running the course. They "got" what it means to be in a race (2003).

Similarly, we have the chance to "get" what it means to be a follower of Christ. An important truth of the Bible is that we are invited to participate in God's work. God does bless us to be a blessing to others. This is a major part of God's story. It means there is more to the story than crossing the starting line—we are invited to run a race with God. But what does that journey look like? That is the continuing story we get to be a part of—God's story that unfolds as we see and participate in the kingdom of God throughout the earth.

The Bible speaks a great deal about kings and kingdoms. Much of the Old Testament is concerned with the kingdom of Israel, both united and divided—united and ruled by Saul, David, and Solomon; and divided as the later kingdoms of Israel and Judah and ruled by many kings. In the Old Testament, there are continuing references to God's kingdom, as in Psalm 145:13: "Your kingdom is an everlasting kingdom, and your dominion endures through all generations. The Lord is faithful to all his promises and loving toward all he has made." In the New Testament, there are even more. In the Gospels, one of the central themes—if not *the* central theme—of Jesus' teaching is the kingdom of God. The idea of God's kingdom is mentioned fifty times in the book of Matthew alone. And of course, it is a recurrent theme in the rest of the New Testament. This theme includes a picture of the fully realized kingdom of God drawn throughout Revelation, a kingdom in which worshippers from every nation, tribe, and tongue surround God's throne in the new Jerusalem where God dwells with men (Revelation 7:9–10, 21:1–5).

Despite the Bible's focus on God's kingdom, the true sense of a *kingdom* is probably a pretty foreign concept for you. Even if you happened to grow up in a country that has a modern monarchy, your idea of kingdom and kingship is likely radically different from that of someone living in the time when this teaching was originally centered. To begin to get at the heart of what the Bible teaches about God's kingdom, it helps to understand the context in which the peoples of the Bible understood a kingdom. James Brownson and others elaborate in their book *StormFront*:

> In order to understand the kingdom of God, we first need to understand the role of the king in the ancient world. This requires an exercise of the imagination, since kingship represents a social structure vastly different from our own experience and assumes a whole pattern of relationships quite alien to our culture. To put it in simplest terms, in the ancient world the king is the richest person around. He commands most of the resources in the country. The king's power, however, comes essentially from generosity. That is, the king gives to others (especially to other nobles) and expects allegiance (both personal and financial) in return.... This reciprocity of generosity and allegiance represents the fundamental "contract" that defines social life in the ancient world. (2003, 38)

Here we see some of the context in which the biblical teaching on kingdom was situated for those who heard it originally. There is an element of reciprocal relationship and an element of generous power in well-functioning historical kingdoms. These qualities are important for us to understand about kingdom life, since they help us translate into our own setting a picture of the idea of allegiance and the authority and power of the king. The idea of authority was the primary concept articulated by Hebrew and Greek biblical terms for kingdom according to theologian George Eldon Ladd, who wrote, "The primary meaning of both the Hebrew word *malkuth* in the Old Testament and of the Greek word *basileia* in the New Testament is the rank, authority and sovereignty exercised by a king.… First of all, a kingdom is the authority to rule, the sovereignty of the king." Ladd distinguishes this primary meaning of kingdom, "rule or authority," from a secondary meaning, "realm." He goes on to define the kingdom of God as having to do with the primary meaning: "When the word refers to God's Kingdom, it always refers to His reign, His rule, His sovereignty" (1959). We should understand the basic meaning of kingdom as first having to do with authority and rule, and second as a realm. Both ideas are important. As Dallas Willard explains in *The Divine Conspiracy*, the kingdom of God is "the range of his effective will, where what he wants done is done" (1998, 25). God has all authority and deserves our allegiance. He is sovereign, and we must always hold the idea of His authority foremost in our understanding of the Bible's teaching on His kingdom. We will explore the idea of realm, which is also very significant, a bit later in this chapter.

"The kingdom of God is the living, breathing presence and purpose and reign of God on our planet."

Upon examining the Gospels, it is immediately clear that Jesus spoke about the kingdom in both concrete, simple terms as well as in parables that are sometimes enigmatic. Many of His teachings about the kingdom of God come through parable or poetic language. The book of Matthew is full of similes about the kingdom, similes that begin with "The kingdom of heaven is like …" and end with words such as *yeast*, *mustard seeds*, and *treasures*. As Ladd notes, "The perplexing fact is that when we turn to the Scriptures, we find an almost equally bewildering diversity of statements about the Kingdom of God. If you will take a concordance of the Bible, look up every reference in the New Testament alone where the word 'kingdom' occurs, write down a brief summary of each verse on a piece of paper, you will probably find yourself at a loss to know what to do with the complexity of teaching" (1959).

In his book *This Beautiful Mess*, pastor and author Rick McKinley describes God's kingdom this way:

> The kingdom of God is the living, breathing presence and purpose and reign of God on our planet. It's beautiful *and* irreducible. To reduce it to a seven-point outline might help you on the quiz, but it won't get you any closer to the experience. It would be like cutting up a corpse to figure out what it means to be human—sure, you'd end

up with identifiable body parts in formaldehyde and maybe a micron photograph of a neurotransmitter, but the wonder of pulsing human life would elude you. (2006, 21)

Even in trying to describe what God's kingdom is, there is a danger of falling into the error of somehow stripping the complexity, life, and reality from the kingdom Jesus spoke about. There is the perilous prospect of reducing something alive to something quantifiable and understandable, but perhaps not so real as it was in the original telling. So it is critical that, as in all matters, we depend on the Holy Spirit to lead us in discerning truths about God's kingdom. Despite the complexity and depth present in the Bible's teaching about the dynamic and living reality of God's kingdom, some basic truths emerge—things that we can see about God's kingdom, which in turn enable us to participate in it.

> *The presence of the kingdom of God is the presence of Jesus.*

Recall the quotation at the beginning of this chapter. In the most basic sense, Newbigin says that the presence of the kingdom of God is the presence of Jesus: "To know what God's kingly rule is, one must believe in Jesus and come with him." Newbigin also says simply, "[The kingdom of God] is the person of Jesus" (2005, 53). Such an equation is suggested by verses such as Acts 8:12, which speaks of the good news—or gospel—as that of both the kingdom and Jesus in the same breath: "But when they believed Philip as he preached the good news of the kingdom of God and the name of Jesus Christ, they were baptized, both men and women." Acts 28:23 and 28:31 make similar pairings. That the kingdom of God is equated with the presence of Jesus is a key element to making sense of the Bible's paradoxical teachings regarding the kingdom of God, some of which Ladd has identified:

- The Kingdom is a present reality (Matthew 12:28), and yet it is a future blessing (1 Corinthians 15:50).
- It is an inner spiritual redemptive blessing (Romans 14:17) which can be experienced only by way of the new birth (John 3:3), and yet it will have to do with the government of the nations of the world (Revelation 11:15).
- The Kingdom is a realm into which men enter now (Matthew 21:31), and yet it is a realm into which they will enter tomorrow (Matthew 8:11).
- It is at the same time a gift of God which will be bestowed by God in the future (Luke 12:32) and yet which must be received in the present (Mark 10:15). (1959, formatting added)

Yet even these seemingly contradictory statements about the kingdom begin to gain clarity when we understand the presence of the kingdom to mean the presence of Jesus. In each of the verses in the above quotation, you can substitute the phrase "presence of Jesus" for "kingdom of God" and, in so doing, enhance understanding without changing the meaning of the passage. Understanding the kingdom of God in terms of the presence of Jesus not only makes it more accessible to us perhaps, but also rightfully centers attention on the person and work of Jesus Christ as the turning point in the work of God to bring about His purpose.

The books of Matthew and Mark both record the first message of Jesus' preaching ministry as an announcement of the kingdom. Mark 1:14–15 says, "After John was put in prison, Jesus went into Galilee, proclaiming the good news of God. 'The time has come,' he said. 'The kingdom of God is near. Repent and believe the good news!' " Matthew 4:17 simply states that "from that time on Jesus began to preach, 'Repent, for the kingdom of heaven is near.' " Jesus is announcing that His presence, His kingdom, has arrived. "When Jesus announced that the kingdom of God was drawing near, many of His hearers must have recognized an echo of those visions recorded in the Book of Daniel," according to *Nelson's New Illustrated Bible Dictionary*. "These prophecies declared that one day 'the God of heaven will set up a kingdom which shall never be destroyed' (Daniel 2:44). Jesus' announcement indicated the time had come when the authority of this kingdom would be exercised."[1] As Stan Nussbaum observes from Luke 4, "Jesus reads to his hometown synagogue from Isaiah 61 and then stuns his hearers by announcing that Isaiah's very down-to-earth messianic prophecy was fulfilled that day" (2005, 26). Here is Christ in the flesh announcing that He is the fulfillment of this Old Testament promise of a triumphant kingdom of God.

> *God's kingdom is both present now, and not yet fully present.*

It is quite evident that Jesus was speaking about a present reality when He announced that the kingdom was at hand. Yet, in other places in the Bible, such as 1 Corinthians 15:50, the kingdom is clearly a future reality as opposed to current life on earth. How do we resolve the seemingly contrary teachings?

In *The Gospel of the Kingdom*, Ladd describes in depth what is sometimes referred to as the "now and not yet" aspect of the Bible's teaching about God's kingdom. God's kingdom is both present *now*, and *not yet* fully present. "God's Kingdom is the realm of the Age to Come, popularly called heaven; then we shall realize the blessings of His Kingdom (reign) in the perfection of their fullness. But the Kingdom is here now. There is a realm of spiritual blessing into which we may enter today" (1959).

Ladd speaks here of a realm that "we may enter today," and this is a tremendously important focus. The kingdom of God is a real realm or dimension of experience that we may enter into at the present time. When we focus only on the "not yet" aspect of the kingdom, we miss out on the very real presence of Jesus and the presence of the kingdom of God that is going on right now all around us on planet Earth in the twenty-first century. Failure to make this connection is perhaps what caused those racers from our earlier parable to miss out on completing the race. Overlooking the "now" aspect of God's kingdom can keep us from joining God in bringing about His purpose. Perhaps we stumble about in part because as finite human beings we are bound by the space-time continuum, whereas God is infinite and not similarly bound. Thus we find it very hard to discover language that adequately describes the present reality of this infinite realm.

> *When we focus only on the "not yet" aspect of the kingdom, we miss out on the very real presence of Jesus and the presence of the kingdom of God that is going on right now all around us on planet Earth.*

One author who does a good job of capturing these dynamics is N. T. Wright, who writes in *Simply Christian*, "And, with [Jesus of Nazareth], God's future has arrived in the present, has arrived in the person of Jesus. In arriving, it has confronted and defeated the forces of evil and opened the way for God's new world, for heaven and earth to be joined forever … not only heaven and earth, but also future and present, overlap and interlock. And the way that interlocking becomes real, not just imaginary, is through the powerful work of God's Spirit" (2006, 221–22).

At the moment of salvation, we enter spiritually into the realm of God's kingdom, as we willingly submit ourselves to God's authority. But one of the things we talked about in the previous chapter is that we are not simply saved *from* something, but that as Christians we are saved *for* something. This something is participation in the kingdom of God—not only in the future as residents of heaven, but in the present moment as residents of this earthly life through the Holy Spirit promised by Jesus.

> He is, at the moment, present with us, but hidden behind that invisible veil which keeps heaven and earth apart, and which we pierce in those moments, such as prayer, the sacraments, the reading of scrip-

ture, and our work with the poor, when the veil seems particularly thin. But one day the veil will be lifted; earth and heaven will be one; Jesus will be personally present, and every knee shall bow at his name; creation will be renewed; the dead will be raised; and God's new world will at last be in place, full of new prospects and possibilities. This is what the Christian vision of salvation … is all about. (N. T. Wright 2006, 219)

If we are willing to accept Jesus as Savior only but not make Him King of our lives, we are much like those racers who cross the starting line and fall all over themselves about the fact that they've simply entered the race. We are missing the point of the reciprocal relationship present in a kingdom. Remember the earlier description of an ancient kingdom—a generous king and subjects who show allegiance to the king? Without living as though Christ is King of our lives, we are missing the part about allegiance. We are missing the invitation to participate more deeply and fully in the adventure God has for us. More devastatingly, we are failing to remove ourselves from the throne of our hearts, and that failure leads to the chaos that always comes when we try to run our lives on our own terms. And what about the impact this me-centered approach to Christianity has on the people around us whom we are called to love and serve? Is it possible to truly obey Jesus' command in Matthew 22:39 to love our neighbors as ourselves if we are simply looking to receive the benefits of salvation but not walking in allegiance to the King who saves us? You will recall from earlier chapters the difference it makes in our perspective when we read the Bible as a story about God rather than about ourselves. The same principle applies to the kingdom of God. Unfortunately, we are tempted continually to miss out on this fact.

Perhaps the complexity of the biblical teaching regarding the kingdom of God is one of the reasons why we tend to overlook it. But there are several other factors that can obscure our vision when it comes to seeing and participating in God's kingdom. The book *Missional Church* points to one factor—thinking of the kingdom as something separate from the message of salvation: "The church has tended to separate the news of the reign of God from God's provision for humanity's salvation. This separation has made salvation a private event by dividing 'my personal salvation' from the advent of God's healing reign over all the world" (Guder 1998, 92). Jesus announced both kingdom and salvation in the same breath, inviting people to *repent*—a term we most often associate with salvation—and *believe* the good news about the kingdom, and thus enter into the kingdom (Mark 1:15). Willard puts it like this: "The reality of God's rule, and all … it involves, is present in action and available with and through the person of Jesus. That is Jesus' gospel" (1998, 28). It is instructive that the Great Commission, which is so firmly identified with evangelization and salvation, comes at the end of Matthew—the account that contains the most teaching on the kingdom of God of all four New Testament Gospels. Look again at the Matthew 28:20 phrase "and teaching them to obey everything I have commanded you." Wouldn't this "everything" have something to do with the teachings previously described by Matthew, including a command found in Matthew 6:33 to seek first the kingdom of God? Surely it would! So, we cannot stop the race just over the starting line and neglect the seeking of His kingdom—a kingdom of generosity and grace to others as we see in the parable of the vineyard workers (Matthew 20:1–16), a kingdom open to all manner and classes of people (Matthew 21:28–32), a kingdom that is such a treasure that it is worth exchanging all we have for it (Matthew 13:44–45).

Thinking of salvation as an individual, private event can also lead to a false divide between private and public life for Christians. Nancy Pearcey writes about the effects of this dichotomy in her book *Total Truth*: "Our lives are often fractured and fragmented, with our faith firmly locked into the private realm of church and family, where it rarely has a chance to inform our life and work in the public realm. The aura of worship dissipates after Sunday, and we unconsciously absorb secular attitudes the rest of the week. We inhabit two separate 'worlds,' navigating a sharp divide between our religious life and ordinary life" (2004, 35). Because we often think of our faith as a private matter, we miss the vision of kingdom: the interest God has in our whole lives and in our offering of our lives in service to those around us. We are not called to be Sunday-only Christians who put up a great-looking facade. We are invited into an experience of kingdom life with God each day of the week, not just the days the church doors are open, and in every facet of our lives, not just the "religious" ones. That is what true allegiance to the King of kings involves.

This idea of keeping one's faith to oneself and out of the public square is certainly reinforced by the messages of the culture around us. Examples abound of Christians who are discouraged, or even outright banned, from expressing their faith in public ways. Perhaps this reality is another reason that we can fail to see and participate in God's kingdom and that we think of the kingdom as only a future reality. The world around us is pretty hostile to many expressions of Christian faith, so how can God's kingdom be present right now in this kind of world? Willard addresses this in *The Divine Conspiracy*:

> One thing that may mislead us about the meaning of "at hand" in Jesus' basic message is the fact that *other* "kingdoms" are still present on earth along with the kingdom of the heavens. They too are "at hand." That is the human condition. Persons other than God, such as you or I, are still allowed on earth to have a "say" that is contrary to his will. A kingdom of darkness is here, certainly, and the kingdoms of many individuals who are still "trying to run their own show."
>
> All of this God still permits…. The "enemies" are certainly here, but we are safe in God's hands even though other "kingdoms" loom over us and threaten us. (1998, 29–30)

This biblical truth of other kingdoms being allowed rule in the interval between the incarnation of Christ and His promised return has to do with the "not yet" element of God's kingdom we talked about earlier. In this regard, it is important to remember that the primary meaning of kingdom is "authority or rule" and secondarily "realm." It is only by God's authority that these other kingdoms are allowed to exist in this earthly realm at the present time. At no time is God's ultimate rule or authority—God's kingdom—threatened, despite the fact that God allows other rulers and powers to exist in our current age here on earth (Ephesians 6:12, Colossians 1:16). In this manner, God's kingdom is "not yet" fully revealed in the sense that His authority, though total, is not fully acknowledged. Even now Christ is in authority over all (Ephesians 1:18–21). And ultimately, every knee will bow before Him (see Isaiah 45:22–24, Romans 14:11, and Philippians 2:9–11). We will look more in depth at the interaction between God's kingdom and other "kingdoms" in the next chapter.

This biblical truth of other kingdoms being allowed rule in the interval between the incarnation of Christ and His promised return has to do with the "not yet" element of God's kingdom.

Perhaps it is the very presence of those who oppose God's kingdom that leads to another false divide that obscures our understanding of the invitation to participate in God's kingdom. Similar to faulty thinking about public and private Christianity is the ancient and false idea that the world is divided into sacred and secular realms. This type of thinking is called dualism. In his book *Exiles*, author Michael Frost notes that Christians have struggled with this from the days of the early Church on. "This dualism has, over 1,700 years, created Christians who cannot relate their interior faith to their exterior practice, and this affects their ethics, lifestyles, and capacity to share their faith meaningfully with others," Frost writes. "It also affects how we see our work.…We can easily think of a friend entering church-ordained ministry as following God, but rarely do we speak of a decision to become a computer programmer or a nurse or a filmmaker or an accountant as similarly following God's calling in our lives" (2006, 185). From thousands of years ago to the present moment, we have struggled with thinking that only certain areas of our lives or certain types of service are honoring to God or are devoted to Him. This is the very opposite of the teaching of the Bible and, particularly, of the teaching on the kingdom of God.

> *We are invited to participate—and come alongside God in His work—to help reveal to those around us the fact of His authority and the reality of another way of living in His realm here on earth.*

We tend to think of those so-called "sacred" professionals—pastors, priests, missionaries, theologians, evangelists—as the only folks called to kingdom building. The rest of us can sit on the sidelines and cheer them on as they advance the kingdom of God. Notice two words used in the previous sentences: *building* and *advance*. Here we have stumbled into another popular fallacy regarding God's kingdom. We are tempted to think of the kingdom of God as something that we are supposed to *build, bring about, establish,* or *advance*. But that is not what the Bible says. "The verbs *to build* and *to extend* are not found in the New Testament's grammar for the reign of God. The announcement of God's reign nowhere includes an invitation to go out and build it, nor to extend it. These are not New Testament ways of speaking about the reign of God" (Guder 1998, 93). And if you remember the idea of the kingdom of God being the presence of Jesus, these types of verbs become all the more nonsensical. How can you build or advance Jesus?

Instead of these aggressive, human-centered verbs, we see in the Bible the words *enter* and *receive* in reference to what we are to do with regard to the kingdom of God. We don't have to advance or build God's kingdom, because God is in charge of that. He does it all and has done it all, through Jesus Christ, the fulfillment and embodiment of the kingdom of God. He is already in total control; His kingdom, in the sense of His rule or authority, is unquestioningly over all things (1 Chronicles 29:10–13, Psalm 145:13, Matthew 28:18). In the sense of the kingdom of God as a realm, we are invited to participate—and come alongside God in His work—to help reveal to those around us the fact of His authority and the reality of another way of living in His realm here on earth. But the power of the kingdom is God's, not ours. We are instructed to receive the kingdom, and we are invited to enter into the kingdom, just as we are invited to receive Christ and enter into relationship with Him. This calls for humility, not hubris. Jesus said, "I tell you the truth, anyone who will not *receive* the kingdom of God like a little child will never *enter* it" (Luke 18:17, emphasis added). These actions are drastically different from advancing and building. "Inherent within the two biblical images of gift and realm are the further issues of repentance and faith. Receiving and entering are actions that mark a turning from other hopes and loyalties that we may accumulate to a singular hope in the one true God. They mark a turning in faith from sinful rejections of God's rule as well as carefree disdain for God's mercy and care. Receiving and entering the reign of God are the ways we 'turn to God from idols' (1 Thessalonians 1:9). This movement indicates that we are involved in an ongoing dynamic relationship with the divine reign" (Guder 1998, 96).

In many ways we are entering into that which cannot be seen, because the kingdom is spiritual in nature. Until the coming age, when God's kingdom will be revealed to all (Philippians 2:9–11), the kingdom of God is something we see more in part than in full, similar to Paul's description found in 1 Corinthians 13:9–12. In a sense, the kingdom of God can be seen but not seen at the same time—another kingdom paradox. Let's try to unpack it. Jesus taught that this kingdom is not observed through natural powers: "The kingdom of God does not come with your careful observation" (Luke 17:20). Instead, it is spiritually discerned, as Jesus told Nicodemus: "I tell you the truth, no one can enter the kingdom of God unless he is born of water and the Spirit" (John 3:5). As Jesus spoke to Nicodemus about spiritual birth, He drew a comparison between the wind and the Spirit (John 3:7–8). Things of the Spirit are similar to the wind: you cannot see the wind, but you can certainly see its effects; you know it is there. The comparison relates to the kingdom of God as well. At the present time, God's kingdom isn't yet fully seen in and of itself, but the effects of the authority and rule of God's kingdom are profoundly apparent to those who have what Jesus called "ears to hear" (Matthew 11:15, 13:9–16; Mark 4:11–12). The kingdom is certainly not wholly unseen. The effects of God's rule and authority—God's kingdom—can be seen just as the wind's effects, and the Spirit's, are visible. Active participation in God's kingdom demonstrates to the world around us a strong witness for the power of Christ. This is why we are called to participate in His kingdom, to join in God's relational, redemptive, reconciling purpose and mission.

"Once, having been asked by the Pharisees when the kingdom of God would come, Jesus replied, 'The kingdom of God does not come with your careful observation, nor will people say, 'Here it is,' or 'There it is,' because the kingdom of God is within you."
—Luke 17:20–21

"Jesus answered, 'I tell you the truth, no one can enter the kingdom of God unless he is born of water and the Spirit.'"
—John 3:5

This is a kingdom of practicing His presence both as individuals and as a community. As God's children, we have the choice every day to participate or not to participate in His kingdom. One of the ways we participate is by developing our own relationship with the Lord to deeper and deeper levels. Yet this type of individualistic approach to the kingdom is clearly not all that God has in mind. The Bible repeatedly challenges us to be in community—meeting together for worship, fellowship, sharing of one another's burdens,

The Kingdom and the Church

"Since the days of Augustine, the [k]ingdom has been identified with the [c]hurch," notes George Eldon Ladd (1959). This is particularly true in much Protestant theological teaching. Though often equated in the minds of many Christians, the kingdom of God and the church are not one and the same. However, they do enjoy a very close and important relationship. To understand these two entities and their relationship, let's begin with some word study.

At the most basic level, a study of the New Testament Greek terms for *kingdom* and *church* reveal very different meanings. The Greek word translated "church" is *ekklesia*, meaning a calling out, "a gathering of citizens called out from their homes into some public place."[1] This term had a very specific meaning in the ancient world. "The most common classical usage of *ekklesia* and its cognates was as a political term, meaning an assembly of citizens," notes Roy Bowen Ward in *Restoration Quarterly* (1958, 164). Ward notes that by the time the New Testament was written, the meaning had shifted: "When *ekklesia* was used, it became what it was because of Jesus Christ; for it became the technical term of that institution which assembled in his name, and which was composed of people who sustained a certain relationship to him, i.e., people 'in Christ' " (179). On the other hand, as we have already discussed in this chapter, the Greek word *basileia* primarily means "rule or authority" and secondarily means "realm" (Ladd 1959). The word *church* comes from a word indicating a very specific physical entity, while the word *kingdom* is from a Greek word that doesn't necessarily have a physical component.

The book *Missional Church* details some of the differences between the kingdom (or reign) of God and the church, noting that the church is a community that both issues from the kingdom of God and is directed toward the kingdom in service. "The church always stands in a position of dependence on and humble service to the divine reign" (Guder 1998, 98). But while recognizing that the kingdom and the church are not the same thing, the book warns against divorcing the two: "The church is constituted by those who are entering and receiving the reign of God. It is where the children of the reign corporately manifest the presence and characteristic features of God's reign. The divine reign expresses itself in a unique, though not exhaustive or exclusive, fashion in the church" (99). So, it is entirely possible for God to act and work by His Spirit outside the entity of the church but not outside the authority and rule of His kingdom. Recognizing the distinction between kingdom and church places the church in proper relationship to the kingdom, or reign, of God. "We are led to capture the biblical sense of the church's calling and vocation this way: *the church represents the reign of God*. This is another way of rendering the fundamental New Testament notion of witness, but promises a fresh and holistic approach to viewing all of the church's life." The church represents the kingdom by pointing "away from itself to what God is going to complete" (101), and the church actively represents the kingdom as its agent and instrument, as its ambassador. "By its very existence, then, the church brings what is hidden into view as sign and into experience as foretaste. At the same time, it also represents to the world the divine reign's character, claims, demands, and gracious gifts as its agent and instrument" (102).

NOTE

1. *The New Testament Greek Lexicon*, s.v. "ekklesia" (by Joseph Henry Thayer and William Smith), http://www.studylight.org/lex/grk (accessed April 17, 2007).

prayer, and instruction and teaching, among other things (Acts 2:42–47). We are admonished not to forsake meeting together (Hebrews 10:24–25). Kingdom life is a team sport! We are designed to live in community and serve one another. Recall one of Jesus' teachings on the kingdom: "The King will reply, 'I tell you the truth, whatever you did for one of the least of these brothers of mine, you did for me' " (Matthew 25:40). When we think of this community in which kingdom life is to take place, our minds are naturally and immediately drawn to the church. But the church and the kingdom of God are not the same thing, though they are closely related. God's rule and authority—His kingdom—are not found only in the church. God's authority extends to all, whether or not it is acknowledged. (Read more in "The Kingdom and the Church" sidebar on page 74.)

If you aren't sure of anything else after reading this chapter, you should certainly know that the kingdom of God is living, real, and paradoxical—both simple and complex, both seen and unseen, both now and not yet. And we are invited to participate, to enter, and to receive! So what does it all mean? We are going to be exploring that question for the remainder of this course, looking at various aspects of God's kingdom mission in a variety of ways, ultimately exploring what God is saying to you about your role in His kingdom. Along the way, we will uncover more and more of the meaning of participating in the kingdom of God. Consider this chapter just the first layer of the onion we are peeling together as we discuss the mission of God, His kingdom, and your place in it.

〇〇

NOTE

1. *Nelson's New Illustrated Bible Dictionary*, ed. Herbert Lockyer Sr., s.v. "Jesus Christ," http://www.ebible.com/dict/NNIBD/jesus (accessed February 19, 2008).

Behind Enemy Lines

One of the things that surprised me when I first read the New Testament seriously was that it talked so much about a Dark Power in the universe—a mighty evil spirit who was held to be the Power behind death and disease, and sin. The difference is that Christianity thinks this Dark Power was created by God, and was good when he was created, and went wrong. Christianity agrees with Dualism that this universe is at war. But it does not think this is a war between independent powers. It thinks it is a civil war, a rebellion, and that we are living in a part of the universe occupied by the rebel.

Enemy-occupied territory—that is what this world is. Christianity is the story of how the rightful king has landed, you might say landed in disguise, and is calling us all to take part in a great campaign of sabotage.

—*C. S. Lewis*

You may be scratching your head a little bit from the last chapter, trying to understand all the different paradoxes related to the kingdom of God. By far, one of the most puzzling aspects we encounter is the tension between the very real kingdom of God present on earth today and the harsh realities of suffering and evil in the world around us—realities that cause so many people to question even the existence of God, much less His supremacy. It is true, there is much suffering and evil in our world. But the Bible teaches that there is another "ruler" at work on earth right now, one whose trade involves deception, lies, and every evil work (Ephesians 2:2, John 16:11). We are instructed in Ephesians 6:11–12 to understand that we are to "stand against the devil's schemes" and recognize that our battle is against "spiritual forces of evil." So, how is the kingdom of God supreme and real right now?

We are going to look at two sources to help explain the tension between the kingdom of God and other kingdoms. Central to understanding God's supremacy even in the presence of evil is the realization that the kingdom of God and the kingdom of God's enemies are *not* equal in nature. God is supreme over all; the enemies of God are allowed their "reigns" subject to God's provision and boundaries. This idea will be explored in more depth later in this chapter, but let's begin with a short piece, "D-Day Before V-E Day," by Pastor Ken Blue. This article draws a helpful analogy of the relationship between God's kingdom and what Blue calls "Satan's pseudokingdom":

> Through His authentic life, perfect sacrifice and victorious resurrection, Jesus effected a transfer of sovereignty from Satan's pseudokingdom to God's kingdom. Now Jesus claims to possess all authority in heaven and earth (Matthew 28:18). God always had this authority, but through the Incarnation it is established in history. And the implications of Jesus' "all authority" are now manifest through the Church in history.

"The kingdom of God has already gone through its darkest night. The most dismal evil in all history found its absolute limits at Calvary."

> Satan is bound and his pseudokingdom is breaking up, yet God has left him room to maneuver. What power and freedom he still possesses and precisely when he is able to exercise these is not entirely clear from Scripture. What is clear from Scripture and increasingly confirmed in our experience is that the kingdom of God has already absorbed the full wrath of Satan's might and survived it. The kingdom of God has already gone through its darkest night. The most dismal evil in all history found its absolute limits at Calvary. After evil had choked on its own venom, it became forever subject to Christ and to us in His name. There is no absolute dualism between God and Satan. The victor at the end of the battle is already crowned. Yet there are still many sick and some demonized people among us who are subjected to the unsanctioned and illegal power of Satan. How are we to understand this ambiguity?
>
> A helpful illustration of how a war already won could continue to be fought comes from the history of World War II. On "D-Day" the allied troops landed successfully at Normandy beach in order to establish a secure beachhead on the European mainland. It was understood by military experts at the time that this operation secured ultimate victory for the allies. There would be, however, many more bloody battles fought before the day on which ultimate victory would be realized: "V-E Day" (Victory in Europe Day).
>
> In God's war with evil, "D-Day" occurred with the death and resurrection of Christ. Ultimate victory is now assured; yet the fight rages on till "V-E Day," the glorious return of Christ. Between these times, the Church presses the battle against the evil which remains in the world. Blood is still shed in these battles, and some of the blood will be ours, but we are assured that the ultimate victory of the past will be fully realized in the future. (1987)

Blue's historical analogy can help us understand better the "now" and "not yet" aspects of God's kingdom as well as the relationship between God's kingdom and the competing "other kingdoms" of the enemy in this current age of history. But to give us an even more-detailed look at this present reality, we turn to author Charles Kraft (2000) and an excerpt from the chapter "Two Kingdoms in Conflict" in the book *Behind Enemy Lines*.

As you read, you will notice that Kraft (2000) uses strong military imagery and phrases such as "taking territory from Satan" and "extend" the kingdom. At first glance, this sort of language may seem to be in conflict with what we learned in the last chapter. We have said that the Bible teaches the kingdom of God not as something to be advanced or built, but rather as something to be received and entered into. It might appear that a phrase like "taking territory from Satan" affirms the idea of building or advancing the kingdom. But if you look deeper, you'll see there isn't really a contradiction. Paul reminds us in 2 Corinthians 4:4, "The god of this age has blinded the minds of unbelievers, so that they cannot see the light of the gospel of the glory of Christ, who is the image of God." The "god of this age" that Paul refers to is, of course, Satan, who seeks to blind as many people as possible to the truth of Christ. This analogy of blindness is apt—as we partner with Jesus to take back territory from Satan, we are inviting those who are blinded to the truth of the kingdom to *receive* the truth and *enter into* life with Christ. We can help remove the blinders by proclaiming truth. The act of receiving Christ translates the formerly blinded one from the kingdom of this world to the kingdom of God, as Paul makes clear in the following:

> As for you, you were dead in your transgressions and sins, in which you used to live when you followed the ways of this world and of the ruler of the kingdom of the air, the spirit who is now at work in those who are disobedient. All of us also lived among them at one time, gratifying the cravings of our sinful nature and following its desires and thoughts. Like the rest, we were by nature objects of wrath. But because of his great love for us, God, who is rich in mercy, made us alive with Christ even when we were dead in transgressions—it is by grace you have been saved. (Ephesians 2:1–5)

> For God, who said, "Let light shine out of darkness," made his light shine in our hearts to give us the light of the knowledge of the glory of God in the face of Christ. (2 Corinthians 4:6)

Just as a candle throws new light on the perspective of one who is in darkness, the truth of Christ lived out and proclaimed by us to the world offers people a firsthand view of the present kingdom of God and the opportunity to receive and enter it. When we participate with Jesus in taking back territory from the enemy, we are not establishing a part of the kingdom that wasn't there before; we are simply helping to reveal God's kingdom that is already present but unseen by many who are blinded by the lies of the enemy. The language in Charles H. Kraft's excerpt that follows should be understood in that context. Let's now turn to that excerpt to learn more about the origins and nature of the conflict between kingdoms, and the battle that we are charged to be a part of.

Dominion by Deceit

God created the earth and created it well. When finished, he filled it with all kinds of living creatures. Last of all he formed his masterpiece, mankind. God's desire was not only to live in fellowship with his creatures, but that they, under him, would rule and reign over earth. "Have many children," he told them, "so that your descendants will live all over the earth and bring it under their control" (Genesis 1:28, GNB).

Just as a candle throws new light on the perspective of one who is in darkness, the truth of Christ lived out and proclaimed by us to the world offers people a firsthand view of the present kingdom of God and the opportunity to receive and enter it.

There was only one thing he required of them as the condition of their authority—obedience. Meet this requirement and all would go well. Disobey and the result would be death (Genesis 2:17). And this death, as we find out later, would involve both the breaking of the perfect fellowship with God for which we are made and the loss of authority over the creation.

But there came a tempter, a powerful and deceptive fallen archangel. Very skillfully, he questioned God's motives in requiring such specific obedience. "If you follow my advice and eat the fruit," he said, "you will be like God and know what is good and what it bad" (Genesis 3:5, GNB).

So God's cherished creatures, his highest creation, the ones he walked with in the cool of the evening, broke the one rule God had made for them. They were tempted and disobeyed God. So they fell from their place of privilege and authority, and all creation fell with them.

What had been created very good now became cursed by God and dominated by the enemy. They now lived behind enemy lines. In their obedience they had had dominion, and every tree and plant that grew had been beneficial to them. But in a cursed and fallen world nothing would come easily.

They would only survive through hard, sweaty work. And even then the ground would produce weeds and thorns as abundantly as it once produced fruit. The world, the cosmos, and the created order all fell under a curse. Satan was free to roam the earth, corrupting God's creation, for humans had given him their authority over the universe.

It was this one act of disobedience that gave Satan the right to say to Jesus, "It has all been handed over to me" (Luke 4:6, GNB). In exchange for Jesus' obedience, Satan could legitimately offer to Jesus the power and authority he gained in the Garden.

From Then On Conflict

From the Fall on, we see in Scripture continuous conflict between the kingdom of Satan and the kingdom of God. This conflict takes place both on earth and in the heavenlies. Though the battles on earth are often obvious, only occasionally is the veil thrown back to allow us to see what is going on behind the scenes.

"From the Fall on, we see in Scripture continuous conflict between the kingdom of Satan and the kingdom of God."

In the first two chapters of the Book of Job, we get to eavesdrop on a conversation between God and Satan. In it, God brags about his servant Job and Satan requests permission to test him. In response, God gives Satan permission to take away from Job all that he has except his life (Job 1:12, 2:6). Job remains steadfast, though not without complaint. In the end, then, the victory is God's and Job is both vindicated and blessed by God with a tenfold return of what he lost.

In Daniel chapter ten we get another glimpse of the conflict between the two spiritual kingdoms. Daniel had apparently prayed and requested God's assistance. It took, however, a full three weeks for help to reach him because the angel sent by God was delayed by "the angel prince of the kingdom of Persia" (Daniel 10:13, GNB). Not until the archangel Michael was sent to help was the first angel able to get through to Daniel.

A further glimpse of heavenly conflict occurs when Jesus announces that he "saw Satan fall like lightning from heaven" (Luke 10:18, GNB) in response to the authoritative ministry of Jesus' disciples. Later, we are told of Satan's desire to sift the disciples "as a farmer separates the wheat from the chaff" (Luke 22:31, GNB). But Jesus prayed for Peter that he would be strengthened in his faith and that, in turn, he would strengthen the rest.

Given these and other scriptural indications of spiritual conflict in the cosmos, we can assume that it continues to our day. As God's kingdom people, then, we live behind enemy lines and, whether we like it or not, are involved in the war in two ways. As those attacked by Satan, we ourselves are a battlefield. And as those commissioned to join with Jesus in taking territory from Satan, we are soldiers in Jesus' army.

Satan's Kingdom

If Satan is "the evil god of this world" (2 Corinthians 4:4, GNB) and the "ruler of this world" (John 14:30, GNB) and if "the whole world is under the rule of the Evil One" (1 John 5:19, GNB), then we all live our lives in enemy territory. It is not, therefore, mere idle boasting when Satan claims that "all this power and all this wealth … has been handed over to me, and I can give it to anyone I choose" (Luke 4:5–6, GNB).

> *"We all live our lives in enemy territory."*

We live as aliens amid the forces of Satan's kingdom. No one, especially Christians, can avoid contact and conflict. But Satan's authority is both delegated and limited. Satan is not in ultimate control even of what he rules.

If, as most Bible students believe, the passage in Isaiah 14 is applied to Satan, we see that his desire was to "climb up to heaven and to place [his] throne above the highest stars. [He] thought [he] would sit like a king…. [He] said [he] would … be like the Almighty" (Isaiah 14:13–14, GNB).

Having been cast out of heaven for rivaling God, Satan attempted to be lord over the earth and lord of all mankind. Though he gained that position by deceit, he knew the promise that one day the Messiah would come and crush his head (Genesis 3:15). For centuries, he tried to destroy the righteous line of descendants through whom his great opponent would come. He tried desperately to destroy Jesus soon after his birth by inspiring Herod to slaughter all male children under three years old in Bethlehem (Matthew 2:13–18).

After Jesus was empowered by receiving the Holy Spirit, he became an even greater threat to Satan's kingdom, and the battle was on in earnest. During the wilderness temptations, Satan sought to defeat Jesus by inducing him to bow down to him (Luke 4:1–13). In Gethsemane the enemy may well have attempted to kill him through his own anguish and the unfaithfulness of his disciples (Luke 22:39–46). Satan's big play, though, was made at the crucifixion, and he thought he had won at last. But on the third day the Father raised his Son and freed him "from the power of the spiritual rulers and authorities" (Colossians 2:15).

Thus thwarted in his ultimate aim, Satan seems to have purposed himself to ruin as much of God's creation as possible, and especially to destroy mankind. If Satan cannot attack God himself or ascend to his throne, his uncontrollable jealousy and hatred drive him to attack and destroy those on whom God has fixed his love.

Satan envies God and humans with their creative abilities that enable them to produce good things. For Satan is unable to create. He can only pervert and ruin things made by someone else. So in jealousy, envy, and hate born of frustration and pride, he goes about counterfeiting and destroying things produced by God and those made in God's image.

His kingdom appears to be well-organized and populated by a large number of fallen angels. In Ephesians 6:12 we read of several types of wicked spiritual forces inhabiting the heavenly world. Among them are "rulers, authorities, and cosmic powers" (Ephesians 6:12, GNB).

Though we don't know exactly how much authority and power Satan has, there is plenty of evidence that it is great. He seems to be on a long tether. Apparently he has been allowed to retain the authority and power he once had as an archangel. *He must, however, work within the limits set for him by God. For God's kingdom and Satan's kingdom are not equal kingdoms. Indeed, the only power Satan has to fight against God is that delegated to him by God. He is dependent on God even for the power to rebel and deceive.*

The Kingdom of God Is at Hand

Into this world controlled by the Evil One, God has planted his own kingdom. This kingdom of God was the constant theme of Jesus' ministry. He spoke of it, he demonstrated it, he illustrated it, and he commanded his disciples to put it first in their lives (Matthew 6:33). After his resurrection, then, he turned the kingdom over to his followers to extend it to the ends of the earth under the guidance and power of the Holy Spirit. For this task he left them (and us) in the world, behind enemy lines as it were. And he armed us with his authority, and commanded us to take as much territory as possible for his kingdom before he returns.

> *"God's kingdom and Satan's kingdom are not equal kingdoms."*

This is a kingdom populated by those who are redeemed and thus freed to attempt to fulfill the mandate God gave to Adam—to obey and depend on him. Its basis is the conscious allegiance, faithfulness, and obedience to God for which humans were designed. Its characteristics are righteousness, truth, light, peace (well-being), joy, and the like.

The characteristics of God's kingdom are just the opposite of those that characterize Satan's. God brings freedom in place of the bondage imposed by the enemy (Luke 4:18–19), freedom in obedience to a loving God. Whether it is from spiritual, emotional, or physical problems, God seeks to bring freedom from satanic captivity. And each time a person comes to Christ and receives physical or emotional healing or is released from a demon's influence, territory is recaptured from Satan's kingdom and claimed for God's.

God's kingdom is even more good than Satan's is evil. It is even more truthful than Satan's is deceitful. It is a kingdom of light in place of the enemy's kingdom of darkness, a kingdom of well-being, of meaningfulness, of joyfulness, of fulfillment of what humans were intended to be.

God's Strategy

There are three primary aspects to God's strategy to counter enemy schemes: God restricts, God protects, and God attacks.

1. *God restricts the enemy by setting limits on his activity and his influence.* Though Satan has great power, we know that "the Spirit who is in [us] is more powerful than the spirit in those who belong to the world" (1 John 4:4, GNB). In the discussion concerning Job, Satan pointed to the restrictions God had placed upon his activity when he said:

> You have always protected him and his family and everything he owns. You bless everything he does, and you have given him enough cattle to fill the whole country. But now suppose you take away everything he has—he will curse you to your face! (Job 1:10–11, GNB)

In response to Satan's complaint, God relaxed the restrictions so that everything Job had authority over—goods, family, and, eventually, even his health—was placed under Satan's power. God said, "All right, he is in your power, but you are not to kill him" (Job 2:6, GNB).

In the New Testament, we find Jesus restricting the enemy when he demanded permission to "sift" the disciples (Luke 22:31). We also see God restricting and releasing Satan for various purposes throughout the Book of Revelation. It was only by God's permission that the enemy was allowed by God to inflict on the apostle Paul a "thorn in the flesh" (2 Corinthians 12:7–10).

If Satan were allowed to work unchecked, the result would be total destruction of the human race (John 10:10). But our merciful God does not allow this (Lamentations 3:22). Instead, whenever we are attacked by the enemy, God restrains and restricts him. Satan is only allowed what God permits.

<aside>

God's Strategy

1. God restricts the enemy by setting limits on his activity and his influence.
2. God's restrictions on Satan's power result in our protection.
3. On occasion, God's strategy is to attack.

</aside>

2. *God's restrictions on Satan's power result in our protection.* God knows we are weak (Psalm 103:4) and need protection from a multitude of harmful things we never know are there. Think of the many germs that don't make us sick or the many accidents that never quite happen to us. We are even protected from bearing the full consequences of many of our mistakes and bad judgments. It is God's protective activity that keeps such things from troubling and destroying us.

Why God doesn't protect people from more of the horrible things that go on, we don't know. Though a certain amount of protection is automatic, God has allowed both satanic beings and humans enough autonomy that they can hurt others. But we are assured that God "will not allow [us] to be tested beyond [our] power to remain firm; at the time [we] are put to the test, he will give [us] the strength to endure it, and so provide [us] with a way out" (1 Corinthians 10:13, GNB). We have a loving God who protects and cares for us as a shepherd protects and cares for his sheep (John 10:11–15). We are, however, instructed by Jesus to pray to the Father to "keep us safe from the Evil One" (Matthew 6:13, GNB), suggesting that we gain more protection when we ask God for it.

3. *On occasion, God's strategy is to attack.* When he called Moses to go before Pharaoh, God went on the offensive; likewise, when Elijah was commanded to challenge the prophets of Baal. The coming of Jesus was, of course, God's most obvious and successful attack on Satan and his kingdom. We are told in 1 John 3:8 that "the Son of God appeared … to destroy what the Devil had done" (GNB). But Jesus did not launch his attack right away. During his early years, he did no miracles and apparently made little impression even on the people of his hometown. They were astounded when he began to teach with authority and to do mighty works (Matthew 13:53–58).

The enemy must have been puzzled during this time, wondering when Jesus would make his move. That didn't happen, however, until Jesus received the empowerment of the Holy Spirit at his baptism (Luke 3:21–22). At that point, he aggressively challenged the kingdom of darkness, declaring war on Satan in the power of the Holy Spirit (Luke 4:14), healing, casting out demons, teaching concerning God's kingdom, and recruiting warriors to assist in the cause.

Each time Jesus healed a person or freed him or her from demons, he was attacking and taking territory from the Evil One. Even his teaching ministry was a part of his offensive against the enemy. When Satan connived to get him killed, then, thinking he had won the victory over Jesus, the Father took the offensive and raised Jesus victorious once and for all over the worst the enemy could throw at him.

"The thief comes only to steal and kill and destroy; I have come that they may have life, and have it to the full."
—John 10:10

The Human Part of God's Strategy

It is God's strategy for humans to play a major part in the defeat of Satan and his hosts. God chose to defeat the enemy in and through the Man, Christ Jesus. It was not in the form of deity that Jesus warred with Satan, it was as the second Adam, as a man.

Jesus limited himself to the empowerment he received from the Holy Spirit, accepting the same limitations as the rest of the human race. It was as a man that Jesus lived under the authority of the Father (John 5:30) in absolute allegiance, obedience, and dependence. He refused to do anything on his own (John 5:19), choosing to teach only what came from the Father (John 7:16, 46; 8:26–28, 38). He worked the Father's works (John 5:17), doing only what he saw the Father doing (John 5:19–20), demonstrating the Father through his deeds (John 10:37–38; 14:11), and in everything pleasing the Father (John 8:29). It was as a man that he declared his intention to release people from Satan in what has been called "the Nazareth Manifesto":

> The Spirit of the Lord is upon me, because he has chosen me to bring good news to the poor. He has sent me to proclaim liberty to the captives and recovery of sight to the blind, to set free the oppressed and announce that the time has come when the Lord will save his people. (Luke 4:18–19, GNB)

"Whether we are fighting to bring wholeness in physical, emotional, or spiritual areas, we are involved in the battle in which Jesus enlisted us–taking territory away from the Evil One."

On earth, Jesus committed himself to training and equipping his followers to continue the war. He set an example that his disciples could follow, saying both "As the Father sent me, so I send you" (John 20:21, GNB) and "Whoever believes in Me will do what I do—yes, he will do even greater things" (John 14:12, GNB). And he gave his followers "power and authority to drive out all demons and to cure diseases" (Luke 9:1, GNB), and commanded them to teach their own followers "to obey everything I have commanded you" (Matthew 28:20, GNB). At the very end of his ministry, Jesus told his disciples to wait in Jerusalem until they received the same gift of the Holy Spirit that had launched him on his ministry. (Compare Acts 1:4 with Luke 3:21–22.) Then they would be empowered to "be witnesses … to the ends of the earth" (Acts 1:8, GNB). And this is where we come in.

Our part in this war is first to receive the Holy Spirit's empowerment. Then we must imitate Jesus' obedience and intimate relationship with the Father. This enables us to follow his example in warfare against the kingdom of Satan. We are to put on the armor God makes available to us (Ephesians 6:10–18) and to fight in the power of the Holy Spirit "against the wicked spiritual forces in the heavenly world" (Ephesians 6:12, GNB).

We are not to run or to hide or to act as if there is no war going on. Whether or not we are carrying out our responsibility, our enemy, the devil, is continually active, roaming around "like a roaring lion, looking for someone to devour" (1 Peter 5:8, GNB). He does not stop his activity and we are not to stop or avoid the task God has given us.

One part of our activity is *defensive*. We are to claim the protection God offers us from the enemy's forces. Our armor is useless unless we put it on (see Ephesians 6:11–17). Defensively we can claim protection for ourselves, our families, and our property. We are given authority to defend people, places, and affairs from the attacks of the enemy by declaring in Jesus' name that they belong to God's kingdom....

Another part of our activity is *offensive*. We are to witness to the lost to rescue them from the Evil One and to bring them into "the glorious freedom of the children of God" (Romans 8:21, GNB). To be effective evangelists we must witness in God's power (Acts 1:8), not simply according to our own abilities. We must take authority over the places and circumstances in which we witness. It is amazing how freely the gospel can be shared when the place has been "cleaned out" of evil spirits beforehand by commanding them to leave in the name of Jesus Christ.

Bringing people to salvation is, however, only a part of the offensive activity to which we have been called as soldiers of God's kingdom. Even after salvation, many remain in considerable bondage to the Evil One in other areas of their lives. Jesus' victory is intended to bring them to freedom emotionally and physically, as well as spiritually.

Whether we are fighting to bring wholeness in physical, emotional, or spiritual areas, we are involved in the battle in which Jesus enlisted us—taking territory away from the Evil One....

... Much we have still to learn. I pray, however, that God will bless you and help you through reading this to take your proper place in his army to fight for his kingdom in whatever ways he leads you. (2000, 18–29; formatting added)

Kraft has traced for us the origins of the cosmic battle between Satan and God, the victory over Satan achieved by Christ's death and resurrection, and both the work of God and our part in revealing more and more of His kingdom to a deceived and fallen world. We are invited to be part of the reconciling work of God—His purpose and His kingdom. Now that we have a better sense of the lay of the land, we can begin to more fully see and embrace our place in the adventure that God has invited us to share with Him.

Review: God's Mission and Purpose

It's hard to believe, but we have already finished nearly a fourth of this course. We have taken a look at the Bible and what it has to say to us—particularly about the mission of God, which is our primary focus. In this foundational study of the Bible, we have looked at many basics about God's story and mission. From here on out, we will continue to examine this story from several different angles—culture, history, and your own call to living out your part of the story. All these lenses will help deepen your understanding of missio Dei, or the mission of God. Throughout history, men and women have taken up the challenge to join God's mission. Abraham is certainly one of them, as are many of the people we read about in the pages of the Bible. And we each have the choice to answer that challenge with our own lives. The idea of joining God on His mission to fulfill His purpose is what is meant by the terms *missional living* or *living missionally*. It is what we have been talking about in this unit—understanding the story God is telling about His purpose, and discovering and living out our part in it.

We are each invited to come into deep and meaningful relationship with the Creator of the universe as He continues His mission to redeem and reconcile the people of the world to Himself. When we talk about living missionally, we are really talking about joining the mission of God or, to put it another way, about participating in God's kingdom. Missional life involves intentionally living out that idea of our "being blessed to be a blessing"—not only in huge, grand ways, but, perhaps even more important, in all the small, seemingly insignificant ways of day-in, day-out life here on planet Earth with all these other people who are precious in God's sight. Our starting point for understanding all of this is the Bible—not just because it is a good book, but because it is God's story. Since God made us and everything that surrounds us, His telling of the story is, quite frankly, the only point of view that matters.

The Bible, from Genesis to Revelation, tells the story of God's purpose.

What Difference Does It Make?

- What have you learned about God by understanding the Bible as His story and understanding that He is the main character? Now that you know those things, what effect will they have on your life?

- Do you read the Bible differently after having studied this unit? If so, what difference does that make in the way you perceive the Bible? What about in the way you live your day-to-day life?

- Most of the time we don't think about the fact that our lives are telling a story to other people. What sorts of truths is the story of your life revealing to those around you? How can you be more intentional about the story your life is telling?

In chapter 1 of this unit, we encountered Lesslie Newbigin's book *A Walk Through the Bible*. In it, Newbigin called the Bible "an interpretation of the whole of history from the creation to its end, and of the human story within that creation" (2005, 5). His telling of the story of the Bible seeks to capture the holistic element—the Bible is *one* story told from the perspective of its author and central character, God. What are the implications of this perspective? The Bible cannot be seen as merely a reference book we turn to when we have a problem or need some guidance in a particular situation. Understanding the Bible as God's perspective on history and the universe points us to God's point of view about everything. And more important, reading the Bible as God's story points us directly to the Author, and it should create in us a desire to get to know Him better.

Think about a best-selling book or a popular movie. Sometimes the story told is so compelling that people want to know more about the author or director who brought the story to life. This was certainly the case when *The Fellowship of the Ring* (Walsh, Boyens, and Jackson 2001), the first movie in *The Lord of the Rings* movie trilogy, was released. People from all walks of life wanted to know more about the director, Peter Jackson. He was everywhere—on television, in magazines—answering questions about the filming of the movies, the decisions he made in adapting the Tolkien books into film form, the costumes, the makeup, the shooting schedule— every little detail. People wanted to know more about this man who had dared to bring such an epic story to life on-screen. How much more exciting it should be for each of us to want to know the God who brought to life such an epic story as the one the Bible tells—an epic story, by the way, that continues to this moment and that you are a part of even as you sit reading this page in this book.

Referencing the people of Europe, Newbigin says that for at least a thousand years "the story told by the Bible was *the* story by which people understood the meaning of their lives" (SE p. 7). This has certainly changed. Our contemporary world, though completely shaped by the Bible's influence, has very little understanding of what the Bible says. Newbigin points out that even though many homes have at least one copy of the Bible in them, owning a Bible doesn't necessarily translate into the understanding of how the Bible is shaping one's life, a common understanding in Western history. The Bible's story, however, is powerfully able to shed light into our lives and their meaning. Engaging the story of the Bible is the first step to understanding the significance and purpose our lives have in an ongoing relationship with God through Christ.

It is worth stopping here to talk a little bit about the power of story. Remember the anecdote at the beginning of chapter 1 about truth clothed in story? Narrative storytelling is an incredibly powerful form of conveying truth. Sometimes we hear a list of truths and they go in one ear and out the other, but stories have a way of sticking with us. The story of God as revealed in the Bible is interwoven in and through the stories of many men and women. Moses would tell one type of story about his own life of being on mission with God, Paul would describe his life of mission differently, and so on. For every character in the Bible, there is a different story of encounter and relationship with God.

You have your own story of relationship with God … Your story is being written every day, and it is told in one way or another to the world around you.

The same is true for you. You have your own story of relationship with God, whether it is a story of intimacy or of estrangement. Your story is being written every day, and it is told in one way or another to the world around you. The story your life tells each day reveals truths to that world. Daily, more and more chapters are being written in this story of you and God, a story that can be a powerful communiqué to the rest of the world. Your story can be one of adventure and fellowship as you follow God's lead through your part in this story. Or your story can be a much-less-inviting picture of your attempts to manipulate God into following your plan for things. Our part of God's story is being written moment by moment as we make choices about who we are going to honor and serve with our lives—God or ourselves. This gets back to perspective. You'll remember from chapter 1 that how we read the Bible reveals a lot about our perspective of how the world works.

The Bible is one big story about God and His purpose, not a lot of little stories or a book aimed at showing you how He will bless you. Some people are guilty of a "yearbook approach" to reading the Bible. You know … when you get your yearbook, the first thing you do is look for pictures of yourself. (C'mon, admit it!) We sometimes do the same thing with the Bible—we dive in looking to see how this book is going to provide answers for the problems in our lives and bring us peace and comfort. Don't misunderstand—the Bible *does* provide answers for our problems, it gives guidance for pursuing peace, its words can comfort us in our darkest times. But this is all true because *the Bible tells the story of God and how His purpose will be fulfilled*, not the story of man and how his wants and needs can be satisfied. Even when we begin to realize that there is a way of reading the Bible that focuses on what God is up to, it is still tempting to pursue our own ends when we turn to God's Word. Consider your own perspective as you read the Bible. What difference does it make in your reading, in your daily life, and in your relationship with God when you approach the Bible as His story?

God's purpose is relationship, redemption, and reconciliation.

What Difference Does It Make?

- Which relationships do you turn to first when you're looking for guidance and support? Does your relationship with God have the same sort of dynamic interaction as some of your other relationships? Should it?

- Would you describe yourself as someone who seeks reconciliation, whether for yourself—reconciliation between you and God or between you and other people—or for others whom you help reconcile with God? What are some situations you see in your world that could use reconciliation?

- What is the importance of relationship—both vertically with God and horizontally with others? Why do you need both? What are you doing in response to God's purpose?

In chapter 2, we uncovered that God's purpose is clearly seen in the story of the Bible. Maybe this was a revelation to you. He is at work with a specific plan that began in eternity past and marches throughout time and space right up until eternity future. We have said that the Bible is the story of God as He acts to achieve a particular purpose or objective throughout history and eternity. And you will remember that God's purpose is relationship, redemption, and reconciliation. We are invited into a redeemed and reconciled relationship with God, the Creator of the universe. This is His original intent for us, and His mission ever since the Fall has been to reconcile us to Himself. Through Christ we have access to redemption and reconciliation with God, but the fullness of relationship with Him doesn't just happen by accident.

As in any relationship, there must be mutual activity and communication for the relationship to be functional. Otherwise, it is a relationship in name only. Throughout this unit, you should have been able to see that relationship with God is to be dynamic, intimate, and reciprocal. It might be interesting to compare the nature of your strongest relationships with people around you to your relationship with God. What characterizes your relationship with your best friend or closest family members? What characterizes your relationship with God? Which relationship would you turn to first in a difficult situation? To whom would you go for counsel? Our relationship with God is so foundational to the adventure He calls us to be a part of that we will continue to look at it in different ways throughout this course. But make no mistake—your relationship with God, whether or not you acknowledge it, is at the heart of your being. You cannot escape the fact that you are in a relationship of some sort with the Creator God. It may be a rich and intimate relationship, or it may be something you have tried to push far from your mind; but whether broken or whole, a relationship of some kind already exists between you and God.

One of the most exciting facets of a reconciled relationship with God is the invitation to participate with Him on mission in the world throughout history. You'll recall from chapter 2 that when we receive the gifts of relationship with God, redemption, and reconciliation, we are charged with the mission and joy of working for reconciled relationships in the world around us. We have both an intake and an outflow capacity when it comes to God's gifts to us.

God invites us to participate in His purpose; He blesses us so that we can bless others.

This brings us to an important reminder from chapter 3—we are blessed in order to be a blessing. Remember Abraham? "Get up out of your comfort zone, Abraham," God basically said. "Go to a place I will show you, and through you I will bless the whole world. On down through history people will still be talking about your faith and obedience. I am going to pour out all kinds of blessing on you, and your job is to let it overflow to the rest of the world." Wow! Even that far back in time God had His eyes on the whole world. The huge thing we are to remember from Abraham's story is that the blessings that come to us are not just for us to enjoy; they are to be shared. And of course, the biggest blessing anyone can ever know is a relationship with Jesus. If you know Him, you are challenged to share that blessing with the world around you.

Something we are going to explore more fully in upcoming chapters is the fact that God is for everyone—not just people like us-but everyone. Just as Abraham had to leave some of the familiar comforts he was accustomed to, we are called to come out of our comfort zones on this adventure with God. To live on mission with Him is to be willing, as Abraham was, to go wherever God sends us, whether it be next door or across an ocean. It often involves some real stepping out in faith to embrace people and places and experiences that may seem foreign or scary. But if we take seriously

What Difference Does It Make?

- What are some of the ways in which you are blessed? Do you see ways you can bless others out of the circumstances of your life?

- Are there hard circumstances in your life that you cannot possibly perceive as containing a blessing? Would you dare trust God to reveal to you His plan of blessing through those circumstances?

- Where are you on the proverbial racecourse mentioned in this chapter? Have you crossed the starting line? Are you jumping around, celebrating being a racer, but not taking a step farther? Are you running out the race? Do you need to be at a different point in your relationship with God?

the invitation to live missionally, as Abraham did by focusing on the purpose set before him, we will have to consider what it means to share our blessings with others.

The Bible clearly teaches that we are blessed in order to be a blessing to others. We spent some time examining the fact that sometimes we miss out on this point, thinking that the Bible is a story of how we are blessed by God and not a story of how God wants us to join Him in blessing all the nations of the earth. Another thing we miss out on is the nature of blessing. Sometimes we let the definition of a blessing be determined by our culture and its values rather than by God and His values. Your idea of a blessing might be a sixty-inch flat-screen television for your room or a date with the most popular person at your school. But God might desire to bless you in ways that don't have to do with material goods, popularity, or even comfort. Many events in the Bible demonstrate that blessing comes in some pretty unusual disguises, so we must have "eyes to see" some of the blessings God provides. Think, for example, of Jesus' words in the Sermon on the Mount: "Blessed are those who are persecuted because of righteousness, for theirs is the kingdom of heaven. Blessed are you when people insult you, persecute you and falsely say all kinds of evil against you because of me" (Matthew 5:10–11). Those are some hard phrases. They particularly go against the grain of the world around us, which screams to us that comfort, ease, stuff, and popularity are the best blessings. Abraham may have thought that it didn't sound like much of a blessing to have to move away from all he knew to an unknown future in an unknown place, but he had faith in God. Sometimes it takes a lot of faith to see the blessings God wants to give us, but they are surely there, and they are surely to be shared for the good of the world around us.

By looking closely at the story of God's relationship with Abraham, we see that God has been pursuing the nations of the world from the very beginning of the Bible story. The fact that God has a heart for all the nations isn't just a New Testament idea. From Genesis forward, *people* are the core of the story that pours out of God's heart. What God has been doing, and continues to do throughout history, speaks of His great love for us and His great desire for relationship with us. He certainly doesn't need us in order to complete His mission, but He has desired that we join Him. The invitation He extended to Abraham to "go where I show you" is the invitation to adventure He offers each of us today.

In chapter 3 we encountered "The Parable of the Race," in which it became clear that we can easily miss the point of what God is trying to do. We get excited about the invitation to join Christ in the race of life, but sometimes we stop just over the starting line to celebrate our blessings, never moving on to live out the race and experience all the blessings in that journey. This analogy of the Christian life as a race is also one that Paul used in Hebrews 12:1, where he wrote, "Therefore, since we are surrounded by such a great cloud of witnesses, let us throw off everything that hinders and the sin that so easily entangles, and let us run with perseverance the race marked out for us." The Bible is clear: We were never supposed to just enter the race. God wants us to run it—not as spectators, celebrating just across the starting line, but as racers, joining God on the adventure of a lifetime.

God's story is unfolding as we see and participate in God's kingdom throughout the earth.

So this brings us to kingdom—this present reality of God's rule that we are invited to live in and participate in on a daily basis. Admittedly, the pictures of God's kingdom that we see in the Bible are paradoxical and filled with layers of meaning. As George Eldon Ladd notes, the Bible's teaching on the kingdom of God is complex and filled with "bewildering diversity" (1959). Because of complexity, we really need to have an intimate connection with the King of kings as we seek to live out kingdom life. Interestingly, the complexity and diversity of the Bible's teaching on kingdom make sense in light of the fact that we are called to be children of God who have a dynamic *relationship* with God, rather than to be robotic slaves who follow a checklist of one-size-fits-all platitudes. In his book *This Beautiful Mess*, Rick McKinley says, "The kingdom of God is the living, breathing presence and purpose and reign of God on our planet" (2006, 21). Note the emphasis on *living* and *breathing*—these adjectives indicate a moving, active state. Although the truth of God is unchanging, the nature of His interaction with us is dynamic, just as His kingdom is a dynamic, active realm. Think of the relationships you have. Aren't they growing and changing as time progresses? Don't they have different facets and seasons? Think about the way your relationships deepen and change in relation to the amount of time you spend with people, the shared experiences you have, the ways you depend on each other. The instant you met some of your friends, were you aware of all the different paths your friendship with them would take? It is highly unlikely.

It is the same way with this kingdom life with God that we are called to. Entering, receiving, and living out the kingdom of God is what missional life is all about. In the ancient world, people who

What Difference Does It Make?

- What are the most puzzling aspects of the kingdom of God? What are some ways you can deepen your understanding of the kingdom of God?

- How much does dualistic thinking influence the way you think about your life and how you live it? How does considering your faith a private matter affect your interaction with the world around you?

- Does it make a difference if you view the world as "sacred and secular"? If Christians are isolated in a separate so-called sacred culture, what does that say about how they view "secular people"? Is that different from how Jesus views people?

were a part of a kingdom knew it and sought the favor, wisdom, and protection of their king. So it is with us. Kingdom life, missional life, a life of dynamic relationship with God—this life requires that we know and cling to the King and not much else.

You have a unique and important role to play in God's purpose.

What? Not much else? Nope. The instructions are fairly simple. Paul said it this way: "Let us fix our eyes on Jesus, the author and perfecter of our faith" (Hebrews 12:2). He said this right after comparing our life in Christ to a race. So, the way we keep going on the racecourse is to keep our eyes on Jesus and get our instructions from Him. We walk in faith that He will never lead us astray. That is the real heart of being on mission with God, and we will look more at keeping our eyes on Jesus in the coming chapters.

The kingdom is at hand. It truly is for you right now. You have a unique and important role to play in God's purpose. Chapter 4 presented the fallacy of thinking that participation in God's kingdom is something for only the experts and professionals who have certain credentials or specific training. Centuries of dualistic thinking have falsely divided the world into the realm of sacred and secular, public and private. We mistakenly believe that there are sacred jobs and secular jobs, and only the sacred ones can be part of kingdom life. Similarly, we think that our faith is a private matter that can be divorced from our public life, as though our lives could be neatly compartmentalized like a well-organized filing cabinet. If you have ever had trouble concentrating on a homework assignment or a test because of an argument you had with another person or because of some other stressful situation, you understand that we are not built for compartmentalizing things into neat little boxes. There is no sacred, private life that can be divorced from secular, public life. Nor does your useful Christian life begin after you have achieved a certain level of education or reached a specific age. There is just life. And it is now.

Author Michael Frost puts it like this: "God is not restricted to some so-called sacred realm. God is no less present in the office or the garden or the stadium than in church services" (2006, 187). Psalm 24:1 declares that "the earth is the Lord's, and everything in it, the world, and all who live in it." That pretty much sounds as if there isn't anywhere or anything on earth that isn't of concern to God. We tend to think that God is interested in sacred things only or that something has to be sacred or holy for God to show up. The Bible doesn't teach this. Nor does it teach that missional living is for a handful of professionals while the rest of us sit on the bleachers.

Think about the founders of the Church—what did their résumés look like? Frost goes on to say that we must "stop assuming that the only people who follow their heavenly Father into the family business are the full-time clergy." We are all called. Ephesians 2:10 says, "For we are God's workmanship, created in Christ Jesus to do good works, which God prepared in advance for us to do." He has already prepared a place for you in His ever-advancing work of relationship, redemption, and reconciliation. As Rob Bell says, "Jesus' desire for his followers is that they live in such a way that they bring heaven to earth" (2005b, 148). That is kingdom life. That is being on mission with God. That is pretty exciting stuff!

The spread of God's kingdom takes place in the context of warfare with Satan.

But as chapter 5 made clear, being a part of that kingdom does not come without opposition. We are, as C. S. Lewis describes, "living in a part of the universe occupied by the rebel." Lewis also calls the world "enemy-occupied territory." Satan and his forces of evil want more than anything to keep God's kingdom from being fully realized here on earth. Even though he is defeated, Satan doesn't act as though that reality is true. As a result, we are engaged in a very real battle as we seek to live on mission with God, joining Him in His kingdom purpose of relationship, redemption, and reconciliation. Lewis reminds us that "Christianity is the story of how the rightful king has landed, you might say landed in disguise, and is calling us all to take part in a great campaign of sabotage" (1996, 51). If the idea of your being involved in cosmic struggle, like Neo in the movie *The Matrix* (Wachowski and Wachowski 1999), appeals to you, then look no further than a purposeful, missional life with God. The enemy is real, but the power of God is even more real. And the power of God gets exercised in some pretty unusual and unexpected ways, some of them more mundane than glamorous. But regardless of the setting and circumstances, being involved in God's work is ultimately the most fulfilling and purposeful thing you can ever be a part of.

As we engage in intentional life on mission with God, we will surely be opposed by the enemy. Kraft reminds us how to prepare: "Our part in this war is first to receive the Holy Spirit's empowerment. Then we must imitate Jesus' obedience and intimate relationship with the Father. This enables us to follow his example in warfare against the kingdom of Satan. We are to put on the armor God makes available to us (Ephesians 6:10–18) and to fight in the power of the Holy Spirit 'against the wicked spiritual forces

What Difference Does It Make?

- One of the ways Satan tries to turn our thinking away from God is through tempting us with the things of this world. What are some prevailing cultural messages that take your thinking away from God's desires for you? How can you lessen your exposure and vulnerability to these temptations?

- What are some areas of your life that are particularly vulnerable to manipulation by Satan? Do you have strategies in place (such as memorizing Bible truths, praying, and being accountable to someone) to defend against such attacks? If not, why not?

in the heavenly world' (Ephesians 6:12, GNB)." Kraft goes on to identify our strategy against the enemy as having both a defensive component and an offensive one. It is important for us to maintain intimate relationship with God in order to be assured of God's protection and truth—both of which defend us against the lies of the enemy—and in order to know how and when to engage in battle offensively (2000, 27).

In the coming chapters we will look more in depth at some of the ways God has been at work throughout history to forward His purpose of relationship, redemption, and reconciliation. It has looked different in various places and eras in history, but God's purpose has always been going forward. God has been active and at work throughout time. We sometimes forget that He desires to work through us to accomplish His plans. Isn't it exciting to think that He wants you to know more and more about how His purpose involves you? In coming chapters we will also consider how God has invited you—with your unique personality, gifts, talents, and interests—to participate in His mission here on earth. We will explore different facets of what it means to live missionally, or on mission, with God.

So, what do we know about missio Dei after looking through the lens of the Bible? We know that God has a purpose. It is to redeem and reconcile us to relationship with Him and with one another. We know we are invited to be a part of that work, that we are blessed so that we can be a blessing. We understand from the Bible that the kingdom of God is at hand, and it is a living, breathing reality of the present that will be fully realized in the future. This kingdom is not just for after we die and go to heaven, for we see in the Bible a call to join God in His kingdom mission right now on earth. He invites us to take up the battle cry against the "powers" of the earth in the present age, recognizing that Christians are indeed living in enemy-occupied territory.

It should certainly be clear from this unit that God has an outward thrust—toward people and reconciled relationship with them. His mission, His purpose, is for us to share that good news with the entire world. The Bible shows us that this outward thrust should also be the hallmark of our lives. Recall again Jesus' identification of the greatest commandment in Mark 12:30–32: " 'Love the Lord your God with all your heart and with all your soul and with all your mind and with all your strength.' The second is this: 'Love your neighbor as yourself.' There is no commandment greater than these." God's heart is for the nations. God's mission is for all people.

Brian McLaren writes about this in *A Generous Orthodoxy* when he discusses the impact of understanding God's mission as being for the good of the world. In exploring the idea of missional Christianity—that is, being on mission with God as we have discussed in this unit—McLaren talks about the life-changing impact of realizing that "Jesus came to preach the good news of the kingdom of God to everyone, especially the poor. He came to seek and save the lost. He came on behalf of the sick. He came to save the world. His gospel, and therefore the Christian message, is Good News for the whole world" (2004, 110). That idea of good news for the whole world will be the focus of our next unit, a unit that will unpack what we can learn about missio Dei through the lens of culture.

Culture Unit
unit two

Unit Introduction

Even though you probably don't spend a lot of time thinking about your culture and worldview, they play an important part in how you think and behave every day. Sometimes we are surprised to discover just how much of the way we view the world is through the lens of the cultural context we live in. We sometimes have cultural blinders that prevent us from really viewing the people of the world the same way God does. We often prefer to surround ourselves with people who are much like us. But none of this surprises God. In fact, the diversity found in His creation is intentional, and it is one of the most profound realities through which He receives glory.

In this unit, we are going to pick up some binoculars and take a fresh look around us. We'll examine how God views culture and how cultural differences have an impact on the way we live with one another. The viewpoint of God always starts with people—the pinnacle of His creation and the apple of His eye. The children's song "Jesus Loves the Little Children" reminds us of this fact: "Red and yellow, black and white, they are precious in His sight." At the heart of living missionally is the task of learning to see the world the way God does—looking through His binoculars, if you will. In the next chapters, we hope to begin to do just that.

In this unit we'll explore the following Big Ideas:

- Effectively communicating God's story requires an intimate understanding of culture and God's view of it.
- The incarnation of Jesus is the model for reaching out to all people, whether within one's own culture or across cultural boundaries. Jesus tells us not only what to communicate but how to communicate it.
- The process of reaching out across cultures can be enhanced by a study of people.
- God's people must learn to connect incarnationally with others in significant cross-cultural relationships.

God's View of Culture

I grew up in Iowa and I knew what to do with butter: you put it on roasting ears [of corn], pancakes, and popcorn. Then I went to France and saw a Frenchman put butter on radishes. I waited for the Cosmic Revenge—for the Eiffel Tower to topple, the Seine to sizzle, or the grape to wither on the vine. But … the universe continued unperturbed.

—Genelle Morain

Unless you have lived on a deserted island for most of your life, you have probably stumbled across the fact that people are very different from one another. Perhaps this reality has made itself known to you through an inability to connect with a person who doesn't speak your language, or maybe you have encountered the frustration that comes when you and another person haven't seen eye to eye on something. Or maybe you have noticed that not everyone looks the same, talks the same, or values things in the same way. Maybe you view this diversity as a great opportunity to learn about different people and new ways of thinking. Or you might find that the stark differences between you and some people can cause you to be fearful or frustrated. In any event, you have stumbled across the reality of different cultures.

There are more than six billion people on the planet.

There are more than six billion people on the planet,[1] and they live in places with vastly differing geography and natural resources. There are bound to be differences between a group of people living along a coastline with an abundant seafood industry and a group of people living in a desert environment where water is a precious commodity. The foods the coast dwellers eat would be different from the foods the desert dwellers eat. Each group would have a different perspective on water and its importance in their daily lives; the coast dwellers might take it for granted, whereas the desert dwellers would likely revere it as precious. Even the words they use frequently or the traditions they have would likely be influenced by the differences between these two terrains. As you begin to understand how an environment can shape and trigger what is important to a group of people, you will uncover some of the forces that shape culture and worldview.

What difference does it make if we acknowledge culture and cultural differences and are able to understand them? It goes back to what we learned in the previous unit about God's purpose and our place in it. God's purpose is relationship, redemption, and reconciliation, and God invites us to participate in His purpose. God's purpose is certainly not limited to the boundaries of one specific culture. As we learned in chapter 3, God's heart is for all people. So the issue of culture is a rather significant one for those who desire to live on mission with God. Effectively communicating God's story requires an intimate understanding of culture and God's view of it.

So what exactly is *culture*? The word gets used in all sorts of ways. A person with "culture" is thought to have excellent intellectual and aesthetic taste. A medical "culture" refers to the process of cultivating living material, such as bacteria, to diagnose illness. We may label influential songs, television shows, blogs, and clothing styles as parts of "pop culture." But for our purposes here, we will define culture in a way that is more aligned with the study of people, as in anthropology and sociology. In this context, the term *culture* is often associated with the closely related term *worldview*. Charles H. Kraft defines culture this way: "The term *culture* is the label anthropologists give to the structured customs and underlying worldview assumptions [upon] which people govern their lives. Culture (including worldview) is a peoples' way of life, their design for living, their way of coping with their biological, physical and social environment." He explains worldview as "the deep level of culture," noting that "worldview is *not separate* from culture. *It is included in culture* as the deepest level presuppositions upon which people base their lives" (1998, 385).

> *Effectively communicating God's story requires an intimate understanding of culture and God's view of it.*

Culture includes the way people live their lives and how they cope with their environment. Just as the culture of a desert-dwelling people would be greatly influenced by the scarcity of water, each of the world's cultures is shaped by external forces. These can range from something as unchangeable as geography to something as arbitrary as war. Culture is also shaped by internal forces, including traditional ways of doing things or communicating, which have been passed down from generation to generation for so long that no one really knows why or how these customs originated. Internal forces that influence culture are often reinforced by members of the culture, such as when the family and peers of someone approve or disapprove of a potential mate for that person. There are many, many variables that shape and define a culture, including language, beliefs, customs, and material objects in the environment. We will be exploring some of these aspects of culture throughout this unit.

> *"Culture (including worldview) is a peoples' way of life, their design for living, their way of coping with their biological, physical and social environment."*

Paul G. Hiebert describes one very interesting phenomenon related to culture:

> So long as we live in our own culture, we are largely unaware of it. When we enter new cultures, however, we become keenly aware of the fact that other people live differently. At first we see the differences in dress, food, language and behavior. Then we learn that there are profound differences in beliefs, feelings and values. Finally, we begin to realize that there are fundamental differences in worldviews. People in different cultures do not live in the same world with different labels attached to it, but in radically different worlds. (1999, 377)

For example, have you ever really stopped to wonder why Americans sleep on beds and sit on chairs when so many other people around the world are perfectly content to sit or sleep comfortably on the floor? Unless you have spent time in another culture, you may not realize that sleeping or sitting on an elevated platform is not the norm universally. Hiebert notes an American "obsession with platforms" and says of Americans, "Behind all these behavior patterns is a basic worldview assumption that floors are dirty. This explains [their] obsession for getting off the floor. It also explains why they keep their shoes on when they enter the house, and why the mother scolds the child when it picks a potato chip off the floor and eats it, even though the floor has just been washed" (1999, 377). In other cultures, such as Japan, the floor is not thought to be unclean. As a result, habits and customs related to sitting, sleeping, and even the wearing of shoes is vastly different from American behaviors in this regard.

Hiebert's observation that we are largely unaware of our own culture until we are confronted with the reality of another culture is a key point. And it brings us back to the importance of our main idea—effectively communicating God's story requires an intimate understanding of culture and God's view of it. In other words, if we are to truly live on mission with God, we must understand how He feels about the variety of cultural differences one finds throughout the world.

Having already studied the first unit of this course, you probably have a good idea that God's view of culture is a positive one. But that isn't necessarily what others, even Christians, believe. Let's look at some of the different ideas about the relationship between God and culture that have been identified by Charles H. Kraft (1996) in his book *Anthropology for Christian Witness*. Kraft's classifications are based on the classic work of Christian sociologist Richard Niebuhr (*Christ and Culture*, New York: Harper & Row, 1956).

> *"So long as we live in our own culture, we are largely unaware of it."*

The first view Kraft identifies is one that says God is a product of culture. This view is generally held by secularists who "do not regard God as anything more than the product of human imagination" (1996, 92). Obviously, a Christian cannot hold this view, and it is clearly incompatible with the Bible. But to hold this view would drastically alter the way you explain and view differences in culture.

A second view says that God is against culture. This view is held by some Christians who point to verses such as 1 John 2:15, "Do not love the world or anything in the world. If anyone loves the world, the love of the Father is not in him." The problem, Kraft points out, is in assuming that "what God means by 'world' is what we mean by 'culture' " (1996, 92). But since the Greek word for *world* used in 1 John 2:15—*kosmos*—is the same as that found in John 3:16, "For God so loved the world," we run into a problem with concluding that God is against culture. "The term is used in two ways—one to designate the people for whom God gave Himself in love, the other apparently used to designate a system governed by Satan," Kraft notes. It may be tempting to embrace the idea that God is against culture, because as Kraft points out, "The truth of this God against culture position is, of course, in the fact that there is much within culture that Christians need to oppose. But it ignores the fact that there is also much cultural behavior that is approvable by Christians" (92–93).

This brings us to the third position described by Kraft, that God endorses a particular culture or subculture. This view, held perhaps unconsciously by some Christians, was also held by many of the Israelites chronicled in the Bible. In our times, this position adopts the mentality that there is one set of superior cultural "forms" that every true Christian should be expected to adopt—from behaviors to worship styles to reading material. Kraft describes this basic mentality of many Christians, who "tend to idealize our culture, as if it were a special Christian culture and, often, our nation as if it were a Christian nation. This is the mistake the Hebrews made. They felt that since God was willing to use their culture, He must be endorsing it as the proper way for *everyone*. Paul, of course, fights such an idea in Acts 15, Galatians, and elsewhere in the New Testament, maintaining that God is willing to use Gentile cultures to reach Gentiles (1 Corinthians 9:19–22). On that basis, [Kraft] would claim that God endorses no culture but willingly uses any culture" (1996, 93; emphasis added). The significant dangers of promoting legalism and limiting God can be found in this mentality regarding God and culture.

The fourth relationship between God and culture that Kraft describes is one that is typically found in deism—God is above culture and is unconcerned with it. "Those who take this stance typically assert that God created the universe, got it going, and then virtually left it" (1996, 93). While this view acknowledges a God above culture, it doesn't allow for God to be intimately interested or acting in the lives of His creation. This is clearly inconsistent with the interaction found in the Bible between God and humankind.

Finally, we come to the fifth of the views Kraft identifies. This last view says that God is both above culture and working through it (1996, 93). In other words, God is not bound or hindered by culture (since He is sovereign), but He chooses to use diversity in culture as a "vehicle" for interacting with His creation. And this is the perspective taught by the Bible's whole story. Once again, the importance of reading the Bible as one great narrative story is affirmed. For if you read snatches and pieces of the story, it might be easy enough to conclude something else about God and His view of culture. But the entire story of the Bible affirms that God acts through culture—whether Israelite or Gentile culture—to redeem, reconcile, and restore humanity to Himself. And He invites us to come along on that mission.

God is above culture—in other words, He is not shaped or bound by culture, but He exists separately from it and above it. As Kraft notes, "The true God exists as He is, outside of culture, whether or not He is accurately perceived by those within culture" (1996, 92).

But God is not opposed to culture; He created it. The significance of understanding a biblical view of God and His view of culture cannot be overstated, since missing it would mean missing out on the heartbeat of God and the ways in which He works.

A key question then, according to Kraft, is, "What is God's view of culture?" The above list demonstrates that even though there are many ways to think about this question, not all of them are in line with the teaching of the Bible. Perhaps the most troubling (and often difficult to detect) aspect about our view of culture as Christians is how much we are tempted to hold the third view in the list above rather than the fifth view. Kraft elaborates on this key question:

> "What is God's view of culture? Is Jewish culture created by God and therefore to be imposed on everyone who follows God? Or is there some indication in scripture that God takes a different position?" I believe we have our answer in 1 Corinthians 9:19–22, where Paul articulates his (and God's) approach to cultural diversity. Paul says, "While working with Jews, I live like a Jew" but "when working with Gentiles, I live like a Gentile." His approach, then, is to "become all things to all men, that I may save some of them by whatever means are possible."

> The early Christians were Jewish. It was natural for them to believe that the cultural forms in which the gospel came to them were the only right ones for everyone. So, they believed, everyone who comes to Jesus must also convert to Jewish culture. But God used the apostle Paul, himself a Jew, to teach his generation and ours a different approach. In the above text, he articulates God's approach. Then in Acts 15:2ff, we find him arguing fiercely against the majority position of the early church for the right of Gentiles to follow Jesus *within* their own sociocultural contexts. God Himself had shown first Peter (Acts 10), then Paul and Barnabas, that this was the right way, by giving the Holy Spirit to Gentiles who had not converted to Jewish culture (Acts 13–14).

> But the Church has continually forgotten the lesson of Acts 15. We have continually reverted to the assumption that becoming Christian means becoming like us culturally. When, after New Testament times, the church required everyone to adopt Roman culture, God raised up Luther to prove that God could accept people who spoke German and worshipped in German ways. Then Anglicanism arose to show that God could use English language and custom, and Wesleyanism arose to let the common people of England know that God accepted them in their culture. And so it has been that there are major cultural issues in the development of every new denomination.

Perceptions of God's View of Culture

1. God is a product of culture.
2. God is against culture.
3. God endorses a particular culture or subculture.
4. God is above culture and is unconcerned about it.
5. God is both above culture and working through it.

But sadly, the problem persists. Communicators of the gospel continue imposing their culture or denomination on new converts.... If, then, we take a scriptural approach, we should *adapt ourselves and our presentation of God's message* to the culture of the receiving people, not misrepresent God as some early Jewish Christians did (Acts 15:1) by requiring that converts become like us to be acceptable to God. (1998, 384–85)

Kraft mentions several New Testament examples that demonstrate God's desire to work through culture, examples that show that God does not demand a single particular cultural expression of Christianity in order to approach Him. And in looking at the entire story of the Bible, there is an even clearer theme that not only does God desire to work through culture, but He actually created diversity as a means of expressing and demonstrating His glory. Many people assume a negative view of culture that stems from the tower of Babel incident recorded in Genesis 11. From children's Sunday school on, many are taught that God created linguistic and cultural diversity strictly as a punishment for human arrogance and disobedience in trying to build a tower to reach the heavens. The natural conclusion is that culture is something God used to separate and punish humankind and couldn't possibly be something He desires or delights in.

But cultural diversity didn't originate at Babel. "At the very outset of the biblical narrative we are presented with a God who revels in diversity, in rich creativity," observes David Smith (1996, 169). The very creation of the world itself speaks of great diversity and difference among creatures and geographies. Many identify Genesis 1:28, the first command God gives to man, as a *cultural mandate*: "God blessed them and said to them, 'Be fruitful and increase in number; fill the earth and subdue it. Rule over the fish of the sea and the birds of the air and over every living creature that moves on the ground.' " Not only are Adam and Eve given rule over all the creatures of the earth, but they are encouraged to increase in number and *fill the earth*. David Cashin, a professor of intercultural studies at Columbia Biblical Seminary and School of Missions, points out that the environmental diversity found in creation necessitates cultural diversity also. As seen in our earlier example of coast dwellers and desert dwellers, the differences of landscape and climate can greatly shape the habits, behaviors, and values of people. So, Cashin says, the cultural mandate of Genesis 1:28 to fill the earth necessarily speaks of an intended cultural diversity (2007). This is further reinforced by the command God

> *God is both above culture and working through it.*

gave to Noah after the flood: "Then God blessed Noah and his sons, saying to them, 'Be fruitful and increase in number and *fill the earth*' " (Genesis 9:1, emphasis added), and "As for you, be fruitful and increase in number; multiply on the earth and increase upon it" (Genesis 9:7). In the subsequent narrative of Noah's line found in Genesis 10–11—particularly in Genesis 10:4, 20, and 31—we see an expression of God's intended cultural and linguistic diversity as the different nations, clans, territories, and languages of Noah's descendants are presented in what is often referred to as the Table of Nations.

The theme of scattering and filling the earth, creating diversity, is one that recurs in the Genesis 1–11 account of the beginnings of the world and throughout the rest of the Bible. And it is exactly this tension between unity and scattering that lies at the heart of the Babel narrative in Genesis 11. The attitude described there stands in rebellious contrast to that which God had commanded and designed from the beginning. Genesis 11:4 describes the heart of the rebellion: "Then they said, 'Come, let us build ourselves a city, with a tower that reaches to the heavens, so that we may make a name for ourselves and not be scattered over the face of the whole earth.' " Note the desire to *not be scattered*, which is in direct rebellion against God's command to Adam and Noah and is in opposition to God's design for the earth. F. Russell Baker, pastor of the First Congregational United Church of Christ in Benton Harbor, Michigan, notes that "humankind, out of *fear*, does not like to be scattered, because we feel alone and exposed—vulnerable. Therefore, we tend to group *together*, particularly with those whom we are comfortable, or are like us" (2004). This fear of scattering and difference is something that humanity has struggled with since the beginnings of time, and it hasn't disappeared yet. Fear, as much as pride, played a role in the rebellion at Babel.

The Tower of Babel

God's actions at the tower of Babel are a restoration of God's intended plan for humankind to fill the earth, to scatter, to embrace diversity in such a way that ultimately brings glory to God.

Far from being created in anger and birthed from punishment, cultural and linguistic diversity serves to reveal something to us about the creativity of God and His ability to express Himself through and be glorified by unity within diversity.

Yes, there is a deserved punishment for rebellion in the Babel narrative (Genesis 11:7–9), but it is not out of that punishment that cultural diversity was created. Instead, God's actions at the tower of Babel are a restoration of God's intended plan for humankind to fill the earth, to scatter, to embrace diversity in such a way that ultimately brings glory to God. Baker observes that "we have been inclined to see *unity* as frequently God's purpose and *scattering* is seen as God's punishment, but it's more *complicated* than that. God's purpose is unity in diversity, not unity in sameness" (2004). Far from being created in anger and birthed from punishment, cultural and linguistic diversity serves to reveal something to us about the creativity of God and His ability to express Himself through and be glorified by unity within diversity, a plan that is far more compelling than unity from uniformity.

Images of this plan of unity within diversity are seen throughout Scripture—from God's promise to Abraham that he would be the father of many nations (Genesis 17:5–6) through the Pentecost narrative of Acts 2, in which the very linguistic diversity expressed is a means that God uses to unify thousands of new believers in Christ. The New Testament reveals the struggles of the early Church to reconcile different understandings of this very issue of culture, particularly with respect to conflicts between Gentile and Jewish means of practicing a life of faith. Against this backdrop, Paul's example reveals that God can and will work through any culture to bring about His purpose (1 Corinthians 9:19–22). God's plan of receiving glory from unity within diversity comes to an ultimate fulfillment before the heavenly throne of God pictured in Revelation 7:9–12, a passage in which we see worshippers "from every nation, tribe, people and language" crying praises before the Lamb of God.

> *God's plan of receiving glory from unity within diversity comes to an ultimate fulfillment before the heavenly throne of God pictured in Revelation 7:9–12.*

So, far from culture and cultural diversity being a simple consequence of God's punishment of rebellion at the tower of Babel, the Bible shows us a picture of a God who desires that the diversity He intended, created, and commanded would come to unity under His headship. This gives us a more far-reaching vision of culture and its purpose than any other interpretation might yield. Leslie A. Klingensmith, pastor of Saint Matthew Presbyterian Church in Silver Spring, Maryland, notes the following: "A presupposition that the diversity of our world is part of God's plan for humanity and all of creation can go a long way toward cultivating a willingness on our part to become acquainted with and appreciate people who are different from us. The potential for unity in our scatteredness, for understanding one another against the odds, is realized in the miracle of the first Pentecost" (2007).

Unity Within Diversity

Many images used in the New Testament to convey the idea of the Body of Christ are pictures of this idea of unity within diversity. See Romans 12:4–8, 1 Corinthians 12, and Ephesians 4:1–16.

God invites us to embrace His perspective of the world and to join in His purpose. We cannot successfully do that without an accurate understanding of God's view of culture, differences, and our place in this rich tapestry. As we explore culture in the coming chapters, we will see more and more the need for utter dependence on God in navigating the waters of cultural difference and communicating His story of love.

∽

NOTE

1. Joshua Project, "Ethne Overview," http://www.joshuaproject.net/ethne.php (accessed April 14, 2008); U.S. Census Bureau, "World POPClock Projection," http://www.census.gov/ipc/www/popclockworld.html (accessed April 22, 2008).

Cultural Pitfalls

Whether we like it or not, our very membership in Western society imprisons us in a set of political, economic, social, and spiritual principles that shape our lifestyles, even when we don't subscribe to it.
—*Brennan Manning*

Among the hardest tasks in life is to divest ourselves of the culture we wear so comfortably.   —*Duane Elmer*

In the last chapter, we described culture as a way of life, a design for living, and a way of coping with biological, physical, and social environments. The forces of a culture can have a powerful shaping influence on both individuals and groups of people. Often this influence is something we don't notice until we are confronted with a culture that is quite different from our own. It is then that the effects of culture can become obvious and can often create some uncomfortable difficulties in communication. Because God has created us to be relational beings that live within community, it is important that we develop a proper and biblical understanding of what culture is, how it can shape us, and how it can affect our ability to communicate with one another. In this chapter, we will begin looking at some of the effects and pitfalls of cultural conditioning, so that we can be more effective communicators of God's story.

In his book *Cross-Cultural Connections*, author Duane Elmer has observed, "Culture is everywhere, and it sneaks up on you" (2002, 35). Elmer illustrates this point by sharing an example of a time when unrecognized cultural differences created a difficult situation in his young marriage. The lessons from this example demonstrate the power of cultural influence.

Snow Tires
by Duane Elmer
Excerpt from *Cross-Cultural Connections*

My wife and I had been married for nearly a year, and I knew I would have to find a special gift for our first anniversary. I put considerable thought into it, because I wanted it to be right. I decided the gift had to meet two objectives: It should be expensive to communicate my love and appreciation for her. And because we would be moving several times over the next few years, the gift should be practical, something she could use, not something decorative that would sit on a shelf and gather dust and maybe get broken in our moving around. This line of reasoning made sense to me. It even seemed like the smart thing to do.

On a chilly mid-December evening I took my bride of one year outside to present her with the "perfect" first anniversary gift. I had prepared her for the event by telling her how much thought and planning had gone into it. With pride I extended the open palm of my hand toward the brand new pair of snow tires on the car. Top of the line. Already mounted on the rims. Shiny black with whitewalls. Metal studs for extra traction. Expensive and practical. The perfect gift.

I noticed a small tear form in the corner of my wife's eye. Thinking she was overcome with joy at my generosity I began congratulating myself on this smashing success. It was my first crack at an anniversary gift and I hit a home run. I began bracing myself for the big hug that would come momentarily. Instead, she turned away and went back inside. She's too cold to hug right now, I reasoned. But as I followed her inside she began to cry profusely—tears not of joy but of bitter disappointment.

My gift reflected the cultural context in which I grew up. Not only was it a rural farming environment but quite a male-dominated one. Life was practical and functional, and my gift reflected this heritage.

My wife, on the other hand, grew up in Zimbabwe (then Southern Rhodesia), Africa. After living with the Shona people for seven years, she went to boarding school where she was transformed into a polite, sophisticated young lady after the British tradition. She grew up attending tea parties with fine china, having men of all ages stand as she entered the room and enjoying the refined life. Born of missionary parents, she was not rich, but was surrounded by a culture that treated women differently than some of us did growing up in the Midwest farming culture of the United States. In both cultures women were valued, but valued very differently according to the dictates of the environment.

So I was doing something that naturally grew out of my cultural history, but her expectations were set in an entirely different direction. Our cultures collided.

Because I did not understand her cultural history, I did not understand why she reacted so negatively. How she could have ever married such an insensitive creature as myself was beyond her. Both of us experienced some culture shocks, because we assumed that the other person saw the world pretty much as each of us did.

By now you have probably concluded that I was really clueless to give my wife snow tires. Even though I have tried to explain my perspective, I doubt that you are persuaded about anything, except that people do not get much dumber than that.

Culture is like that. It sneaks up on us, and we tend to make decisions based on our cultural background rather than trying to understand the cultural background of the other person first. When something goes wrong we tend to judge negatively and quickly. To withhold or suspend judgment means that we refuse to think negatively about the other person or culture until we have made deliberate attempts to understand. Now, let's finish the story.

We were poor, sometimes having to wait a few days for a check to come so we could buy milk or bread. My wife was putting me through school by working as a public health nurse. Her job took her into the really poor and often dangerous areas of the city. With the winter days growing dark before she would leave these areas and with snow piling up, I feared for her safety. I sensed she was anxious too. The snow tires might bring her an added sense of safety and a little more peace of mind for both of us. I cared for my wife deeply and wanted to show it in the best way I could. But was this the best way? Probably not. Yet, you see my frame of reference. So did my wife. Enlarging our frame of reference may not make things right, but it helps us understand and be less harsh in our judgments.

We usually communicate from our own frame of reference. Snow tires communicated from my frame of reference and my cultural heritage. But the gift completely missed my wife's frame of reference and her cultural heritage. It caused her pain when I wanted so desperately to bring her joy. It put a strain on our relationship when I wanted to make it stronger. It communicated insensitivity when I wanted to communicate love and devotion. Fortunately, my wife is a forgiving person and usually sees my heart when my actions miscommunicate.

What should I have done? Knowing what I know now, I should have given her some roses or perfume or a necklace or something that would have been appreciated from her perspective and said later, "Oh, by the way, I put some new snow tires on the car because I love you very much and want you to come home safely every night." (36–39)

Of course, issues of cultural communication and miscommunication exist on a much-broader scale than just that of two individuals who were reared in significantly different circumstances. As we studied in chapter 2, God created us to be in relationship and community. The nature of relationships and community create cultural ties in and of themselves. But, as we learned in the last chapter, the Bible shows that God doesn't desire that we become locked into one particular culture, and often He instructs us to "scatter" to places and to be with people groups that are unfamiliar to us. In order to live missionally with God, we must be prepared to go—even if it is to the unknown, just as Abraham did. Whether that "going" is around the world or around the block, we are likely to encounter cultural differences.

The forces of a culture can have a powerful shaping influence on both individuals and groups of people. Often this influence is something we don't notice until we are confronted with a culture that is quite different from our own.

We now turn to an excerpt from the article "Cultural Differences and the Communication of the Gospel" by Paul G. Hiebert (1999). The first portion explains three basic dimensions of culture: beliefs (cognitive level), feelings (affective level), and values (evaluative level). The second part explains three pitfalls related to each of these three dimensions of culture—misunderstanding of cultural beliefs, ethnocentrism related to cultural feelings, and premature judgments related to cultural values.

At the heart of a culture is the shared beliefs, feelings and values of a community of people. Through their experiences, people form mental pictures or maps of their world. For instance, a person living in Chicago has a mental image of the streets around her home, those she uses to go to church and work, and the major arteries she uses to get around town. Obviously, there are a great many streets not on her map and as long as she does not go to these areas, she has no need for knowing them.

Not all our ideas reflect the realities of the external world. Many are the creations of our minds, used to bring order and meaning to our experiences. For example, we see a great many trees in our lifetime, and each is different from all others. But it would be impossible for us to give a separate name for each of them, or to each bush, each house, each car—in short, to every experience we have. In order to think and speak we must reduce this infinite variety of experiences into a manageable number of concepts by generalizations. We call these shades of color "red," those "orange," and the third set "yellow." These categories are the creations of our minds. Other people in other languages lump them together into a single color, or divide them into two or more colors. Do these people see as many colors as we? Certainly. The fact is, we can create as many categories in our minds as we want, and we can organize them into larger systems for describing and explaining human experiences. Culture is a people's mental map of their world. This is not only a map *of* their physical world, but also a map *for* determining action. It provides them with a guide for their decisions and behavior.

Beliefs

Shared beliefs about the nature of reality make communication and community life possible. They provide people with the categories and logic they use to experience the world. Beliefs also tell people what

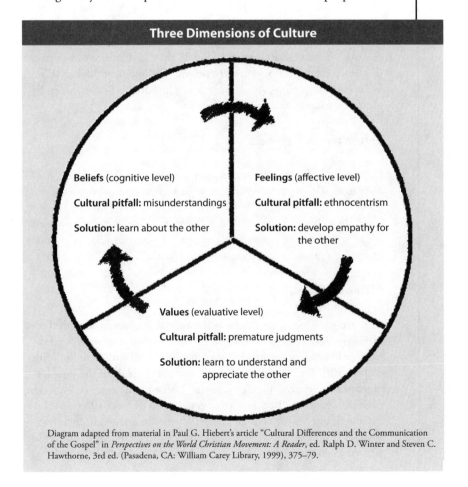

Three Dimensions of Culture

Beliefs (cognitive level)

Cultural pitfall: misunderstandings

Solution: learn about the other

Feelings (affective level)

Cultural pitfall: ethnocentrism

Solution: develop empathy for the other

Values (evaluative level)

Cultural pitfall: premature judgments

Solution: learn to understand and appreciate the other

Diagram adapted from material in Paul G. Hiebert's article "Cultural Differences and the Communication of the Gospel" in *Perspectives on the World Christian Movement: A Reader*, ed. Ralph D. Winter and Steven C. Hawthorne, 3rd ed. (Pasadena, CA: William Carey Library, 1999), 375–79.

exists and what does not. For instance, most Westerners believe in atoms, electrons, gravity and DNA, although they have never seen them. South Indian [Southern India] villagers believe in fierce *rakshasas*—spirits with big heads, bulging eyes, fangs and long wild hair, which inhabit trees and rocky places, and jump on unwary travelers at night. Not all Indians believe in *rakshasas*, just as not all Americans believe in God. But all must take into account the categories that exist in their culture.

Feelings

Culture also has to do with the feelings people have—with their notions of beauty, tastes in food and dress, likes and dislikes, and ways of enjoying themselves or expressing sorrow. People in one culture like their food hot, in another, sweet or bland. In some cultures people are encouraged to sing in sharp, piercing voices, in others to sing in deep, mellow tones. Members of some societies learn to express their emotions and may be aggressive and bellicose; in others they learn to be self-controlled and calm. Some religions encourage the use of meditation, mysticism and drugs to achieve inner peace and tranquility. Others stress ecstasy through frenzied songs, dances and self-torture.

The affective dimension of culture is reflected in standards of beauty, and taste in clothes, houses and food. It also plays an important part in human relationships—in our notions of etiquette and fellowship. We communicate love, hate, scorn and a hundred other attitudes, by our facial expressions, tones of voice and gestures.

Values and Allegiances

Culture includes the values by which people judge the experiences of their lives. These values determine what is right and wrong, what is good and what is evil, in the culture. For example, in ancient Japan it was a sin to beat a horse while it is lying on its back, and to sow seed where someone else has already done so. In parts of India, losing one's temper is a greater sin than sexual immorality....

Misunderstandings

After we get beyond our initial culture shock, we are faced with three lifelong problems. The first has to do with cognitive misunderstandings [or beliefs]. Some missionaries in Congo had trouble in building rapport with the people. Finally, one old man explained the people's hesitancy to befriend the missionaries. "When you came, you brought your strange ways," he said. "You brought tins of food. On the outside of one was a picture of corn. When you opened it, inside was corn and you ate it. Outside another was a picture of meat, and inside was meat, and you ate it. And then when you had your baby, you brought in small tins. On the outside was a picture of babies, and you opened it and fed the inside to your child!" To us, the people's confusion sounds foolish, but it is all too logical. In the absence of other information, the people must draw their own conclusions about our actions. We do the same about theirs. We think they have no sense of time when, by our culture, they show up late. We accuse them of lying, when they tell us things to please us rather than as they really are (although we have no trouble saying "Just fine!" when someone asks "How are you?"). The result is cultural misunderstanding, and this leads to poor communication and poor relationships.

Edward Hall points out how different views of time can lead to confusion [The Silent Language, Garden City, NY: Doubleday, 1959]. When, for example, two Americans agree to meet at ten o'clock, they are "on time" if they show up from five minutes before to five minutes after ten. If one shows up at fifteen after, he is "late" and mumbles an unfinished excuse. He must simply acknowledge that he is late. If he shows up at half past, he should have a good apology, and by eleven he may as well not show up. His offense is unpardonable.

"Our first task in entering a new culture is to be a student of its ways. Whenever a culture 'makes no sense' to us, we must assume that the problem is ours, because the people's behavior makes sense to them."

In parts of Arabia, the people have a different concept or map of time. If the meeting time is ten o'clock, only a servant shows up at ten—in obedience to his master. The proper time for others is from ten forty-five to eleven fifteen, just long enough after the set time to show their independence and equality. This arrangement works well, for when two equals agree to meet at ten, each shows up, and expects the other to show up, at about ten forty-five.

The problem arises when an American meets an Arab and arranges a meeting for ten o'clock. The American shows up at ten, the "right time" according to him. The Arab shows up at ten forty-five, the "right time" according to him. The American feels the Arab has no sense of time at all (which is false), and the Arab is tempted to think Americans act like servants (which is also false).

Misunderstandings are based on ignorance of the beliefs, feelings and values of another culture. The solution is to learn how the other culture works. Our first task in entering a new culture is to be a student of its ways. Whenever a culture "makes no sense" to us, we must assume that the problem is ours, because the people's behavior makes sense to them.

Ethnocentrism

Most Americans shudder when they enter an Indian restaurant and see people eating curry and rice with their fingers. Imagine diving into the mashed potatoes and gravy with your hand at a Thanksgiving dinner. Our response seems natural, to us. Early in life each of us grows up at the center of our own world. In other words, we are egocentric. Only with a great deal of difficulty do we learn to break down the circle we draw between me and you, and learn to look at things from the viewpoint of others in our group. Similarly, when we first encounter other cultures, we find it hard to see the world through other cultural eyes. We are ethnocentric.

The root of ethnocentrism is our human tendency to respond to other people's ways by using our own affective assumptions, and to reinforce these responses with deep feelings of approval or disapproval. When we are confronted by another culture, our own is called into question. Our defense is to avoid the issue by concluding that our culture is better and other people are less civilized.

But ethnocentrism is a two-way street. We feel that people in other cultures are primitive, and they judge us to be uncivilized. Some North Americans were hosting a visiting Indian scholar at a restaurant, when one of them who had never been abroad asked the inevitable question, "Do you really eat with your fingers in India?" Implicit in his question, of course, was his cultural attitude that eating with one's fingers is crude and dirty. North Americans may use fingers for carrot sticks, potato chips, and sandwiches, but never for mashed potatoes and gravy or T-bone steaks. The Indian scholar replied, "You know, in India we look at it differently than you do. I always wash my hands carefully before I eat, and I only use my right hand. And besides, my fingers have not been in anyone else's mouth. When I look at a fork or spoon, I often wonder how many other strangers have already had them in their mouths!"

Ethnocentrism occurs wherever cultural differences are found. North Americans are shocked when they see the poor of other cultures living in the streets. People in those same societies would be just as appalled to observe how we North Americans surrender our aged and sick and the bodies of our departed to strangers for care.

The solution to ethnocentrism is empathy. We need to learn to appreciate other cultures and their ways. But our feelings of superiority and our negative attitudes toward strange customs run deep and are not easily rooted out.

Premature Judgments

We have misunderstandings on the cognitive level and ethnocentrism on the affective level. On the evaluative level we tend to judge another culture too quickly, before we learn to understand and appreciate them. Our initial assessment is often that they are somehow inferior and ignorant.

As people learn to understand and appreciate other cultures, they come to respect these cultures as viable ways of organizing human life. Some are stronger in one area, such as technology, and others in other areas such as family ties. But all "do the job," that is, they all make life possible and more or less meaningful. Out of this recognition of the integrity of all cultures, emerged the concept of cultural relativism: the belief that all cultures are equally good—that no culture has the right to stand in judgment of others.

This position of cultural relativism is very attractive. It shows high respect for other people and their cultures and avoids the errors of ethnocentrism and premature judgments. The price we pay, however, in adopting total cultural relativism is the loss of such things as truth and righteousness. If all explanations of reality are equally valid, we can no longer speak of error, and if all behavior is justified according to its cultural context, we can no longer speak of sin. There is then no need for the gospel and no reason for mission.

What other alternative do we have? How do we avoid the errors of premature and ethnocentric judgments and still affirm truth and righteousness? There is a growing awareness that all human activities are full of judgments. Scientists expect one another to be honest and open in reporting their findings and careful in the topics of their research. Social scientists must respect the rights of their clients and the people they study. Businessmen, government officials, and others also have values by which they live. We cannot avoid making judgments, nor can a society exist without them.

On what basis, then, can we judge other cultures without becoming ethnocentric? We have a right as individuals to make judgments with regard to ourselves, and this includes judging other cultures. But these judgments should be well informed. We need to understand and appreciate other cultures *before* we judge them. Our tendency to make premature judgments is based on ignorance and ethnocentrism.

As Christians, we claim another basis for evaluation, namely, biblical norms. As divine revelation they stand in judgment of all cultures, affirming the good in human creativity and condemning the evil. To be sure, non-Christians may reject these norms and use their own. We can only present the gospel in a spirit of redemptive love and let it speak for itself. Truth, in the end, does not depend on what we think or say, but on reality itself. When we bear witness to the gospel, we do not claim a superiority for ourselves, but affirm the truth of divine revelation. (1999, 375–79)

Hiebert goes on to pose the very significant question, "But what keeps us from interpreting the Scripture from our own cultural point of view, and so imposing many of our own cultural norms on other people?" (1999, 379). You will recall from the last chapter that Acts 15 and many other portions of the New Testament demonstrate the struggles of the early Church in dealing with exactly this issue. Jewish followers of Christ wanted at times to impose their own cultural forms of worship on Gentile followers of Christ. This same issue that so plagued the early Christians is a difficult and pressing issue for today's believers as well. And missionaries throughout history have often with the best of intentions erred on the side of exporting much of their own home culture as the gospel to newly evangelized areas.

Obviously, an awareness of our own cultural beliefs, feelings, and values is a great asset for us to have. But our first step must always be to focus on our relationship with God, which includes obeying His instructions and accepting His invitation to us. We must remember that God is above earthly culture. His purpose is for His kingdom, not any kingdom of this world. He can and will choose to work through different cultures to bring about His purpose, often in ways that may initially surprise us. A great example of this is Peter's experience with Cornelius recorded in Acts 10. As we have stated before, it is critical that we be utterly dependent on God when we seek to communicate His story to others. With that in mind, we will turn in the next chapter to the most significant model of cross-cultural communication that any Christian can find—the example of Jesus Christ's coming to earth as a man in order to communicate God's love to the world as one of us.

The Incarnation

*A halfway house on the way to God would not do for a lost humanity,
and so God had to come down to man, not halfway but the whole way.*
                                        —*Michael Frost and Alan Hirsch*

Several years ago, a singer named Joan Osborne had a hit pop song
with the words "What if God was one of us?" ("One of Us," written
by Eric Bazilian, on Osborne's CD titled *Relish*, Island/Mercury,
1995). The writer of the lyrics wonders what it would be like if
God were one of us, "just a stranger on the bus, trying to make his
way home?" The tune is catchy, and the lyrics are indeed thought-
provoking—what *would* God be like if He were one of us? Would
we recognize Him? What would that mean for our lives?

Osborne's song dances around the edges of a key truth of the
Christian faith—God did become one of us. In the event theologians call the Incarnation, God became man in the person of Jesus
of Nazareth. The God of the universe came to the world as a baby.
Sometimes we find ourselves so accustomed to knowing and accepting this Bible teaching that we don't stop to really reflect on the significance of this act of God. In many ways it is impossible to grasp
all the dimensions involved in God becoming man—we are finite
beings, after all! But in this chapter we look again at this timeless truth
of God's love for us, and what the Incarnation signals to us about our
own role in communicating the truth of God's love to others.

We begin with a simple story made popular by radio commentator Paul Harvey through his rendition of it for so many years on

Christmas Eve. This story, whose author is unknown, has been told in many different forms, but each version seeks to bring light to the Incarnation and its motivation.

The Christmas Geese
by Unknown Author
Made popular by the late Paul Harvey

There was once a man who didn't believe in God, and he didn't hesitate to let others know how he felt about religion and religious holidays, like Christmas. His wife, however, did believe, and she raised their children to also have faith in God and Jesus, despite his disparaging comments. One snowy Christmas Eve, his wife was taking their children to a Christmas Eve service in the farm community in which they lived. She asked him to come, but he refused.

"That story is nonsense!" he said. "Why would God lower Himself to come to Earth as a man? That's ridiculous!" So she and the children left, and he stayed home.

A while later, the winds grew stronger and the snow turned into a blizzard. As the man looked out the window, all he saw was a blinding snowstorm. He sat down to relax before the fire for the evening. Then he heard a loud thump. Something had hit the window. Then another thump. He looked out, but couldn't see more than a few feet.

When the snow let up a little, he ventured outside to see what could have been beating on his window. In the field near his house he saw a flock of wild geese. Apparently they had been flying south for the winter when they got caught in the snowstorm and couldn't go on. They were lost and stranded on his farm, with no food or shelter. They just flapped their wings and flew around the field in low circles, blindly and aimlessly. A couple of them had flown into his window, it seemed.

The man felt sorry for the geese and wanted to help them. The barn would be a great place for them to stay, he thought. It's warm and safe; surely they could spend the night and wait out the storm. So he walked over to the barn and opened the doors wide, then watched and waited, hoping they would notice the open barn and go inside. The geese just fluttered around aimlessly and didn't seem to notice the barn or realize what it could mean for them. The man tried to get their attention, but that just seemed to scare them and they moved further away. He went into the house and came back out with some bread, broke it up, and made a breadcrumbs trail leading to the barn, but they still didn't catch on.

Now he was getting frustrated. He got behind them and tried to shoo them toward the barn, but they only got more scared and scattered in every direction except toward the barn. Nothing he did could get them to go into the barn where they would be warm and safe. "Why don't they follow me?" he exclaimed. "Can't they see this is the only place where they can survive the storm?" He thought for a moment and realized that they just wouldn't follow a human.

"If only I were a goose, then I could save them," he said out loud.

Then he had an idea. He went into barn, got one of his own geese, and carried it in his arms as he circled around behind the flock of wild geese. He then released it. His goose flew through the flock and straight into the barn—and one by one the other geese followed it to safety!

He stood silently for a moment as the words he had spoken a few minutes earlier replayed in his mind: "If only I were a goose, then I could save them!" Then he thought about what he had said to his wife earlier. "Why would God want to be like us? That's ridiculous!"

Suddenly it all made sense. That is what God had done. We were like the geese—blind, lost, and perishing. God had His Son become like us so He could show us the way and save us. That was the meaning of Christmas, he realized! As the winds and blinding snow died down, his soul became quiet and pondered this wonderful thought. Suddenly he understood what Christmas was all about, why Christ had come. Years of doubt and disbelief vanished like the passing storm. He fell to his knees in the snow, and prayed his first prayer: "Thank You, God, for coming in human form to get me out of the storm!"

> *The Incarnation is a single, simple act motivated by the most tremendous and pure love of all—the love of God for His creation.*

In one respect, the Incarnation is a single, simple act motivated by the most tremendous and pure love of all—the love of God for His creation. But because of the simplicity and familiarity of the Christmas story, we can often overlook the profound nature of what God did in that moment. In that one instant, the whole universe changed. As Max Lucado notes, it was "a most remarkable moment" that was like no other. He says, "For through that segment of time a spectacular thing occurred. God became a man" (1987, 25). In *The Shaping of Things to Come*, Michael Frost and Alan Hirsch describe the Incarnation this way: "When we talk of the Incarnation with a capital *I* we refer to that act of sublime love and humility whereby God took it upon himself to enter into the depths of our world, our life, and our reality in order that the reconciliation and consequent union between God and humanity may be brought about" (2003, 35).

For some, perhaps one of the most startling aspects of the Incarnation is how fully human God in Jesus became. The humanity of Christ can make us uncomfortable because it is so filled with humility. Many are well able to grasp that Jesus is worthy of worship; believers generally have no problem affirming Jesus' majesty and giving Him praise. They are less able to confront that He became fully human and that he came humbly to serve us. "When God chose to connect with humans, he did so as a servant," notes Duane Elmer (2006, 21). "The first earthly image we get of Jesus at the very beginning of his life is as a baby born in a barn, surrounded by livestock. The scene announces humility, lowliness, vulnerability, weakness, exposure. The last image we get of Jesus as he ends his earthly life is as a broken body hanging on a cross. The scene communicates humiliation, suffering, failure and, to many, defeat" (22).

Max Lucado draws an even more realistic portrait of the humanity of Christ in *God Came Near: Chronicles of the Christ*:

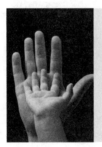

The Humanity of Christ
by Max Lucado
Excerpt from *God Came Near: Chronicles of the Christ*

The omnipotent, in one instant, made himself breakable. He who had been spirit became pierceable. He who was larger than the universe became an embryo. And he who sustains the world with a word chose to be dependent upon the nourishment of a young girl.

God as a fetus. Holiness sleeping in a womb. The creator of life being created.

God was given eyebrows, elbows, two kidneys, and a spleen. He stretched against the walls and floated in the amniotic fluids of his mother.

God had come near.

He came, not as a flash of light or as an unapproachable conqueror, but as one whose first cries were heard by a peasant girl and a sleepy carpenter. The hands that first held him were unmanicured, calloused, and dirty.

No silk. No ivory. No hype. No party. No hoopla.

Were it not for the shepherds, there would have been no reception. And were it not for a group of stargazers, there would have been no gifts.

Angels watched as Mary changed God's diaper. The universe watched with wonder as The Almighty learned to walk. Children played in the street with him. And had the synagogue leader in Nazareth known who was listening to his sermons …

Jesus may have had pimples. He may have been tone-deaf. Perhaps a girl down the street had a crush on him or vice-versa. It could be that his knees were bony. One thing's for sure: He was, while completely divine, completely human.

For thirty-three years he would feel everything you and I have ever felt. He felt weak. He grew weary. He was afraid of failure. He was susceptible to wooing women. He got colds, burped, and had body odor. His feelings got hurt. His feet got tired. And his head ached.

To think of Jesus in such a light is—well, it seems almost irreverent, doesn't it? It's not something we like to do; it's uncomfortable. It is much easier to keep the humanity out of the incarnation. Clean the manure from around the manger. Wipe the sweat out of his eyes. Pretend he never snored or blew his nose or hit his thumb with a hammer.

He's easier to stomach that way. There is something about keeping him divine that keeps him distant, packaged, predictable.

But don't do it. For heaven's sake, don't. Let him be as human as he intended to be. Let him into the mire and muck of our world. For only if we let him in can he pull us out. (1987, 25–27)

Some of us have little difficulty picturing the humanity of Jesus, so much so that we forget He was and is also God. We have nothing in our day-to-day experience that prepares us for a being that has both a fully human and a fully divine nature at the same time. It is a bit mind-boggling to embrace that Jesus is truly one of us—fully human—and yet He is still fully God. As Michael Frost notes in *Exiles*, "[The Incarnation] reminds us of the radical capacity of Jesus the man to seamlessly embrace humanity and divinity equally and successfully" (2006, 54). This fact isn't just a radical capacity; it is *unique* in all of history. Some call Jesus the 200 percent man—because He is both 100 percent man and 100 percent God. This concept of both a divine nature and a human nature being united in the one person of Jesus Christ is referred to by theologians as "hypostatic union." John 1, a poetic, majestic telling of the Christmas story of Incarnation, beautifully recounts the two natures expressed in the one person of Jesus: "In the beginning was the Word, and the Word was with God, and the Word was God. He was with God in the beginning. Through him all things were made; without him nothing was made that has been made" (vv. 1–3). "The Word became flesh and made his dwelling among us. We have seen his glory, the glory of the One and Only, who came from the Father, full of grace and truth" (v. 14).

Without question, it is beyond our human ability to discern the day-to-day specifics of how the presence of these two natures in one person worked itself out in Jesus' life. But the questions are worth pondering, if only for the sense of awe we find in trying to understand such a mystery (see the "Twenty-five Questions for Mary"

Twenty-five Questions for Mary

- What was it like watching him pray?
- How did he respond when he saw other kids giggling during the service at the synagogue?
- When he saw a rainbow, did he ever mention a flood?
- Did you ever feel awkward teaching him how he created the world?
- When he saw a lamb being led to the slaughter, did he act differently?
- Did you ever see him with a distant look on his face as if he were listening to someone you couldn't hear?
- How did he act at funerals?
- Did the thought ever occur to you that the God to whom you were praying was asleep under your own roof?
- Did you ever try to count the stars with him … and succeed?
- Did he ever come home with a black eye?
- How did he act when he got his first haircut?
- Did he have any friends by the name of Judas?
- Did he do well in school?
- Did you ever scold him?
- Did he ever have to ask a question about Scripture?
- What do you think he thought about when he saw a prostitute offering to the highest bidder the body he made?
- Did he ever get angry when someone was dishonest with him?
- Did you ever catch him pensively looking at the flesh on his own arm while holding a clod of dirt?
- Did he ever wake up afraid?
- Who was his best friend?
- When someone referred to Satan, how did he act?
- Did you ever accidentally call him Father?
- What did he and his cousin John talk about as kids?
- Did his other brothers and sisters understand what was happening?
- Did you ever think, *That's God eating my soup*?

From *God Came Near: Chronicles of the Christ* by Max Lucado (Portland, OR: Multnomah Press, 1987), 43–44.

sidebar). It is fitting to recognize that the Incarnation is indeed a mystery—a paradox—that must be embraced in faith. Even so, we can learn much from reflecting on the Incarnation and the life of Christ. The Incarnation is the model for reaching out to all people, whether within one's own culture or across cultural boundaries. Jesus tells us not only what to communicate but how to communicate it. And the primary way He did and does that is through His humanity, His ordinariness. Though it is hard to grasp, He was truly one of us. He walked on earth, struggled as humans do, and overcame as Hebrews 4:15 indicates: "For we do not have a high priest who is unable to sympathize with our weaknesses, but we have one who has been tempted in every way, just as we are—yet was without sin." And as Frost points out, "His ordinariness invites us to follow him by providing us with a template of how to be Godlike even as an ordinary human being" (2006, 37).

> *"His ordinariness invites us to follow him by providing us with a template of how to be Godlike even as an ordinary human being."*

We are invited as believers to be disciples—to model our lives after that of Christ. As Paul writes in 1 Corinthians 11:1, "Follow my example, as I follow the example of Christ." But what does that mean? What is the example of Christ I am to follow as I accept the invitation God gives to join His mission, to participate in His purpose?

The act of the Incarnation itself is a model for us—it represents the most significant crossing of a cultural divide that could ever be imagined. If God is willing to go to such lengths to demonstrate His love for us—to enact His plan of relationship with us, redemption, and reconciliation—what does that suggest about our response? If we serve a God who is so oriented toward the service of others, so willing to sacrifice in love, so humble as to embrace our finite, limited, and mere existence, what does that speak to us about how we are to be oriented?

It isn't just the act of the Incarnation itself that is a model for us, either. In Christ's life, we have a great portrait of servanthood, love for others, and cross-cultural ministry. Jesus was perfect in His pursuit of not only those of His immediate Jewish culture, but also those in various cultures He encountered throughout His ministry. In *Eternity in Their Hearts*, Don Richardson identifies several cross-cultural encounters Jesus had that served as examples—not only to His disciples, but also to us—that He has always intended to go to all people. The Roman centurion who sought Jesus' healing of his paralyzed servant (see Matthew 8:5–13) was praised by Christ as having more faith than anyone in Israel. "As in many other discourses, Jesus exploited the occasion to teach His disciples that Gentiles have just as great a potential for faith as Jews! And they make just as valid objects for the grace of God too!" writes Richardson (1981, 155). Jesus healed the demon-possessed daughter of a Canaanite woman (see Matthew 15:21–28), and at least one of the ten lepers Jesus healed along the border between Samaria and Galilee was a Samaritan (see Luke 17:11–19). Richardson notes, "Jesus' penchant for holding up non-Jews as examples of righteousness for Jews—who, of all people on Earth, were supposed to be leaders in righteousness—is even more dramatically illustrated, however, by His Good Samaritan story" (157). Jesus was intentional about reaching out to others in love and about seeing beyond and exposing the cultural bias and ethnocentricity of the people around Him.

Cross–Cultural Encounters

Matthew 8:5–13
Matthew 15:21–28
Luke 17:11–19
John 4:4–42

Perhaps the most famous example of Christ's intentional reaching out beyond the barriers of culture and custom is found in the encounter chronicled in John 4:1–42—the encounter with the woman at the well. Jesus and His disciples were traveling from Judea to Galilee (John 4:3–4). The shortest route was through Samaria, but because of animosity between Jews and Samaritans, most Jews traveled *around* Samaria rather than *through* it. Jesus intentionally took the route that would place Him in contact with this culture that was viewed as inferior by His contemporaries. Once in Samaria, Jesus started a conversation specifically with a Samaritan woman. This was a radical act on two accounts: First, Jews did not associate with Samaritans, whom they viewed as an inferior, pagan nation. Second, Jewish men in Jesus' time traditionally did not speak with women unless they were family members; at the very least, women were considered second-class citizens by the customs of that time. Jesus' act of approaching a Samaritan woman for a drink of water was a scandalously inclusive act, which led not only to her conversion but also to the conversions of many other Samaritans. John 4:27 gives us more than a hint that this sort of behavior is highly unusual when it notes the surprise of the disciples to find Jesus talking to this woman. In this story, we see the intentional and radical way in which Jesus reached out to serve others—regardless of their status or ethnicity. This is a critical model for us to bear in mind.

Being on mission with God is a lifelong journey, and the missional life of following Christ's example is one that is engaged in daily over the course of a lifetime. So, no simple one-size-fits-all, cookie-cutter template exists for the demands that journey will make on your life. But at the heart of it, Frost notes, "Christians must be prepared to go where Christ would go: to the poor, to the marginalized, to the places of suffering. They must be prepared to die to self in order to follow Jesus' radical lifestyle of self-giving and sacrifice" (2006, 54). Frost and others identify this willingness as incarnational living or incarnational mission. David Ruis, in the book *Practitioners*, reflects on the Incarnation and on Jesus' life:

> We see missionality incarnated in Christ, and the concept [of missional living] becomes clearer. It becomes clear that Jesus is the exact representation of God. Sometimes we think in our heads, "*Oh boy, if I could just see God.*" Well, we do see Him in a very clear sense, in the pages of the Gospels and in the reflections of other biblical writers.
>
> He's the exact representation of God, and here again we see this completely upside-down approach to the journey of the Kingdom. Jesus absolutely refused to let His disciples depend on Him. Have you ever noticed that? He rarely drew attention to Himself as a man. That's one of the tensions of the faith, you know—the goodness of Jesus and the humanity of Jesus.
>
> There was an early heresy that swirled around the Early Church called Docetism. It was the idea that God simply couldn't take on a body. So there were all sorts of spiritualizations and wrestlings by which people tried to deal with the nature of God in Jesus Christ.
>
> I've really come to the conviction that Christ fully took humanity on Himself. He didn't just wear it; He became it. He didn't just cloak Himself with humanness; He stepped into the entire depth of what it means to be human. I believe that Jesus learned, stretched, grew and wrestled with obedience. Hebrews 4:15 says that He even faced temptation.
>
> So as a man that you could touch and smell and sit with and eat with and interact with and ask questions of, He constantly refused to have the disciples rely on Him. He always said things like, "I'm leading you to the Father," "I'm taking you to another place," "I'm giving you authority," "I'm giving you power."
>
> One of the most stunning verses in Scripture is this: "Anyone who has faith in me will do what I have been doing. He will do even greater things than these" (John 14:12).
>
> To me, that verse isn't about power; rather, it's one of the most awesome declarations a leader can make. Jesus wasn't here to prove anything. He was here to do what His Father does and, as He said in John 5, to invite us into that kind of partnership.

I see it modeled again and again in Jesus. He's constantly moving people toward the Father, toward the Father, toward the Father. There is this attitude of leaning into God and leaning into dependence on the Holy Spirit, which is absolutely critical in living life this side of heaven, this side of the return of Jesus Christ.

Jesus fascinates me because He was missional, because He truly interacted with people. Maybe that was the perceived blasphemy of Christ. Maybe that's what, in some ways, got Him stuck up on a cross. People might have said, "Oh, no, no, no! You can't be God. God doesn't have children jumping up and down on His lap and yanking on His beard and pulling His hair. No! God does not have prostitutes standing behind Him, weeping and touching Him and standing in His presence. No!"

It wasn't just the claim to be the Messiah and the One sent from God; it was His simple action. Many of the teachers and religious minds in the time of Christ had been raised on Scripture. They could quote long passages of Scripture without blinking. And yet there was God right before them in the flesh, and they couldn't see Him. They couldn't see Him!

See, I don't think we can understand the mission of God if we don't understand God Himself. (2005, 126–27)[1]

Through the Incarnation we have a picture of God with skin on, what He looks like walking around and talking with us as one of us. It is in Jesus Christ that we see the heart of God—a heart full of love for His beloved creation, a heart full of humble service to even His enemies. That is the heart of the One who bids us, "Come and follow Me."

❧

Note

1. David Ruis, "Missionality as Relationship with God," in *Practitioners: Voices Within the Emerging Church*, ed. Greg Russinger and Alex Field, 122–45 (Ventura, CA: Regal Books, 2005). Used by permission.

God's View of People

Let us live daily in the rhythms of Jesus, where moving over and experiencing the other, the stranger, become as natural as breathing.
—*Greg Russinger*

Talk about living among "the other," as Russinger talks about above! In a most shocking and humiliating act of Incarnation, God in Christ became one of us. In the life and death of Jesus of Nazareth the entire nature of the universe changed—not least in terms of the creation of new and free access to relationship with our Creator God. A popular evangelism tract visually depicts this reality by showing the Cross as a bridge that spans the chasm that separates us from God. Indeed, in Christ a bridge is created.

But to stop at only the bridge Christ created between us and God is to stop at a limited understanding of the bridges Christ built in His earthly ministry. It is also to stop short of grasping the types of bridges that God desires for you to build and to cross as you join Him in His purpose. As Edward R. Dayton notes, "God is in the business of redeeming this world.... Our responsibility is to become involved with Him in carrying out His good purposes for the world" (1990, 164). In meditating on the example of Christ's incarnation, we find that Jesus reached out to all—regardless of their "other-ness." Class, ethnicity, tradition, social mores, economics, or any other classifications we use to divide ourselves didn't stop Him. Jesus is a bridge not just for you, but *for every single person* in the world to be able to come to the Father. Moreover, He formed bridges of understanding between groups that had never previously been able to see eye to eye. Just think of the mix of characters that made up His twelve disciples—a tax collector, a group of fishermen, at least one religious zealot, and a couple of Greek-speaking men. How often would these folks normally even share a meal together? Yet these men traveled and labored side-by-side with Christ for several years and on after His ascension. The example of the early Church and the unity found between Jew and Gentile in Christ is but the beginning of the legacy created by the inclusiveness of Christ's love for all people.

If we are honest, this idea of love for all people is a hard thing to grasp. After all, people are so *different*. And there are so many! According to the U.S. Census Bureau, as of 2008 there are more than six billion people in the world.[1] That is a difficult figure to wrap one's mind around, much less begin to understand. Nevertheless, Christ models for us a life and ministry of enormous cross-cultural proportions. He calls us to share His love to all people by following Him down the road—a road that offers reconciliation, restoration, and relationship with God to the world around us. This process of reaching out across cultures can be enhanced by a study of people.

To start with, we should begin to recognize the vast diversity of the world around us. Most of the time we tend to think of the world as being very much like "us," though the opposite is really more the case. In 2002, Duane Elmer presented the statistical snapshot found in "The Global Village" sidebar.

In his book *Cross-Cultural Connections*, Elmer notes that the "North Americans, Europeans and Japanese (just over 11 percent of the population) own nearly 90 percent of the wealth in the world and consume more than half of its products." And the statistics show that in the area of religion, 330 of these 1,000 global villagers are Christians, leaving 670 non-Christians. Among those classified as non-Christians, Muslims are the largest group, represented by 198 people. They are followed by 126 nonreligious people, 135 Hindus, and 60 Buddhists, and the balance includes tribal religions, atheists, New Agers, and other smaller groups (2002, 20).

Statistical pictures such as these begin to give us a sense of how diverse the world is, and they broaden our understanding of the limits of our own cultural context. As Elmer notes, "Sometimes we fail to see beyond our experience and fail to realize the vast array of differences" (2002, 20). This limitation can be a crippling blind spot if we are serious about following Christ and joining God in

---

The Global Village

"Imagine a village of 1,000 people that represented the world's population.

- 206 would be Chinese

- 167 would be Indian

- 79 would be from Central and South America

- 50 would be from the former Soviet Union (Eastern Europe)

- 51 would be North American

- 45 would be Western European

- 33 would be Indonesian

- 21 would be from Japan

- 22 would be from Bangladesh

- 21 would be from Nigeria

- 24 would be from Pakistan

- 118 would be from other sub-Saharan African and other Asian countries" (Elmer 2002, 19–20)

His plans for the world. But thinking about the world's diversity of people only in terms of geographical or political boundaries, such as countries or nations, doesn't always give an accurate picture of cultural difference either. One of the challenges of understanding people is in understanding that their cultural contexts can be far more complex than what is suggested by identifying someone by nationality or language only.

In chapter 3 we discussed briefly the idea of nations as it is described in the Bible. At the heart of the term often translated "nations" in the Bible is the concept of *ethnos*, a Greek word meaning "a tribe, nation, people group."[2] This Greek term is the root of our English words *ethnic* and *ethnicity*, which have to do with race and people groups. Understanding this concept of people groups gives us an even richer picture of the world's diversity, which in turn gives a greater picture of the magnificent, creative, and loving heart of God. It can also play an important role in understanding just how much of the world has yet to be introduced to Christ.

One of the most basic ways we categorize people is in terms of "us" and "them"—those who are like us and those who aren't. In the simplest terms, a people group is made up of people who share the conviction that they are an "us." Outside the people group are the "thems." But for more detail, let's turn to an explanation from missiologist Edward R. Dayton:

> Although we usually think of other nations as countries with geographic locations, when the Bible refers to "nations," it is referring to groups of people sharing the same language and culture. For example, the "Kurds" are people with the same language and culture who live in regions located in Iran, Iraq, Turkey, and Russia.
>
> In 2000, the *U.S. Government World Factbook* said there were over 267 countries in the world. They come in all sizes. They range from an estimated 1.2 billion people in China, down to only 1,876 in Niue, South Pacific....
>
> One way of thinking about ... that world is *one people group at a time*, not one country at a time, because countries vary so much. India, with over 1 billion people, has 18 official languages and thousands of castes, tribes, and other social groups....
>
> Let us use an illustration to explain what we mean by a people group....
>
> First, your language is English. Who are the people with whom you have been communicating naturally in English? Which ones do not speak the language? Let us draw a "boundary" that represents language.

Do you live among different ethnic groups? Which one is yours? Hispanic? Indian? White? Black? Asian? Notice how in the illustration the boundary is reduced because of your ethnic group.

You live on the south side of Chicago. For many people, where they live and the people they live close to determine who they consider to be part of their group. Again, in our illustration your group is becoming better defined by country or region.

If you are black, do you relate to some people better than others? Do you think of yourself as belonging to a particular class or caste? Perhaps you think of yourself as belonging to a specific occupation or profession. Your parents came to America from Libya, North Africa. You relate best with other North Africans. Another boundary goes up because of social relationships.

What kind of people do you worship with? In other words, what is your religion? For many people, religion is one of the primary ways they identify themselves with a group. You happen to be a Muslim like your parents. A boundary of religion is formed.

All these boundaries are both inclusive and exclusive. They define a particular people group. And they exclude those people who are not part of the people group.

Every country is filled with people groups. At first glance we may believe that all the people in our country are "just like us." But closer examination will show a vast mosaic of differences. Take, for example, the city of greater Los Angeles. The numbers of Asians, Hispanics, and blacks now make up 53 percent of the population (U.S. Census [as published in] 2000), and 43 percent speak a language other than English in their home. There is no longer an ethnic white majority in L.A. This changes the whole look of the city. Already there is not just one Asian community but multiple communities of Koreans, Chinese, Japanese, etc. In the schools, teachers often need Spanish to communicate with their students from Latin American countries.

The situation in Los Angeles is duplicated in cities and rural areas throughout the world. (1990, 162, 164)

As Dayton mentions, you get quite a different picture of the world once you look beyond traditional geopolitical classifications such as countries and languages. Our world is far too complex for those limited classifications. According to David Smith's Mapping.com, "there may be anywhere between 168 and 254 nations, depending on who is doing the counting."[3] But the picture becomes much more diversified when you think in terms of people groups. According to its website, the Joshua Project—which defines a people group as the largest group within which one doesn't encounter barriers of understanding or acceptance (in other words, a group that considers itself an "us")—has identified more than sixteen thousand people groups in the world. Thinking of the world in terms of sixteen thousand different people groups instead of two hundred fifty nations can really expand one's vision of the wonderful diversity that God has created!

One of the insights gained by thinking in terms of people groups rather than countries or language groups is an understanding of the idea of cultural distance. It is quite possible for two groups of people to be neighbors geographically and yet still have vast cultural distance between them. An excellent example of this is found in Iraq where, even though the population is largely made up of Iraqi-born Muslims, you find deep and significant divisions between Sunni and Shiite Muslims. Though they may live near each other geographically, their cultural distance prevents even the most basic communication or understanding between them. Such stark examples are found almost anywhere around the globe where sectarian violence and strife occur. But closer to home even, consider the cultural distance in any major urban American city that contains one or more groups of immigrant communities. It is possible in many areas of this country for you to live less than a mile from people who are also Americans, who also speak English, who work and shop where you do, but who are vastly different from you in terms of culture and worldview.

Ralph Winter describes a phenomenon called "people blindness" that is related to this idea of cultural distance. He defines it as "blindness to the existence of separate *peoples* within *countries* … The Bible rightly translated could have made this plain to us. The 'nations' to which Jesus often referred were mainly ethnic groups within the single political structure of the Roman government. The various nations represented on the day of Pentecost were for the most part not *countries* but *peoples*" (1974). This blindness, Winter notes, is highly prevalent in the United States and is the type of thing that can prevent us from seeing the type of life and witness we should have if we truly want to follow the cross-cultural example of Christ. Jesus reached out and loved across all levels of cultural distance. Understanding the different levels of cultural difference and how significant some of our cultural distances may be is a key step in preparing ourselves to embrace the call of God to join Him in His purpose for the whole world.

A familiar passage of instruction from Jesus can help illustrate the difference in cultural distance and shed light on Jesus' intention that we were never designed, as children of God, to live our lives only within the comfortable familiarity of our own people group. In Acts 1:8 Jesus gave His disciples this last word of instruction before His ascension: "But you will receive power when the Holy Spirit comes on you; and you will be my witnesses in Jerusalem, and in all Judea and Samaria, and to the ends of the earth." Thus, He gives specific attention to the worldwide nature of God's heart with an emphasis on the specific differences in not just geography but also culture. Winter notes the following: "At first glance you might think that he is merely speaking geographically, but with more careful study, it seems clear that he is not talking merely about *geographical* distance, but about *cultural* distance. The clue is the appearance of the word *Samaria* in this sequence. Fortunately, we have special insight into what Jesus meant by *Samaria*, since the New Testament records in an extended passage the precise nature of the evangelistic problem Jews faced in trying to reach the Samaritans" (1974). You will remember from our last chapter that although Samaria was near Jerusalem geographically (situated between Galilee and Jerusalem), there was a tremendous cultural difference between Jews and Samaritans.

For a Jew of Jerusalem, communicating with Judeans and reaching out to them would have been a relatively simple matter. There was no significant barrier of language or cultural distance between the two; the cultures were very much the same. Ralph D. Winter developed a scale of cultural distance in which Jerusalem to Judea represents an E-1 relationship that has no significant cultural barriers to cross for communication and outreach to occur (1974). According to Winter's E-Scale (Winter and Hawthorne 1999b), the only frontier of distance is that which exists between a believer in Christ and a nonbeliever. You probably have friends who share much in common with you but who don't know Christ. These would be the people with whom you have an E-1 relationship—largely, you are able to comfortably communicate with them and would have no real barriers in communicating effectively with them.

Samaria represents a second level of cultural distance (what Winter calls E-2) in which there is a second frontier of cultural distance to cross in order to communicate intimately and effectively. "The Bible account shows that although it was relatively easy for Jesus and his disciples to make themselves understood to the Samaritans, the Jew and the Samaritan were divided from each other by a frontier consisting of dialectal distinctions and some other very significant cultural differences" (1974). This "second frontier" of cultural distance makes it an E-2 relationship because it is between people of different cultural orientation. You may have people in your school or community who share many common experiences with you, but who are culturally distant from you because their first language is not your first language or because their cultural traditions are vastly different from yours. An example would be an international exchange student who attends classes with you but who has a very different cultural background.

Finally, Jesus' last realm of concern, "the ends of the earth," involves what Winter would call an E-3 relationship, in which the greatest cultural distance exists between parties. As Winter says, "The people … in this third sphere live, work, talk, and think in languages and cultural patterns utterly different from [one's own]" (1974). For most of us, E-3 relationships are rare because of the great cultural

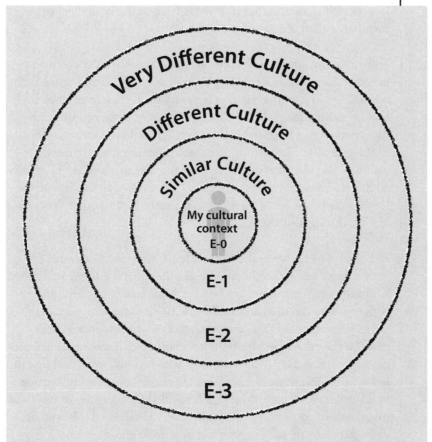

Diagram based on Ralph D. Winter's E-Scale described in "The Highest Priority: Cross-Cultural Evangelism," a paper sent to congress participants prior to Lausanne 1: The International Congress on World Evangelization in Lausanne, Switzerland, 1974, quoted in *Perspectives on the World Christian Movement: A Reader*, ed. Ralph D. Winter and Steven C. Hawthorne, 3rd ed. (Pasadena, CA: William Carey Library, 1999), 339–53.

distance they require us to cross. But it is very possible that there are people who are geographically near you—in your city, county, or state—who may indeed represent an E-3 cultural distance from you.

All this talk of cultural distance and E-Scale is important in the sense that it reveals something deeper to us about how different people are and how distant we can be from many of those we are called in Christ to love. It is apparent that all but the E-1 relationships require a certain degree of intention and preparation. Unfortunately, we are often prey to the "people blindness" Winter references because we are, as human beings, apt to seek the comfort of the familiar. If we are serious about following Christ and joining God in His purpose, living on mission with Him, then we must be serious about imitating His desire to reach out to the whole world in love. This is why understanding the vastness of the world around us can be so significant in catching the same sort of vision God has—a vision that reaches in love far beyond the bounds of our own particular cultural comfort zone.

Jesus went far outside His cultural zone to come to the earth and become one of us. His ministry demonstrates again and again the way He saw the world—one person at a time, each in need of a loving, healing touch from Him. Examples abound of His reaching beyond even His earthly, Jewish religious-leader culture. Think of the eyebrows His actions often raised among the Pharisees, for instance, because of His forgiveness extended to a woman caught in adultery, His acceptance of the hated Zaccheus, His healing of the lepers. The list of Jesus' intentional ministry to the "other" goes on and on throughout the Gospels.

Look up the story in Luke 7:36–50.

In Luke 7:36–50, we find a story of Jesus' acceptance of a sinful woman who burst into the middle of a dinner at the home of Simon, a prominent Pharisee, only to weep at Jesus' feet, wipe them dry with her hair, and then anoint them with perfume. Can you imagine the scene this caused? Yet, even though this woman ignored "her place" within the expectations of her culture, Jesus embraced her and chastised His socially prominent host who had judgment and disdain in his heart. "Simon wanted to quickly dismiss this woman because, in his day, any woman whose touch fulfilled the pleasures of men was ostracized. In contrast, Jesus created space. He allowed this woman to *be*, without any judgment, without any conditions, without any confusion. He allowed this woman—He allows the stranger, you and me—to come and sit, knowing that His touch, truth, time and relentless tenderness transform the human heart" (Russinger 2005, 39).

The example of Christ is to reach out in love to the "other." We are called to do no less if we want to live on mission with God. Beginning to understand the vastness of His creation, the tremendous variety among the people that He loves, is the beginning of learning to love them ourselves.

ॐ

NOTES

1. U.S. Census Bureau, "World POPClock Projection," http://www.census.gov/ipc/www/popclockworld.html (accessed April 22, 2008).

2. *The New Testament Greek Lexicon*, s.v. "ethnos" (by Joseph Henry Thayer and William Smith), http://www.studylight.org/lex/grk (accessed July 17, 2007).

3. David Smith's Mapping.com, "Countries of the World," http://www.mapping.com/countries.html (accessed November 1, 2007).

Between a Rock and a Hard Place

Incarnational living emphasizes living out Christ in any and all situations and contexts.... So what do I have to do to live incarnationally? … All I know is that when Christ is incarnated through you and me, we will strive to find new ways to pour ourselves out in service to the Father by serving others as the Holy Spirit leads us. We will become active participants in all of creation being reconciled to Christ.

—*Scott Sharman*

The Word became flesh and blood, and moved into the neighborhood. We saw the glory with our own eyes, the one-of-a-kind glory, like Father, like Son, generous inside and out, true from start to finish.

—*John 1:14, The Message*

In the last chapter, we looked at the vast diversity of the world we live in. One of the ways we can begin to follow the model of Christ is by learning more about people and how to reach out across boundaries of cultural distance with the love of God. As you likely know, this is not always an easy task! Reaching out to those who are different from us (and who isn't different from you?) carries with it a certain element of risk. But difficulty and hardship is never an excuse to shrink back from the places God calls us to go, and He definitely calls us to love our neighbor. And if you recall the parable of the good Samaritan (Luke 10:25–37), our neighbors aren't always who we would choose them to be. As God's people, we are called to learn to connect incarnationally with others in significant cross-cultural relationships.

What does it mean to connect incarnationally? Well, at the most basic level it means to connect with others in the way that Jesus did with us. Jesus connected with humans by coming to us and identifying fully with us, or, as John 1:14 says in The Message, "The Word became flesh and blood, and moved into the neighborhood." Moving into the neighborhood is an act of reaching out, entering into a new context—maybe a terribly unfamiliar one—and setting up house. Moving into the neighborhood involves making a commitment, spending time there, putting down roots. To connect incarnationally with others in significant cross-cultural relationships may mean to literally move into a new neighborhood. Or it may mean simply to be intentional about seeking out new people to get to know instead of waiting for them to come to you. At either end of the spectrum, connecting in an incarnational manner involves reaching out to others and sharing in their lives.

Michael Frost talks about four aspects of incarnational living. He derives these aspects from the example of Christ. The first aspect is an active sharing of the life of the community or person you are reaching out to, including walking alongside someone's "fears, frustrations, and afflictions." The second aspect is use of the "language and thought forms of those with whom we seek to share Jesus. After all, he used common speech and stories: salt, light, fruit, birds, and the like. He seldom used theological or religious jargon or technical terms." The third aspect Frost mentions is that idea of moving into the neighborhood—"a preparedness to go to the people, not expecting them to come to us." Finally, the fourth aspect of connecting with others incarnationally is "a confidence that the gospel can be communicated by ordinary means, through acts of servanthood, loving relationships, good deeds" (2006, 55). At the heart of it, Jesus reached out to people in very simple and practical ways—meeting needs, loving, and forgiving. Christ's example is indeed simple, but that doesn't necessarily mean that it is easy to follow.

> *Jesus reached out to people in very simple and practical ways—meeting needs, loving, and forgiving.*

In this chapter, we begin to look at the realities of how challenging it can be to connect incarnationally with others in significant cross-cultural relationships. There are many ways that misunderstandings and even hard feelings can surface as we reach out—especially cross-culturally—in pursuit of living on mission with God. To get you thinking about the realities of living as Jesus did, reaching out to others in significant relationships no matter the cultural distance, we will look at an article by Elliot Paulson, an American Christian who has lived in the Middle East for nearly two decades. In the following piece, "Between a Rock and a Hard Place," Paulson shows us some of the challenges of incarnational living in a very different cultural setting.

Between a Rock and a Hard Place
by Elliot Paulson
Excerpt from *Mission Frontiers*

I love it when Americans ask me where I live these days. My answer: "Between a rock and a hard place." Not many people can say that. Here's why. English-speakers usually pronounce Iraq as "eye rack" or "a rack." However, when Middle Easterners say Iraq, it sounds closer to "a rock." Therefore, given the countries we share borders with, we can literally say we live between Iraq ("a rock") and a hard place. Several hard places, actually. Look at a map. It's a rough neighborhood.

But lately I flinch when Muslims ask me where I am from. My answer: "Nice weather today, isn't it?" Seriously. Here's why.

Exactly ten days before the Second Gulf War officially started, I hopped in a taxi on the way to the airport. I was on a journey of about 4,000 frequent flyer miles, which is not all that interesting except that I was flying on a Muslim country's flagship carrier (complete with direction finder for Mecca for those who want to pray en route), I would be flying on the edge of Iraqi airspace, and I would be changing planes in a Muslim country smack in the middle of the Gulf. That's not all that interesting either, except that I would be reversing my route just hours before every commentator was predicting missiles would start falling on Baghdad.

As the taxi driver effortlessly navigated his 1600-cc, LPG-fueled tin can through red lights, angrily honking at motorists who dared to try to pass through the intersection on the green, my wife's parting words were ringing in my ears. "Try to stay inconspicuous. Don't advertise the fact you are an American."

I promised I would heed her warning and even joked with her that on my trip, if I had to speak English in public places I would pronounce words with a Middle Eastern accent.

My taxi driver was a sociable fellow, and during the normal pleasantries he innocently asked, "Where are you from?"

We'd already noted the temperature and precipitation in our chitchat, so I obviously couldn't divert his attention with, "Nice weather, isn't it?"

So I offered him another deflection. "I'm from Anchovy Province." This made him jerk his head toward me and squint his eyes in a fiercely doubtful examination of my facial features. (This also meant, of course, that he took his eyes off the road, but that had little practical effect on his driving.)

During our conversation he'd picked up clues that I wasn't a local, so before he could blurt out an expletive of incredulity, I slowly raised my right index finger to my olfactory organ and said with a grin, "Isn't it evident from my nose?"

He chuckled and glanced back out front just in time to cut off a bus and barely miss a push cart.

The natives of Anchovy Province are famously proud of their Roman noses, and mine, though not as noble as their benchmark profile, is nonetheless more prominent than most here. My driver glanced at me again and laughed, pleasantly surprised at my knowledge of his culture.

I seized my chance to make him forget his original question about my origin. "Where are you from?"

"Tea Province."

"Why, that makes us practically neighbors," I said. Anchovy and Tea Provinces are next to each other.

"You know," I went on, "if you ask me, I think that Tea Province is the most beautiful province in the whole country." (Note: If my kids ever tell you that I say this to every taxi driver, no matter which of the 80-some provinces he is from, I will deny it.)

His smile showed that he agreed with me, and I could tell his thoughts wandered back to the pristine air and the hillside tea groves of his homeland, displaying their thousands of shades of green framed by sapphire skies. But he snapped back to reality as an overloaded and seriously listing minibus belching black diesel exhaust roared past us on our left, cut in front of us and swerved to the right curb, squealing his brakes and tossing his human cargo about, just to pick up a single passenger for whom there was no room. After leaving his own skid marks and cursing the minibus chauffeur, my driver shifted into first and pulled back into the traffic flow.

"No, really, where are you from?" he repeated.

Seeing no way out, I gave an honest answer, but camouflaged in a cough. "Amggouffhhhkkhaa."

"What?" he persisted, with furrowed brow.

"America," I said as quietly as possible. Then louder, "But don't blame me, nobody asked me where I wanted to be born."

Now, before you accuse me of being unpatriotic, let me explain. When I meet a Middle Easterner, I can't always tell immediately what his opinion of Americans, and therefore of me, is going to be. A man sporting blue jeans and a golf shirt might be as anti-American as one who is clothed in 7th-century Arab garb. I've found that my joke about my choice of birthplace usually softens even the most prejudiced Middle Easterners, whether they are anticapitalist leftists or anti-Christian Muslims. Once I have shown them I am not a stereotypical American, we can have a decent, mutually respectful dialogue. But as much as possible, I avoid smashing into the rock of brandishing my passport.

Now don't get me wrong. I am thankful I was born in America. I grew up in relative prosperity, peace and health. I had the luxury of choosing a university, a course of study, and a profession. I had the freedom to both select a faith and to practice it with little or no discrimination or social cost. I am deeply aware of my blessings, and thankful for them. So total denial of my American heritage would put my conscience in a very hard place.

Some may ask, "Being thankful is one thing, but aren't you proud to be an American?"

Well, I prefer to say that I am grateful to be an American. But I certainly cannot say I am proud of everything that is known as American culture or of American foreign policy. Living for 18 years in a Muslim country has given me a broader worldview than most Americans have.

But infinitely more important, I know that it is no great personal character virtue to have been born in a given place. I am not the only human being who had no choice where he or she was born. And certainly, no one can claim any personal merit from his or her birthplace. In fact, we have nothing that we have not been given, including our natural talent, intelligence, and health. So, along with our birthplace, finding any of these things as a source of pride is totally in vain (1 Corinthians 4:7).

In addition, Jesus said that the more we've been given, the more we will have to give account for (Luke 12:48). Along with the great privilege of being an American Christian comes a great burden of responsibility to do good to all nations (Genesis 12:3, Matthew 28:18–20).

This phrase, American Christian, leads me to a second between-a-rock-and-a-hard-place situation we constantly live in. Your average

Muslim here has never met either a Christian or an American. Not that they make the distinction: they think that all Americans are Christians. If you are born there, you are a Christian, just like if you are born here, you are a Muslim.

The fact is, Muslims get literally all of their impressions of Christians and Americans from Hollywood and/or the Islamic press. They see every American actor and every American politician as Christian. So, if I voluntarily identify myself as a Christian to Muslims, they hear me confessing that I am immoral, imperialistic, or both. That is the rock on my one side. To avoid hitting my head on it, I almost never use the word *Christian* when describing my faith to Muslims.

But some may protest, "First, you are not proud to be an American and now you are ashamed of being a Christian. Repent! The Bible says we are not to be ashamed of the gospel!" (see Romans 1:16).

To which I reply, "Being ashamed of the gospel is one thing. Distancing myself from Muslims' uninformed and prejudiced opinion of Christians is another. When I have a chance, I say that I am a follower of Jesus the Messiah by choice, not by birth. I tell them they can call me by a variety of names: Messianic believer, disciple of Jesus, member of the fellowship of Jesus. Sure, these are strange terms for Muslims, and when I see their faces contort with incomprehension, I put them out of their misery by saying, "Or you can call me a True Christian."

"But by the time I reached my destination, an American Christian and a Middle Eastern Muslim had agreed on lots of important principles: innocent people should not die in war; the motives of politicians are rarely clear, let alone pure; the Middle East situation is a lot more complicated than either Europeans or Americans comprehend; evil men should not have the means to destroy others whether individually or en masse; and God is ultimately sovereign."

I know that sounds like arrogance, just the opposite of the humility that Jesus taught us to have. Who am I to say that I am a true Christian, implying that someone else is not? Yet, I am in a hard place. I must still somehow show Muslims that I am different than the bulk of the Hollywood stars and Washington pundits who come to their media-manipulated minds. So I quote Jesus himself, hoping they'll get the point: "Not everyone who calls me 'Lord, Lord' will enter the kingdom of heaven; only those who do the will of my Father will enter" (Matthew 7:21).

If you think that I could soften up that hard place by simply explaining to Muslims the distinctions between the varieties of nominal, liberal and conservative/evangelical American Christians, and if you then think that by identifying myself with conservative evangelicals I will enhance my credibility and reputation with Muslims, think again. Sadly, most Muslims are unaware or have forgotten that a Nobel Peace prize-winning and evangelical Christian former president opposed this war. But informed Muslims know full well that many of the most hawkish politicians and a large slice of the current president's constituency are Bible-believing and Bible-quoting Christians. In short, Muslims see these Christians as the ones launching the missiles. Like I said, a rock and a hard place.

But back to my taxi ride. My Muslim driver had not yet revealed his opinion of my being an American. He probed some more. "What do you think of your president?"

"Which one?" I replied with a grin. He took his eyes off the road one more time and glanced at me.

"Do you mean the American one or the one here, in my adopted homeland?" His smile and nod showed he appreciated my identification with his people.

He never did say what he thought of Americans, and therefore, of me. But by the time I reached my destination, an American Christian and a Middle Eastern Muslim had agreed on lots of important principles: innocent people should not die in war; the motives of politicians are rarely clear, let alone pure; the Middle East situation is a lot more complicated than either Europeans or Americans comprehend; evil men should not have the means to destroy others whether individually or en masse; and God is ultimately sovereign.

As I paid my fare, I placed my hand on his shoulder and sighed, "You know, younger brother, if only they would ask us, you and I could solve the problems of the world, couldn't we?"

Handing me my change, he smiled one more time. "You're right, older brother, you're right." (2003, 14–16)

12

Cross-Cultural Case Studies

All good people agree,
And all good people say,
All nice people, like Us, are We
And every one else is They:
But if you cross over the sea,
Instead of over the way,
You may end by (think of it!) looking on We
As only a sort of They!

　　　　　　　　　　—Rudyard Kipling

Loving someone in Christ across cultural distance can often create difficult situations. Many times the Bible is clear about how to handle questions that may arise, but often there are no easy answers. Sometimes the most profound cultural distance can be found between a Christian and a predominantly nonbelieving culture in which the Christian lives—a situation you may be familiar with depending on where you live or what your family history is. Sometimes even what seems like a simple issue of honoring one's parents or following accepted cultural norms can clash with the Bible and the example of Christ in ways that we do not expect.

The following case studies are designed to help you think through some of the issues of cross-cultural life and ministry. The first and last case studies are from the book *Case Studies in Missions*, and the middle one, "Honor Your Mother and Father," was written by Dr. Daniel Egeler, vice president of international ministries for the Association of Christian Schools International, from his own experiences in missions. You will notice that in these stories drawn from the experiences of Christians serving cross-culturally in many different parts of the world, the "rest of the story" is missing. The case studies are intentionally presented in an open-ended fashion in order to give you the opportunity to consider what you might do in these situations. As you read, try to insert yourself into the scene, evaluating your own response in terms of your worldview and culture.

Food Offered to Idols
by Simon P. David

Rajasekaran looked across the room at the large picture of the blue-faced god Krishna, heavily garlanded with marigolds and tinsel, and then at the printing-press workers gathered around the small shrine set up before the god. It was Friday, and Rajasekaran realized that he had arrived just at the completion of weekly prayers to Krishna, the patron god of the press. Like many businessmen in this city in South India, the proprietor provided money to purchase coconuts, bananas, and sugar to offer to the deity at the weekly *puja*. He believed that the prosperity of his shop was due to the blessing of the god for his faithful offerings.

As assistant editor of a Christian magazine, Rajasekaran was responsible for working with the press workers in order to make certain that the publication was properly printed on schedule. Today there had been some urgent matters to take care of, so he had come earlier than usual. He had hurried into the room, and Mani, the press foreman, had seen him before he realized that the *puja* ceremonies were still going on.

Over the past months, Mani and the editor had developed a close friendship as they worked together. Rajasekaran hoped someday to win his friend to Christ, but right now Mani was pulling him by the hand toward the group receiving the food that had been offered to Krishna and having *kunkumam* (colored powder) placed as spots on their foreheads to signify that they had been purified by eating the leftovers of the god. Rajasekaran knew that for many Hindus, including Mani, eating the food offered to a god was a sign of goodwill, much like receiving a Christmas present. But he also knew that for orthodox Hindus, partaking of the food and the *kunkumam* was part of the worship of an idol. Rajasekaran did not want to harm his relationship with Mani, but he also did not want to compromise his Christian witness. He saw Mani hold out the platter of food, and he ● ● ●

(Hiebert and Hiebert 1987, 38–39)

Honor Your Mother and Father
by Daniel Egeler

Suji had just come to a saving knowledge of Jesus Christ while attending an international Christian school. She was the child of recent immigrants from Taiwan, and she was sincere in her desire to have an authentic and uncompromising walk with God. Suji was in grade 8 in the middle school.

Suji's Bible class had been studying the book of Daniel, and she was particularly receptive to the book's portrayal of lives of uncompromising obedience to God's commands. In particular, she was deeply moved by the example of Shadrach, Meshach, and Abednego's refusal to bow down to the image of gold that King Nebuchadnezzar had set up (Daniel 3).

Suji's parents had sacrificed to have Suji attend an international school. Her parents were willing to have their children adopt aspects of a new culture, but they also wanted them to have a sense of history, understanding, and empathy for their home culture. As part of that heritage and culture that they wanted to instill in their children, her parents expected her to bow down before images of their ancestors to honor their memory.

Suji wanted to honor her parents by paying homage to her ancestors, but she also wanted to obey God's standards. She approached her Bible teacher with her dilemma. After giving her teacher the background of her family, she asked the following questions: "If I bow down before an image of my ancestors, am I compromising my faith in Jesus Christ? Or should I follow the biblical example of Shadrach, Meshach, and Abednego and refuse to bow down, but dishonor my parents by turning my back on my heritage and culture?"

After considering the situation, Suji's Bible teacher responded by saying ● ● ●

(Egeler 2000)

To Bribe or Not to Bribe?
by Teg Chin Go

Pastor Luke looked with despair at the immigration official seated behind his large desk. He could offer the man a small sum of money and then receive the visa permitting Revered John to enter the country, or he could refuse and no visa would be granted. The choice was his.

Pastor Luke was the elderly pastor of a large church with more than a thousand members among the Chinese in the Philippines. He had labored hard, but now he was in poor health and the load was too heavy. The people complained that they were being neglected, and he knew that the outreach of the church in the community had almost stopped. But where could he find help? He had searched widely throughout the Philippines for a younger assistant, but even in the Bible schools and seminaries there were almost no young Chinese training for the ministry. To find one in the country was almost out of the question.

In discussing the matter with other pastors, Pastor Luke found out that there were Taiwanese pastors willing to work in the Philippines. Their language abilities and cultural backgrounds were well suited to his Chinese-speaking congregation. So he and some church elders had traveled to Taiwan, where they found Reverend John, an able and willing worker.

However, when Pastor Luke applied for a work permit for the Taiwanese pastor, he ran into a serious problem. The officer in charge of immigration expected some money, and the pastor had heard that in some cases it had taken five to ten years for an application to be processed when no money was offered. With a suitable sum changing hands, the matter could be resolved in a matter of a few days.

When Pastor Luke brought the problem to the board of elders, most of them explained that the giving of money to an official should be thought of as a "gift" and not a "bribe." Many of them were involved in business, and they admitted that giving "gifts" to those in authority was a cultural practice in the country. They faced similar situations in business, and if they did not follow the accepted pattern they could not continue their work. Pastor Luke raised an objection. Were they not in danger of compromising with evil, of not speaking out against corruption, no matter the cost? Was the giving of money to officials so much a part of the culture that they should accept it as a church and comply in order to carry out the work of the church? Or were the elders right when they said that it was only a "gift" to the officials for their assistance? Throughout the years, he had been firm in his preaching that Christians should not be involved in bribery.

When Pastor Luke hesitated to go along with the elders who asked him to pay the money, they threatened to remove him from office and install the new pastor in his place. If, however, he agreed to give the money, would he not compromise his own convictions and lose the respect of those in the congregation who knew of his firm stand on the issue? Pastor Luke looked at the official seated before him and said ● ● ●

(Hiebert and Hiebert 1987, 136–37)

13

Review: The Lens of Culture

When you begin to get serious about living on mission with God, you cannot escape the role that culture plays in both uniting and separating people from one another. Unfortunately, our natural human tendency is to develop our most intimate and sustaining relationships with people who are the most like us. But God clearly has more than that in mind for those who want to join His mission of relationship, redemption, and reconciliation. It is impossible to take seriously the call to follow Christ as a disciple without recognizing His example of mission even to those who would reject Him. In Christ we find the most compelling example of reaching out in love regardless of the cultural distance that must be crossed. We are talking, of course, about the Incarnation.

In this unit we have looked at missional life through the lens of culture. God's story demonstrates to us that the heart of God is for *people*—people of all colors, shapes, and sizes. God desires that the hearts of His followers be atuned to people in the same way that His is. To begin to understand the role of culture in missio Dei, we have to turn to the heart of God.

Effectively communicating God's story requires an intimate understanding of culture and God's view of it.

What Difference Does It Make?

- Which of Kraft's five views of God and culture best describes your own view? Is it difficult for you to see that God values all cultures and can work through them?

- How aware are you of the different cultural influences that shape you? What are some of the most predominant cultural influences in your life?

- What are some evidences of cultural diversity that you see in your own community? Is there more or less diversity surrounding you than what you thought?

We began in chapter 7 with an overview of the fact that our planet of more than six billion people contains a great deal of diversity. Even though we have a hard time grasping all those differences, we must realize that not only does God have no trouble comprehending the differences, but He is ultimately glorified by unity within that diversity. We see this pictured in Revelation 7:9–10: "After this I looked and there before me was a great multitude that no one could count, from every nation, tribe, people and language, standing before the throne and in front of the Lamb. They were wearing white robes and were holding palm branches in their hands. And they cried out in a loud voice: 'Salvation belongs to our God, who sits on the throne, and to the Lamb.' "

One way that we are accustomed to discussing the differences between people is by using the terms *culture* and *worldview*. On the basis of the work of Charles Kraft, those terms were defined in chapter 7 in this way: *Culture* is "a peoples' way of life, their design for living, their way of coping with their biological, physical and social environment." *Worldview* is "included in culture as the deepest level presuppositions upon which people base their lives" (1998, 385). Interestingly, it is much easier to point out the distinctives of an unfamiliar culture than it is to recognize the distinctives of our own culture and how they affect us. Because of this, unless we take some time to study and reflect on the ways in which we are shaped by our own culture, we do wear some blinders to the powerful influences of our culture.

We can have all sorts of different ideas about how God views culture. The popular views of the relationship between God and culture range from the idea that God hates culture to the idea that He prefers one culture (perhaps a so-called Christian culture?) above all others. But as we learned in chapter 7, there is only one relationship between God and culture that squares with the teaching of the Bible: God is sovereign above all culture and is working through culture to bring about His purpose. In "Culture, Worldview and Contextualization," Kraft (1998) mentions several New Testament examples that demonstrate the desire by God to work through culture, examples that show that God does not demand a single particular cultural expression of Christianity in order to approach Him. And in looking at the entire story of the Bible, there is an even clearer theme that not only does God desire to work through culture, but He created diversity as a means of expressing and demonstrating His glory.

Of course, the glory of God is demonstrated most fully when the diversity He intended and created is unified under His headship, as we see pictured in Revelation 7. Also, in poetic prophecies such as Isaiah 11:1–10, we find strong images of unity within diversity: "The wolf will live with the lamb, the leopard will lie down with the goat, the calf and the lion and the yearling together; and a little child will lead them" (v. 6). That prophecy culminates with an image of Christ unifying many peoples: "In that day the Root of Jesse will stand as a banner for the peoples; the nations will rally to him, and his place of rest will be glorious" (v. 10). These images of unity are a picture of how God views culture, how His tremendous power can bring about unity within such seemingly vast differences. And that is the picture we must begin to develop for ourselves if we are to live missionally for Him.

Of course, as we learned in chapter 8, we will encounter a lot of snares and pitfalls when we set out to live in community with those who are different from us. Even if we have the best of intentions, we can blunder terribly, as Duane Elmer reminds us in his candid story about trying to buy his wife an anniversary present. His "perfect" gift of snow tires somehow didn't square with her expectations of a romantic first-anniversary gift. Some of these cultural pitfalls are *misunderstandings* based on what we think or know about another culture, *ethnocentrism* based on how we feel about culture, and *premature judgments* based on how we evaluate other cultures.

The snow tire story Elmer told demonstrates the way ignorance of his wife's feelings led to a roadblock in communication. This is an example of misunderstanding. Paul G. Hiebert reminds us that "misunderstandings are based on ignorance of the beliefs, feelings and values of another culture. The solution is to learn how the other culture works" (1999, 378; SE p. 121). But even in learning how the other culture works we have problems, many of them having to do with ethnocentrism. Simply put, ethnocentrism is the attitude that stems from the belief that one's own group is superior to other groups, and therefore the worldview and actions of one's own group are also superior to those of others. Unless we are particularly vigilant, this attitude can permeate the way we think when we encounter cultural differences. Hiebert notes, "The solution to ethnocentrism is empathy. We need to learn to appreciate other cultures and their ways. But our feelings of superiority and our negative attitudes toward strange customs run deep and are not easily rooted out" (378–79; SE p. 122).

What Difference Does It Make?

- How willing are you to learn about different cultures, particularly ones that are very different from your own?

- Do you recognize your own ethnocentrism? What specific areas of your culture do you think of as being superior to others? Why? Do these views square with the Bible?

- Do you try to make God fit into your worldview, or are you open to fitting into His?

By learning more about other cultures and working to develop empathy with people who are different from ourselves, we set the stage for avoiding the premature judgments that can create deep cultural divides. Such cultural divides hamper our ability to follow the invitation God gives to live on mission with Him. Chapter 8 concluded by reminding us that an awareness of our own cultural beliefs, feelings, and values is a great asset for us to have. But our first step must always be to focus on our relationship with God by obeying His instructions and accepting His invitation to us. We must remember that God is above earthly culture. His purpose is for His kingdom, not any kingdom of this world. He can and will choose to work through different cultures to bring about His purpose, often in ways that may initially surprise us. Of course, one of the most surprising (if not *the* most surprising) cross-cultural events of all times occurred when God sent His own Son to become one of us.

The incarnation of Jesus is the model for reaching out to all people, whether within one's own culture or across cultural boundaries. Jesus tells us not only what to communicate but how to communicate it.

What Difference Does It Make?

- What do you think is the most puzzling aspect of the Incarnation? Why?

- Do you think of yourself as being "sent" into the world to be God's ambassador of love, just as Jesus was sent to the world to demonstrate God's love?

- What particular elements of Jesus' example do you believe are the most significant for your spiritual journey at this point? Are you willing to seek to understand them and live them out more fully?

For many of us, the story of the Incarnation is incredibly familiar. The Christmas story of Jesus' coming to earth as a tiny baby has been a part of our lives since we were first old enough to learn the song "Away in a Manger." Perhaps because we know the story so well, we often overlook the significance of what happened that night in Bethlehem so many years ago. God became one of us.

In many ways, the simple truths of the Incarnation are tremendously difficult for us to grasp. The Gospel writer John testifies of Jesus: "In the beginning was the Word, and the Word was with God, and the Word was God" (John 1:1) But what are the full implications of the line a few verses later that says, "The Word became flesh and made his dwelling among us" (John 1:14)? Can we begin to understand the depths of that love? The willing choice to put aside glory for a life marked with servanthood and suffering? The crossing of the divide between eternal life and love in intimate fellowship with Father God to be subject to the limitations of finite flesh and blood? In this life, perhaps we shall never fully grasp the depths of meaning found in the Incarnation. But the Incarnation speaks volumes to us about how seriously God takes His mission of relationship, redemption, and reconciliation.

Meditating on the act of Christ's coming to us allows us to discern some tremendous truths and principles for our own lives. As we take up the invitation to live on mission with God, we can follow Christ's powerful example of intentionally reaching out beyond the familiar. As chapter 9 reminds us, Jesus was intentional about reaching out to others in love and about seeing beyond and exposing the cultural bias and ethnocentricity of the people around Him. Not only that, but Jesus seemed to specifically delight in going to the marginalized—the ones who lived on the edges or far outside the bounds of polite Jewish society. One need look no further than the story of the woman at the well (see John 4) to recognize that Jesus' mission wasn't limited by the boundaries of cultural bias or ethnocentrism. And the list of outsiders doesn't end with that Samaritan woman—think of the lepers Jesus healed, the woman caught in adultery He forgave, the tax collectors He befriended and even included in His inner circle. As Michael Frost notes, "Christians must be prepared to go where Christ would go: to the poor, to the marginalized, to the places of suffering. They must be prepared to die to self in order to follow Jesus' radical lifestyle of self-giving and sacrifice" (2006, 54).

The incarnation of Christ and His life on the earth remind us that we are to be willing to be *sent* as Christ was. We are to be willing to *go* to the "other" in humble service. We can't sit back and wait for people to come to us, and we can't discriminate against a particular group of people because they are different from us. The willingness of Christ to come to us stemmed from His deep well of love for people. Similarly, living missionally calls us to abide in Christ until we are flooded with that same motivating love.

The process of reaching out across cultures can be enhanced by a study of people.

> **What Difference Does It Make?**
>
> - Do you notice those in your community who are from people groups that differ from yours, or are they largely invisible to you? How do you feel about people from other groups?
>
> - How intentional are you about getting to know people who are different from you? Have you ever taken the time to try to bridge the cultural distance between you and another person? Why or why not?

Chapter 10 began with a simple look at how diverse our world really is. Despite the fact that it is easy to feel that most people are at least somewhat like you, the statistics show us otherwise. Even if you are part of the largest ethnic group, the Chinese—as some 20 percent of the world is—there is still 80 percent of the world that is not ethnically the same as you. If you are a Christian, you are not in a majority in the world, since Christians make up only a third of the population of the global village when it is divided by religious affiliation. So, although it is easy to feel that you are in the majority, the truth is, the world is a tremendously diverse place. There are so many different kinds of people with so many different ways of thinking and acting. And as Duane Elmer observes, "Sometimes we fail to see beyond our experience and fail to realize the vast array of differences" (2002, 20).

As we read in chapter 10, learning to see people in all their diversity—or learning to see beyond "us" to the "thems" of the world—is a crucial part of missional living. Jesus didn't go only to those who were familiar and safe; His life embodied risk taking and eyebrow raising. So, neither are we to be content to live and love within the familiar confines of our cultural comfort zones. We must be open to the Lord's leading us outside our home base. Chapter 10 gave us tools to begin to see the world and its complexity a little more clearly. In understanding not only geopolitical distinctions but the distinctives of people groups, we can see a richer and more-detailed picture of the peoples of the earth.

With a grasp of the concept of people groups, we can then see the importance of learning to think about cultural distance. A bull's-eye

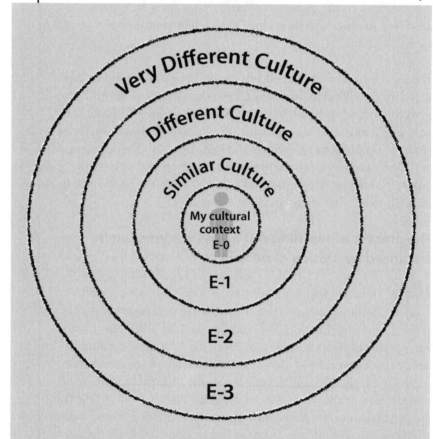

Diagram based on Ralph D. Winter's E-Scale described in "The Highest Priority: Cross-Cultural Evangelism," a paper sent to congress participants prior to Lausanne 1: The International Congress on World Evangelization in Lausanne, Switzerland, 1974, quoted in *Perspectives on the World Christian Movement: A Reader*, ed. Ralph D. Winter and Steven C. Hawthorne, 3rd ed. (Pasadena, CA: William Carey Library, 1999), 339–53.

can illustrate the concepts of cultural distance that exist between individuals or people groups.

While it is tempting to stay among the familiar faces of your E-0 home base, living missionally may call you to take up the work necessary to reach out to those who are one, two, or even three layers of cultural distance removed from your own people group. Ralph Winter describes a concept known as "people blindness," which prevents us from seeing the separate peoples within a country, something we are especially prone to doing in the United States. Developing eyes to see the various levels of cultural distance between peoples in your own community is a part of the missional life we are called to in Christ. Any city or town with an immigrant population or a college or university is a place where opportunities for reaching out across several layers of cultural distance exist.

Chapter 10 concluded by telling us that the example of Christ is to reach out in love to the "other." We are called to do no less if we want to live on mission with God. When we begin to understand the vastness of His creation, the tremendous variety among the people that He loves, we begin to learn to love them ourselves.

God's people must learn to connect incarnationally with others in significant cross-cultural relationships.

Significant cross-cultural relationships are not without challenge. As the various case studies presented in chapters 11 and 12 demonstrate, there are not always clear-cut paths in cross-cultural ministry. Often many layers of misunderstanding and premature judgments must be worked through. As Elliot Paulson's *Between a Rock and a Hard Place* demonstrates, there is an element of risk taking and an extending of trust that must take place in authentic cross-cultural relationship. We are called to connect incarnationally with others, something that is impossible to do in our own power. We are dependent on the Holy Spirit for guidance, and we must seek to follow the example of Christ in our lives. Only in dwelling deeply in that relationship will we be able to navigate the tricky waters of significant cross-cultural relationships.

In chapter 11, we looked at four aspects of incarnational living that author Michael Frost wrote about in *Exiles*. The first aspect is an active sharing of the life of the community or person you are reaching out to, including walking alongside someone's "fears, frustrations, and afflictions." The second aspect is use of the "language and thought forms of those with whom we seek to share Jesus. After

What Difference Does It Make?

- What does Paulson's experience demonstrate to you regarding the difference between studying about cross-cultural ministry and really living it out?

- Do you agree with Paulson's perspective? How does it differ from your own way of thinking? How does it compare with Jesus' life and ministry?

- Explain how well the interaction described by Paulson demonstrates the idea of incarnational living.

all, he used common speech and stories: salt, light, fruit, birds, and the like. He seldom used theological or religious jargon or technical terms." The third aspect Frost mentions is that idea of moving into the neighborhood—"a preparedness to go to the people, not expecting them to come to us." Finally, the fourth aspect of connecting with others incarnationally is "a confidence that the gospel can be communicated by ordinary means, through acts of servanthood, loving relationships, good deeds" (2006, 55). At the heart of it, Jesus reached out to people in very simple and practical ways—meeting needs, loving, and forgiving. We will continue to explore specific ways that you can live this out as we continue our discussion of missio Dei.

Of course, meeting needs, loving, and forgiving can be complex, and the complexity grows when elements of cultural distance are introduced. The case studies in chapter 12 intentionally draw attention to this fact. You may be tempted to conclude that there is no standard for our behavior in some cross-cultural situations, especially when the Bible seems to be silent on a particular issue. However, we are never left without the counsel of the Holy Spirit and the principles of God's Word to guide us. Despite the challenges and the sometimes outright mystery of living and serving cross-culturally, we are not left to bridge uncertain gaps on our own. In fact, quite the opposite. Missional life—joining God in His mission—means seeing where He is already at work and aligning ourselves with that work, coming alongside His method of fulfilling His purpose. As this unit reminds us, God is at work all around the globe, in many different cultural contexts, some of them perhaps quite surprising to us. He invites us to join Him. Though the journey may be different than we imagined and more difficult than we would like, living on mission with God is the best adventure you could spend a lifetime being a part of.

What Difference Does It Make?

- In what ways do you encounter similar tricky situations while living out your faith in your own context? Do you have peers who misunderstand your choices?

- Is your relationship with God deep enough to help you weather a difficult encounter with a nonbeliever? What strength do you draw on at such a time?

History Unit
unit three

UNIT INTRODUCTION

Have you ever wondered what God has been up to since the end of the New Testament story? Do you realize that throughout the past two thousand years God has been at work, inviting men and women around the globe to participate in His ongoing mission? He wasn't just working through the lives of the men and women we read about in the Bible, but throughout history He has faithfully continued His story of relationship, redemption, and reconciliation—a mission that will come to an ultimate fulfillment in the future.

In this unit, we will continue to trace the story begun in Genesis 1—the remarkable story of God's mission. Think of this as a travelogue about journeying with God, a travelogue that contains the story of those who have already taken the trip. We will see how God has invited people to participate with Him all along. As we explore the circumstances and people He has used to further His work, we will take a deeper look at how He works and how people are a part of His plans. As you spend time in this travelogue, take note of what it has to offer you: information about points of interest, experiences you don't want to miss, pitfalls you'll want to avoid, and other hints you can glean about how your journey with God can be the best travel possible.

In this unit we'll explore the following Big Ideas:

- God initiates and advances His purpose throughout human history.
- History reveals the challenges, successes, and shortcomings that people throughout history have experienced as they have participated with God in completing His purpose.
- God's redemptive purpose will come to an ultimate completion in human history.

14

How God Works Through History

My Father is always at his work to this very day, and I, too, am working.
—*Jesus (John 5:17)*

Mission is not ours; mission is God's. Certainly the mission of God is the prior reality out of which flows any mission that we get involved in.
—*Christopher J. H. Wright*

You will recall from the first unit of this course that the Bible tells the story of God's purpose of relationship, redemption, and reconciliation. You will also recall from chapter 3 that God specifically invites us to participate in His purpose; He blesses us in order that we might be a blessing to others. In other words, our God is a God of mission, and throughout history He has invited people to participate in His mission. And in the last unit, we learned that this invitation is not limited to one particular people or place. God can and does use all cultural expressions to bring glory to Himself. The unity found in the Body of Christ, despite its members' diversity, is beautifully expressed as a picture of the ultimate fulfillment of God's purpose described in Revelation 5:6–10 and 7:9–12. Ultimately, worship of God will come from every nation, tribe, people, and language.

In this unit, we will examine the story of God's mission and the way people have participated in it throughout history. In the coming chapters, we will be exploring God's story as it has extended beyond the pages of the Bible and marched down through the ages toward its ultimate fulfillment as expressed in the book of Revelation. We shall see that God continues to invite people to participate in His purpose and that despite our fallibility and frailty as human beings, God continues to use us to accomplish His will. We also

Revelation Passage

"Then I saw a Lamb, looking as if it had been slain, standing in the center of the throne, encircled by the four living creatures and the elders. He had seven horns and seven eyes, which are the seven spirits of God sent out into all the earth. He came and took the scroll from the right hand of him who sat on the throne. And when he had taken it, the four living creatures and the twenty-four elders fell down before the Lamb. Each one had a harp and they were holding golden bowls full of incense, which are the prayers of the saints. And they sang a new song: 'You are worthy to take the scroll and to open its seals, because you were slain, and with your blood you purchased men for God from every tribe and language and people and nation. You have made them to be a kingdom and priests to serve our God, and they will reign on the earth.'"

— Revelation 5:6–10

know that despite our weaknesses and failings, God's purpose will be fulfilled: "The plans of the Lord stand firm forever, the purposes of his heart through all generations" (Psalm 33:11). God initiates and advances His purpose throughout human history.

You don't have to read very far in the Bible before you see that God works in and through people to accomplish His purpose. But that is not to say that people are supposed to accomplish His purpose on their own or according to their own wisdom. God is always at work; He is the initiator, the equipper, the one who advances His plan. In the following excerpt from the book *Experiencing God*, Henry T. Blackaby and Claude V. King describe the work of God in calling and equipping men to achieve His purpose:

> Moses had an assignment as an administrator and a national religious leader. Moses, however, didn't think he was gifted for this assignment, so he argued with God.
>
> God knew exactly what He was doing when He called Moses. Moses' success was not dependent on Moses' skills, abilities, likes, preferences, or past successes. God first gave Moses an assignment, and then God equipped him with His Holy Spirit to administrate and lead. When Moses obeyed God, he used his "spiritual giftedness." The results revealed that God was at work through Moses doing things that Moses could not do on his own. (1994, 74)

Other biblical examples that show how God initiates and advances His purpose can be found in the lives of the Old Testament judges, of David, and of the workmen who built the Tabernacle. "Throughout the Old Testament, the Spirit of God was always present to equip an individual to carry out a divine assignment. God didn't give a person some *thing*. God *Himself* was the *Gift*. The Spirit manifested His presence by equipping each individual to function where God had assigned him. The results reflected God's activity" (Blackaby and King 1994, 75).

This Old Testament pattern is what the authors of *Experiencing God* describe as "the kindergarten for understanding the Holy Spirit's work in the New Testament" (Blackaby and King 1994, 74). Jesus explained to His disciples the role of the Spirit: "But the Counselor, the Holy Spirit, whom the Father will send in my name, will teach you all things and will remind you of everything I have said to you" (John 14:26). But the Spirit of God is not a promise given only to Jesus' disciples. Paul's letter to the Ephesian believers tells us that the Holy Spirit will come to all who believe in Christ: "And you also were included in Christ when you heard the word of truth, the gospel of your salvation. Having believed, you were marked in him with a seal, the promised Holy Spirit, who is a deposit guaranteeing our inheritance until the redemption of those who are God's possession—to the praise of his glory" (Ephesians 1:13–14). Paul writes in another letter: "Because you are sons, God sent the Spirit of his Son into our hearts, the Spirit who calls out, '*Abba*, Father' " (Galatians 4:6). Missional life is impossible without the Spirit of God. The Holy Spirit is God living and working in the life of the believer. In this manner, God initiates and advances His purpose into the present day through the lives of believers, who are invited to join His mission, "for it is God who works in [each believer] to will and to act according to his good purpose" (Philippians 2:13). God initiates all mission to fulfill His purpose; we are invited to be a part of His work. We are not to do work for God and then ask for His blessing on our endeavors. But the temptation to run ahead of Him is certainly there.

You will recall that in Genesis 12 God invited Abraham into a missional relationship with Him—a relationship that had long-range and wide-range implications. God initiated the conversation with Abraham and enabled him to obey. Then, through Abraham's direct heir Jesus, God extends blessing to all nations of the earth. But as Abraham's story unfolds in the pages of the Bible, we see a tension between faith and doubt—a tension that is one of the hallmarks of human frailty. On the one hand, Abraham exhibits an incredible richness of faith and obedience. Indeed, Abraham is listed in the Hebrews 11 "roll call of faith" as an example of great faith. On the other hand, we see the reality that Abraham fell prey to the temptation to step out in his own "wisdom" from time to time. Though God had promised Abraham a son (Genesis 15:4), Abraham and his wife, Sarah, got impatient with God's timing. In seeking to "lend God a hand" in fulfilling His promise, they came up with a scheme to produce an heir through Abraham's servant Hagar (Genesis 16:1–6).

> *As Abraham's story unfolds in the pages of the Bible, we see a tension between faith and doubt—a tension that is one of the hallmarks of human frailty.*

The result was not the son of promise from God, but it was Ishmael, of whom God said, "He will be a wild donkey of a man; his hand will be against everyone and everyone's hand against him, and he will live in hostility toward all his brothers" (Genesis 16:12). Despite the impatience of Abraham and the heartache caused to both he and Sarah, not to mention Hagar and Ishmael, God promised Abraham that Sarah would be the mother of a son with whom God would make a covenant of blessing (Genesis 17:19–21).

The presence of this tension between faith and doubt—between obedience and disobedience to God's callings, leadings, and plans—is found throughout the pages of the Bible. It is also found throughout the pages of church and mission history. In the coming chapters, we will explore the complexities of understanding the history of God's mission over the past two millennia while keeping an eye on both sides of this coin. In doing so, it is critical to recognize and rejoice in the sovereignty of God to bring about His purpose.

An exciting mission unfolds throughout the pages of history. We are invited to join what God is doing around the world.

What God promises, He will do. What He initiates, He will complete. Isaiah 14:27 reminds us of this: "For the Lord Almighty has purposed, and who can thwart him? His hand is stretched out, and who can turn it back?" Ultimately, the plans of the Lord will stand, as we see in Isaiah 43:13: "Yes, and from ancient days I am he. No one can deliver out of my hand. When I act, who can reverse it?" Not only can we rejoice that God is at work and that He will accomplish His purpose, we can rejoice in His leading and directing of us as we join in His mission. As we are reminded in the following passage from Proverbs, if we let Him lead and equip us, He will accomplish His purpose through us: "Trust in the Lord with all your heart and lean not on your own understanding; in all your ways acknowledge him, and he will make your paths straight" (3:5–6). Verse 6 in the King James Version says, "In all thy ways acknowledge Him, and He shall *direct thy paths*" (emphasis added).

Does it seem illogical that God would use fallible and finite human beings to further His purpose or that He would allow people's failures and mishaps to intermingle with His plans? Perhaps it does to us, with our finite understanding. But we must recall God's words in Isaiah 55:8–9: " 'For my thoughts are not your thoughts, neither are your ways my ways,' declares the Lord. 'As the heavens are higher than the earth, so are my ways higher than your ways and my thoughts than your thoughts.' " Just as in the Bible we find reassurance of God's grace in the face of failure and we watch His purpose going forward despite humankind's fumbling, we will see the same thing as we study the continuing story of God's mission throughout the past two thousand years. There are certain chapters of the history of mission that may seem particularly unsavory or even abhorrent to us—many would name the Crusades as one example—but God's purpose is moving forward during those pages nonetheless. In fact, the story of God as He continues to advance His kingdom throughout the earth is one of great victory and glory to Him. An exciting mission unfolds throughout the pages of history. We are invited to join what God is doing around the world. Robert A. Blincoe describes it this way: "The world has turned around many times since Yahweh made His covenant with Abram, the moon-worshiper from Chaldea (Joshua 24:2–3) forty centuries ago. From generation to generation, from Jerusalem to the ends of the earth, God is wooing rebellious humanity, winning nations from sin and Satan and death, and inviting the peoples to His coming banquet. That is the mission He gave to Abraham's children" (2003, 110). This is the work that God is doing. God's mission marches on beyond the pages of the Bible. Where the New Testament narrative ends in time, the pages of history pick up. They tell a rich story of God at work as He leads and directs throughout the different eras of mission. In the chapters that lie ahead, we will explore the ways in which God's work has unfolded through the years.

15

Era One: The Beginnings of the Church

At the time of Jesus' birth, Israel had become integrated into the Roman political system.... Except for brief periods of limited national sovereignty, Israel had long been a small nation caught up in the swirl of events of a wider international history.... The first Christians emerged from this crucible.... Christianity entered a world that was inhabited by a host of other religions and gods.... It was a world of great cultural diversity as well. Languages, customs, and practices varied from region to region, and even from street to street in the cities.
—*Dale T. Irvin and Scott W. Sunquist*

In the previous unit, we talked about the incarnation of Christ—an event that changed history forever. In his book *God Came Near*, Max Lucado calls the birth of Jesus "a most remarkable moment" that was like no other. He also writes, "For through that segment of time a spectacular thing occurred. God became a man" (1987, 25). But another moment like no other—the resurrection of Christ three days after His cruel crucifixion and death at the hands of Rome—marked a turning point in world history. It was this moment that has continued to echo down through the many centuries that have followed. It was this moment, and the impact that Jesus' resurrection had on those who were witnesses to it, that spurs on the continuing mission of Christians from the first century to the present day. And then at Pentecost, a geographically diverse crowd of listeners from lands far north, south, east, and west of Jerusalem heard the wonders of God being proclaimed in their own tongues (Acts 2:6–11). This event both foreshadowed and laid the groundwork for the spread of the gospel of Jesus Christ to "the uttermost" parts of the earth.

At the time of Pentecost, Jerusalem was part of the powerful Roman Empire, nestled in the Mediterranean basin. Yet, as indicated by the presence of the many geographically far-flung pilgrims to Jerusalem at Pentecost, this location was a prime crossroad of empires and civilizations in the first century. "The eastern Mediterranean was part of a much wider network of cities and civilizations that stretched ... across a wide expanse of the ancient world," note historians Dale Irvin and Scott Sunquist (2001, 3). Included in this network were the Roman and Persian empires and, farther east, the countries of India and China. Among these four civilizations was an even further myriad of ethnic cultures and traditions. (See the "First Era Snapshot" sidebar for more details.) Beyond these great civilizations of the first century lay nomadic tribes to the north and the many tribes and people of the African continent to the south. Jerusalem—situated within the rule of the Roman Empire, one of the most vast and advanced civilizations to exist until that moment in history—was indeed at an intersection of many cultures.

It was into this geographical and historical backdrop that the Son of God came—lived, died, and rose again—creating a new way for God's mission of relationship, redemption, and reconciliation to go forward in history. You will recall from the last chapter that people throughout history have participated in completing God's purpose. The message of salvation through faith in Jesus Christ was birthed in the perfect location and time for it to be shared with people from many different cultural traditions by those who had joined God's invitation to mission in this time period following Christ's ascension.

There are a number of factors that reveal the perfect groundwork God laid for successful Christian mission in the first century. As we said, a wide range of cultural diversity that centered in the empires of this period created an opportunity for the message of Christ to reach many different people groups. In addition, several first-century realities allowed the gospel message to spread quickly and widely during this time. Relative ease of both travel and communication across cultures existed in the first century in ways that later deteriorated and didn't exist again until the nineteenth century. Historian Stephen Neill notes, "The Roman Empire had imposed on a large area of the world such a massive unity as it had never known before.... Where the Romans went, there they built roads, paved, well-engineered, running undeviatingly forward over hill and dale. Later, when the Roman order had collapsed and the roads were neglected, a great part of mankind lived in isolated villages ... But in the Roman days it was not so; travel was safer and more rapid than at any later time till the nineteenth century" (1986, 24). Extensive trading networks existed beyond the borders of the Roman Empire, thus facilitating the travel of merchants across the expanse of the Asian continent, into Africa, into major cities of the time. (See the "First Era Snapshot" sidebar.) Additionally, a common language, *koine* Greek, was widely used in trade across the Roman Empire and beyond (Irvin and Sunquist 2001, 8). The Roman Empire had adopted Greek as the language of trade and of primary conversation among educated individuals (Neill 1986, 24). Although many native languages and dialects (such as the Hebrew and Aramaic of Jesus and His disciples) continued to exist, Greek-speaking men and women were found across the known trade and travel routes of the first century.

But perhaps more indicative of the foundations God had prepared for the early spread of the gospel is the widespread presence of Jews in large numbers throughout the Roman Empire, a result of *diaspora*, or "scattering," that dates from Old Testament periods of captivity and exile. As Acts 2 indicates, Jews were living in many nations on all sides of Jerusalem, and they continued to maintain their religious identity. "Throughout the diaspora, Jews built synagogues in cities where they lived that served as both prayer houses and community centers," note Irvin and Sunquist (2001, 20). These synagogues and the presence of "God-fearers" and of proselytes (or pagan converts) to Judaism would play a key role in the spread of Christianity among the Gentiles in the first century. Synagogues in cities outside Jerusalem initially provided a natural "starting place" for preaching by itinerant evangelists such as Paul and Barnabas. Both the God-fearers and the Greek-speaking proselytes to Judaism represent a sort of bridge in bringing the gospel message to the Gentiles, as we will examine shortly. So, the foundations of Christian mission were laid by God in a place and time ripe for the cross-cultural spread of the gospel.

In this chapter, we will look specifically at the shape of that mission going forward in the first several decades after Christ's resurrection. It is important to remember that, as has been the case throughout God's story, God invited people—fallible, finite people—to be the bearers of His purpose, and history reveals the challenges, successes, and shortcomings that people have experienced in their attempts to participate in God's purpose. We will see this more fully as we unpack the shape of Christian mission throughout the ages.

The earliest events of Christian mission are familiar to us through our reading of the Gospels and the book of Acts. Following the resurrection of Jesus, He appeared to many during the forty days before His ascension. At His ascension, He gave this word to His assembled disciples: "But you will receive power when the Holy Spirit comes on you; and you will be my witnesses in Jerusalem, and in all Judea and Samaria, and to the ends of the earth" (Acts 1:8).

Proselytes and God-Fearers

The presence of Gentile converts to Judaism played a significant role in the first-century spread of the gospel to the Gentiles. There were generally two types of Gentile converts to Judaism: (1) a full convert, or proselyte, who had undergone circumcision and was considered fully a member of the Jewish people, and (2) a "God-fearer," who was devout in synagogue attendance and devotional practice, but had not undergone circumcision. Cornelius, Peter's first Gentile convert (see Acts 10), is described as a God-fearer. Significantly, these proselytes and God-fearers—called Hellenists, or Greek-speaking Jews—represent a cultural difference from Hebrews (Aramaic-speaking Jews) who, as Stan Nussbaum says, "eventually proved decisive … leading in about fifty years to the emergence of 'Christianity' as a religion separate from Judaism" (2005, 17).

As described in Acts 2, that power, which came at Pentecost, led to the proclamation of the gospel to a multiethnic audience and resulted in the increase in the disciples' numbers by about three thousand people who were baptized. From this time on, key events such as the stoning of Stephen and subsequent scattering of believers, the conversion of Saul, and Peter's encounter with Cornelius (Acts 10) formed the basis of God's unfolding mission of reconciliation to the world. Of course, the most revolutionary hallmark of this early period is God's leading of Peter and others to proclaim salvation through Christ to the Gentiles. The story of first-century mission is largely the story of the emergence of the redemptive message of Christianity, how it became a separate religion from Judaism and spread across a number of cultures within a relatively short period of time.

> *The word began spreading to both Jews and Gentiles, through not only Peter and the first apostles but also an emerging network of scattered believers. Mission was not something for a select few. Every believer was a witness.*

Although the familiar events of the vision God gave to Peter and Peter's preaching to Cornelius, the God-fearer, in Acts 10 are generally thought to make up the primary New Testament story of the coming of the gospel to the Gentiles, there are threads of another story—a larger story—found in the pages of Acts. Following the stoning of Stephen, a great persecution broke out against the church at Jerusalem. According to Acts 8:1, believers were scattered "throughout Judea and Samaria," and, as noted in Acts 8:4, "those who had been scattered preached the word wherever they went." This story picks up again in Acts 11:19–21, which says, "Now those who had been scattered by the persecution in connection with Stephen traveled as far as Phoenicia, Cyprus and Antioch, telling the message only to Jews. Some of them, however, men from Cyprus and Cyrene, went to Antioch and began to speak to Greeks also, telling them the good news about the Lord Jesus. The Lord's hand was with them, and a great number of people believed and turned to the Lord." So, the word began spreading to both Jews and Gentiles, through not only Peter and the first apostles but also an emerging network of scattered believers. Mission was not something for a select few. Every believer was a witness. Stan Nussbaum notes, "Mission is the core of [the first-century church], not an incidental matter" (2005, 42). Neill notes his agreement in the following: "The Church of the first Christian generation was a genuinely missionary Church. There were, of course, the whole-time workers, such as Saul and Barnabas, specially set apart with prayer for the prosecution of missionary endeavour (Acts 13:1–4).… Apart, however, from these special workers, the Church could count on the anonymous and unchronicled witness of all the faithful" (1986, 21–22).

Many of these witnesses followed the pattern of mission that Paul used when entering a new city: "It was Paul's custom to settle for a time in one of the great cities of the empire, and through his younger helpers to radiate out from that centre to the smaller cities of the region…. As soon as a church had taken root and showed signs of being able to stand on its own feet under its local leaders, Paul felt free to move onward towards a further fulfilment of his plan, that all the Gentiles might hear the word of the Lord and so the end might come" (Neill 1986, 27). In Romans 15:20, Paul sums up his motivation and the method behind his mission: "It has always been my ambition to preach the gospel where Christ was not known, so that I would not be building on someone else's foundation." And this is likely the case for many of those anonymous first-century men and women who, like Paul and other named missionaries of the Bible, strove to share the good news of Christ with as many as would hear it.

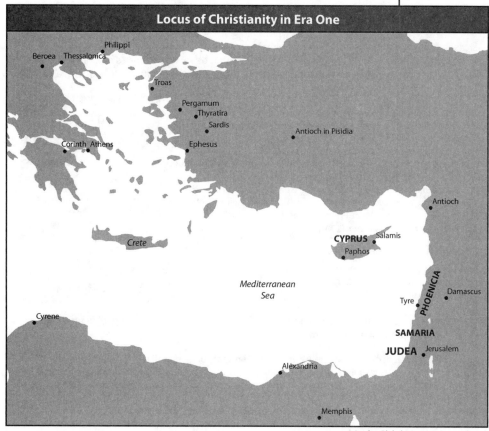

Map by Global Mapping International.

First Era Snapshot

During the first century AD …

The location of world mission was centered in Jerusalem, which was situated in a network of major empires stretching from the Mediterranean basin eastward to the Pacific Ocean. Historians Dale T. Irvin and Scott W. Sunquist describe the geographical and cultural powers of the time (2001, formatting added):

- On the western end was the Mediterranean basin, a civilization that had incorporated a multitude of ancient cultural traditions including Egyptian, Ethiopian, Greek, Jewish, Mesopotamian, Persian, and Latin. Usually referred to by scholars today as Greco-Roman civilization, by the time of Jesus it had become unified by the diffusion of a common Greek language and culture, under the imperial rule of the city of Rome. (3)

- East of the Mediterranean basin … centered politically in the region today known as Iran, the Persian empire likewise incorporated a multitude of cultures and traditions, including Greek, Jewish, Mesopotamian, Iranian, and Indian. (3)

- A third cultural field extended east and south of Persia, encompassing the Indian subcontinent and sections of southeast Asia beyond it. This was the civilization of India. (3)

- At the eastern end of this urban belt of civilization, across the Himalaya Mountains and Tibetan plateau, was China, the fourth great cultural complex in this network. (4)

- To the north of this string of urban civilizations in the first century lived an extensive number of nomadic tribal peoples, scattered from Siberia across central Asia into modern Russia and northwestern Europe. A shared linguistic and religious heritage linked various tribes together into several major families of Celtic, Germanic, Slavic, Turkish, and Mongol cultural identity. (8)

- South of the Mediterranean on the continent of Africa were numerous tribes and peoples.… The ancient city-kingdom of Meroë (in Northern Sudan) [was] the dominant political entity in the first century. (8)

Travel and cross-cultural interaction across these empires were facilitated by major trade routes fueled by interconnected economic interests. Historian Stephen Neill says that travel was safer and more rapid during the time of the Roman Empire than in any other period until the nineteenth century (1986, 24). Irvin and Sunquist describe the trade routes as follows:

> Among the most significant trade routes of the ancient world was the Silk Road, which stretched westward from the Great Wall of China into India, and to the Mediterranean coast.… On the other end of the Silk Road in Syria and Arabia, caravans regularly crossed the deserts to carry goods between cities and to the seacoasts. Ships navigated the Mediterranean Sea, Red Sea, Arabian Sea, Indian Ocean, and parts of the Pacific to bring goods from India or China to markets in the cities of Alexandria, Carthage, or Rome. An extensive system of Roman-built roads helped link the various urban centers of the Mediterranean world into an efficient economic network by the first century. (2001, 5)

Further facilitating the spread of the gospel was a common language in much of this part of the world. "*Koine* Greek [was] a common form of the language that was spoken and understood from the Pyrenees to the Himalaya Mountains" (Irvin and Sunquist 2001, 8).

Citizens of these empires—particularly the Roman and Persian empires—lived in a variety of different ways, as described by Irvin and Sunquist in the following:

> Scattered across these ancient civilizations were numerous cities that concentrated high numbers of people, material wealth, and political power in relatively small geographical areas of space. Cities were home to the ruling elite of the ancient world … Outside the cities' walls the vast majority of people in the ancient world lived in small villages or in the countryside. Their lives were dominated by agriculture and herding, supported by various forms of light production (pottery, weaving, carpentry, and some metal working). (2001, 4)

You will recall that God had provided a widespread network of Jews in many parts of the Roman Empire and beyond through the scattering of Jews over previous centuries. The presence of these Jewish communities and synagogues in so many cities facilitated a natural starting point for preaching the risen Christ in all directions from Jerusalem. It was to exactly these locations that both the persecuted believers scattering from Jerusalem and the specially set-apart missionaries sought to take the good news. And as is so often described in the missionary journeys chronicled in Acts, witnesses would go first to the synagogue and preach. Irvin and Sunquist note, however, that even though often the synagogue "was the place where contact with other Jews was first made[,] Christian evangelists met others out on the streets, in the marketplace, in workshops, and around public buildings. The main form of communication in ancient cities was word of mouth" (2001, 32). This gives us a picture of the pervasive nature of the gospel message in the lives of the average believers. They spoke of their experiences wherever they went, living an organic, unstructured, and powerful missional life of witness. Although the synagogue may have been the typical starting place for evangelism in the early days of Christianity, ultimately—and especially with the spread of the gospel to more and more Gentiles—the locus of the Christian movement shifted from synagogues to private homes. The examples of Paul, Barnabas, Silas, Timothy, John Mark, and other missionaries named in the New Testament are certainly typical of the first century. But alongside these teachers and preachers, earliest Christian mission is something that all believers engaged in as they went about the ordinary business of life, inviting others into home fellowships in which worship, ministry to the poor, and the celebration of the Eucharist formed the basis of Christian community.

The Bible tells us that Antioch was the place where believers were first called "Christians." According to Irvin and Sunquist, the use of this name indicated that the believers "were clearly setting themselves apart from the synagogue in their new community" (2001, 28). This new identification is one of the ways in which we see Christianity emerging with a separate identity from traditional Judaism. By the middle of the first century—some fifteen to twenty years after the resurrection of Christ—mission to the Gentiles had strong roots in Antioch and the surrounding regions of Syria and Cilicia (Acts 15:23). The God-fearing Greeks spoken of earlier were the group in which "the preaching of the Gospel found its most ready and its most immediate response" (Neill 1986, 25). Indeed, these God-fearers were an integral part of God's means of propelling Christian mission forward in the first century. The success of mission among the Gentiles led to what Acts 15 describes as the council in Jerusalem—the first of many councils held throughout the first centuries of Christian history to address questions of doctrine and practice. This first council at Jerusalem, believed to have been held around the year 48, was to address the question of whether "the Gentiles must be circumcised and required to obey the law of Moses" (Acts 15:5). The resulting inclusion of Gentiles without the requirement of circumcision signaled a significant way in which Christianity was becoming a separate practice from that of its Jewish roots.

Earliest Christian mission is something that all believers engaged in as they went about the ordinary business of life, inviting others into home fellowships in which worship, ministry to the poor, and the celebration of the Eucharist formed the basis of Christian community.

Another turn of events in the first century marked definitive change for the early Christian movement. A revolt against the Roman government on the part of Judean Jews began in the year 66 and resulted in the destruction of Jerusalem and, more specifically, the temple there in the year 70 (Irvin and Sunquist 2001, 50). This unmooring from the early Christian movement's physical roots goes hand in hand with the fact that the destruction of Jerusalem also marked the end of the Christian's view of Jerusalem as the location of the mother church of the Christian world. Neill notes, "Since AD 70 the Christian Church has never had one local centre; it has learned to look only to the living presence of the Lord within itself" (1986, 21).

Rather than the events of that year causing the infant Christian movement to lose momentum, the destruction of Jerusalem seems to have served only to strengthen the growing mission of the early Church. Irvin and Sunquist elaborate on the way in which early Christian communities flourished despite geographical separation and the destruction of Jerusalem:

> The collective apostolic memory was the ground out of which a common church emerged.... The connectedness the apostles had with one another through their common experience with Jesus in Galilee and Jerusalem was understood to continue in the communities they had founded in various parts of the world, even after the church in Jerusalem effectively ceased to exist.

> In an important sense this form of apostolic connection embodied what they believed to be Jesus' own trans-regional presence through the Spirit....

… The dispersion of the apostles to regions beyond Jerusalem did not lead to the breakup of the movement. Their unity, they believed, was found in the person of Jesus, who beckoned them from the edges of history. (2001, 40–41)

God's mission continued to move forward with the energy of the Holy Spirit propelling individuals to bear witness to God's grace and love to the far reaches of the Roman Empire and beyond.

As we discussed in the last unit, the message of God and His story is one that transcends culture. It is through this very transcendence that God worked so powerfully in the first century. You will recall from chapter 7 that God is glorified through unity within diversity, and His plan of receiving glory in this manner comes to an ultimate fulfillment with worshippers "from every nation, tribe, people and language" crying praises before the Lamb of God on His heavenly throne (Revelation 7:9–12). This truth pulses through the early spread of the gospel. In writings throughout the New Testament, "Paul provided a powerful theological argument for a trans-cultural experience that was emerging in the [early Christian] movement. Early Christian communities embraced several cultural identities within their ranks. Gentiles and Jews alike brought much of their past with them when they joined the Christian movement. Some elements … they were strictly instructed to give up. Others they began to modify…. Christian life and Christian worship thus began to look different in different locations. At the same time, a lively sense of trans-regional connection emerged among the churches" (Irvin and Sunquist 2001, 39–40). Here in the New Testament church, we see God at work to bring about the unity within diversity that He so desires. According to Andrew F. Walls, a professor and theologian, this timely sharing "of faith in Jesus across cultural lines" (1996, 16) was the foundation for Christian mission throughout the centuries. In other words, Walls says, "cross-cultural communication saved Christian faith for the world" (18).

??

- What do the events of the early Church teach you about how to live on mission with God? Early believers shared their faith wherever they found themselves. Do you see among believers today the same sort of enthusiasm for missional life that the members of the early Church demonstrated?

- What characteristics of the earliest believers in Christ would you most like to see in your own life? Why?

16

Era Two: AD 100 to 600

It should not bother us that, during the epoch under discussion, the Christian faith was perceived and experienced in new and different ways. The Christian faith is intrinsically incarnational; therefore, unless the church chooses to remain a foreign entity, it will always enter into the context in which it happens to find itself.   —*David J. Bosch*

In the last chapter, we looked at the first era of Christian mission—the spread of Christianity in the first century. God prepared a rich environment for the message of the risen Christ to spread rapidly across geographical distance in a short time. We saw that a powerful feature of Christian mission is the ability of the gospel to speak into a variety of cultures. In completing His mission, God works through cultures without being fenced in by them. Not only is this a feature of Christian mission in the first century, but it continues to be a hallmark of His mission as the gospel spreads in the next centuries. In this chapter, we will examine the rapid changes and growth in mission during the second era of Christian mission, the years 100 to 600.

Over the course of the next several hundred years, Christianity passed from a first-generation "breaking news story" about the resurrection of Christ to a creed and doctrine.

Over the course of the next several hundred years, Christianity passed from a first-generation "breaking news story" about the resurrection of Christ to a creed and doctrine (Nussbaum 2005, 49). It emerged from its first-century identity as a loose network of widely spread small churches to become an organized institution with formal doctrine and leadership hierarchy. The leadership of the church passed from the first-generation apostles to bishops and church leaders. Some historians—

when referring to the significant role these church leaders, or church fathers, played in shaping and guiding the formation of orthodox doctrine—have called this era the Patristic Period. By the year 600, Christianity had been transformed from its simple, first-century roots into a large-scale institution that influenced world events.

Christian mission moved forward through a host of changing realities in the world between the years 100 and 600. The Roman Empire during this time was initially the dominant political force, as it was in Jesus' day. By AD 300, the Roman Empire extended all the way from the Atlantic Ocean into parts of northern Africa and eastward to the Mediterranean basin. Outside the Roman Empire to the east, Christianity was becoming established in places such as Edessa, Armenia, and, according to tradition, India. To the south, the gospel had reached Ethiopia by the early fourth century. "By the third century, prayers were being offered in Syriac, Greek, Latin, Egyptian, and other tongues" (Irvin and Sunquist 2001, 103).

During this second era, the Roman Empire was still the center of most Christian activity. In terms of Christian mission, one can

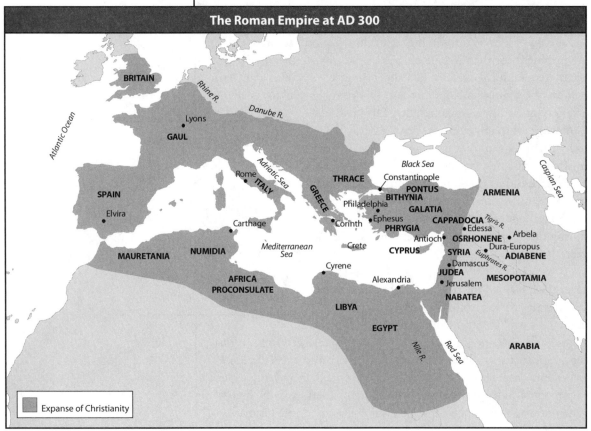

The Roman Empire at AD 300

Map by Global Mapping International.

think of dividing the more than five hundred years into two nearly equal halves. The first half, from 100 to 313, was a time in which believers still lived in a state of uncertainty and without formal recognition. Christianity, standing in contrast to the officially sanctioned practice of emperor worship, was an outlawed religion in the Roman Empire. Thus, Christians were subject to a number of forms of persecution ranging from taxation to the burning of Christian books and meeting places, to the most dramatic form of persecution—martyrdom. Christians were put to death in sporadic bursts of severe persecution occurring during the reigns of at least three emperors during the third century. "Persecution diminished the ranks of the Christians in the short run but aided Christian growth in the long run" (Irvin and Sunquist 2001, 111). Indeed, the faithfulness of these martyrs served as one of the means of mission in this time period. Neill recounts, "There are a number of well-authenticated cases of conversion of pagans in the very moment of witnessing the condemnation and death of Christians; there must have been far more who received impressions that in the course of time would be turned into a living faith" (1986, 39).

"Defend the faith or die for it" is the way Nussbaum describes another major force of mission at this time. "The second- and third-century church fathers were known collectively as the 'apologists,' that is, those involved in apologetics (defense of the faith), not those 'apologizing' for it. Many who spoke up for the faith were martyred for it.… By sealing their arguments with their own blood, these Christians showed what mission looks like under fire" (2005, 51). These apologists were church fathers whose writings and defense of the faith formed the basis for formalized doctrines of belief later on. But in the early years, apologetics and defending the faith were a significant means of mission—particularly in trying to win to Christ those among the upper classes who influenced society.

We noted in the last chapter that Christianity began to become distinct and separate from Judaism at the close of the first century. In the second through fourth centuries, we begin to see a shift in the orientation of Christian thought from a Jewish worldview to a Greek, or Hellenistic, worldview. And it is through this shift in thinking that God moved Christianity into a wider field of influence in the world. These apologists and church fathers strove to present Christian truth in a way that would make sense to a Hellenistic mind. As we have seen, God works through diverse cultures to achieve His mission. Hellenism was the dominant cultural form of thinking and learning in the Roman Empire for hundreds of years. Acts 17:16–32 reveals that even in Paul's day, believers were putting

Hellenism

Though you may think of the terms *Hellenism* and *Hellenistic* as having to do exclusively with the culture of ancient Greece, they also describe the influence of Greek thinking, which greatly affected the Roman Empire. Therefore, historians often refer to this Greco-Roman world as having a Hellenistic cultural outlook.

Christian truths into the Hellenistic context, described as "talking about and listening to the latest ideas" (Acts 17:21). Thus, during the second and third centuries, believers speaking of Christian truths in terms of the cultural forms of Hellenism created the opportunity for more widespread understanding of the gospel. Along with an emphasis on ideas, one of the characteristics of Hellenistic thinking was philosophical orderliness. As Bosch observes, the primary impact of this mind-set was the "ever-growing tendency to define the faith and systematize doctrine" (1991, 194). It was from this period that we see the beginnings of theology and creeds, and we see the defining of what is orthodox in Christian belief.

A major turning point for Christian mission came in 313 in the form of the Edict of Milan, an imperial directive granting freedom for Christian worship throughout the Roman Empire. "In the early second century, Christianity was a banned religious movement in the Roman Empire," notes Nussbaum. "Early in the fourth century, the ban on Christianity was lifted, and by the late fourth century all citizens in the Roman Empire were required by the emperor to be Christians" (2005, 49). This freedom of religion accompanied growing support for Christianity from Emperor Constantine, who by 324 had "declared his unreserved allegiance to Christ and Christianity" (Irvin and Sunquist 2001, 162). Neill describes the dramatic change resulting from this endorsement: "The favourable attitude of the emperor produced a complete change in the situation of the Christian Church. From obscurity it emerged into brilliance, from obloquy to the height of popularity.... It seems likely

---

Second Era Snapshot

During the years AD 100–600 …

- The location of Christian mission was still centered in the Mediterranean basin at the beginning of the second century. Stephen Neill notes, "In the second century there were three outstanding centres of Christian life in the Mediterranean—Antioch, Rome, and Alexandria" (1986, 22).

- By the year 600 the central locations of Christianity were Rome in the west and Constantinople in the east. Though the Eastern and Western churches didn't officially separate until 1054, even by AD 600 Rome was the center of Latin-speaking churches we know today as Roman Catholic. Constantinople was the center of Greek-speaking churches we know today as Eastern Orthodox (Irvin and Sunquist 2001; Neill 1986).

- Travel continued to be facilitated to some degree by the great Roman road system and the Silk Road to the east. Yet during the third and fourth centuries, the invasions by the barbarians ultimately diminished freedom of travel, particularly to the west (Neill 1986).

- Similarly, the unity of language found in the Roman Empire deteriorated along with the empire itself, giving way to a patchwork of languages and dialects among the different cultures found in the region in the latter half of this era (Irvin and Sunquist 2001; Neill 1986).

that the number of Christians in the empire at least quadrupled itself in the century that followed Constantine" (1986, 41). In the space of just a few years, Christianity went from being an outlawed and persecuted religion to the official creed of the Roman emperor and the members of the widespread Roman Empire.

The second half of this era, from the early 300s to the year 600, saw the emergence of an institutionalized church, fully protected and supported by the government and, in some cases, being used by the government to further the government's own aims of unity within the Roman Empire. "As churches became more visible and accepted in the civil arena, they absorbed more influences from the world around them.... Now Christian identity seemed to require less of a break with previous lifestyles and even religious practices than it had once demanded.... Imperial embrace brought with it new forms of imperial domination.... Bishops who found themselves recipients of imperial funds were also burdened with new political responsibilities" (Irvin and Sunquist 2001, 163–64). Alongside the challenges of the emperor's endorsement of Christianity, however, came tremendous opportunity for the growth and spread of Christian faith. Among the lasting effects of this period are many familiar elements of current faith and practice. By the year 500, the church had identified which books were to be included in the Scriptures and had given "the New Testament equal canonical status with the Old. Through the work of the great Councils it had settled many questions of doctrine, and had laid down the limits within which Christian thought has moved ever since.... In the great Councils it had developed a marvellous instrument for the expression and the maintenance of Christian unity. In spite of troublesome disputes ... Christians in every part of the world felt themselves to be one with all other Christians" (Neill 1986, 52).

Indeed, the creation of an organized church with formalized doctrine and worship practices served as the foundation for church-sponsored mission. In the period from 300 to 600, we see the development of mission practice as a function of the church. According to the thinking of this time, says Ion Bria, mission meant "calling people to become members of the Christian community in a visible concrete form" (1980). Nussbaum elaborates on this: "As more people join the church, its diameter increases and it can pipe more of God's life and love into the world. This is 'service' to God, for it releases more of the love that is pent up in him, eager to deluge the world. The more his life and love flow out, the more things will be brought into harmony as they were meant to be and the more glory and praise will flow back to him—the ultimate aim of mission" (2005, 51). The liturgy, or rites of worship, of the church itself were also thought of as a principal means of mission. According to Bria, "Mission is thus centripetal rather than centrifugal … It 'proclaims' the gospel through doxology and liturgy. The witnessing community is the community in worship; in fact, the worshiping community is in and of itself an act of witness" (1980).

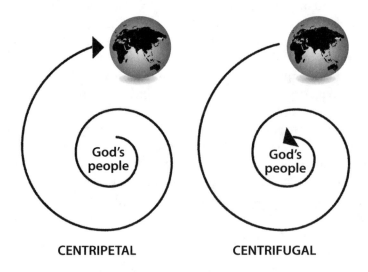

CENTRIPETAL   CENTRIFUGAL

Even with such an emphasis on attracting the pagan world through the worship and life of the church, there were also mission patterns during these years that resembled the itinerant preachers of the first century. According to Irvin and Sunquist, "Monasticism carried on the spiritual heritage of self-sacrifice and extreme conviction that the martyrs had often exemplified. It was also the major vehicle for the missionary expansion of Christianity beyond the borders of its existing churches" (2001, 158). Today, we think of monks as being shut away in a cloistered environment, but early, formalized monasticism was a way of establishing a Christian community in a new location. Monks received visitors, brought new converts into their communities of worship, led mass, and taught. But the model of successful mission was to bring converts into the church, so even monasticism was very church-centered: "The missionaries were ambassadors of the bishops, whose task was to incorporate converts into the church" (Bosch 1991, 202).

Up to this point, we have considered mission in the years between 100 and 600 exclusively within the confines of the Roman Empire and its growing church, which was centered in Rome. By the late fifth century, the Roman Empire ceased to exist as the dominant political entity it once was. The western part of the empire basically collapsed in 476, though Greco-Roman influence and leadership

Monasticism

Though ultimately a major force in the spread of the gospel, Christian monasticism has its roots in a group of men who, beginning in the third century, lived isolated, ascetic lives in the deserts of Egypt. Often called the Desert Fathers, they secluded themselves from the outside world and spent much of their time in prayer and in meditation on God. "Yet precisely because they had renounced the material ways of the world in order to pursue a deeper spiritual life, they proved to be attractive to the large numbers of people who traveled out into the wilderness areas who went to seek out their blessings," note authors Dale T. Irvin and Scott W. Sunquist (2001, 210). In the fourth century, Athanasius, the bishop of Alexandria, wrote *The Life of St. Antony*, which chronicled the life of one of these ascetics and drew even more pilgrims to seek wisdom from the Desert Fathers (Cornish 2005, 46). Eventually these isolated monks began a more communal life—perhaps in part to accommodate the growing number of men (and, in some cases, women) attracted to this devout lifestyle. By the early fourth century, the Egyptian ascetic Pachomius drew up guidelines for shared monastic life in communities. "Pachomius's rule caught on, and within several decades of his death the number of ascetics who were living by it in community had swelled to the tens of thousands" (Irvin and Sunquist 2001, 212). It was from these roots that monasticism grew into a major force of spreading the gospel in the coming centuries.

continued in the eastern part of the empire (often called the Byzantine Empire) centered at Constantinople.

Christian mission moved forward from Constantinople and also from churches located outside the borders of the former Roman Empire. "These churches were often far more actively involved in mission than the increasingly monolithic 'main' church" (Bosch 1991, 203). Churches farther east, such as in Persia, didn't experience the governmental blessing and protection that occurred in the Roman Empire beginning with Constantine, and this absence of blessing and protection may have caused their methods of mission to be more similar to those of first-century believers. "By AD 225 … the Syrian church had carried the Christian faith halfway across Asia to the edges of India and the western ranges of China" (Moffett 1987). Bosch says, "Its ascetics-turned-missionaries … healed the sick, fed the poor, and preached the gospel." Also outside the Roman Empire, Nestorian Christians from Persia became what Bosch describes as "the major missionary force in non-Roman Asia" (1991, 204), spreading Christianity throughout central and eastern Asia during the Middle Ages. Saint Patrick, a person familiar to

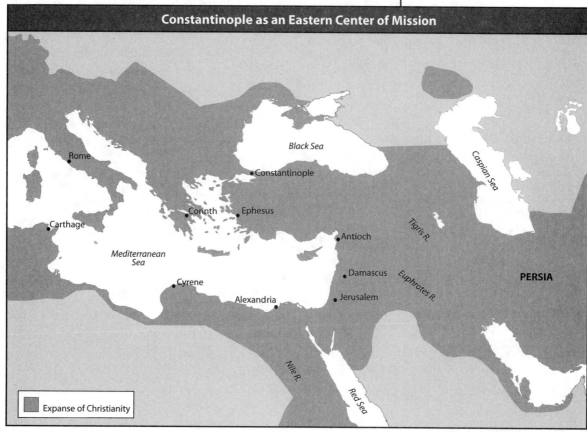

Constantinople as an Eastern Center of Mission

Black Sea

Rome

Constantinople

Corinth

Ephesus

Carthage

Caspian Sea

Tigris R.

Antioch

Mediterranean Sea

Damascus

Euphrates R.

PERSIA

Cyrene

Alexandria

Jerusalem

Nile R.

Red Sea

Expanse of Christianity

Map by Global Mapping International.

many largely because of his participation in God's mission during this era, went on mission to Ireland in the fifth century—mission that also took place outside the auspices of the Roman church. By the time of Patrick's death around 460, Ireland was primarily a Christian nation that would serve as the base of much Christian mission at the hands of Celtic monasticism in the years to come (Irvin and Sunquist 2001; Neill 1986; Tucker 2004).

Outside the growing Roman church came mission to the Gothic tribes through Ulfilas, an Arian Christian from North Africa. As early as the fourth century, nomadic Germanic tribes of barbarians known as Goths began warring against the northern areas of the Roman Empire. Ulfilas' mission to these warriors resulted in a rapid spread of the gospel to the north. The fourth-century ministry of Ulfilas had widespread influence, largely because of his translation of the Bible into the Gothic language—a feat that was a significant step in cross-cultural adaptation of Christian practice into a local context. "Ulfilas first had to render the Gothic language into written form, literally creating the script.... With the translation of the scriptures, Christianity quickly spread among the Goths, and

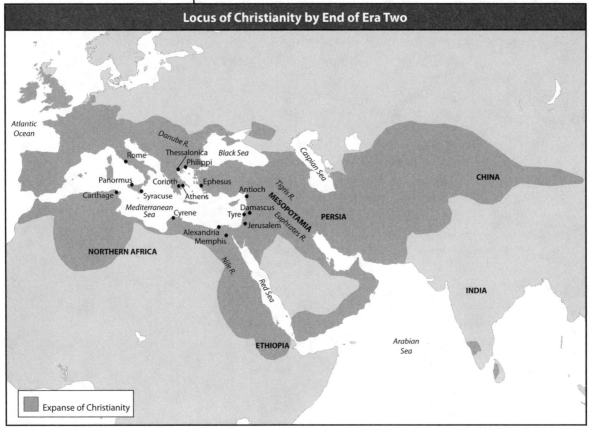

Locus of Christianity by End of Era Two

Map by Global Mapping International.

from them to other Germanic tribes. Within in a matter of several decades the Goths had converted en masse to Christianity.... We know that the Christian faith also spread quickly to other Germanic tribes on the northern Roman frontier" (Irvin and Sunquist 2001, 179–80).

By the year 600, the land extending as far as the Atlantic Ocean to the west, the Tigris and Euphrates rivers to the east, the Danube to the north, and the Mediterranean basin of North Africa to the south had a population that was predominantly Christian. Christianity also had centers of worship to the east in Mesopotamia, Persia, and India, and as far south as Ethiopia.

To further His mission, God used many circumstances in history, including political recognition of Christians in the Roman Empire and the conversion of rulers such as Emperor Constantine in the fourth century and the Frankish tribal leader Clovis in the fifth century. Additionally in these years, God used a myriad of believers, such as the martyrs and the monks, to be witnesses through their lives of exemplary faithfulness, and He used the testimony of the ever-present and more-organized church. As we turn our eyes to the next era, we will see how God continued to build on the foundations of these early years to bring about His mission to farther and wider spheres.

??

- Emperor Constantine endorsed Christianity as the state religion of the Roman Empire in the fourth century. What are the benefits of a close relationship between church and state? What are the dangers? How would your life be different if Christianity were banned where you live?

- Do you ever experience suffering because of your faith in Christ? How can suffering and persecution be beneficial to the spread of the gospel? What are you willing to experience and endure for the sake of Christ?

Constantine and Clovis

In the early eras of Christianity, one significant means of extending mission to larger and larger numbers of people came through the conversions of the leaders of empires or other groupings of people. The conversion of Roman Emperor Constantine in the fourth century marked a significant turning point in the life of the church and the spread of the gospel. More than a hundred years later, the conversion of Clovis, the leader of barbarian Frankish tribes to the north of the Mediterranean, played a significant role in bringing the gospel to people groups outside the Roman world.

An interesting facet of the conversion to Christianity by these leaders is that their subjects followed suit, often en masse. We have already seen the dramatic results of the conversion of Constantine in bringing Christianity to the Roman Empire. Authors Dale T. Irvin and Scott W. Sunquist recount the dramatic example of mass conversion that occurred in AD 496 among Clovis and his men: "Under the influence of his wife ... Clovis abandoned the practice of his ancestral religion and was baptized. He was shortly followed into the waters by some three thousand members of his army" (2001, 238). Yet, the practice of mass conversion was not limited to the example of these two leaders. There are instances throughout history, to present day, of mass conversions among a people group or a tribe.

God used the conversion of leaders to spread His mission. But these leaders' lives, just like those of Old Testament patriarchs and New Testament disciples, were sometimes marred by questionable behavior and selfishness, as historical records reveal. This is yet another manifestation of God's commitment to invite men and women, despite their shortcomings, to join His mission.

17

Era Three: AD 600 to 1500

Much has been written about the harm done to the cause of the gospel
when Constantine accepted baptism … But could any other choice
have been made? When the ancient classical world … ran out of spiritual fuel and turned to the church as the one society that could hold a
disintegrating world together, should the church have refused the appeal
and washed its hands of responsibility for the political order?… And yet
we have to ask, would God's purpose … have been better served if the
church had refused all political responsibility?   *—Lesslie Newbigin*

It is important to realize that, in spite of what meets the critical
human eye, the missionary contribution of the Middle Ages was not
only something to lament.… The point is that medieval Christians
responded to the challenges they faced in the only way that made
sense to them.   *—David J. Bosch*

In the last chapter, we explored a period of tremendous transition
for the Christian movement. Over the course of five hundred years,
Christianity grew from a loosely organized and outlawed religion
in the Roman Empire to a formally organized church that received
official sanction by the government. God used the church to fulfill
His mission both in the Mediterranean world and in locations farther afield. These first years provided a foundation for God's story
of mission that continues to unfold to this day.

From here we turn our attention to a third era of Christian mission,
which took place between 600 and 1500—the period of time com-
monly called the Middle Ages. Over the course of nine hundred
years, there was tremendous turmoil that produced change in world
political leadership. That turmoil was reflected in great change
within the church as well. Even so, God's mission went forward
through what today we would call rather dark times. Interestingly,
though this period spans nine centuries, there were consistent
modes of mission throughout those centuries. As we shall see, the
two dominant forms of mission in this era seem almost diametri-
cally opposed to one another—one peaceful and constructive, one

violent and destructive. No matter what our feelings are toward some of the events of Christian expansion during the Middle Ages, we must remember two things: First, God remains sovereign and His purpose will go forward through history. Second, the events of any era in Christian mission take place within a specific context and without the benefit of hindsight. In other words, people act and respond in ways that make sense to them, given their circumstances.

Over the course of five hundred years, Christianity grew from a loosely organized and outlawed religion in the Roman Empire to a formally organized church that received official sanction by the government.

During this period, church and state continued to be heavily intertwined to the point that an enemy of the state was easily viewed as an enemy to Christianity and vice versa. This was a view with often-unpleasant consequences. Because of the oppressive facts of life in the Middle Ages, with the constant reality and threat of invasion and domination by a variety of non-Christian influences, it is in some ways astonishing that a vibrant Christianity emerged from this period. God is able to take what is intended for evil and use it for good (Genesis 50:20). What He did for Joseph in the earliest days of Israel, He continued to do through the Middle Ages and continues to do for us today.

Two Conflicts

Stephen Neill notes that there were "two conflicts which the Church found on its hands in the years following AD 500—the struggle with the barbarians, and the unending battle with Islam" (1986, 53). In both instances we see great conflict, not only in the annals of history but in the history of Christian mission as well. As mentioned in the last chapter, invading barbarian tribes troubled the Roman Empire as early as the third century. In addition, Islam arose in Arabia in the seventh century, and its rapid advance conquered many of the most widely known centers of earliest Christianity, including Jerusalem and Alexandria. "The East Roman (or Byzantine) empire within a single generation lost more than half its territories to the Arabs. Gone … were Syria, Palestine, Egypt, and Roman North Africa" (Irvin and Sunquist 2001, 259).

In the ninth century, Rome was plundered. "By 902 Sicily was a Muslim country, and strongholds had been established on the South Italian coast" (Neill 1986, 54). Warfare in Asia Minor continued until "at last in 1453 Constantinople fell to the Turks, and the Eastern Roman Empire, the bulwark of Christendom for a thousand years, was at an end" (55).

Life under Muslim rule was different for Christians who had previously lived under the jurisdiction of the former Roman Empire, though not substantially different for those who had been living as a minority religion in Persia and other places. Irvin and Sunquist note that Christians were extended some freedoms of worship under Muslim rule, but they could not evangelize among the Muslims. "Despite the restrictions imposed upon them, Christian communities managed to survive and sometimes even to grow in number during the first centuries of Islamic rule" (2001, 276). However, Christianity suffered significant attrition in Muslim-dominated lands. Even though Christians generally were not compelled to convert to Islam, they were encouraged to do so and many did. Thus, in the regions under Muslim control, Christian mission was significantly curtailed. "The Muslim conquests, and their control of many of the great trade routes … involved a notable shift in the whole perspective of the Christian world. Christianity became an almost completely European religion" (Neill 1986, 56).

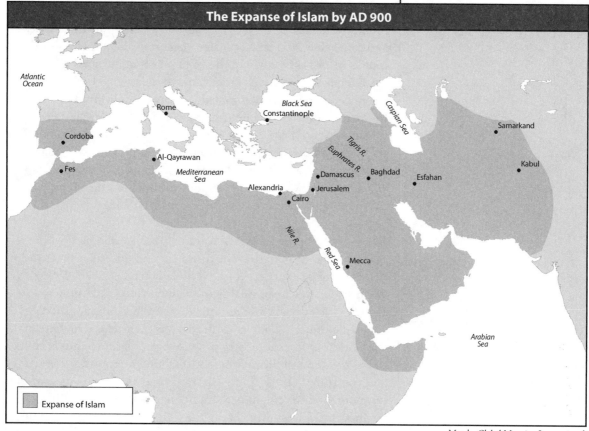

The Expanse of Islam by AD 900

Map by Global Mapping International.

Western Front of Christendom

Let us now turn our attention to the western front of Christendom, where the barbaric tribes in the west captured much of the attention of the church. During the early years of the Middle Ages, significant mission outreach to these peoples went forward in what is present-day Europe. "For five hundred years the major task of the Western Church was that of wrestling with the barbarians and with barbarism in the effort to make their conversion something more than nominal," notes Neill. "Far more difficult than the task of first bringing these peoples into the Church was that of making Christian faith effective in their lives, of bringing proud, undisciplined, and illiterate natures under the yoke of the Gospel" (1986, 53–54, 57).

A primary force of accomplishing this was monasticism, which was at the center of Christian mission for many centuries. Over the course of nine hundred years, differing types of monasticism emerged. One of the earliest was Celtic, through the Irish monks descending from the fifth-century work of Saint Patrick. Nussbaum says that these monks probably did not think of themselves as ambassadors of the gospel. "They were simply serving God and renouncing the down side of the world" (2005, 59). Celtic monks were fond of wandering pilgrimages of personal penance, and somewhat "accidental mission" occurred along the way as the monks helped others whom they met on their journeys. In time, the Benedictine monastic order came to replace the Celtic, and the Benedictine order dominated Roman Catholic monasticism for many centuries. The Benedictines "became involved in explicit missionary enterprises, in an even more significant way than did the Celtic monks. It was Gregory the Great, himself a Benedictine monk, who first conceived the idea of a planned 'foreign mission,' when he sent the monk Augustine … to initiate a missionary venture among the pagan English" (Bosch 1991, 235).

Bosch notes that monks demonstrated patience and hard work that served as a contrast to the turbulent and uncertain times the neighboring peasants experienced in daily medieval life (1991, 232). Theirs was a "spirituality of the long haul," according to Patrick G. Henry (1987), not one that produced instant success. Bosch continues, "Coupled with this was their refusal to write off the world as a lost cause or to propose neat, no-loose-ends answers to the problems of life, but rather to rebuild promptly, patiently, and cheerfully" (1991, 233). This quiet and steadfast witness of the power of God to bring peace amidst chaos won many of the monks' neighbors to Christ. Mission by the Celtic and Benedictine monks over the years 600 to 1000 spread Christian faith among the many tribes who inhabited western Europe. Meanwhile, similar monastic activity was also going forward in the east. "The expansion of the Christian movement east of Persia after the year 600 was primarily the work of East Syrian monks, priests, and merchants who traveled the trade routes across Asia" (Irvin and Sunquist 2001, 305).

Monastic Christian mission was formally spreading the gospel to new lands despite the losses to Islam in many areas that had previously been Christian. Irvin and Sunquist sum up some of this activity:

> Constantinople opened up a new mission in the ninth century to the Bulgars and the Slavs who had established kingdoms to its north. This was followed in the tenth century by the conversion of the ruling household among the Russian people. Meanwhile, in the West, the ninth and tenth centuries witnessed the advance of Christianity among the inhabitants of Scandinavia, who were brought into the family of churches that looked toward Rome as the bearer of tradition. This new wave of expansion reached as far as Iceland in the year 1000. Thus at the end of the first millennium, the movement that began in Galilee and Jerusalem reached from China and India in the

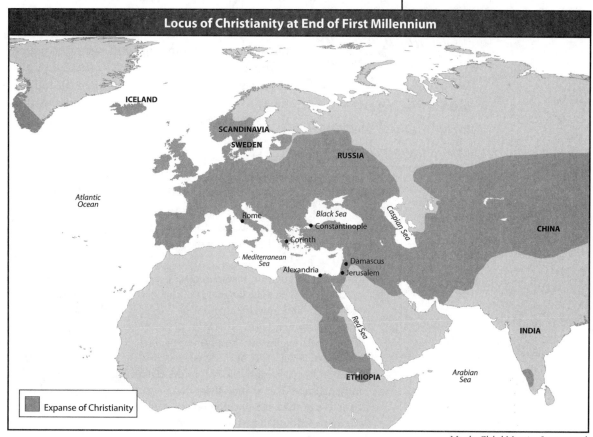

Locus of Christianity at End of First Millennium

Map by Global Mapping International.

east; to Ethiopia in the south; to Russia and Sweden in the north; and to Iceland in the west. (2001, 259)

Between the years 1000 and 1200, the Christian world had extended to the lands of Scandinavia, Denmark, Norway, Iceland, Greenland, Sweden, and Finland. Beginning in 1200, the rise of two new Roman Catholic monastic orders, the Franciscans and the Dominicans, was used by God to extend Christian mission to Ukraine, Mongolia, India, Azerbaijan, and Georgia, though much of the gains in Asia were wiped out in the later Middle Ages by the advance of the Turks across the continent.

Unity Within Diversity

An interesting facet of Christian mission during the Middle Ages is the varying approaches to creating and maintaining Christian unity within the diverse cultures in which the gospel was being proclaimed. Generally speaking, mission that went forward under the auspices of the Eastern Church at Constantinople was more open to incorporating new cultural forms into Christian worship and practice. For example, Irvin and Sunquist note the following: "Christians joined missionaries from other religions who were journeying across central Asia into China, and by all appearances learned much from them. In India, the Christian community accepted a place within the caste system … [thus] being integrated into the Indian religious cosmos without abandoning their own identity as different" (2001, 322). Eastern mission to China involved translation of the Scriptures from Syrian into Chinese. The issue of language for worship is one in which several approaches were taken, and each approach demonstrated a different view of maintaining unity within diversity. Neill elaborates in the following:

> Rome had throughout insisted on Latin as the sole liturgical language of the West. The languages of the barbarians were uncouth, uncultured, and unwritten, and were judged to be ill-adapted to the dignity of liturgy; Latin came with all the prestige of antiquity and of the civilizing power. The advantage gained by this method was the creation of a real unity of the Western world, in which Latin was the common language until the end of the eighteenth century and a great unifying force. The weakness was that worshippers understood little, if anything, of what was going on in Church. The sense of mystery was increased; intelligent participation was at a minimum.

An interesting facet of Christian mission during the Middle Ages is the varying approaches to creating and maintaining Christian unity within the diverse cultures in which the gospel was being proclaimed.

The attitude of Constantinople was entirely different. Orthodox Christians were familiar with Armenians and Syrians, who had a different alphabet and their own liturgical traditions … it always seemed natural to Byzantine churchmen that as new peoples were brought within the Church they should be encouraged to build up their Church and their national culture on the basis of their local language…. this measure of tolerance for local usage, and the at least partial recognition of the independence of the local Churches, has been one of the strong factors in fostering Orthodox unity. (1986, 73–74)

It would be unfair, however, to say that the Roman church was opposed to any cross-cultural translation of the gospel. As Irvin and Sunquist note, "Western monks and nuns were also translating Christianity, this time from its urban, Mediterranean context to a mostly rural, Germanic one" (2001, 258). Neill describes this process as the transformation of the Roman church from an imperial church into a feudal one (1986, 54). This was a feudal church that, owing in great part to a unified Latin language for worship, maintained its unity in the face of the ongoing fragmentation of Europe into many different kingdoms and power centers—particularly after the year 900 (Irvin and Sunquist 2001, 342).

This idea of unity in worship style—so central to the dominant Roman Catholic Church, or western branch of Christianity—was found not only in matters of liturgy, but in other matters as well. We mentioned earlier the ongoing close relationship between

Third Era Snapshot

During the period AD 600–1500 …

- "During most of the Middle Ages Europe was, for all intents and purposes, a self-contained island, cut off from the rest of the world by Islam. To the East, Islam had penetrated into Central Asia, from where it formed an unbroken chain via Western Asia, the Middle East, and North Africa into Spain and as far as the Pyrenees" (Bosch 1991, 226).

- "The successes of the Muslims had cut the world in two. Having taken to the sea, they had made the Mediterranean unsafe for Christian traffic, and in Indian waters they were the dominant power. This state of things continued unchanged until … the end of the fifteenth century … By land most of the familiar trade routes were in [Muslim] hands, though some of the northern routes through Central Asia were still open to Christians, and Byzantium was not wholly deprived of its trade relations with Cathay" (Neill 1986, 81).

- Linguistically the world was a much more diverse place than it had been in previous years when Greek was widely used as a language of literature and trade. Individual tribes and kingdoms throughout what became Europe spoke their own individual languages and dialects. In areas under Islamic rule, Arabic was the primary language spoken. In countries under Christian leadership, there was some linguistic unity, at least for worship and liturgy. In Christendom's west, the primary language was Latin. In Christendom's east, Greek was the primary language spoken (Bosch 1991; Irvin and Sunquist 2001; Neill 1986).

church and state. In such a climate of unified thinking about politics and faith, it was easy for the enemies of the state to be viewed as enemies of Christendom and vice versa. This medieval idea of church unity included the prevalent Western Christian mind-set that there was no salvation outside formal membership in the Roman Catholic Church. Therefore, "it was to people's own eternal advantage if they could be made to join this body" (Bosch 1991, 237). From this climate springs a defining characteristic of the Middle Ages—that of compulsion to faith, whether directly or indirectly, through conquest and war.

Conversion by Force

Initially, we see what is termed *indirect missionary war*, whose aim was "the subjugation of the pagans, which was regarded as the basis for *subsequent* missionary activity under the protection of the state; peaceful proclamation of the gospel could now take place" (Erdmann 1977; Rosenkranz 1977). For example, Pope Gregory I, in the sixth century, "praised fighting [the] barbarians to ensure that Christianity could be preached to the conquered" (Houweling and Siccama 1988, 43). But as Bosch notes, "the dividing line between 'indirect' and 'direct' missionary war was, however, very thin. It was only a matter of time before the second would evolve from the first" (1991, 224). An example of this blend from indirect to direct mission wars may be found in the methodologies of Charlemagne in his campaigns against the Saxons beginning in 772: "Once a German tribe had been conquered, its conversion was included in the terms of peace" (Neill 1986, 68). But, as Irvin and Sunquist observe, this pattern of forced conversion was dangerous: "With the baptism of the Saxons, we see the first full-scale use of military force and violence to compel a people to convert to Christianity.... Charlemagne set a precedent, one that Christian rulers all too often came to follow" (2001, 336). We find a similar example when the Christian Swedish ruler Erik IX initiated a campaign against Finland in 1155 and demanded baptism of the conquered (Neill 1986, 93). In the thirteenth century we see conquests in Prussia by the Teutonic Knights, a venture in which "the whole apparatus of medieval Christianity [was] brought in as an accompaniment to military conquest" (95).

Of course, the military events most often associated with Christianity in this era are the Crusades. "Pope Urban II at a council in southern France in 1095 issued a call for a military campaign under the sign of the cross (*crusade*) against the Muslims in the Holy Land.... The time had come, the pope declared, to liberate the Christian lands of Palestine and Spain from the rule of Muslim unbelievers" (Irvin and Sunquist 2001, 383–84). Historians offer different interpretations of the motivations and practices of crusaders. One can question whether the Crusades of the next two centuries should best be viewed as missionary wars or as attempts to return Christian holy sites to Christian rule by freeing them from Islamic rule. But whatever the accurate label for the motivations of the Crusade, one cannot help but see this entire period in history as a dark time. Neill notes that "the Crusades involved a lowering of the whole moral temperature of Christendom" (1986, 98). Even after the fall of the last crusader stronghold at Acre in 1291, the crusading spirit lived on in various forms. "In western Europe, crusading unleashed new violence against those who were considered to be infidels, or Christendom's outsiders. Before long the same crusading spirituality was turned … against groups in the West who were identified as heretics by the Catholic church" (Irvin and Sunquist 2001, 405).

Mission Going Forward

The Middle Ages were indeed a time of much violence on the part of pagans and Christians alike. But even as distasteful as these times and methods may seem to us, God's mission was going forward despite less-than-desirable circumstances. One example of this is the spread of the gospel through those who were enslaved as a result of conquest. For example, "Viking raiders unintentionally helped introduce Christianity into their homelands," observe Irvin and Sunquist. "Christians taken captive and brought back as slaves quickly introduced the practice of their faith there" (2001, 373). This type of Christian mission—preaching the truth of Christ whatever the circumstances—is similar to New Testament mission, and though obscured by larger events of history, it continued unabated throughout the years of the Middle Ages. It would appear that there have always been those who quietly accept God's invitation to mission and carry it out wherever they are.

It may be tempting to wonder why God allowed the challenges to His mission, such as those caused by the advances of the pagan barbarian tribes or the Muslims, but once again we recall the facts of Isaiah 55:8–11. The ways of God are not our ways, and His Word will not return to Him empty, for He says, "[It] will accomplish what I desire and achieve the purpose for which I sent it." It may not seem logical to us that God would allow such widespread obstacles as those encountered by Christian mission in the years between 600 and 1500, but there is a long view—a continuing

??

Daily life in era three was often filled with violence, oppression, uncertainty, and chaos; yet God continued to bring hope and reconciliation in the midst of such strife. What circumstances of chaos and strife are you struggling with? Do you trust God to be with you through those circumstances? How can you focus your hope on Him and not on your circumstances?

story—unfolding in even these pages of history. By the year 1500, even while Christianity had suffered attrition in areas such as North Africa and the Middle East, it had gained strength in what is now Europe. It was from these European countries that God's mission went forward in the centuries to come—something God knew and prepared for even in years referred to as the Dark Ages.

The end of this third era of Christian mission can be marked by several events, not the least of which was the fall of Constantinople to the Ottoman Turks in 1453, the event that marked the end of more than eleven centuries of Christian leadership from the city Constantine founded in 330. Indeed, the rise of the Turkish Empire spelled the reversal of many gains that had been made for the gospel in central Asia. By the end of this era, "the majority of the world's Christians resided in the European West" (Irvin and Sunquist 2001, 504).

In the closing years of this third era, we begin to see the winds of change sweeping through what had been the dominant ideas of mission between the years 600 and 1500. Some work prefigured the coming of the Reformation in the next era. Among these efforts

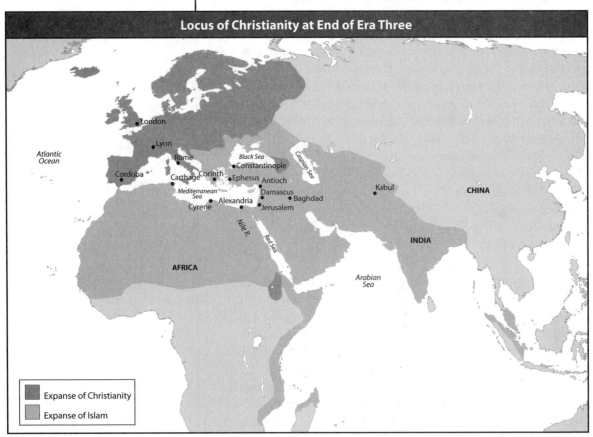

Locus of Christianity at End of Era Three

Expanse of Christianity

Expanse of Islam

Map by Global Mapping International.

was John Wycliffe's fourteenth-century translation of the Bible into English, a task performed so that the Bible could be read by people who didn't know Latin. These winds of reform would usher in a new paradigm of mission as well, and God would work through people in fresh ways to bring His message of love and reconciliation to the world of the Renaissance. We will examine this time of reform and change in our next chapter.

18

Era Four: AD 1500 to 1800

In 1514, Copernicus, the Polish astronomer, privately circulated his manuscript claiming that the earth revolves around the sun—a challenge to ancient authority that would require a new cosmology. Two years later, Erasmus produced the first printed Greek New Testament, making the original text available to any educated person of the day. In 1517, Martin Luther nailed his ninety-five theses to the church door in Wittenberg, thereby launching the Protestant Reformation. A paradigm shift was underway in northern Europe.   —*Norman E. Thomas*

As we have seen in our journey through the history of God's mission, there are times when the weakness of men and women appears to overshadow God's purpose and keep it from going forward. It may be hard for us, with our contemporary vantage point, to have a charitable point of view about the way people have participated in various portions of the story of God's mission. We may even be tempted to believe that this divine mission was interrupted completely by the events of certain eras in history. But just as God moved His purpose forward during periods of difficulty, captivity, and exile in the life of Israel, so has He been moving His purpose forward throughout periods of difficulty and challenge for the church, for His followers. We shall continue to see God's mission of relationship, redemption, and reconciliation move forward in the pages of history as we look in this chapter at the next three hundred years.

The fourth era in the history of Christian mission roughly spans the years 1500 to 1800. In the beginning of this era, the mission efforts of the Roman Catholic Church were the predominant means of God's mission going forward, and Christianity was largely confined to what today we would call western Europe. The confluence of several events at the beginning of the sixteenth century propelled mission far beyond those boundaries. In a thirty-year period (between 1490 and 1520), two events unfolded that would set the stage for

Christian mission on a scale previously unknown in the world. One was the Protestant Reformation, whose greatest effect on Christian mission would take several centuries to fully ripen. Another was the Age of Discovery—marked by the voyages of explorers such as Christopher Columbus, Vasco da Gama, and Amerigo Vespucci—which broadened the horizons of what constituted the known world.

The Protestant Reformation

As mentioned at the close of the last chapter, winds of change were blowing throughout Europe during the fifteenth century. The Renaissance, a rebirth of classical ideas in arts and science, had begun in Italy and moved through Europe. As a result, inventions and innovations brought about dramatic changes. One such innovation was the movable type printing press, introduced to Europe around 1440 by German Johannes Gutenberg. The printing press enabled wider-scale production of texts at a fraction of the cost of hand-copied books.[1] As a result, for the first time, the Bible would become more available to the layperson. This availability, taken together with events such as John Wycliffe's earlier translation of the Bible into English, set the stage for an even more dramatic and widespread change—the Protestant Reformation.

The Reformation officially began in 1517 when Martin Luther posted his grievances against the Catholic Church, his Ninety-five Theses, on the door of the church at Wittenberg, Germany.[2] The ensuing reformation led to the formation of new communities of worship and eventually, over several centuries, new life in global Christian mission. In a nutshell, "the Protestant Reformation replaced the authority of the popes with the authority of the Bible, as interpreted by the local church" (Tannenbaum 1973, 309). But as mission scholar Ralph Winter reminds us, revitalization occurred both outside and inside the Catholic Church: "This great decentralization of Christendom was in many respects the result of an increasing vitality which ... was just as evident in Italy, Spain and France as in Moravia, Germany and England. Everywhere we see a return to a study of the Bible and the appearance of new life and evangelical preaching" (1999b, 209–10).

One of the reformers' core beliefs was that justification came by faith (Romans 1:16–17), a uniquely individual expression of relationship with God. According to Stephan Pfürtner, "The question about salvation became the personal question of the individual ... in a thousand different forms believers would insist on the personal and subjective experience of a new birth by the Holy Spirit, as well as on the responsibility of the individual over against the group" (1984). This issue is related to the theme of unity within diversity that we have been studying, because the Reformation brought into question the ways in which individuals versus groups function in Christian unity. Could individual believers engage in relationship with God and Christian life without the mediation and guidance of priests and leaders of the Catholic Church? What would such emphasis on the individual do to the unity of the faith? Could such an allowance for diversity possibly result in the unity of faith that the Bible exhorts believers to live in? These questions may seem odd to us, but they were very heatedly debated during the era of the Reformation. Individualism as we think of it was largely a new concept—particularly in matters of faith, which had traditionally been governed by the church and its hierarchy.

Many scholars have identified the Renaissance, which began in the late Middle Ages, as a period in which the individual began to emerge from the group in a host of ways. The Protestant Reformation sharpened this focus on the individual, particularly in relation to the doctrine of the *priesthood of all believers*, which was an understanding that "the believer stood in direct relationship with God, a relationship that existed independent of the church." Bosch describes this doctrine as a reintroduction of the view of the early Church in that every Christian has a calling and responsibility to serve God (1991, 242–43). You will recall from chapter 15 that a feature of early Christian life was that individuals on mission were propelled by their personal relationship with God and fueled by the Holy Spirit. As Neill notes, not only were there specifically set-apart, full-time workers, such as Paul and Barnabas, who were forces of mission, but also "the Church could count on the anonymous and unchronicled witness of all the faithful" (1986, 21–22). And as Irvin and Sunquist remind us, "the dispersion of the apostles to regions beyond Jerusalem did not lead to the breakup of the movement. Their unity, they believed, was found in the person of Jesus, who beckoned them from the edges of history" (2001, 41).

Mission During the Reformation

With Protestant theology emphasizing so many elements of individual responsibility and personal calling to serve God, you would imagine that mission would be a significant and immediate feature of the new expressions of Christian faith. Yet, despite a fundamentally mission-oriented theology on the part of reformers such as Luther and Calvin, "very little happened by way of a missionary outreach during the first two centuries after the Reformation"

Renaissance

The phrase *the Renaissance* is traditionally used to describe a period in European history that began during the late Middle Ages. The term *renaissance* is actually French for "rebirth." It is an apt description of a period in history characterized by a revitalization of both the arts and the sciences. *Merriam-Webster Online Dictionary* defines the Renaissance as "the transitional movement in Europe between medieval and modern times beginning in the 14th century in Italy, lasting into the 17th century, and marked by a humanistic revival of classical influence expressed in a flowering of the arts and literature and by the beginnings of modern science."[1] The many advances of the Renaissance had a profound influence on much that followed this period. In particular, from the Renaissance comes the foundation of Enlightenment thinking that we will examine in chapter 19 in connection with the nineteenth century.

NOTE

1. *Merriam-Webster Online Dictionary*, s.v. "renaissance," http://www.m-w.com/dictionary/ (accessed April 22, 2008).

From the *Merriam-Webster Online Dictionary* ©2008 by Merriam-Webster, Incorporated (www.Merriam-Webster.com).

(Bosch 1991, 245). Nussbaum notes a predominant inward focus for survival: In the early days of the Reformation, Protestants scrambled to define the "true" church. "All the definitions of the church revolved around 'what happens inside its four walls, not in terms of its calling in the world' " (2005, 62). Clearly, in this climate, the churches that were in the process of reformation faced obstacles to missionary endeavor. Bosch elaborates as follows:

> To begin with, Protestants saw their principal task as that of reforming the church of their time; this consumed all their energy. Second, Protestants had no immediate contact with non-Christian peoples.… Third, the churches of the Reformation were involved in a battle for sheer survival … Fourth, in abandoning monasticism the Reformers had denied themselves a very important missionary agency; it would take centuries before anything remotely as competent and effective as the monastic missionary movement would develop in Protestantism. Fifth, Protestants were themselves torn apart by internal strife … little energy was left for turning to those outside the Christian fold. (1991, 245)

Though it may seem strange to us today, a primary belief among reformers was that the apostles in the early Church had fulfilled the mandate of the Great Commission. A major theme of Reformation theology during this time period was that "all initiative [for] salvation lay with God alone," writes Bosch. "The attitude was that no human being could undertake any mission work; God would, in his sovereignty, see to this" (1991, 250). This theological point of view was dominant for several centuries, and it was expressed in different ways by major figures of the Reformation. This view certainly diminishes a focus on joining God's mission. "Instead of saying, 'We ought to have missions, and we will have them, as soon as the Lord opens the door,' the Protestants [of the sixteenth century] tended to say, 'Missions are neither obligatory nor desirable, and our lack of them cannot be held against us as blindness or unfaithfulness' " (Neill 1986, 189).

Though it may seem strange to us today, a primary belief among reformers was that the apostles in the early Church had fulfilled the mandate of the Great Commission.

There were, however, some exceptions to the idea that Christian mission wasn't a responsibility for Protestants. There were voices, though few, calling for service to God in the form of obedience to the Great Commission. Among them was the sixteenth-century Dutch theologian Adrian Saravia, whose writings would eventually have far-reaching effects on world mission. In a 1590 work, "Saravia argued that the apostles themselves could only in limited measure have carried out the Great Commission. Two centuries later,

William Carey would popularize Saravia's contention that the Great Commission applies to the whole Church in all subsequent times" (Thomas 1995, 41). In addition to such writings, there were some Protestant movements actively pursuing evangelism and mission work. It is to these movements we turn now, paying special attention to the ways in which these early Protestant mission endeavors would grow into the worldwide mission activity of the nineteenth and twentieth centuries.

Three movements on the margins of the Reformation did the most significant mission thinking and work in the sixteenth, seventeenth, and eighteenth centuries—respectively, the Anabaptists, the Puritans, and the Pietists. In the sixteenth century, Anabaptists radically embraced the idea of priesthood for all believers and a missionary calling. They rejected the Catholic and the Reformation notion that geographical territories are to be governed by a particular branch of the church as dictated by the ruler. Thus, they selected and systematically sent preachers into many parts of Europe (Bosch 1991, 246).

Mission work of the Puritans, a branch of reformers centered in England, went forward in the seventeenth century. Perhaps most famously, some of these British believers traveled to the new world of North America in an effort to escape increasing religious persecution in England. But, as R. Pierce Beaver chronicles, "the participation of Protestants in world mission began early in the 17th century simultaneously with the evangelistic work of the chaplains of the Dutch East Indies Company and the New England missions to the American Indians.... It was the Puritan missions to the American Indians that would provide the missions of a later day with inspiration and models" (1999, 244). Indeed, later generations were deeply influenced by accounts of John Eliot's seventeenth-century evangelization of Native Americans and translation work for them and by the eighteenth-century diary of American David Brainerd, which chronicled the essence of his missionary work among Native Americans in Massachusetts and Pennsylvania. Puritan mission work, though perhaps not tremendously widespread, did lay a foundation for future pages of the story of God's mission around the world.

The Pietists, a Lutheran group, "gave up on the mission potential of the Lutheran Church ... as a whole," writes Nussbaum. "The Pietists established a small revived community to be the bearer of mission. They did not wait to be sent by political authorities into the colonies but simply went when and where Christ was sending them" (2005, 67). The first Protestants on mission to Asia were Pietists Bartholomew Ziegenbalg and Heinrich Plutschau. These men were "the first of about 60 Pietists who went to India in the eighteenth century" (Pierson 1999, 264). Perhaps the most famous Protestant mission endeavor of the eighteenth century was that of the Moravians, who had roots in Pietism. Emerging from a small group of exiled believers fleeing anti-Reformation persecution in Bohemia and Moravia, they were a remarkable group of people devoted to God's mission and calling in the Protestant climate of much theological debate and little action. "Known for their 24 hour, 100 year prayer watch, they were a highly disciplined, monastic-like community of married men and women devoted to win 'souls for the Lamb.' During their early years, one of every 14 members became a missionary, often going to the most difficult fields" (265). Among the early Moravian mission fields were Greenland, the West Indies, and Dutch Guiana (Neill 1986).

> *In the fullness of time, God used the events of the Age of Discovery to propel men and women to new frontiers of Christian mission. The effects of that age on Christian mission were swift and far-reaching. These events provided the perfect opportunity for God's mission to go forth to previously unknown lands and peoples.*

In addition to these three examples of Protestant mission of this era were also eighteenth-century preaching and revival that God would use to stir passion for mission in the hearts of believers in the next century. Pierson writes, "The fourth stream leading to the Protestant missionary movement flowed from the *Wesleyan/Evangelical* revival in England, with John Wesley as its best known leader, and the First Great Awakening in North America" (1999, 265). God was planting seeds through these events that would give birth in the nineteenth century to a Protestantism finally focused on the mission of God.

The Age of Discovery

In the fullness of time, God used the events of the Age of Discovery to propel men and women to new frontiers of Christian mission. The effects of that age on Christian mission were swift and far-reaching. These events provided the perfect opportunity for God's mission to go forth to previously unknown lands and peoples. "It is impossible to exaggerate the enlargement of views which these discoveries brought both to the European mind and to the outlook of the Christian Church," notes author Stephen Neill (1986, 120). Da Gama's voyage to India around the Cape of Good Hope opened a new route to the Far East—through Muslim-controlled sea trade routes. Columbus, Vespucci, and others brought awareness of new lands and new peoples to the minds of church leaders and political leaders of Europe. God used the dominant sea powers of the time—the Catholic countries of Portugal and Spain—to spread His gospel far and wide around the globe.

In the sixteenth century, Central and South American lands saw swift exposure to the gospel, if not also swift conquest and occupation by European settlers. Neill chronicles the methods of mission in Latin America during this era:

> The approach of [Spain and Portugal] to the New World of the West was always marked by three considerations—conquest, settlement, and evangelization. The peoples of these unknown lands were to be brought permanently under the dominion of the Christian kings, to whom God through the Pope had given sovereignty. This domination was to be maintained through the presence of a considerable number of Europeans as permanent settlers and residents … The purpose of this Christian rule was to create Christian peoples out of those who were regarded by their conquerors as members of barbarous and pagan races. (1986, 143)

Language learning by the missionaries and translation work to provide Christian literature were widely accepted first steps. Generally speaking, evangelizing native peoples involved gathering them into villages where churches and schools were built and where priests and their representatives carried out strict discipline and religious instruction. But there was no true effort to support indigenous ministry (Neill 1986, 147–48). No doubt a serious impediment to fruitful and lasting work was the documented cruelty of colonists, and this period of mission is marked by cycles of native uprisings resulting in the massacre of missionaries. However, seeds of the gospel were rapidly being planted all over lands that had previously never heard the name of Christ.

The Jesuits

"With every expedition for exploration or conquest came priests and friars. The major part of the work was undertaken by Franciscans and Dominicans, with the Jesuits following a little later" (Neill 1986, 144). Pope Paul III created the Jesuit order in 1540 with the express purpose of mission to those who didn't know Christ. "Within the next hundred years Jesuits were to lay their bones in almost every country of the known world and on the shores of almost every sea" (127).

Christian mission was also going forward in the Far East—for example, in India, Japan, and China—particularly through the

Jesuit monastic order. A notable example is found in Francis Xavier. Neill describes the significance of Xavier's work in Japan:

> These early contacts with the Japanese produced a change in Xavier's understanding of the nature of Christian missionary work which was to be of the greatest significance for the whole future of the enterprise. In earlier years he had been inclined to accept uncritically the doctrine of the *tabula rasa*—the view that in non-Christian life and systems there is nothing on which the missionary can build, and that everything must simply be levelled to the ground before anything Christian can be built up. This was the general view of the Spanish missionaries in Latin America and the West Indies; in his dealings with the simple and illiterate fishers in South India, Xavier had seen no reason to modify it. But now that he was confronted by a civilization with so many elements of nobility in it, he saw that, while the Gospel must transform and refine and recreate, it need not necessarily reject as worthless everything that has come before. This new idea was to be fruitful in results—and also in controversies. (1986, 133)

To our ears, the ideas of respect for a new culture and of integrating Christian teaching into already present cultural forms and patterns may sound obvious. But this was not the predominant thinking of this era, in which the primary means of mission was more along the lines of creating a separate "Christian culture" rather than integrating Christian truth and life into existing cultural forms. But change was coming, however slowly. Xavier's insights into mission methodology influenced other Jesuits. Resulting attempts at cultural sensitivity and accommodation gave way to the difficult questions that come when ministering cross-culturally—such as, What is the appropriate apparel to wear in a new culture? Are there equivalent native terms for Christian concepts? How far can ancient cultural customs be integrated with Christian teaching? It was precisely these kinds of questions regarding methodology that led to controversy, change, and ultimately decline in Roman Catholic mission in the coming years.

The Decline in Roman Catholic Mission

The first profound change for Catholic mission came in the seventeenth century. Instead of Catholic mission coming to new lands through exploration and colonization by the Spanish national churches and the Portuguese national churches, Catholic mission was centralized through Rome after 1622. Thus began numerous positive changes, including emphasis on developing indigenous clergy, openness to different cultural forms in the evangelization of new lands, and mission training for clergy outside the monastic orders. However, carrying out the openness of these new policies led to controversy. Neill (1986) points out that almost every approach to mission work had been attempted in diverse work that was going forward during this era—accommodation of local customs and insistence on abolishing them; conversion of individuals and groups; ordination of indigenous priests and the banning of ordination of indigenous believers; mission that targeted primarily the leaders and the wealthy rather than the poor and the outcast. With each strategy came passionate arguments of support and opposition, arguments that created strife in a system that was very dependent on central leadership through Rome. "The second half of the eighteenth century was a period of tragic collapse for the Roman Catholic missions," summarizes Neill. The ongoing theological conflicts and religious wars that defined the early years of the Reformation had international impact as well. As Neill observes, "The two hostile camps into which Christendom had been divided by the wars of religion extended their quarrels overseas." Whereas in the early years of discovery and colonization the primary navigational powers were from Catholic countries, "from 1600 onwards, the Protestant powers—England, Holland, and Denmark—began to enter what the Roman Catholic nations had regarded as their exclusive [domain]" (173). Even so, in the three hundred years between 1500 and 1800, Neill records that Catholic mission had gone forward in India, China, Japan, Central America, and South America, with limited work in Africa and North America.

Though initially lacking in zeal for mission, the theological and organizational changes wrought in the church by the Protestant Reformation did indeed create a climate in which believers could recapture a first-century sense of individual responsibility to serve God and to answer His invitation to mission.

What had been a largely European religion at the beginning of this era had, in the space of three hundred years, expanded to having at least some footing in lands that had previously been unheard of, much less evangelized. God used the rapid discovery and exploration of new lands as a vehicle for the spread of the gospel. Through technological and scientific advances of the day, such as the printing press and navigational prowess, He furthered life and witness in these new lands. And though the means by which some mission work went forward may have been intermingled with all-too-human motives for wealth and power, God was still sovereign in marching His purpose and mission forward through time. As always, He was using people and circumstances for good in the midst of brokenness. Though initially lacking in zeal for mission,

- Ethnocentrism and cultural superiority were often exhibited during era four, even in the realm of Christian mission. Do you have underlying beliefs and attitudes that are counterproductive to effective missional living? Do you find yourself prejudiced against certain cultural practices or groups of people?

- The Age of Discovery offered new avenues for sharing the gospel during era four. What are some circumstances in your life that seem to be advantageous for developing new cross-cultural relationships? How could you take advantage of those opportunities?

the theological and organizational changes wrought in the church by the Protestant Reformation did indeed create a climate in which believers could recapture a first-century sense of individual responsibility to serve God and to answer His invitation to mission. By the end of this fourth era, we see a road being paved for Christianity to finally become truly international in scope.

છ

NOTES

1. *Microsoft Encarta Online Encyclopedia*, s.v. "printing," http://encarta.msn.com/encyclopedia_761562769/Printing.html (accessed June 20, 2008); Mary Bellis, "Johannes Gutenberg and the Printing Press," About.com:Inventors, http://inventors.about.com/od/gstartinventors/a/Gutenberg.htm (accessed June 20, 2008).

2. *The Columbia Encyclopedia*, s.vv. "Reformation," "Martin Luther," http://www.bartleby.com/65/ (accessed June 20, 2008).

19

Era Five: Nineteenth and Twentieth Centuries

The progress of the Gospel is not tied to the political or economic fortunes of any one part of the human race, but as long as men live in human and very physical bodies, it will not be possible completely to separate the religious from other aspects of the human situation.

—*Stephen Neill*

Of course, Christianity did not disappear after the Enlightenment; on the contrary, it has since spread across the entire globe.

—*David J. Bosch*

Throughout our tracing of the story of how God has worked in the world over several millennia, God has given us just a taste of how He shepherded the spread of His story through a variety of cultural, social, and political realities. We have seen that He used people in each era, from all circumstances—slave or free, educated or uneducated, clergy or layperson—to write additional chapters of His story of redeeming and reconciling His people to relationship with Himself. This mission continues to go forward through time, regardless of the different circumstances. In each era, people have responded to His invitation to join missio Dei. This is certainly no less true in the nineteenth and twentieth centuries of era five.

Historians refer to the years 1789–1914 as a period of time that "was pre-eminently the European century in world history, the period in which Europe was able to impose its will and its ideas on the whole of the inhabited world" (Neill 1986, 207). Events such as the French Revolution in 1789 and the widespread impact of the Industrial Revolution by 1800 marked a turning point in world history in many ways. And it was no less a turning point for Christian mission, as several events in the 1790s paved the way for the remarkable spread of Christian mission that occurred in the next two hundred years. European dominance in this era draws the focus of our chapter primarily to European and North American

Steam and Revolution

One of the factors that enabled rapid growth of mission around the world in era five was the development of swifter forms of travel and communication. This came about largely with the Industrial Revolution, which was in full force as the nineteenth century began. Stephen Neill writes the following: "It is strange to reflect that the Emperor Napoleon could travel no more speedily than the Emperor Augustus. The most rapid form of motion known to men was that of the galloping horse or camel … The rapidity of communication which set in with the invention of the steam engine and the steamship did more than anything else to make possible the birth of the new world in which we live" (1986, 209). With these inventions, travel reached a level of ease not known since the days of the great Roman roads in the centuries surrounding the life of Christ.

In the last chapter we saw that by the end of the eighteenth century, mission under the leadership of the Roman Catholic Church had entered a period of decline. This was exacerbated by the events of the French Revolution and the subsequent rule of Napoleon, who asserted his own authority and rule over that of the pope. When Napoleon met his defeat at Waterloo in 1815, the Papal States were reestablished, and attention almost immediately returned to the work of mission both through monastic orders and through new emphasis on the laity. As Stephen Neill notes, "All the old Orders gradually reorganized themselves, and took up again their share of missionary labour…. From 1815 onwards, serious attempts were made to interest the laity, and to make ordinary Christians in the world feel that the work of missions was something in which they too were intimately concerned" (1986, 336–37). Neill goes on to say that scholars identify the papacy of Gregory XVI between 1831 and 1846 as the period in which the renewal of Catholic mission was accomplished on a large scale.

In the Eastern Orthodox universe, Muslim domination during the previous millennia shifted the center of this historic church to Moscow, Russia. Russia's politically based efforts at Westernization in the late eighteenth century resulted in a new spirit of openness to other religious practices in Russia and a corresponding decline in mission energy within Russian Orthodox churches. However, the nineteenth century saw a renewal in Orthodox mission endeavor, with successful work in Central Asia, Siberia, Japan, and other places (Neill 1986).

Protestant mission. And though the Protestants were dominant on the scene during this period, they were not the only people God used on mission during this time period. (See the "Catholic and Orthodox Mission" sidebar on this page.)

Much of the thought about the world and the Christian mission that developed more fully in the nineteenth and twentieth centuries will seem familiar to us. Indeed, these centuries have likely made a deep impact on your own worldview. As discussed in the unit on culture, a person's worldview profoundly shapes the way in which that person responds to the environment and to the invitation of God to join His mission. For that reason, as we trace the contours of mission history in era five, we will also examine the ways in which this period shaped our own era. But before we go forward, we need to take a brief step backward to talk about an earlier intellectual movement called the Enlightenment.

The Influence of the Enlightenment

"The modern world has been shaped by the intellectual movement of the seventeenth century known as the Enlightenment," notes historian Wilbert R. Shenk. "No area of life in the West has been exempted from its influence" (1999, 21). He goes on to describe some of the intellectual hallmarks of the movement:

> The universe was conceived to be an orderly machine governed by laws that ensured predictability…. In contrast to the medieval tradition, where authority resided in tradition, the modern outlook took scientific fact to be the source of authority…. Science and technology were indispensable; religion was increasingly consigned to the realm of superstition….
>
> The Enlightenment was possessed of a strong purpose to make the world over in its own image. It infused the Western worldview with a great sense of buoyancy, self-confidence, and optimism. (155)

Enlightenment thinking also included a tremendous faith in the principle of progress: in exploring new lands, discovering and developing new things, moving forward. Another facet was a tremendous faith in the ability of humans—as free and autonomous beings—to solve problems. In terms of progress, Neill notes that a division between East and West came about as a result of the Industrial Revolution, largely with "the application of mechanical power to manufacture…. The acquisition of the new resources, and the breakdown of the old order in the French Revolution, sent Europe out conquering with a new self-confidence, and increasingly, as the century advanced, with a new sense of mission to the world" (1986, 209–10). This larger sense of mission, however, was not Christian mission or even a religious mission; it was a mission of science, reason, and progress.

For perhaps the first time in history, large portions of the world engaged in thinking that in many ways tried to eliminate God's authority. Humankind became the measure of all things. In medieval times and earlier, Nussbaum explains, "nature and society were always defined in relationship to God," but in the wake of the Enlightenment came the development of the natural sciences and then the social sciences, both of which emphasized *careful observation* by a human being … God was not needed to help human beings observe things" (2005, 73). Because science and reason were pursued independently from faith in anything else, human beings became the arbiters of reality through their powers of observation. As Bosch observes, "Religion was assigned to [the] realm of values since it rested on subjective notions and could not be proved correct" (1991, 266). But, he says, "the Enlightenment on the whole did not deny religion a place under the sun.… The Christian faith became just one among several 'religions.' In essence, it was considered to be the same as any other" (268).

Despite this pessimistic-sounding backdrop, we soon see God using the circumstances of this era to bring about one of the most far-reaching and effective periods in mission history. "Of course, Christianity did not disappear after the Enlightenment; on the contrary, it has since spread across the entire globe" (Bosch 1991, 268). Indeed, the nineteenth century marked a time when Christianity finally and fully became a world religion, a result that was by no means a certainty in the year 1800. Christian mission had been severely limited in the Far East by persecution and outright bans. India saw limited success, no real impression had been made on Islamic lands, and Africa saw Christianity confined to coastal areas. Despite so much hand-in-hand exploration and mission work in the previous era, in 1800 "Christianity was still mainly the European's religion" (Neill 1986, 208). Yet not only did modern thinking influenced by the Enlightenment propel scientific and technological progress, but it also emboldened a whole generation of Christians to believe and act on the idea that God could use them to reach the entire world. "The Enlightenment idea of *progress* had a huge impact on mission thinking in the nineteenth and twentieth centuries," notes Nussbaum (2005, 73). Bosch elaborates on this: "Sometimes it manifested itself as the belief that the entire world would soon

Defining Modern

When historians use the term *modern*, they usually do not simply mean something contemporary. *Modern* typically refers to a specific mode of thinking characterized by Enlightenment values of rational thought, scientific superiority, and a belief in progress. In historical terms, this type of thinking began influencing almost all realms of Western thought in the late eighteenth and early nineteenth centuries. It dominated thinking in much of the twentieth century as well. Generally, historians describe the present twenty-first century as belonging to the *postmodern* era, thus indicating that some of the characteristics of modern thinking have shifted.

Discussions on the history of mission follow the same trend. The modern period in mission is generally held to be that of the nineteenth and twentieth centuries.

be converted to the Christian faith; at other times Christianity was regarded as an irresistible power in the process of reforming the world, eradicating poverty, and restoring justice for all" (1991, 271).

Protestant Mission Going Forward

Of course, it would be erroneous to assign mission progress simply to a burst of energy brought about by Enlightenment ideals and belief in progress during this period. This confident attitude about converting the world to Christianity was but one of many ways that God propelled His mission forward. In the last chapter, we mentioned how the First Great Awakening planted seeds that bore fruit in nineteenth-century mission. In the decades on both sides of 1800, we see the Spirit of God at work stirring up the mission passions of Christians in both Europe and North American through events known as the Second Great Awakening in America and a similar movement called the Evangelical Revival in England. "The new mood [of the Second Great Awakening] spawned a missionary spirit. By 1817 the missionary cause had become the great passion of the American churches" (Chaney 1976). "It was not very different in Britain," notes Bosch (1991, 279).

Earlier we noted that several events in the 1790s paved the way for the remarkable spread of Christian mission. These revival periods were certainly much of that catalyst, but within these revivals a specific trigger worth mentioning would be the preaching of William Carey, who is often called (though somewhat erroneously, according to some scholars) the father of Protestant mission. "William Carey was not the first Protestant missionary," writes Ralph D. Winter. Indeed, as we saw in the last chapter, there were several earlier movements of Protestant mission that emerged following the Reformation. But it is accurate to say that William Carey's emphasis on obedience to the Great Commission found in Matthew 28:18–20 was another spark that set Protestants on fire with zeal to participate in Christian mission. As we noted in the last chapter, most theologians prior to Carey considered the Great Commission to have been completed in some form by the apostles. Our contemporary ideas about the mandate of the Great Commission we owe largely to the emphasis on this passage that Carey articulated in his small 1792 book titled *An Enquiry into the Obligations of Christians to Use Means for the Conversion of the Heathens*. Winter calls this book "the Magna Carta of the Protestant mission movement.… [Carey's] little book, in combination with the Evangelical Awakening, quickened vision and changed lives on both sides of the Atlantic" (1999a, 254–55). Bosch points out that "Carey's famous slogan

'Expect great things from God, attempt great things for God!' expressed the prevailing mood well. And it can hardly be doubted that the Enlightenment had reinforced this mood and helped to bring the entire world within reach of the gospel.... Many believed that, through the explorations of [eighteenth-century explorer James] Cook and others (now purely secular and mercantile enterprises and no longer intimately linked to the church and the spreading of the gospel) God in his providence was opening a way for missions also" (1991, 279–80).

The Great Century of Christian Mission

Kenneth Latourette identified the nineteenth century as "The Great Century" of Christian mission (Shenk 1999, 142). The foundation of mission societies and a new mood of voluntarism resulted from Carey's teaching and the revival spirit in Britain and America. Bosch describes mission societies as "individual Christians, frequently belonging to different churches, banded together for the sake of world mission" (1991, 280). The voluntary mission society had a tremendously widespread impact in the nineteenth and twentieth centuries, and "it differed from all previous structures in that it was open in its membership, that lay people were as much

---

Voluntary Mission Society

The first voluntary mission society was the Baptist Missionary Society founded by William Carey in 1792 (Beaver 1999). From this humble beginning sprung a rapidly growing movement—within 25 to 30 years, a dozen or so had formed on both sides of the Atlantic Ocean. "The later years of the nineteenth century," writes Andrew F. Walls, "saw the development of a multitude of new missionary societies" (1996, 252). Over the course of this century, missionary societies engaged in many different facets of mission—educational, agricultural, and medical, among others—that went hand in hand with the work of evangelism and individual conversion. William Carey's outlook on holistic mission was typical of the period: "[Carey's] primary goal was to lead people to personal faith in Jesus Christ and eternal salvation; however he saw no conflict between that goal and his other activities in education, agriculture, and botany. Carey labored widely to withstand social evils and bring change in Asia" (Pierson 1999, 265). R. Pierce Beaver describes some of the ministries at Serampore, India—ministries that influenced much of nineteenth-century mission:

> The Baptist "Serampore Trio" of [William] Carey, [Joshua] Marshman, and [William] Ward was especially influential in the early period. Although Carey sought individual conversions, he wanted to foster the growth of a church that would be independent, well sustained by a literate and Bible-reading laity, and administered and shepherded by an educated native ministry.... At Serampore there were schools for Indians and for foreign children. The vast program of Bible translation and printing ... established the high priority of such work among all Protestants....

> Furthermore, this famous Trio worked for the transformation of society under the impact of the gospel, and they became a mighty force for social reform. (1999, 247)

Alongside evangelistic, educational, and social-reform mission work, the mid-nineteenth century saw the advent of medical mission as a formal means of sharing the gospel. The first doctors sent abroad were primarily there to take care of missionary families, but it was soon realized what a significant form of mission medical ministry could be, and societies devoted to this form of mission emerged.

---

involved as ministers, and that its organization was rooted in a mass membership, who felt responsibility for it and contributed generously to its support" (Walls 1996, 242). (See the "Voluntary Mission Society" sidebar for more details.) These mission societies were formed both inside and outside of denominational structures, but "whether church-related or independent, a missionary society was sustained by individuals committed to world mission" (Shenk 1999, 143).

This type of mission represents a significant shift from the way Christian mission was carried out in the preceding centuries, when monastic orders and "professional" clergymen were by and large the only formal, organized agents of mission—though throughout history God has certainly used the witness of individual men and women sharing their faith. The nineteenth century marks the first time since the early-Church era that individuals felt responsibility to respond to God's invitation to mission on such a wide scale. "The sheer scale of the missionary movement in the nineteenth century finds no precedent in history. Although the Christian church was self-consciously missionary in its first decades, it was largely a spontaneous and organic movement outward. In the nineteenth century formal organization and conscious strategizing became hallmarks of this movement to reach the ends of the earth with the message of Jesus Christ" (Shenk 1999, 144). "The Enlightenment ideal of the emancipated, autonomous individual found its corollary in the autonomous voluntary missionary society" (Thomas 1995, 52). So, though we can no doubt name negative qualities about the individualism of Enlightenment thinking, there is a way in which that emphasis was used by God precisely to restore a passion in individual Christians to live a life of service to Him.

Reaching Inland

The mid-nineteenth century witnessed another major change in Protestant mission—a change that was to have a lasting impact to the present day in terms of understanding the nature and scope of God's desire for mission. Up to this point, the majority of mission had penetrated only the coastlands of larger nations. Ralph D. Winter writes about an Englishman named Hudson Taylor, who in 1865 raised the question of taking the gospel to the inland peoples of China. Taylor was initially opposed by people who told him there was no way to get there and who asked him if he would be willing to bear responsibility for the blood of those who would surely perish in the effort. "This accusing question stunned and staggered him. Groping for light, wandering on the beach, it seemed as if God finally spoke to resolve the ghastly thought: 'You

Women in Mission

Another feature of nineteenth-century mission that marks a change from the previous eras is the inclusion of previously marginalized or oppressed groups of people, such as women. In many cultures, men could not have contact with most women; thus, as R. Pierce Beaver notes, "realistic strategy demanded that adequate provision be made for [ministry to] women and children, but the [mission] boards and societies were stubbornly resistant to sending single women abroad for such work. Finally in desperation the women in the 1860s began organizing their own societies and sent forth single women. A whole new dimension was thus added to mission strategy: the vast enterprise to reach women and children with the gospel, to educate girls, and to bring adequate medical care to women" (1999, 250). Winter describes the advent of women's missionary prayer groups and mission societies as "a trend which led to women becoming the main custodians of mission knowledge and motivation" (1999a, 255). "By 1900, over forty denominational women's societies existed, with three million active women, some despite sustained hostility from the men of the church" (Hill 1985). "Publicizing projects through their mission magazines, women in local church auxiliaries nickeled and dimed their way into building hospitals and schools around the world, paying the salaries of indigenous female evangelists, and sending single women as missionary doctors, teachers, and evangelists" (Robert 1996, 129).

are not sending young people [into] the interior of China. I am.' The load lifted." With this confirmation, Taylor founded the China Inland Mission, a faith mission that depended solely on prayer for the provision of its needs and ultimately supported more than six thousand missionaries working in China's interior. The faith mission became a model for many future mission societies. At the time Taylor founded his organization, "all existing agencies were confined to the coastlands of Africa and Asia, or islands in the Pacific," notes Winter, who also records that "it took 20 years for other missions to begin to join Taylor in his special emphasis—the unreached, inland frontiers" (1999a, 257). Despite initial hesitancy toward this type of challenging pioneer work, the emphasis on unreached frontiers continues to this day, and we will examine it more thoroughly later in this chapter.

In support of this type of mission to the unreached, inland frontiers, "God brought forth a student movement ... the Student Volunteer Movement for Foreign Missions, history's single most potent mission organization" (Winter 1999a, 258). This movement, officially organized in the late 1880s, had as its slogan "The evangelization of the world in this generation" (Nussbaum 2005, 82). It was an outgrowth of events that can be traced back to an event called the Haystack Prayer Meeting at Williams College in 1806. Between the founding of the movement in the early 1800s and its waning in the 1940s, it is estimated conservatively that more than twenty thousand students had reached the mission field, and those students had thousands more students committed to supporting their efforts (Howard 1979; Winter 1999a). The Student Volunteer Movement was exemplary of the tremendous optimism and fervor that God was bringing about in the years between 1890 and 1914. "Enlightenment belief in progress and confidence that every problem can be solved found its missionary spokesperson in John R. Mott who, amid the general euphoria in 1900, wrote that 'there is no insuperable obstacle to world-wide evangelization' " (Thomas 1995, 52; format changed). Throughout the nineteenth century and up until the First World War, a strong belief in the imminent conversion of the world had emerged among mission-minded Christians. Perhaps the apex of this fervor was the 1910 Edinburgh World Missionary Conference, chaired by Mott. The ecumenical gathering of more than twelve hundred delegates from mission societies in North America, Europe, South Africa, and Australia "represented the all-time highwater mark in Western missionary enthusiasm" (Bosch 1991, 338). As Nussbaum notes, the conference assumed that "the final victory of Christian mission was just around the corner. There were more missionaries in more places reporting more success stories than ever before" (2005, 82). However, the advent of World War I a few years later virtually shattered this optimism.

The spirit of optimism and passion for mission that marked the Edinburgh conference of 1910 was quickly dampened by the realities of war and global conflict in the form of the two world wars. That is not to say that mission completely disappeared from the landscape, but World War I took a major toll on optimism, especially "as 'Christian' nations fought each other to the death. Optimism about mission evaporated" (Nussbaum 2005, 82). Three decades later, World War II significantly redrew the balance of Western domination both in world affairs and in mission. These years mark a time of transition for the geopolitical balance of the world as well as for Christian mission. But before we examine how God brought His work forward through the twentieth century, let's cast an evaluative look over one facet of the nineteenth century.

Colonialism and Imperialism

The darker side of this faith, along with confidence in progress and expansion (the influence of Enlightenment thinking), can be seen in the colonialism, the imperialism, and the mission progress that marked the nineteenth century. "Where European powers expanded their colonies in the eighteenth and nineteenth centuries, missionaries of those nations were not far behind. Almost always these missionaries became advocates for colonial expansion.... David Livingstone advocated an alliance for 'commerce, civilization and Christianity.' This became a common motive for mission among British Protestants in the colonial era" (Thomas 1995, 51). Colonization was an outgrowth of Enlightenment sensibilities and Western ethnocentrism; it was also an economic and political agenda founded on the previous era of exploration and expansion. Because the thinking of the time considered non-Western cultures in need of "civilizing," a pattern of cultural superiority took hold in Christian mission and in political, economic, and educational enterprises. In the minds of some, Christian mission is a guilty partner to the ills of the colonial mind-set. And the charge is not without some merit. Beaver writes the following:

> Even in countries with a high culture, such as India and China, European missionaries stressed the "civilizing" objective as much as their brethren in primitive regions because they regarded the local culture as degenerate and superstitious—a barrier to Christianization....
>
> With regard to the other religions, mission strategy was aggressive, seeking their displacement and total conversion of the peoples. This

aggressive spirit declined towards the end of the century, and something of an appreciation of the work of God in the other faiths grew slowly until by 1910 many regarded them as "broken lights" which were to be made whole in Christ and as bridges to the gospel. (1999, 247, 250)

From our vantage point today, we can readily critique the imperial/colonial mind-set. Neill summarizes it for us: "Whether we like it or not, it is the historic fact that the great expansion of Christianity coincided in time with the world-wide and explosive expansion of Europe that followed on the Renaissance;… and that in the main, Christianity was carried forward on the wave of Western prestige and power" (1986, 414). But as we have seen in several previous eras, God sovereignly works through a variety of circumstances—pleasant or not—to carry His plans forward. To be fair to the men and women God used in the nineteenth century, not all was dark and damaging. A genuine desire to improve the lives and fortunes of those being evangelized resulted in medical missions, agricultural and economic assistance, and educational programs that ranged from elementary to higher education. At the dawn of the twentieth century, God had taken His mission to virtually every geographical portion of the world, though there were still many people yet unreached.

At the dawn of the twentieth century, God had taken His mission to virtually every geographical portion of the world, though there were still many people yet unreached.

Twentieth Century

The twentieth century was a century of transition for the world. At the opening of the century in 1900, the automobile was still not in widespread use, and human speech had just been transmitted by radio waves for the first time. By 2000, jet travel was available virtually worldwide, and instant global communication was possible via the Internet. Geopolitically, the twentieth century marked a time of increasing nationalism, and the dominance of Europe and North America as colonial powers was waning—all as a result of two world wars and independence movements around the globe, among other factors. The mid-twentieth century saw a rapid shift in the world balance of power. As Winter notes, "By 1945, Europeans had achieved virtual control over 99.5% of the non-Western world.… Twenty-five years later, the Western nations had lost control over all but 5% of the non-Western population of the world" (1999b, 210). The rapid changes going on in the world certainly meant a time of transition and change for Christian mission as well.

Changing Worldview of Human Beings

Era Three
600–1500
Medieval Cosmology

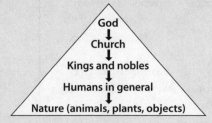

Notice that humans in general were under the authority of three layers, yet nature was considered below humans.

Era Four
1500–1800
Renaissance and Reformation Cosmology

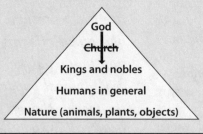

Events of this era, particularly the Reformation, diminished the authority of the church over humans.

Era Five
1800–2000
Age of Revolution
(late 18th century)

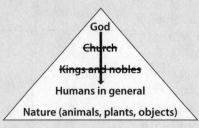

Events such as the American and French revolutions diminished the authority of kings and nobles over humans.

Era Five
1800–2000
Age of Science
(17th century and following)

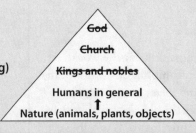

Events such as the Industrial Revolution, as well as scientific and technological advances, gradually eliminated God from general cosmology, and nature was seen as self-validating. Humans were validated because they were a part of nature.

Adapted from a diagram in Stan Nussbaum's *A Reader's Guide to "Transforming Mission"* (2005, 70).

Throughout time, one can trace the movement of Western thought from the medieval outlook to the modern outlook. Events such as the Reformation and the Renaissance began to take the church out of its place in the order; the Age of Revolution (primarily the American and French revolutions) removed the kings and nobles from this equation, so that "the ordinary people now saw themselves as being, in some measure, related to God directly, no longer by way of king or nobility and church" (Bosch 1991, 263). Here are early stirrings of democracy. The Age of Science largely eliminated God from society's validation structure—this would more fully develop toward the turn of the twentieth century. "Two scientific approaches characterized the Enlightenment tradition: the Empiricism of Bacon ... and the Rationalism of Descartes ... Both these approaches operated on the premise that human reason had a certain degree of autonomy. However, neither Bacon nor Descartes saw their theories on scientific progress as in any sense jeopardizing the Christian faith. Bacon, in particular, operated completely within the Puritan paradigm and presumed a complete harmony between science and the Christian faith. Still, in the period following their pioneering work, science was increasingly regarded as being in opposition to faith" (263–64).

As nationalism expanded and the world was becoming a different place, "the mind and temper of the Christian Churches was becoming afflicted by a new kind of uncertainty" (Neill 1986, 417). This uncertainty evidenced itself in a growing critique of colonialism and its relationship to Christian mission, and in divisions between liberal and conservative theological thinking. "Western man had learned how much there was in his colonial record of which he had to be ashamed. He was much less sure than he had been of the uniqueness and finality of the Christian Gospel" (419). And this uncertainty at times meant that a Western focus on global mission, which had been so enthusiastically and confidently embraced in 1910 at Edinburgh, became harder to sustain. Andrew Walls describes the twentieth century as a time of "substantial *recession* from the Christian faith among the European peoples" (1996, 21), leading many to label Europe and North America as "post-Christian" by the latter half of the twentieth century. But as Ralph D. Winter and David A. Fraser note, "at no time in the 20th century was the grass-roots Christian movement ever extinguished" (1999, 354).

In the twentieth century, one of the prominent themes of global mission work was frontier mission to unreached people groups.

Indeed, despite some waning of mission enthusiasm in the West during certain decades, there was a core of ongoing work. In the twentieth century, one of the prominent themes of global mission work was frontier mission to unreached people groups, rooted in the earlier work of various individuals, such as Hudson Taylor with the China Inland Mission. In 1934, God used the work of two men to spark new life into this frontier of Christian mission. Cameron Townsend in Guatemala was engaged in translation work that emphasized linguistic groups. He had been challenged by the question of a Guatemalan Indian: "If your God is so smart, why can't he speak our language?" At the same time Donald McGavran, working in India, was beginning to recognize the challenges of India's social barriers. McGavran recognized the power of "homogeneous units," which we would now call "people groups" (Winter 1999a, 260). Although it would take several decades for the strategic-mission thinking of these men to be widely noticed, the focus of global missions by the 1950s was becoming more attuned to the forgotten peoples of the world. From this emphasis emerged tribal mission work such as that undertaken by Jim Elliot, Nate Saint, Ed McCully, Peter Fleming, and Roger Youderian—five men who were martyred in Ecuador in 1956. The story of their martyrdom stirred a renewal in mission commitment, particularly among young people in the United States.

At the same time, a shift in the locus of mission was occurring. We noted that Christianity was largely centered in Europe and North America at the beginning of the nineteenth century; Western nations served as the primary sending force for foreign mission. But over the course of the twentieth century, Christian mission has become decentralized from its centuries-old Northern Hemisphere home base. Walls writes of this as a "massive movement towards Christian faith in all the southern continents—sub-Saharan Africa, Latin America, certain parts of Asia, the Pacific Islands—which means that Christian profession in the southern continents now outnumbers that in the northern" (1996, 68). It is in this fact—the southward shift of Christianity globally—that we find fruit borne from the previous centuries' mission work that God led steadily outward from its home in the Mediterranean basin and moving through Europe and around the globe. Latin American theologian Samuel Escobar describes the new locus of mission as "the gospel from everywhere to everyone," the subtitle of his book *The New Global Mission* (Downers Grove, IL: InterVarsity Press, 2003). The emergence of new points of global leadership in Christian mission is reflected in the global mission conferences of the latter quarter of the twentieth century—conferences that are the grandchildren of the 1910 World Missionary Conference in Edinburgh. Key among them was the 1974 International Congress on World Evangelization in Lausanne, Switzerland, where more than twenty-three hundred evangelical leaders from 150 countries met.[1] A host of other global mission conferences were held in the final decades of the twentieth century, each with delegates from around the globe representing mission agencies from both the Northern and Southern hemispheres as well as from Protestantism, Catholicism, and Orthodoxy.

> *God is moving His people in a paradigm shift that is, in reference to the last era, quite new. But in reference to the larger, longer story of God's mission, the situation in which we find ourselves may really be a very old one.*

Perhaps the contours of God's mission in the twentieth century can best be summed up in the words of Andrew Walls:

> The high hopes once entertained of the evangelization of the world in one generation had by [1920] drained away into the trenches of the First World War. But we can see now that it was enough. The seeds of Christian faith had been planted in the Southern continents; before long they could be seen to be fruiting abundantly. All the world Empires, except the Russian, have now passed away; the European hegemony of the world is broken; the recession of Christianity among

the European peoples appears to be continuing. And yet we seem to stand at the threshold of a new age of Christianity. (1996, 21–22)

Indeed, many recognize our present day to be one in which God is moving His people in a paradigm shift that is, in reference to the last era, quite new. But in reference to the larger, longer story of God's mission, the situation in which we find ourselves may really be a very old one. At the dawn of the twenty-first century, the Christian cultural context has shifted, much as it had in the closing years of the first century, when crossing cultural boundaries ensured the very survival of the Christian faith. We will turn to some of these themes in the next chapter, which will focus on the present and future mission God invites us to be a part of.

❧

NOTE

1. Lausanne Movement, http://www.lausanne.org.

In what ways can you see the influence of Enlightenment ideas in your own thinking about the world? How does this affect your concept of Christian life? of truth? of God?

Review: The Ultimate Completion of God's Purpose

Christian history reveals the faith often withering in its heartlands, in its centers of seeming strength and importance, to establish itself or begin its margins. It has vulnerability, a certain fragility, at its heart—the vulnerability of the cross, the fragility of the earthen vessel.
—*Andrew F. Walls*

But we have this treasure in jars of clay to show that this all-surpassing power is from God and not from us.   —*2 Corinthians 4:7*

As we journeyed through two thousand years of the history of mission in this unit, it may have seemed messy, and it may have appeared at times that God was not working. The messy part is real, but the part about God not working couldn't be further from the truth. Cycles of human success and failure in participating in God's mission have continued throughout history. At no point in time, however, has the mission of God been in jeopardy. None of the events of the past have been surprising to God, nor have they been beyond His use in fulfilling His mission.

God initiates and advances His purpose throughout human history.

Indeed, the manner in which people have failed and succeeded in participating in God's mission seems to have swung from high points to low points throughout recorded time, beginning in the days of Israel, as again and again the Old Testament documents times of apostasy and rebellion followed by times of obedience and service to God. These cycles of high and low run throughout—from the story of Israel's deliverance from Egypt to the conquest of the Promised Land, through the time of the Judges to the period of the divided kingdom, and into Israel's periods of captivity and exile. In each period, God's purpose was going forward, but faithful

What Difference Does It Make?

- What do you think the story of others' participation in God's purpose throughout time can teach you about your own journey with God?

- Do you perceive God as being a present-day actor in the events of today? Why or why not?

human participation swung from hot to cold throughout. Even at the moment in history when Jesus Christ—God Himself—arrived in the flesh, there were many who failed to see Him as Messiah. Certainly there were those who accepted Jesus' invitation to mission wholeheartedly, as the New Testament reveals. But others, failing to recognize the amazing opportunity of redemption at hand, rejected this invitation. And yet, a certain truth of the Bible, borne out by history, is that God works through even our failures in order to accomplish His purpose and mission. As 2 Corinthians 4:7 reminds us, God is the source of power. He is the one who initiates and advances His purpose—His mission—throughout human history. Even though He invites us to participate in His purpose, without a doubt He is still sovereign. And God's redemptive purpose will come to an ultimate completion in human history.

History reveals the challenges, successes, and shortcomings that people throughout history have experienced as they have participated with God in completing His purpose.

In this chapter, we continue to examine the overarching story of God's mission going forward through time as we keep our gaze firmly fixed on the assurance we have of the ultimate completion of God's redemptive purpose. In the previous five chapters, we have looked in some detail at how people have participated in God's mission during specific historic eras and circumstances. In sifting through the details of history, we must not lose sight of what God's purpose is. In chapter 2, we stated that God's purpose is relationship, redemption, and reconciliation. The mission of God is to complete His purpose—to bring about a restored relationship with His creation through the process of redemption and reconciliation. Yet, we also discussed that Christians have often lost sight of this mission. Even today, we often struggle with maintaining a focus on the mission of God and on the invitation He has given us to join Him.

Remember "The Parable of the Race" (McLaren and Campolo 2003, 26–27) from chapter 3? Sometimes we are tempted to be like those racers who were rejoicing just to have made it over the starting line, and we fail to realize that there is more to our journey with God than just meeting Him. Perhaps this limited viewpoint is a result of having grown up with Enlightenment-influenced thinking about individualism. Our culture's prevailing emphasis on the individual makes it challenging to see other people and community as significant or even noteworthy. Relationship to God *and to others*

What Difference Does It Make?

- Do you believe that God continues to work through people as He did in the Bible to accomplish His plans? If not, then why not? Do you see Him directly initiating and advancing His purpose in the world around you? If so, in what ways?

- One extreme that is related to the invitation God gives to join His mission is to ignore the invitation; another extreme is to run ahead of God and "do things for Him" without His leading or equipping. Do you tend toward one of these extremes in your relationship with Him? What are some examples?

- What roles do faith and doubt play in your own understanding of how God is at work in your life and in the world around you? Like Abraham, do you ever feel as though you need to "help God out" with His plans? Do you find it difficult to wait on God's timing and leading in your life?

is the center of the gospel and the center of God's concern, according to Jesus. When asked by the Pharisees what the greatest commandment is, Jesus said to them, " 'Love the Lord your God with all your heart and with all your soul and with all your mind.' This is the first and greatest commandment. And the second is like it: 'Love your neighbor as yourself.' All the Law and the Prophets hang on these two commandments" (Matthew 22:37–40). Love God. Love your neighbor. Everything that God has revealed is based on this, Jesus told them. This has been God's purpose for us from the beginning, and things have not changed in thousands of years of history. Nor will they change before God's mission comes to completion in human history. God speaks of this in Isaiah 46:9–11:

> Remember the former things, those of long ago; I am God, and there is no other; I am God, and there is none like me. I make known the end from the beginning, from ancient times, what is still to come. I say: My purpose will stand, and I will do all that I please. From the east I summon a bird of prey; from a far-off land, a man to fulfill my purpose. What I have said, that will I bring about; what I have planned, that will I do.

God's redemptive purpose will come to an ultimate completion in human history.

Psalm 33:11 also reminds us of this truth: "But the plans of the Lord stand firm forever, the purposes of his heart through all generations." What are these plans—these reflections of God's heart—that stand through all generations? We know from the story about God that is told in the Bible that His purpose—His mission—is to redeem and restore His creation to unbroken relationship with Himself. Unbroken relationship and intimate fellowship with God the Father, God the Son, and God the Holy Spirit is the ultimate fulfillment of God's mission. What we are talking about here is the fulfillment of the "now and not yet" aspect of the kingdom of God. It is the announcement pictured in Revelation 11:15: "The seventh angel sounded his trumpet, and there were loud voices in heaven, which said: 'The kingdom of the world has become the kingdom of our Lord and of his Christ, and he will reign for ever and ever.' " This is the ultimate completion of God's redemptive mission in history. Richard J. Mouw, writing about this in *When the Kings Come Marching In*, reminds us of God's delight in people from every tribe, tongue, and nation:

> "Red and yellow, black and white, they are precious in his sight." These words from the children's song express a profound biblical truth. God's redeeming love reaches out to people from all tribes and

What Difference Does It Make?

- What difference does it make to you personally to know that God's purpose will be fulfilled? Are you willing to commit yourself to God's purpose even if you won't see it completed in your lifetime?

- What does the past have to teach us about the future in terms of the mission of God? What does it have to say to us about His faithfulness?

nations. God was not satisfied to limit his covenant promises to the Hebrew people; he has called many nations to come and dwell in his City. And this has been his plan even from ancient times, when he said to his prophet: "It is too light a thing that you should be my servant to raise up the tribes of Jacob and to restore the preserved of Israel; I will give you as a light to the nations, that my salvation may reach to the end of the earth" (Isaiah 49:6). (2002, 83–84)

Indeed, God's redemptive purpose will come to an ultimate completion in human history.

A Look Back: Emerging Themes

1 God invites people to participate.

Several themes have emerged from our study of over two thousand years of history. These themes are important not only because they say something to us about the continuity of God's mission throughout history, but also because they give us an indication of

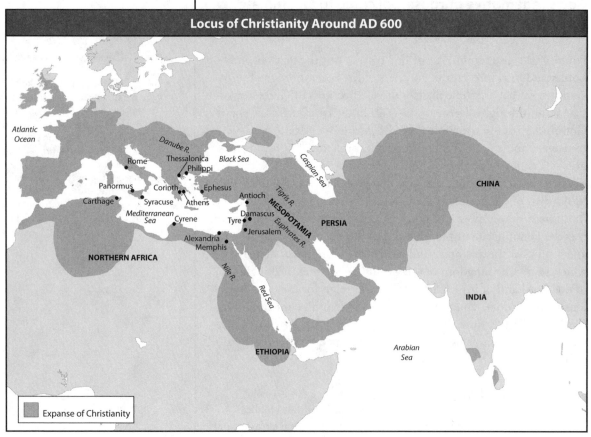

Locus of Christianity Around AD 600

Map by Global Mapping International.

how God will continue to work in the future as He brings His mission to fulfillment. As we have already mentioned, an inescapable theme of mission history is that God uses people to participate in His mission. We have seen throughout history a variety of methods that people have used to share the love of Jesus with others. These range from formal monastic orders to the institutionalized movements of mission (whether through a church or through voluntary mission societies), to slaves in captivity bringing Christianity to a new land, to the simple passions of individual believers sharing Christ in the interactions of their daily lives. Mission participation has ranged from accidental to programmed in a thousand different contexts and with numerous strategies over the past two thousand years. Yet at the heart of it all, we find people who have willingly yielded their lives to God's invitation. Successful mission has always had at its foundation a surrendering to the leadership and strategy of God. Our relationship with Him is the basis for any mission endeavor, for it is His purpose, not ours, that is going to be fulfilled. Participation in missio Dei has always been, and will continue to be, dependent on the participants' recognition that God is the one who is giving the instructions, providing the tools, and sustaining the work.

2 God shapes history regardless of circumstances.

Another theme we discussed earlier is that God has been at work throughout history regardless of the circumstances of that age. He works through the circumstances of a particular era and shapes them into use for furthering His mission. In the years following Christ's resurrection, there was a confluence of many favorable circumstances that helped the story of Jesus travel across many miles within just a few decades. Jerusalem was at the intersection of many cultures, and the great network of Roman Empire roads led to even more lands where a common merchant language made communication much easier than during later times. In the following two hundred years, the fact that Christianity was an outlawed religion didn't stop its growth, and even the torture and martyrdom of believers propelled God's mission further still. The fourth-century conversion to Christianity of not only Emperor Constantine but, in effect, the entire Roman Empire brought both formal recognition and benefits to the growing Christian movement. But we also witnessed how this entwining of matters of faith with matters of state presented challenges. Even so, by the year 600, the land extending as far as the Atlantic Ocean to the west, the Tigris and Euphrates rivers to the east, the Danube to the north, and the Mediterranean basin of North Africa to the south had a population that was predominantly Christian. Christianity also had centers of worship to the east in Mesopotamia, Persia, and India, and as far south as Ethiopia (SE p. 195).

Throughout the Middle Ages, instability and war marked the life of many people. Against the backdrop of barbarian invasions and the advance of Islam, Christianity offered a stabilizing influence in society through the uniform practice of liturgy and worship. The chaotic centuries of instability, war, and captivity offered many believers the challenge of being exiled to new lands, yet they took their faith with them. The development of monasticism in this time period further spread the gospel to new areas. By the year 1000, Christianity had spread to the north in Slavic and Scandinavian countries, despite attrition in areas such as North Africa and the Middle East. By 1500, Christianity was strengthened in Europe, from where God would launch the next major wave of Christian expansion through the Age of Discovery. The period 1500–1800 saw European powers explore and colonize lands around the globe, creating opportunities for Christians to travel with the gospel to

Locus of Christianity in the Present Day

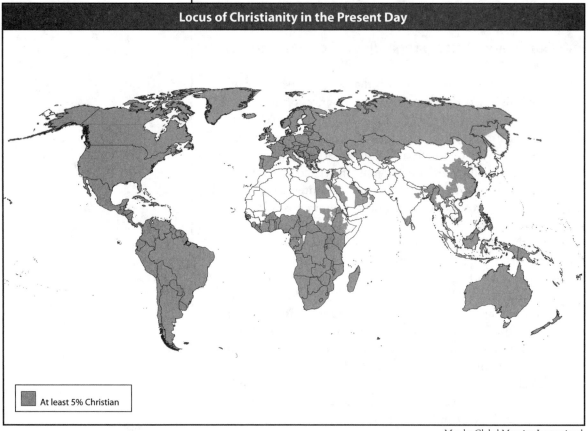

At least 5% Christian

Map by Global Mapping International.

lands that were previously unheard of. The "New World"—North America, South America, parts of Africa, and many parts of the Far East such as China, Japan, and India—had been reached in part through Christian witness by means of sea travel and advancing exploration. And with growing dominance of Western ideas springing from the Industrial Revolution and the Enlightenment, Christian witness could be found around the globe by the twentieth century, though not yet within every tribe, tongue, and nation.

From the record of Christian expansion in the face of seemingly the best and the worst of circumstances over time, we can be sure that God will continue to use people to reach "the uttermost part of the earth" (Acts 1:8, KJV) regardless of the challenges and opportunities of any future age. He is able to work through circumstances even in times when Christianity is a banned and outlawed practice; He is able to work through circumstances when a government favors or embraces Christianity. He can work through times of war and times of peace, through periods marked by deep corruption and periods marked by noble and faithful submission to Him. The testimony of those who have participated in God's mission throughout history, regardless of the circumstances, is surely that of the apostle Paul's in Philippians 4:12–13, in which Paul said, "I know what it is to be in need, and I know what it is to have plenty. I have learned the secret of being content in any and every situation, whether well fed or hungry, whether living in plenty or in want. I can do everything through him who gives me strength."

3 Christ is the center.

Another interesting theme that emerges from a study of two thousand years of mission history is that God isn't interested in establishing a cultural or geographical center for His mission and Christian faith. Instead, He has established Christ as the center. As Stephen Neill notes, "Since AD 70 the Christian Church has never had one local centre; it has learned to look only to the living presence of the Lord within itself" (1986, 21). God has always directed His people back to this truth. In era one, we see the destruction of Jerusalem by Rome in AD 70, an event that forced believers to rely on Jesus as the center of Christian faith rather than to rely on the city of Jerusalem and its body of believers. Even with the official sanction of Christianity by the Roman Empire during era two, we still see more than one "center of leadership" for the church: Rome, Constantinople, Alexandria, and other cities were places with major churches, but believers both inside and outside the Roman Empire were united under Christ's headship rather than under one ecclesiastical governing body. In era three, the geographical locus of Christianity was certainly centered in Europe, since Islam ultimately subdued many of the cities that had previously been Christian centers. But in the coming years, Europe served as a jumping-off point for exploration and mission that literally circled the globe. The Protestant Reformation, too, can be seen as an agent of decentralization because it emphasized individual, personal relationship with God rather than reliance on the mediation of a particular Christian body or Christian leader.

As mission spread around the globe in the nineteenth and twentieth centuries, we also saw the fruit of years of Christian mission to distant places. Today, the largest number of Christians in the world is found in the Southern Hemisphere—in places such as South America and Africa—and in parts of Asia. Increasingly, North America and Europe are being identified as "post-Christian," a label that indicates that these nations have moved away from a predominantly Christian-oriented political or social leadership. Yet this should be no cause for discouragement; it is simply a reminder that our center as believers is never a particular place or earthly power center. Andrew Walls reminds us: "A place which had been a Christian heartland, a shining center of Christian devotion and activity, ceased to have this function; the light burned down or burned out, and the candlestick was taken out of its place. But [this decline did not] mean the disappearance of the Christian faith or the end of Christian witness—rather—the reverse.… The Christian story is serial, its center moves from place to place. No one church or place or culture owns it. At different times, different peoples and places have become its heartlands, its chief representatives. Then the baton passes on to others" (1996, 385). For the Christian, the center of our faith and our life is within Christ, not within the circumstances or the location one is found in. The circumstances of today have a bit in common with the circumstances of the first-century Church, that minority group of "outlaw" believers who turned the world upside down with their obedience to Christ.

4 There is unity within diversity.

Another theme that we can trace throughout the past two thousand years is that of how God, by His continual assertion of the *cultural transcendence of the gospel* and by His emphasis on the theme of *unity within diversity*, over the years has directed His followers back to the truth of Christ as the center. Shenk describes the origins of this as having come at Pentecost, when "a new people, drawn from the nations, whose linguistic particularity is the means for each to hear about 'the mighty acts of God' (Acts 2:6, 11), is called forth. Its unity is expressed neither through culture nor ritual but in worship of the God revealed in Jesus the Messiah (Acts 2:14–36)" (1999, 14).

Throughout the five historical eras, we have seen a variety of people who served as bearers of God's purpose and mission. People participating in God's mission have always come from a variety of ethnic and linguistic backgrounds and have intentionally gone to people and places of ethnic and linguistic backgrounds different from their own. Along the way, a major recognition of the cultural transcendence of the gospel took place, and it resulted in translation of the Bible into the languages of different peoples. "Lamin Sanneh argues that the simple decision to translate the scriptures into local languages was in itself a key concession to native cultures … The mere act of translation proved that no single language was privileged as a vehicle of salvation.… Through the act of translation, too, and the use of familiar local terms and concepts, the scriptures are forced to become relevant to each individual culture" (Jenkins 2002, 113). As we studied history, we noted some examples of introducing the gospel into new languages and cultural contexts. One was the creation of a Gothic alphabet by Ulfilas in the fourth century so that he could translate the Bible into the Gothic language (SE p. 194). Another was present-day recognition of the cultural distinctiveness of different people groups (SE p. 229). The record of history has at times not spoken favorably about Christians' methods or ideas about cross-cultural mission, and the historical record certainly bears out the extreme challenges and complexities of cross-cultural ministry. But God's purpose will be accomplished in this as well.

In the New Testament, the story of the early years of the Church demonstrates this forging of the "unity within diversity" concept for Jewish and Gentile believers in Christ. Paul reminds us in Ephesians 2:17–19 that this unity comes from Christ: "He came and preached peace to you who were far away and peace to those who were near. For through him we both have access to the Father by one Spirit. Consequently, you are no longer foreigners and aliens, but fellow citizens with God's people and members of God's household." To put it another way, we turn to Richard Mouw, who writes the following:

> The God who in ancient times called a specific ethnic people, the tribes of Israel, into a special relationship with himself has begun in

these latter days to establish a "holy race" made up of people from every tribe and tongue and nation. The God of Israel has addressed the Xhosa as "my people" and has called Polish laborers "the works of my hands." Mexicans have become "Abraham's offspring," and Koreans have been named "heirs according to the promise." The Lord has assembled together Scots and Swedes, Iranians and Navajos, and has addressed them, saying: "Once you were no-people, but now you are my people." (2002, 97)

These reminders from both the apostle Paul and Richard Mouw affirm what we have already studied in this unit: We as believers must move beyond ethnocentrism and cultural superiority to participate in the mission of God. In previous chapters we saw strains of ideas greatly influenced by ethnocentrism, such as the belief that a true Christian would have to behave the same as a civilized western European or that indigenous forms of expression and worship would have to be eradicated before a person could be truly Christian. Philip Jenkins notes that when Christianity settled into Europe during the Middle Ages, "European Christians reinterpreted the faith through their own concepts of social and gender relations, and then imagined that their culturally specific synthesis was the only correct version of Christian truth" (2002, 6–7). We may be tempted to judge these attitudes, but we are in no less danger of adopting them than those who came before us. As we have already mentioned in this chapter, the majority of Christians in the world are not in North America and western Europe as they had been for many years. We are living in an era of global Christianity. As the Kenyan Anglican archbishop, Benjamin Nzimbi, says, "The West used to send missionaries to Africa and the third world … But now the third world is sending its missionaries to the West."[1] At the present moment and into the future, we need an understanding of the global nature of Christianity if we are to move beyond our interpretation of a "proper Christian culture" that looks like just a cleaned-up version of our own culture. Shenk reminds us, "Jesus the Messiah invited individuals from all classes and clans to repent and submit their lives to God's rule, creating one new people from among the peoples" (1999, 12). It is important that we are mindful of the lessons and themes of history which show that God doesn't prefer one geographic or political center for His people, that His fingerprint is the creation of unity within diversity, and that the gospel transcends any one specific cultural or temporal form.

Missio Dei Going Forward

What we have been studying in this unit is a picture of how God has continued to invite people to join Him in bringing forward His mission throughout time. Similarly, today God invites each of us to participate in missio Dei—the mission of God. This is the participation in kingdom life that Jesus preached about. The authors of *StormFront* remind us of this:

> Hearing the gospel entails recognizing, entering, and receiving this surprising reign of God, in which God's presence and action intrude mysteriously and unexpectedly into our lives and invite us to participate in something greater than ourselves, greater than what we could accomplish on our own. The announcement of the gospel is an invitation to be caught up in God's surprisingly new way of working in the world, where the poor sit down at rich banquet tables, the sinners and the pious eat together, where old divisions come crashing down, where the sick are healed, demons are cast out, the proud are humbled, fearful hearts are given fresh courage, and the powerful are left on the sidelines. It is this sense of God's reign and God's purposes that has led many [scholars] to speak of the centrality of the missio Dei—*the mission of God*—rather than *our mission for God*. (Brownson et al. 2003, 41; emphasis added)

This is the gospel that so many men and women throughout history have shared with others in different ways, places, and times. History is the story of men and women who participated in this mission even when they didn't see much fruit, who continued in faith that God's purpose will stand and be fulfilled. As Shenk notes, "The reign of God is a mystery we do not grasp fully.… In the end, the kingdom could be apprehended only through eyes of faith" (1999, 10). As we look through eyes of faith, we too are assured of the ultimate completion of God's redemptive purpose.

And that is the final theme that we will highlight from this unit of study—God's mission has gone forward, and it continues to do so. We can see it through the lens of the story of the Bible and through the lens of a historical survey of the past two thousand years, and we can expect to continue seeing it in the coming years. Circumstances and cultural contexts will change. Difficulties and trials, victory and progress—all these will come. Through all of this, God invites us to participate with Him. As participants in God's mission throughout history, human beings have been vessels through which God's love and purpose have been revealed—truly the *jars of clay*

What Difference Does It Make?

- How would you describe the attitude of the culture around you toward the message of the gospel? What means of communicating the love of Christ are most powerful in influencing those around you?

- Where do you see yourself in the ongoing, unfolding story of God's mission in the coming years?

containing unspeakable treasure that Paul describes in 2 Corinthians 4:7. Samuel Escobar echoes this point:

> An overview of the history of missions is a picture of peaks and troughs. In twenty centuries the church has moved from being a sect of Judaism to becoming an immense global family of diverse peoples, cultures and languages who confess Jesus Christ as Savior and Lord.... An honest reading of history shows just how true the words of the apostle Paul [in 2 Corinthians 4:7] are: the glorious treasure of the gospel has indeed been carried by earthly vessels. It will continue to be so because the Holy Spirit, who moves the church to become a missionary body, does not wait until perfect celestial instruments appear. (2003, 53)

As you go forward in your own journey with God, it is important to recognize His fingerprints on the invitation He has given you to join Him.

We can move forward in our own lives as participants in missio Dei with full assurance of the truths that God is in control (as He has always been) and that His purpose will be fulfilled. This is good news for those of us who want to participate but who recognize our own frailties and inadequacies. Fortunately, as Christian author Patsy Clairmont has observed, "God uses cracked pots" (1999). What assurance the above truths should give each of us as we consider in the next unit the shape of God's invitation and as we explore what missional life is all about. Your challenge is to seek the specifics of your own invitation from God. As shown in Ephesians 2:10, He has uniquely gifted you to participate in His mission in a way, place, and time that is specifically for you.

❧

NOTE

1. Associated Press, "U.S. Priests Consecrated in Kenya Say American Church Has Lost Its Way," *Global South Anglican*, August 30, 2007, http://www.global-southanglican.org/index.php/comments/us_priests_consecrated_in_kenya_say_american_church_has_lost_its_way (accessed February 7, 2008).

Practices Unit
unit four

UNIT INTRODUCTION

So, what does it look like to be on mission with God? Where do we pick up now that we understand more about God's story in the Bible, God's love of unity within diversity, and people's ways of participating in the mission of God during previous times? That is the heart of this final unit—practices. What are some ways in which we accept our personal invitations to live missionally with God?

Being on mission with God looks different for different people. In this unit, you won't find a one-size-fits-all label. There aren't any cookie cutters here. Instead, you'll find some general principles and some stories about what being on mission with God can look like and what it has looked like for others. Just as no two people pack exactly the same items in the same way in their backpacks as they prepare for a hike, your life with God will take on additional shades of depth and personal meaning that make it uniquely your own. Think of these chapters as a bundle of basics that you should take along on any journey, basics that are the essential items for the back-pack—including highlights you won't want to miss as you journey on your adventure with God. The topics in this chapter are essential components of participating in missio Dei—the stuff you want to have along in your backpack as you go. Happy travels!

In this unit we'll explore the following Big Ideas:

- Participating in missio Dei requires a personal intimacy with God.
- Participating in missio Dei requires spiritual passion.
- Participating in missio Dei is lived out in the context of community.
- Missio Dei culminates in the gathering of every tribe, tongue, language, and nation around the throne of God.

21

Intimacy with God

The man who enters by the gate is the shepherd of his sheep. The watchman opens the gate for him, and the sheep listen to his voice. He calls his own sheep by name and leads them out. When he has brought out all his own, he goes on ahead of them, and his sheep follow him because they know his voice. —*John 10:2–4*

If you take the time to recognize the threads of God's voice, then words, images, dreams, and scriptures all blend into the mosaic of what he's already said. You begin to recognize God's inferences in the same way you can interpret a slightest glance from the person you know the best. —*Susan D. Hill*

Imagine being able to talk with God about every little detail of your life—hearing His thoughts on the circumstances you are going through, the questions you have, and even the direction you should go in life. Imagine the God who made the whole universe talking to you about what science project to do, where to go to college, who to date, or even where to find the overdue library book you've been searching for.

That idea seems nuts to many people. To others, it sounds more like a big exception than a rule. Maybe you get suspicious or even jealous when you hear people say, "God told me …," as though He were sitting right next to them. Perhaps you think, "God doesn't talk to me like He talks to you." As if people can have a friendship with God, anyway. Maybe you're thinking, "Adam and Eve had that in the Garden, and so did many other Bible characters. But for me … well, that's another story." You may be pretty sure God doesn't care about such things as your next science project, your prom date, or your SAT test, though you may wish that He did. But here's the thing—He does care about those details in your life (along with a lot of other details!). And He wants to walk and talk with you as a close friend would, just as He did with the people we read about in the Bible. That is normal Christian life, the way God intended our relationship with Him to be.

But believing that can be such a struggle. As author Brennan Manning says, some of us "prefer to read the map rather than visit the place" (1996, 20). In other words, we study a lot about God and know lots of facts *about* Him. But we don't actually take the journey of coming to know God the same way we get to know our closest friends or family members. There are plenty of Christians who live that way for years, even a lifetime. There are even a few who believe that God doesn't really speak to His people anymore. Dallas Willard notes, "We can get by in life with a God who does not speak. Many at least think they do. But it is not much of a life, and it is certainly not the life God intends for us or the *abundance* of life that Jesus Christ came to make available" (1999, 186). The fact is, God's story—the story of the Bible—is a story of relationship. And it's not just a cold, dead, "in name only" relationship, but it's a living relationship of intimacy and trust. If we are to join God on His mission, we need not only to *understand* this, but to *live* it. Participating in missio Dei requires a personal intimacy with God.

Participating in missio Dei requires a personal intimacy with God.

What Difference Does It Make?

- Do you believe that God is really concerned and interested in the day-to-day decisions and events of your life? Why or why not?

- If you could hear God's perspective on your circumstances, feelings, and decisions, how would that change the way you make decisions? Would you want that kind of relationship? Why or why not?

- How would a conversational relationship with God affect your participation with Him in the work He is doing to fulfill His purpose?

Pastor and author John Ortberg notes that this kind of intimacy is *the* story of the Bible: "The central promise in the Bible is not 'I will forgive you,' although of course that promise is there. It is not the promise of life after death, although we are offered that as well. The most frequent promise in the Bible is 'I will be *with* you' " (2005, 16). You may recall from chapter 2 that the mission of God is His purpose of relationship, redemption, and reconciliation. But as that chapter asks on SE p. 45, if you don't speak to one another or spend time together, do you really have much of a relationship? Sadly, too many people settle for a life of having an underdeveloped relationship with God. As author Susan D. Hill observes, "If Christianity is a story about restoring *relationship* with God, there must be more to it" (2008, 4), more than head knowledge alone, more than reading the map and not visiting the place.

So, what is that "more" we're talking about? We need to have a DTR (define the relationship) conversation. What do we mean by personal intimacy? We're going to look at it several ways. Let's start by defining some terms. The *Merriam-Webster Online Dictionary* defines *intimacy* as "the state of being intimate"[1] and *intimate* as "characterizing one's deepest nature"; "marked by very close associa-

By permission. From the *Merriam-Webster Online Dictionary* ©2008 by Merriam-Webster, Incorporated (www.Merriam-Webster.com).

tion, contact, or familiarity"; and "marked by a warm friendship developing through long association."[2] But if a simple dictionary definition isn't enough for you, let's look at the Bible's picture of intimacy with God.

As we have already mentioned, the Bible is full of God's promise to be with us. We see it in both the Old and New Testaments. In the beginning God was with Adam and Eve. Later we see Him with Abraham, Isaac, Jacob, Moses, and many others. God told Joshua that He would be with him when the Israelites entered the Promised Land (Joshua 1:9). Through the prophet Isaiah, God promised to be with the Israelites when they experienced trials (Isaiah 43:2). Through the Incarnation, Jesus Himself came to be with us-the "God with us" Immanuel, as foretold in Isaiah 7:14 (see also Matthew 1:23). Jesus promised to be with us to the end of the age (Matthew 28:20). He promised that the Holy Spirit would be with us forever and live in us (John 14:16–17). And the Bible's picture of the new Jerusalem in Revelation 21:3 promises the following: "Now the dwelling of God is with men, and he will live with them."

"We can get by in life with a God who does not speak. Many at least think they do. But it is not much of a life, and it is certainly not the life God intends for us or the abundance of life that Jesus Christ came to make available."

We also see in the Bible different pictures of that intimacy—the "being with" that is such a continuous promise of God's story. Jesus speaks of His followers not as servants, but as His friends (John 15:15). Jesus also says, "If anyone loves me, he will obey my teaching. My Father will love him, and we will come to him and *make our home with him*" (John 14:23, emphasis added). To paint this picture of intimacy another way, Paul speaks in Ephesians 1:5 of adoption as sons through Jesus Christ. In Galatians 4:6, he explains further: "Because you are sons, God sent the Spirit of his Son into our hearts, the Spirit who calls out, '*Abba*, Father.' " Brennan Manning and Jim Hancock write that "*Abba* is a rather intimate Aramaic word for *father*, roughly equivalent to the English words *daddy* or *papa*" (2003, 8). Do you begin to get what this idea of intimacy is all about? Friendship. Living as a beloved child. Having the God of the universe make His home with you. According to the Bible, there is a lot more to knowing God than just knowing *about* Him. It seems to be expected that we will relate intimately with God.

So far, we have defined the relationship as something that is as close as friendship or family and that involves God's presence. But while we're on the subject of DTR, let's look at a little wordplay that paints another dimension of the picture of intimacy. In the following, John Ortberg redefines DTR as a spiritual DTR—not just about "defining the relationship," but also about "the Dust of The Rabbi":

> " 'May you always be covered by the dust of your rabbi.' That is, 'May you follow him so closely that the dust his feet kicks up is what cakes your clothing and lines your face.' "

Biblical scholar Ray van der Laan notes that the first-century Jews had a blessing that beautifully expresses the commitment of a disciple to stay in the presence of the one he followed: "May you always be covered by the dust of your rabbi." That is, "May you follow him so closely that the dust his feet kicks up is what cakes your clothing and lines your face." …

So let the letters D.T.R. take on one more meaning: "Dust of The Rabbi." That represents how Jesus invites us to define the relationship: to intend to live so much in his presence that we are dusty disciples. (2005, 54)

So there you have it, several different angles on defining the relationship—all that paint a picture of the intimacy that is normal and expected in Christian life. From the perspective of God, the expectation of intimacy hasn't changed since the beginning of His story. And why would that picture change? As Susan Hill says, "Living in a different time, under different circumstances, shouldn't exclude me from that sort of relationship" (2008, 4). Even though in light of our present-day experiences it might be tempting to conclude that God doesn't speak to us, the Bible is filled with stories that show otherwise. John Eldredge speaks about this in *Walking with God*:

> Now, if God doesn't *also* speak to us, why would he have given us all these stories of him speaking to others? "Look—here are hundreds of inspiring and hopeful stories about how God spoke to his people in this and that situation. Isn't it amazing? But you can't have that. He doesn't speak like that anymore." That makes no sense at all. Why would God give you a book of exceptions? *This is how I used to relate to my people, but I don't do that anymore.* What good would a book of exceptions do you? That's like giving you the owner's manual for a Dodge even though you drive a Mitsubishi. No, the Bible is a book of *examples* of what it looks like to walk with God. (2008, 14–15)

God speaks. This isn't just something that happened for people who lived in Bible days. God speaks today. Pastor Charles Stanley writes about this in his book *How to Listen to God*: "We might ask, 'Why would God still want to talk to us today? Hasn't He said enough from Genesis to Revelation?' " Stanley notes four reasons God speaks today. First, "[*God*] *loves us just as much as He loved the people of the Old and New Testament.*" Second, "*we need His definite*

God Speaks

In *Hearing God's Voice*, Henry and Richard Blackaby have written a chapter titled "For the Record: God Speaks," in which they detail the numerous ways God speaks, as recorded in the Bible. The following list and sample biblical references are drawn from their book. As the authors point out, however, this list is not exhaustive: "No doubt God spoke in countless other ways as well, ways we do not read about in the Scriptures. Obviously the key is not how God spoke. God steadfastly refused to limit himself to only one way of communicating" (2002, 38).

God speaks through ...	
creation	Genesis 9:11–17; Psalm 19:1–2; Romans 1:18–20
angels serving as messengers from God	Genesis 16:7, 19:1–13; Daniel 9:20–23; Matthew 1:24, 2:13; John 20:12; Acts 5:19, 8:26, 10:30–33
prophets relaying God's messages to people	Deuteronomy 18:18–22; 2 Samuel 24:10–12; 1 Kings 12:22–24; Acts 11:28, 21:10–11
dreams	Genesis 37:5–11; Daniel 2:1–45; Matthew 2:12–13
visions (similar to dreams, but the recipient is awake)	Ezekiel 1, 8–10, 37, 40, 43; Daniel 7–12; Acts 9:10–12, 10:9–17, 18:9–10
lot-casting	Leviticus 16:8; Numbers 34:13; Proverbs 16:33; Acts 1:23–26
Urim and Thummin (special objects used by priests in the Old Testament)	Numbers 27:21; Nehemiah 7:65
a gentle voice	1 Samuel 3:4; 1 Kings 19:11–14
fire	Deuteronomy 4:33, 36; Judges 6:17–21; 2 Chronicles 7:1–2
a burning bush	Exodus 3:1–4
preaching	Jonah 3:4–10; Romans 10:14–15; 1 Thessalonians 2:13
judgments (to communicate God's offense at sin)	2 Chronicles 6:24–31, 7:13–14; Amos 4:6–12
symbolic actions (often enacted by prophets)	Isaiah 20; Jeremiah 32:6–15; Hosea 1:2
signs, wonders, and miracles	Exodus 4:1–8, 7:8–11:10; Joshua 4:1–24; Isaiah 7:3; Matthew 11:20–24; John 20:30–31
a writing on the wall	Daniel 5
a donkey	Numbers 22:21–35
trumpet blasts	Exodus 19:16, 19; Jeremiah 4:5, 6:1; Joel 2:1, 15
thunder, lightning, smoke, and storms	Exodus 19:16, 20:18; 1 Samuel 12:17–18; Job 40:6
a fleece	Judges 6:36–40
the sound of marching in the treetops	2 Samuel 5:22–25; 1 Chronicles 14:14–17
personal guidance	Nehemiah 2:12, 7:5; Jeremiah 31:31–34; Ezekiel 3:3–4, 10
the risen Christ	Luke 24:13–35; John 20:14–18, 24–29; Acts 9:3–5; Revelation 1:9–16
prayer (often seen as a two-way conversation between God and man)	Acts 22:17–21
Scriptures	Matthew 4:4, 7, 10; Luke 24:27, 45; Acts 1:20, 2:16–21, 7:2–53
the Church	Acts 4:31; 1 Corinthians 12
a direct word from the Father	Matthew 16:17; Luke 3:22, 9:33, 35
the Holy Spirit	Matthew 10:19–20; John 14:26, 16:7–8, 13; Acts 8:29; Romans 8:26; 1 Corinthians 2:9–16
various unspecified ways	Genesis 8:15, 12:1; Exodus 24:12; Joshua 7:10; 1 Samuel 16:1; Zephaniah 1:1; Acts 16:6

Chart adapted from *Hearing God's Voice* by Henry and Richard Blackaby (Nashville, TN: B&H Publishing, 2002), 22–38.

and deliberate direction for our lives" as much as they did. Third, "*we need [His] comfort and assurance*" just as much as they did. Finally, "*the most important reason God is still talking today is that He wants us to know Him*" (1985, 3). Remember, it is not what you *know about* God but rather, do you *know* God?

God seeks us out. Remember reading Lesslie Newbigin's book *A Walk Through the Bible* in chapter 1? In it Newbigin describes God's seeking us out—God's earnest longing for us—as a story that runs throughout the whole of the Bible (SE p. 10). God longs for us. And He knows us. Remember, He is our Creator. Psalm 139 is filled with this truth. Matthew 10:30 and Luke 12:7 remind us that God knows exactly how many hairs are on our head. This is getting at intimacy—knowing and being known. "An unexpected tranquility comes when you know God is utterly aware of your life, sees what you see, and feels what you feel, but always has a much larger story in mind for you" (Hill 2008, 84–85).

"So," you might think, "God desires intimacy with me. He speaks." And your thoughts continue, "Well, of course He does. He speaks through the Bible. I read it. I see what He says. I try to obey. End of story." But that is not the end of the story. You can have—God desires you to have—a conversational, intimate relationship that is personal and unique to you and Him. Indeed, He does speak to us through the Bible. That is, in fact, the center of how He speaks to us. But it isn't the only way He speaks to us. By the Bible's own account, God speaks in a host of ways (see the "God Speaks" sidebar). We'll explore this more a bit later. But first, let's look in part at what it takes to participate in an intimate, conversational relationship with God. Hill says, "A big part of intimacy with God involves a basic trust in his character" (2008, 18). It may be hard to believe that God is interested in loving you or that He wants to spend time with you or speak with you. But He does. Trusting in that—trusting His goodness and His love—is foundational, just like the role trust plays in any relationship. "It all comes down to faith—believing that God wants to be with you and talk to you, to show you the mystery and wonder of his ways. But more than that, he longs to tell you that you're loved, even adored" (208).

Another foundation to conversational intimacy with God is to realize that intimacy gets right down into our beings. It goes beyond outside appearances. An intimate relationship with God isn't having a "cleaned-up look." As Nancy Ortberg says in *Looking for God*, "God's vision for restoring and reconciling people to Him is not about behavioral modification or an outside cleanup. It is about an internal heart change that reflects the heart of God" (2008, 176). In a way that's similar to how the people you spend time with can shape the way you think and act, personal intimacy with God gets down into your soul and makes you whole. God has us "as the focus of his love, to be made whole and holy by his love" (Ephesians 1:4, The Message). Intimacy with God changes us.

It is important to recognize that it is only through relationship with God—intimate and personal conversation with Him—that we will ever get a handle on living out much of what the Bible models for us. We can work so hard at trying to "do" Christian life that we miss the fact that we can never do it on our own. We weren't made to. This can even be the case in developing our relationship with God. We can get trapped into thinking that the relationship is something we must "make happen," like one more item on a to-do list. Some of you will get all tied in knots about how to "create" an intimate relationship with God. But here's some good news … you can *facilitate* a relationship with God, but you cannot *force* it. Just as in developing any relationship, you must have faith and hope that it will come to be, but you cannot make it happen by yourself. Yet, any relationship requires effort. It is all a matter of what you might call "plugging in."

Faith is like a conduit—like the plug on an appliance. An unplugged toaster sitting on the kitchen counter next to the electric outlet can stay right there next to the power source all day without ever getting hot. The only way the toaster is going to do what it is designed to do (get hot) is by putting the plug into the wall and turning the toaster on so that electricity can flow from the outlet into the toaster. This analogy also gives a little insight into what John Ortberg observes as the difference between *being in the same room as* someone and *being with* someone. Being with another person requires interaction (2005, 86). Similarly, we can be in the same "room" as God—knowing that we have put our trust in Christ, even living a life of obedience. But we aren't *with Him* intimately until we interact, plugging in to an ongoing, two-way conversation with Him by faith.

> *We can be in the same "room" as God—knowing that we have put our trust in Christ, even living a life of obedience. But we aren't* with *Him intimately until we interact, plugging in to an ongoing, two-way conversation with Him by faith.*

Faith is at the core of intimate relationship with God. First we have to have faith that He is speaking to us—individually, personally, and in the present moment. Then we have to have faith that He will enable us to recognize His voice. As Job 33:14 says, "For God does speak—now one way, now another—though man may not perceive it." He does speak. We just miss it a lot of times, or we write off His speaking to us as something else, maybe coincidence or something equally in line with our rational, empirical minds. Disbelief that God ever (much less, on a daily basis) has something personal and specific to say to us is, obviously, a huge barrier to having a conversation with Him. There are other barriers, such as our pain or our unconfessed sin, that can keep us from hearing Him as clearly as He wants us to, but not believing that someone will talk to us is definitely a relational "buzzkill." Perhaps a person will have to cry out to God like the man did in Mark 9:24: "I do believe; help me overcome my unbelief!" Susan Hill says simply,

> *"There is no trick to hearing God's voice. It has nothing to do with the number of years someone's been a Christian. Nor is it about being more spiritual than another."*

"There is no trick to hearing God's voice. It has nothing to do with the number of years someone's been a Christian. Nor is it about being more spiritual than another. Once the barriers are cleared away, it comes down to noticing things, taking a second look, and pausing to reflect" (2008, 77).

Could it really be that simple?

Yes. But simple doesn't mean automatic. And it doesn't even mean easy. It just means uncomplicated. Just like learning any new skill, developing ears to hear the loving voice of God takes practice. But the good news is that God is even present in the practicing with you. As Isaiah 2:3 says, "He'll show us the way he works so we can live the way we're made" (The Message). We're made to live in true and intimate relationship with God. But we're going to have to practice.

Our earlier *Merriam-Webster Online Dictionary* definition of *intimate* included "marked by a warm friendship developing through long association."[3] This gives you a clue about the need to work at developing this intimacy, especially early on as you learn to listen for God's "voice"—a voice that probably will not be audible, but more likely, will be sensed in your "inner being" (Ephesians 3:16) or in your "gut," as some like to describe it. As you practice listening, you will develop more assurance about discerning His voice.

By permission. From the *Merriam-Webster Online Dictionary* ©2008 by Merriam-Webster, Incorporated (www.Merriam-Webster.com).

Eldredge explains it this way:

> If you want to make music, you have to learn how to play an instrument. And in the beginning, it doesn't sound too good—all the squawks and squeaks and bad timing. You really *are* on your way to making music. It just sounds like you're strangling a pig. If you stick with it, something beautiful begins to emerge. Or how about snowboarding—learning to do that is really awkward at first. You fall down a lot. You feel like an idiot. But if you hang in there, you come to enjoy it. You get better. It starts to feel natural. That's when it becomes fun. This holds true for anything in life.
>
> Including our walk with God. It takes time and practice. It's awkward at first, and sometimes we feel stupid. But if we hang in there, we do begin to get it, and as it becomes more and more natural, our lives are filled with his presence and all the joy and beauty and pleasure that come with it.
>
> It is something learned.
>
> And it is worth learning. (2008, 17)

You will have to start with baby steps and grow from there.

Spending time reading your Bible and meditating on what you find there is a good starting point for hearing and discerning God's voice. As we've already said, the Bible isn't the only way that God speaks to His children, but it is the filter through which any other conversations with God must be viewed. Charles Stanley reminds us, "Since almighty God never tells us to do anything to contradict His Word, the better we know it, the more readily we will identify His speaking voice" (1985, 45). This fact is important to remember, because as Henry and Richard Blackaby note, "The world is abuzz with voices all clamoring for your response. This is a dangerous environment for someone who is incapable of distinguishing between God's voice and the competing voices of self, Satan, and the world" (2002, 215). Susan Hill says, "I'm leery of people who say they hear from God but don't know their Bible. It's too easy to make God what you want him to be, instead of *who he is*" (2008, 200). Spending time reading the Bible and learning what God says there is very important.

"When [God] says something to you, it will be in your own language, significant in a personal and specific kind of way. It will be exactly what you need to hear."

But having said that, you should also know that God can and will speak to you individually—in a way that you will connect to. There isn't a one-size-fits-all approach here. As Nancy Ortberg says, "Molds are fine for Jell-O. But not for people" (2008, 26). Think of all the different options you have for "talking" with your friends: in addition to speaking with them face-to-face, you could send an instant message or a text message, chat on Facebook, post a video clip on YouTube, or call on the phone. And think of the different means through which you can choose to communicate: words both spoken and written, a sketch, a video, photographs, songs, poems … you get the picture. You no doubt have some preferences about communicating with others. God knows this about you. So, why would God choose only one way to speak to you instead of reaching out in ways you are most likely to connect with? And though comparing what others say to what the Bible says is critical in learning to discern God's voice, comparing His way of speaking *to you* with His way of speaking *to other people* isn't helpful. Hill writes, "When he says something to you, it will be in your own language, significant in a personal and specific kind of way. It will be exactly what you need to hear" (2008, 95).

Sure, God is on record as having spoken through burning bushes and talking donkeys. But He also talks through a "still, small voice," prayer, and creation itself. Hearing from God isn't always going to create a huge spectacle, although it certainly can. "God is just as present in the days that all run together, days when nothing really stands out, as he is in the extraordinary days.… God is so great and so everywhere that even the ordinary is sacred" (N. Ortberg 2008, 64). We should practice looking for Him in the nondescript, ordinary, everyday stuff. At times we will see repetition or patterns in things—like hearing a Bible verse repeated over the course of a couple of days, getting a line of a song stuck in our heads, or seeing the same number or word over and over again. Sometimes these are God's way of initiating conversation, and we will simply miss it. "Too often we merely say, 'Wow. What a coincidence.' We look at it like a two-headed rooster perched on our windowsill and then go have a sandwich. We never do anything with it. And so we lose the gift God is trying to give. Or miss the warning he is sending up like a flare" (Eldredge 2008, 105). Next time you encounter a coincidence, get still and ask God if He is trying to show you something. This is but one way we can learn to "connect the dots" of our daily life in a way that helps us hear Him better.

Listening is a really big part of developing an intimate relationship. You probably know from your own friendships that a good listener is a real find! But listening, of course, takes practice. John Ortberg says, "Listening can involve a variety of practices: reading, solitude and silence, conversations, watching the beauty of a sunset, listening to great music" (2005, 98–99). And listening and intimacy also involve focus and attention. "Building intimacy with him requires nothing so much as paying attention. How easily we delete his messages like junk mail. We're chronically distracted. The noise of earthly life commandeers our waking thoughts.... We need a quiet space to hear him whether we realize it or not (Hill 2008, 153–54). Another way to practice listening is to just get still somewhere, ask God a question, and wait to find out what you hear in response. This may take time, but it is time well spent when the outcome is more intimacy with God. There are plenty of good questions to ask (see the "Conversation Starters" sidebar).

At this point some of you may be very skeptical, perhaps even scared, to try out this practicing to hear God's voice. You may be fearful of trying to develop intimacy because you are afraid to fail. You might be thinking, "What if I get it wrong?" Guess what? You will, at least some of the time. And that's OK. Can you think of anything that you do correctly 100 percent of the time? God offers His grace and forgiveness for mistakes in all arenas of our lives; can you imagine that He wouldn't offer that same grace in this one thing? Nancy Ortberg echoes 1 John 4:18 when she says, "There is something very powerful about dispelling fear by realizing that your mistakes are not stronger than God's love for you" (2008, 155). Have you ever seen a parent with a baby who is learning to walk, as the baby tentatively works out those first little steps? There are lots of encouraging words, hands eagerly extended, the parent's face filled with joy and expectation. Even if the baby fails and falls, the parent smiles, helps the baby get back up, and offers more words of encouragement. When the little tot puts together a few steps in a row, the real celebration begins, with high fives, clapping, and choruses of "You did it! Great job!" Imagine our heavenly Father, His eyes filled with love as He watches us lean into taking those first steps of listening for His voice. "God's voice may surprise you, but the texture of his words and his tone will be unmistakably about his love" (Hill 2008, 216).

So what difference would it make if we pursue personal intimacy with God? Quite simply, it is the difference between having just life and having life more abundantly (John 10:10, NKJV). A life filled with intimate, conversational relationship with God brings joy. We have the privilege of communing with the God who created the universe and who created us. It puts us in a position to really follow

Conversation Starters

In his book *Walking with God*, John Eldredge (2008) shares some of the questions he asks God in order to get a conversation rolling. Here are some of his suggestions:

- *"What are you saying, Lord?"* (75)
- *"What is the life you want me to live?"* (28)
- *"What would you have me read today?"* (47)
- *"How am I doing, God? How do I think I'm doing, and how do you think I'm doing?"* (140)

He also reminds us of the importance of asking what we should pray for (101) and asking follow-up questions to get more detail or more depth about specific things God reveals to us. As Henry and Richard Blackaby observe, "At times people get an assignment from God, then they race off to do it without waiting for the specifics of how and when he wants them to carry it out" (2002, 54).

Of course, there are literally thousands of questions you can ask God. Your circumstances and imagination will obviously determine many of the questions you will ask. But those listed above are a good start!

God instead of trying to "pilot our own ship." And it remakes us, creating in us the character that God desires for us to have. It is part of participating in His kingdom. Intimacy with God is what fuels the spiritual passion that drives our participation in His mission, our involvement in the kingdom of God now, our living incarnationally, and so many other things we have talked about in this course. A personal and intimate relationship with God is the only way we can ever serve Him out of spiritual passion rather than religious duty. And that topic is what we want to explore in the next chapter.

∽

NOTES

1. *Merriam-Webster Online Dictionary*, s.v. "intimacy," http://www.merriam-webster.com/dictionary/ (accessed September 4, 2008).
2. *Merriam-Webster Online Dictionary*, s.v. "intimate," http://www.merriam-webster.com/dictionary/ (accessed September 4, 2008).
3. Ibid.

22

Spiritual Passion

God steers us in the direction of His kingdom, His purpose, His passions. His desire is not to conform us, but to transform us.
—*Erwin Raphael McManus*

We were created to be passionate.   —*Floyd McClung*

You may have noticed that it is pretty difficult to get very far in a car that has an empty gas tank. Fuel is essential to the movement of the vehicle. No gas, no go. In many respects, human beings are much like cars. We have to have some sort of fuel to keep us going. It's pretty easy to identify what that fuel is for us in a physical sense; it is food. But what about beyond our physical needs? John Eldredge writes, "There is a secret set within each of our hearts. It often goes unnoticed, we rarely can put words to it, and yet it guides us throughout the days of our lives. This secret remains hidden for the most part in our deepest selves. *It is the desire for life as it was meant to be*" (2007, 1; emphasis added).

We are so driven by this desire at a core level that we spend an incredible amount of our time and energy chasing after one thing or another, hoping that something will satisfy our empty "gas tanks." There are a whole lot of dead-end pursuits that we can run across in our search for life as it was meant to be. And some of them are really hard to detect. But eventually, the inadequacies of these dead-end pursuits reveal themselves, and the results are similar to what happens when you put regular gasoline into a car designed to run on diesel: you will end up with a big mess and an engine in need of repair. If these breakdowns happen often enough, people stop trying to find the right fuel and just try to deaden the pain of their unfulfilled emotional longing. If you think about it, a lot of the brokenness in the world around us stems from the measures people take to deal with the pain that comes from too many dead ends and unfulfilled longings. The fact is that spiritually we are people of desire and passion whether we choose to acknowledge it or not.

Christ's invitation to us to be restored to a holistic relationship with the Creator of the universe calls out to our deepest longings for life as it is meant to be. Not only are we offered the opportunity of relationship with God, but we are invited to join Him in His purpose. It is a grand and epic mission, filled with adventure enough to satisfy even our deepest cravings for meaning, significance, and purpose. We are challenged in a missional life to share our blessings with others, to live incarnationally, and to pursue, with abandon, intimacy with God. And yet, even in Christian life we can easily find ourselves feeling as though we're in a car sitting on empty—having no gas, no go, and a big dose of tire-kicking frustration. We cannot manage the demands of missional life in our own strength. We cannot join God without the fuel that comes from Him. Participating in missio Dei requires spiritual passion.

Passion is a word that you are probably familiar with. If you type it into an online search engine, you will find hits on everything from dating services to an independent women's football league team. You'll find websites related to emotions, Christianity, literature, television and film, bands, songs, and even a Broadway musical called *Passion*. You name it, someone has a passion for it. As author Floyd McClung notes, "The term *passion* is used to describe everything from romance to hunger pangs" (2008, 188).

But what does having passion really mean? And what is spiritual passion? We're going to spend some time sorting that out in this chapter. Let's start with the word *passion* itself, which today is most often thought of as a strong emotion. But it is one of those words whose usage has changed over time. Its history conveys more depth in its meaning. The *Dictionary of Changes in Meaning* traces this history:

> The earliest "passion" was recorded in English in the twelfth century, and was the suffering of pain, and in particular the sufferings of Christ.… In the fourteenth century, the sense expanded from physical suffering to mental, and entered the emotional fields of strongly experienced hope, fear, love, hate, joy, ambition, desire, grief and much else that can be keenly felt.… In the seventeenth century, "passion" gained its inevitably weakened sense (after so much strength) as merely "great liking for." (Room 1986, 200–201)

<aside>

What Difference Does It Make?

- What are you passionate about? Are your passions characterized by the fruit of the Spirit or by something else? Where does your passion come from? The world? Your own pleasure? God's desires for you?

- What are you willing to suffer for? What are you willing to sacrifice comfort, time, money, or other things for?

- What is the difference between being a believer and being an experiencer (p. 276)? Which are you in your relationship with God? Which do you have more of: information about God or intimacy with God?

- Do you fall prey to engaging in facsimiles of spiritual passion? Do you ever find yourself trying to fake spiritual passion? What can you do to stay focused on the true source of spiritual passion when you feel dry or feel as though you're on the wrong track?

</aside>

Another source explains the following: "In the Latin of Tertullian, early father of the church, is found the word *passio*, 'suffering,' and Christianity carried this word into English as the *passion*, or suffering, of Christ during the crucifixion" (Funk 1950, 274). You may be familiar with this original definition because of the movie *The Passion of the Christ*, directed by Mel Gibson.

Isn't that interesting? Today, we think of passion as having to do with emotion, romance, or love. And so often we misuse or overuse the word *love* to describe things we merely have "a great liking for"— like certain foods, songs, or cars. And yet as we saw above, the term *passion* originally comes to English as a description of incredible intensity: the suffering of Jesus on the cross. Historically, passion is about the most true and greatest love. It is about the "first love" of God (see 1 John 4:19 and Revelation 2:4). Passion describes the intensity with which God pursues you—He loves you so much that He died for you. It also describes the intensity with which we need to pursue God. We need to recover passion in its fullness, in its original Christian context. "If you grew up in the church, you might have been taught that passion is sinful," writes Leonard I. Sweet in his book *The Gospel According to Starbucks: Living with a Grande Passion*. "The spiritual passion that is evidenced by a consuming desire for God might have gotten obscured by all the warnings against lust, envy, pride, and greed, as if passion were concerned *only* with the satisfaction of sinful appetites. Don't lose the full meaning of this word" (2007, 20).

> *Passion describes the intensity with which God pursues you—He loves you so much that He died for you. It also describes the intensity with which we need to pursue God.*

Our current usage of *passion* as "an aim or object pursued with zeal"[1] does convey one aspect of spiritual passion: adoration, which is another way of describing worship. As recorded in John 4:23–24, when Jesus spoke with the woman at the well, Jesus explained quite simply what we can describe as spiritual passion: "It's who you are and the way you live that count before God. Your worship must engage your spirit in the pursuit of truth. That's the kind of people the Father is out looking for: those who are simply and honestly *themselves* before him in their worship. God is sheer being itself— Spirit. Those who worship him must do it out of their very being, their spirits, their true selves, in adoration" (The Message, emphasis added). This passage describes adoration, worship, and intimacy that are without barriers, no holds barred, which sounds a lot like the "strongly experienced" emotional facet of meaning you find in the word history of *passion*.

McClung narrows the focus even further: "I don't know what it means to you, but for me passion means whatever a person is willing to suffer for.... It is what you desire so intensely that you will sacrifice anything to have it" (2008, 188–89). This definition captures the fullest sense of the word *passion*. And when we place passion in the context of our relationship with God, it becomes *spiritual passion*—a desire for God and His purpose that is so consuming that we are willing to sacrifice and even suffer for it. How many of us can describe our relationship with God and our daily experiences with Him with that level of commitment and intensity? Yet that is the capacity with which we are created to experience God.

Often we shy away from—perhaps even fear—that level of intensity because it is filled with so much abandon, so much of the unknown, and therefore discomfort. Pastor and author Erwin Raphael McManus describes it this way:

> We have become believers rather than experiencers. To know God in the Scriptures always went beyond information to intimacy. We might find ourselves uncomfortable with this reality, but the faith of the Scriptures is a mystical faith. It leads us beyond the material world into an invisible reality. We become connected to the God of eternity. Who you are at the core is spirit. God is Spirit. To walk with God is to journey in the spiritual realm. (2005, 61)

In our contemporary life that requires proof and logic to validate experience, it is easy and tempting to ignore the realities of living by the power of the Spirit. But we are invited to embrace the adventure of spiritual passion that will take us to the place where our deepest longings for purpose and meaning are fulfilled—alongside God, participating in the greatest story ever told. Spiritual passion is a passion that is "Spirit of God controlled." It is cultivated and ignited through the kind of personal and intimate relationship with God that we discussed in the last chapter.

We've talked a good bit about what spiritual passion is. But let's look at some things that spiritual passion is not. First of all, spiritual passion isn't just mere enthusiasm. Enthusiasm doesn't sustain the journey of participating in missio Dei over the long haul. Spiritual passion does. Enthusiasm could be compared to cheering from the sidelines, whereas spiritual passion would be the level of commitment a person needs to get into the game, to sacrifice the time and energy needed for practice, and to suffer through hits from the opposing team.

Am I Really Passionate?

So, if spiritual passion means a willingness to sacrifice and suffer, you might be thinking, "I'm not suffering a whole lot. Am I really spiritually passionate?" Before you beat yourself up, think about these things:

- A *willingness* to put aside self-preservation is what is required, although we aren't to intentionally seek to put ourselves in situations of suffering just for the sake of suffering. All our actions must be motivated and directed by God; otherwise, we aren't joining His mission, but we're manufacturing experiences to make ourselves feel as though we are.

- Passion springs from intimacy with God. If you aren't cultivating an intimate relationship with Him, you aren't able to cultivate spiritual passion. So, if you are suffering and sacrificing outside of an intimate relationship with God, you are not doing so out of spiritual passion, but out of some other motive.

- The Bible describes a whole range of sacrifices—each of them costly to different degrees for different people. First Peter 2:5 describes us as offering "spiritual sacrifices" to God. Some of these include the sacrifices of offering praise (Hebrews 13:15), of giving material gifts (Philippians 4:18), of doing good to others and sharing with them (Hebrews 13:16), and of offering our bodies as "living sacrifices" (Romans 12:1; see also Romans 6:13 and 1 Corinthians 6:20).

Spiritual passion also isn't religious duty. There has been confusion on this point since the time when Jesus walked the earth. One of the ongoing conversations Jesus had with the religious leaders of His day was regarding their attitude toward external religious duty rather than passion for God. In Matthew 23, Jesus repeatedly called the Pharisees hypocrites. Among His charges was this: "You are like whitewashed tombs, which look beautiful on the outside but on the inside are full of dead men's bones and everything unclean. In the same way, on the outside you appear to people as righteous but on the inside you are full of hypocrisy and wickedness" (Matthew 23:27–28). We can do all the "right things" on the outside and not be one step closer to spiritual passion than the Pharisees were.

Eldredge notes that "the Pharisees miss the boat entirely. Their hearts are hardened by the very law they claimed would bring them life" (2007, 39). He goes on to say that the same problem exists today. "The promise of life and the invitation to desire have again been lost beneath a pile of religious teachings that put the focus on knowledge and performance" (39–40).

How Much of Myself Must I Give?

C. S. Lewis writes in *Mere Christianity* about how much we are called to give of ourselves to God. As he explains in the excerpt below, this choice is the difference between a frustrating religious duty and the fulfillment of spiritual passion:

The ordinary idea which we all have before we become Christians is this. We take as starting point our ordinary self with its various desires and interests. We then admit that something else—call it "morality" or "decent behaviour," or "the good of society"—has claims on this self: claims which interfere with its own desires. What we mean by "being good" is giving in to those claims. Some of the things the ordinary self wanted to do turn out to be what we call "wrong": well, we must give them up. Other things, which the self did not want to do, turn out to be what we call "right": well, we shall have to do them. But we are hoping all the time that when all the demands have been met, the poor natural self will still have some chance, and some time, to get on with its own life and do what it likes. In fact, we are very like an honest man paying his taxes. He pays them all right, but he does hope that there will be enough left over for him to live on. Because we are still taking our natural self as the starting point.

… Make no mistake: if you are really going to try to meet all the demands made on the natural self, it will not have enough left over to live on. The more you obey your conscience, the more your conscience will demand of you. And your natural self, which is thus being starved and hampered and worried at every turn, will get angrier and angrier. In the end, you will either give up trying to be good, or else become one of those people who, as they say, "live for others" but always in a discontented, grumbling way—always wondering why the others do not notice it more and always making a martyr of yourself.…

The Christian way is different: harder and easier.…

… The terrible thing, the almost impossible thing, is to hand over your whole self—all your wishes and precautions—to Christ. But it is far easier than what we are all trying to do instead. For what we are trying to do is to remain what we call "ourselves," to keep personal happiness as our great aim in life, and yet at the same time be "good." We are all trying to let our mind and heart go their own way—centered on money or pleasure or ambition—and hoping, in spite of this, to behave honestly and chastely and humbly. And that is exactly what Christ warned us you could not do. As He said, a thistle cannot produce figs. If I am a field that contains nothing but grass-seed, I cannot produce wheat. Cutting the grass may keep it short: but I shall still produce grass and no wheat. If I want to produce wheat, the change must go deeper than the surface. I must be ploughed up and resown. (1996, 168–70)

Author Eric Sandras offers this insight:

> Most of us have been trained to read [Jesus'] words as rules and doctrine first, believing that obedience to the externals of those rules will produce goodness inside us. But if we focus on being obedient in the externals, we remain hollow internally. We orient our lives around the *effects* of God's kingdom—being good, not telling outright lies, not cheating on our spouse, writing a check to feed the poor—and not the core of the kingdom—loving the Lord our God with all of our heart, soul, and mind (see Matthew 22:37–39). Yet if we truly invest in making sure that our core is right, the godly behaviors will flow naturally from that place. (2004, 21)

Spiritual passion is truly centered in "the first and greatest commandment" of Matthew 22:37, to "love the Lord your God with all your heart and with all your soul and with all your mind."

Religious duty suggests that there is a formula—if you can just follow along with the correct to-do list, you will have the control and safety that come through comfortable predictability. But that illusion of control is a counterfeit of authentic life with God, which is a life fueled by intimacy with Him that ignites spiritual passion for Him. In her book *Closer Than Your Skin*, Susan Hill quotes the following from an unknown author: "Religiosity was the counterfeit of all I had hoped for, like owning a state-of-the-art kitchen, studying recipe books, and cooking fantastic meals—but never eating. The people in its grip are starving to death and don't know why. It's going through the motions, the trappings, and the appearance of faith, but missing the substance of it" (2008, 41). Sadly, this is where a lot of people camp out. And it kills our souls. Religious duty is the opposite of spiritual passion, which is the foundation for a life that is authentic, spontaneous, and responsive to the world around it. Religious duty tries to put us in the driver's seat—just as the old bumper sticker does that displays the words "God is my co-pilot." Spiritual passion is ignited, grown, and lived out with God in the driver's seat, on His throne where He belongs. Religious duty we control. Spiritual passion God controls.

Here's another thing spiritual passion is not. Spiritual passion is not about self-preservation. We often behave as though Christianity is designed to make for us what John Eldredge calls "a happy little life." He says, "We really believe that God's primary reason for being is to provide us with happiness, give us a good life. It doesn't occur to us that our thinking is backward. It doesn't even occur to us that God is meant to be our all, and that until he is our all, we are subhuman" (2008, 86).

Nancy Ortberg points out that "often the words we choose imply that God works for us" (2008, 88). And Eldredge expounds further: "We see God as a means to an end rather than the end itself. God as the assistant to our life versus God *as* our life" (2008, 87). This is the case despite the fact that our invitation from Jesus says, "If anyone would come after me, he must deny himself and take up his cross and follow me" (Matthew 16:24; also Mark 8:34 and Luke 9:23). According to Sweet, "The gospel was not meant to be comfortable or safe. Jesus does not invite lukewarm faith, the brand practiced by the church of Laodicea. Instead, God promises to spit the lukewarm out of God's mouth" (2007, 33). The New Testament, along with the annals of history since that time, is filled with story after story of Christ-followers who experienced trials, sacrifice, and suffering. "Love always moves to sacrifice, which is exactly where He calls us to go. We shouldn't be surprised, then, that to follow Christ is to abandon the luxury of safety and security. If we are to be like Him, we must always risk for love. We are invited to follow Him with reckless abandon. The call of God is more than a leap of faith; it is a life of faith" (McManus 2005, 116).

Despite our general hesitancy to pursue activities that require sacrifice and suffering, Jesus' radical call is not something to be avoided, but it "is the source of true passion," according to Floyd McClung. "All other passions are imitations of, mere replacements for, the holy passion of God's love" (2008, 188). As McClung suggests, enthusiasm, religious duty, self-preservation, and other passions are imitations. They are poor substitutions for true spiritual passion. The Bible teaches that a tree will be known by its fruit (Matthew 7:15–20). Naturally, true spiritual passion is marked by the fruit of the Spirit: "love, joy, peace, patience, kindness, goodness, faithfulness, gentleness and self-control" (Galatians 5:22–23). When you see these things in action, you can know that you are dealing with the Spirit of God.

Certainly there are deceptive, false, dead-end passions. But the key to avoiding them is to cultivate a spiritual passion that is marked with the fingerprint of God's Spirit, a passion that comes from a deep intimacy with God and that allows us to trust both our passions and the desires of our hearts. "If He has won your heart, then to follow your heart will always lead you to follow the heart of God" (McManus 2005, 14). Psalm 37:4 says, "Delight yourself in the Lord and he will give you the desires of your heart." We often take that to mean that if we delight in God, He will give us the stuff we want. But it really has more to do with His placing within us transformed desires.

Hot or Hurl

Author Leonard Sweet owns an unusual bookmark that is a graphic reminder of God's perspective on the subject of lukewarm faith. He describes it in this excerpt from *The Gospel According to Starbucks*:

In Revelation 3, God speaks to the church of Laodicea in language that translators have laundered, thereby proving the reason for God's warning in the first place.

"Would that you were hot or cold," God says, "but because you're lukewarm [or more precisely, play-it-safe, middle-of-the-road, mediocre], I'm going to spit [or spew, or in the best translation of the Greek, vomit] you out of my mouth."

You didn't know there was a God-vomit verse in the Bible, did you? Above this verse I have written in the margins this paraphrase: "You make me sick, pew-potato church." That's why my bookmark is a Continental Airlines barf bag.

Whenever I want to join the crowd, or start to become faithful in my mediocrity: whenever I get growing a garden-variety soul, I get out my barf bag and remember that God loves variety that is vigorous and audacious....

One of my favorite gifts to pastors is a personalized vomit bag on which I write the abbreviated form of the warning this God-puke verse issues to every person and church: "Hot or Hurl." I then sign it "God." You can't have a love affair with lukewarm. (2007, 59–60; bracketed text in original)

In Christianity the goal of the spiritual journey is the transformation of our desires. God's intention in transforming our hearts is not the elimination of desire, but something quite different. To have no desires is to be without passion. A person who lives without passion is someone who is literally apathetic. When we delight in God, we become anything but apathetic. In fact, we become intensely passionate. These desires of our hearts are born out of the heart of God." (McManus 2002, 49)

Jesus was confident enough in the transforming power of intimacy with God that He did not hesitate to say, "If you remain in me and my words remain in you, ask whatever you wish, and it will be given you" (John 15:7). This verse is just one of several places in the Bible where we are taught that if our hearts are aligned with His in a reciprocal relationship, then He will do anything we ask. That may seem stunning to us. But if we are truly remaining in Christ, our desires will be in line with the desires of God. As McManus says, "When we turn to God, His love transforms us and ignites a new passion within us. All that we have loved is consumed by the passions of a new heart" (2005, 101).

When the Spirit of God is transforming us, we cannot help but grow in spiritual passion. "To be filled with the Spirit of God is to be filled with dreams and visions that are too compelling to ignore," writes McManus in *The Barbarian Way* (2005, 100). The truth is, many folks are uncomfortable with big dreams and visions except in an abstract sense. We profess that we have big dreams, but we are frightened to take a step into unknown waters to live out those big dreams. Stepping into the uncharted territory of spiritual passion requires faith. You'll recall, from the previous chapter, our toaster analogy in which faith is the conduit of power. Faith is the cord that plugs you (the toaster) into God (the power source). Here's the interesting thing about a power cord: once it is plugged into an electrical outlet, it has no choice but to conduct electricity. When by faith you are plugged into an intimate relationship with God, the result will be the ignition of spiritual passion. You won't be able to help it. It will just flow through you, like electricity flowing through a power cord. But the reverse is true as well. Spiritual passion—a consuming desire for God and His purpose—cannot happen apart from connection with the Spirit of God. It cannot be ignited apart from intimacy with God any more than an unplugged toaster can toast bread. True spiritual passion cannot be manufactured, no matter how hard you try to muster it in your own strength. It flows from the heart of God through faith into your life. It transforms you. It makes over your character and your heart.

In *Chasing Daylight*, McManus writes, "With the depth of godly character comes an intensity of godly passion. It is in this process of transformation that we find the fuel to engage with confidence the opportunities placed before us" (2002, 49). Some of those opportunities will not necessarily be ones we would think to choose for ourselves. Remember, we are talking about joining God on His mission, journeying along with Him in the places where He is at work. True spiritual passion will lead us into the story God is telling. "We followers of Christ have such potential to participate in something much bigger than ourselves," writes Eric Sandras. "We can release our full potential by learning to move in harmony with God's kingdom" (2004, 35). Spiritual passion causes us to follow God into His story; it causes us to want to join His mission. And His mission is going on all over the place and in circumstances we cannot predict or even begin to imagine.

Jesus says this: "The wind blows wherever it pleases. You hear its sound, but you cannot tell where it comes from or where it is going. So it is with everyone born of the Spirit" (John 3:8). And so it is with spiritual passion and joining God on His mission. We may not know where we are going or what we will be asked to do on this journey, but by the power of God our faith-driven spiritual passion will serve to fuel us in those situations. This is a walk "by faith, not by sight" (2 Corinthians 5:7). We may not always see that we are being transformed into His likeness or that we have the ability to meet the challenges of the situations we face. But we can have faith that God is going ahead of us, that He is transforming us day by day. As we saw in the last chapter, developing personal intimacy requires practice and an ongoing investment of time and energy. If spiritual passion is an outgrowth of personal intimacy with God, it is logical to recognize that it, too, is a process and a journey. Journeys take time. Spiritual passion, like intimacy with God, is cultivated over a lifetime.

Faith is required of us on this front because we live in times of instant gratification. Our culture conditions people to expect results immediately. If the real thing isn't available, we are coached by our culture to accept a reasonable facsimile. Eric Sandras writes the following:

> In a world of artificial sweeteners, pseudo-intimacy via the Net, virtual airplane rides, and silicone body parts, I've found something real. It's not some secret formula or thirty-day money-back guarantee to sainthood, but it is some insight into the only person who has ever fully lived what we blithely call a "relationship with God": Jesus

Walk by Faith, Not by Sight

When Joshua and the Israelites were entering the Promised Land, they had to cross the Jordan River at flood stage (Joshua 3:5–17). There was no bridge, and the plan for getting across the river was simply this: "Tell the priests who carry the ark of the covenant: 'When you reach the edge of the Jordan's waters, go and stand in the river'" (Joshua 3:8). It wasn't "first the water will be cut off, and then step out."

We, too, are asked to put our toe into the water in faith. We don't always get to see first. "Now faith is being sure of what we hope for and certain of what we do not see" (Hebrews 11:1). The priests were certain of what they did not see—a way across the river. They had to put their feet in the water, even though they didn't know how deep the water was or how they were going to cross. But as Joshua told the Israelites: "See, the ark of the covenant of the Lord of all the earth will go into the Jordan ahead of you" (Joshua 3:11). God will go ahead of you.

Christ. Maybe you will find, as I have, that it is the *pursuit* of the kind of relationship with the Father that Jesus had, and not the expectation of attainment in this lifetime, that we've needed all along." (2004, 21)

The world doesn't need any more "I have arrived; I have it all together" pretend spiritual passions. We don't need any more Pharisaic substitutes that masquerade as having fully arrived on the outside while rotting away on the inside. The world needs to see true spiritual passion.

Ever-increasing skepticism toward Christianity is certainly evidence that the world doesn't see enough true spiritual passion. The book *UnChristian* documents some of this skepticism that has much of it centered on the fact that our rhetoric and our actions don't line up. In other words, the world doesn't see us as representing Christ very well. "Using descriptions like 'hypocritical,' 'insensitive,' and 'judgmental,' young Americans share an impression of Christians that's nothing short of … unChristian," says the book jacket's back cover (Kinnaman and Lyons 2007). In recent years, Christians have tried to "mark" themselves in a number of ways—with fish on cars, W.W.J.D. bracelets on wrists, crosses on practically everything—so that the world will know who they are. While there is nothing wrong with those types of identifications, the thing that really marks us as Christians to the world is passion for Christ and the things He is passionate for. In John 13:34–35, Jesus told us how to live so the world would recognize us: "A new command I give you: Love one another. As I have loved you, so you must love one another. By this all men will know that you are my disciples, if you love one another."

We don't need any more Pharisaic substitutes that masquerade as having fully arrived on the outside while rotting away on the inside. The world needs to see true spiritual passion.

At the heart of the matter, love is the theme in this whole spiritual passion-fueled journey with God. Jesus was passionate for it, and we must be as well. McClung says, "All those who are passionate for Jesus are passionate for what Jesus is passionate for" (2008, 191). We'll be looking at that more closely in the next chapter.

ɔ

NOTE

1. *Oxford English Dictionary*, 2nd ed. (Oxford, England: Clarendon Press, 1989), s.v. "passion."

23

The Spiritual Passion of Jesus

The life of faith opens up a full life—not a new set of moral standards or a longer list of religious requirements. The spiritual life is grande passion—life on an EPIC scale. —*Leonard I. Sweet*

We concluded the last chapter with the desire of getting to know what true spiritual passion is by looking at the things that Jesus was passionate about. After all, Jesus is God in the flesh, Emmanuel, God with us. As we first discussed in chapter 9, all the fullness of God is represented in Jesus. Therefore, to look at Him is to see God and to see what He is all about. In fact, Jesus said to His disciple Philip, "Anyone who has seen me has seen the Father" (John 14:9). If we are going to be passionate about God and about the things He is passionate about, we have no better place to look than to Jesus.

But where do you start? In the Bible we see Jesus doing and saying quite a number of things. In fact, discussions of the things that Jesus is passionate about can fill up hundreds of bookshelves. Did you know that literally tens of thousands of books have been written on the life of Jesus? (A search on Amazon.com returns more than 60,000 results for the phrase "the life of Jesus.") People have been disagreeing over the nuances of His life for years and years. It is important to recognize that you can (and should) spend a great deal of time meditating on and exploring the different dimensions of those things. That is part of developing intimacy with God and spiritual passion that are needed for the journey of missio Dei. But for our purposes in this chapter, a simple starting place is best. So we will go straight to the source and begin with the simplest, most straightforward, and most comprehensive statements of Jesus' passion in all of the Gospels.

During the last week before His crucifixion, Jesus was teaching in the temple. Some of the different religious leaders were questioning Him, mostly with the goal of trapping Him in His own words and trying to discredit Him as a teacher. At one point, an expert in the law asked Jesus, "Teacher, which is the greatest commandment in the Law?" Here is what Jesus said—the thing that Jesus identified as the most important commandment: " 'Love the Lord your God with all your heart and with all your soul and with all your mind.' This is the first and greatest commandment. And the second is like it: 'Love your neighbor as yourself.' All the Law and the Prophets hang on these two commandments" (Matthew 22:34–40; there is also a record of this conversation in Mark 12:28–31). From these passages we see that there is basically one thing to focus on. This one thing has two parts to it, and everything else that is significant hangs on these two parts of this command: Love God. Love people.

> *We are to be passionate for God. Love God. Passionately. Passion for God naturally leads us to the second part: Love people.*

Now you could argue that in this particular context Jesus wasn't really talking strictly about what He is passionate about. And it is true that He wasn't answering the question, What are you passionate about? But if you look at the actions and words of Christ in the Bible, there is nothing that falls outside this "greatest commandment." Jesus is always loving God and loving people. These things are His passion. Remember from the last chapter that the original meaning of *passion* is "suffering." Loving God and loving people are what Jesus was willing to (and did) suffer for.

Looking at Matthew 22:37–40 in The Message reveals an interesting word:

> Jesus said, "Love the Lord your God with all your passion and prayer and intelligence." This is the most important, the first on any list. But there is a second to set alongside it: "Love others as well as you love yourself." These two commands are pegs; everything in God's Law and the Prophets hangs from them.

Did you see it? *Passion.* Right there at the beginning of that first commandment. We are to be passionate for God. Love God. Passionately. Passion for God naturally leads us to the second part: Love people. After all, God's passion is people. As we studied at the beginning of this course, the whole story of the Bible is the story of the plan and mission of God to bring people back into relationship with Him.

Let's look a little more at loving God. It may seem hard to know how to do this. What do you give the person who has everything? Well, there is one thing that you have that He may not have, and that is your heart and your devotion. The first and most important way that you can love God is by giving yourself completely to Him. We certainly see this in Jesus' example. Jesus loved God the Father through giving Himself completely to God's plan and purpose. Jesus explained it this way: "I tell you the truth, the Son can do nothing by himself; he can do only what he sees his Father doing, because whatever the Father does the Son also does" (John 5:19). Jesus later said, "I seek not to please myself but him who sent me" (John 5:30). These words are echoed, too, in Jesus' devotion to God's plan and purpose in the Cross. Jesus says in the Garden of Gethsemane, "My Father, if it is possible, may this cup be taken from me. Yet not as I will, but as you will" (Matthew 26:39). In the darkest and most bleak period of His life, Jesus was still willing to follow God's plan. Despite what it cost Him personally, He wanted to follow His Father's lead. This is really what obeying God means.

In fact, obeying God is a way that we love Him. The Bible tells us, "This is love for God: to obey his commands. And his commands are not burdensome" (1 John 5:3). Did you see that? His commands are not burdensome. We so often forget that, because we think of obedience in terms of slavishly following a set of rules, usually ones that seem arbitrary to us or ones that we don't enjoy. Our concept of obedience is based on the idea of following a list of things we cannot do. But what we see modeled in the life of Jesus isn't a lot of rigid "thou shall nots." What we see is a life of obedience that was simply following the lead of God the Father, a life that was never boring or dull, a life that was full of adventure. Following God's lead caused Jesus to live a life of giving and of loving those He encountered. To many people in the world around us, Christians are known more for what they won't do rather than what they are willing to do. Jesus was definitely known for what He did rather than what He wouldn't do. Following Jesus' example, we can express our love to God by being willing to follow Him and participate in the work He is doing on His mission of relationship, redemption, and reconciliation.

Now, the members of the popular band the Beatles probably won't go down in history as great theologians, but they did have their teaching right on one count when they sang the lyrics "all you need is love." The heart of God's commands, and therefore God's passion, is love. As 2 John 6 says, "This is love: that we walk in obedience to his commands. As you have heard from the beginning, his command is that you walk in love." Take a few moments to slowly read the next few sentences. Let the truth of the command of love sink in.

> *God leads us into love. He is passionate about loving people. Yet some people aren't all that easy to love. And love isn't always simply a mushy, warm, fuzzy feeling. Sometimes it is biting and hard-edged. Sometimes it is radical. Sometimes the way of love is lonely because others cannot understand it.*

This is the message you heard from the beginning: We should love one another. (1 John 3:11)

Do not seek revenge or bear a grudge against one of your people, but love your neighbor as yourself. I am the Lord. (Leviticus 19:18)

No one has ever seen God; but if we love one another, God lives in us and his love is made complete in us. (1 John 4:12)

Be imitators of God, therefore, as dearly loved children and live a life of love, just as Christ loved us and gave himself up for us. (Ephesians 5:1–2)

A new command I give you: Love one another. As I have loved you, so you must love one another. By this all men will know that you are my disciples, if you love one another. (John 13:34–35)

God leads us into love. He is passionate about loving people. Yet some people aren't all that easy to love. And love isn't always simply a mushy, warm, fuzzy feeling. Sometimes it is biting and hard-edged. Sometimes it is radical. Sometimes the way of love is lonely because others cannot understand it. But nevertheless, the bottom-line command is that of love. Spiritual passion is infused with love. And love comes from God (1 John 4:7). Following God's lead may not always be easy. But Jesus said that if we have faith in Him, we will do what He did and more: "I tell you the truth, anyone who has faith in me will do what I have been doing. He will do even greater things than these, because I am going to the Father" (John 14:12).

What are some of the other things we see Jesus doing? There are plenty of places in the Bible that show us other aspects of Jesus' life that relate to such topics as compassion, justice, health, poverty, and practicing mercy. Yet when you think about it, *all of these things are rooted in Christ's love for God and for others.* All of Christ's acts of mercy and grace were motivated by love—love of God and love of people. Let's look at just some of the fingerprints of love that Jesus left during His ministry on earth. One picture comes from Chap Clark and Kara E. Powell in *Deep Justice in a Broken World*:

> When we look carefully at the life, heart, ministry, and teaching of Jesus, it seems we are called to a "radical" lifestyle that is much more than simply being militant....
>
> Our radical King is a defender of the weak, the poor, and the outcast. Our King is radical because, unlike most leaders in the world, he tells us we are to love those who hate us, to give our enemies double what they seek from us, and to be peacemakers. The message and justice work of Jesus, the King of Kings, is so radical that only those who are willing to become like little children can enter his kingdom. When his disciples were arguing over who would be the greatest in his kingdom, Jesus' response was radical:
>
>> Jesus called them together and said, "You know that the rulers of the Gentiles lord it over them, and their high officials exercise authority over them. Not so with you. Instead, whoever wants to become great among you must be your servant, and whoever wants to be first must be your slave—just as the Son of Man did not come to be served, but to serve, and to give his life as a ransom for many." (Matthew 20:25–28) (2007, 73)

Another look at the fingerprints of Jesus—the marks of His passion, you might say—comes from Pastor Rudy Rasmus, author of the book *Touch*:

> I like the way John described it in his first letter. He said that if we say we are really following Jesus, we will "walk just as He walked." What in the world does that mean? Here's my list of what I think it means (you may have your own list):

> • Jesus didn't use love as leverage. He didn't love people to get them to change. He just loved them and let them respond. Some of them repented and found love and hope; some hated Him and plotted to kill Him.

> • He didn't own much (a tunic, sandals, and maybe some lip balm), and He never seemed to care about acquiring things. In fact, He was really wary about the destructive power of things. Freedom and joy seemed to come from giving stuff away.

> • He loved people and used a few rules—not the other way around.

> • Jesus regularly hung out with riffraff, sick folks, prostitutes, and other outcasts.

- He wasn't afraid of powerful, rigid people.

- He asked really hard questions, and when people asked Him questions, He didn't give simple answers—if He gave any answers at all.

- He loved people so much that He was severely criticized for it.

- At least once or twice, He used calculated violence to make a point. (I probably shouldn't have included this one, but it's the truth. Maybe protesting is the same thing for us.)

- He was rigidly nonpolitical ("Render to Caesar …")

- He taught and modeled a powerful combination of truth and grace.

- He accepted everybody, but He never abandoned the brutal truth to accommodate differences.

- As almighty God in human flesh, Jesus was infinitely superior, but common people felt completely comfortable with Him because He loved them without patronizing them.

- Rigid, self-righteous, power-hungry, political people felt threatened by Him and hated Him.

- He prayed often, long, and hard.

- He had such a clear sense of His purpose and strong trust in the Father that He was never in a hurry, even though the weight of the world was on His shoulders.

- Popularity and success never went to His head. He always moved toward people in need, not toward people who would give Him applause and power.

- Interruptions (like four guys lowering a paralyzed friend through the ceiling in the middle of His talk) never fazed Him. He saw every moment as an opportunity to do the Father's will.

  After looking at how Jesus related to the Father and to people, it's easy to see that He was quite different from anyone else who ever lived. If God's direction to me is to "walk just as He walked," I have to ask myself, *how much am I really walking like Jesus?* And I'll ask you the same question: *How much are you walking like Jesus?* (2007, 114–15)

As we've already said, there are many distinct dimensions to the way Jesus walked and lived on earth. But you will not find anything among those dimensions that falls outside the simple precept Jesus shared in Matthew 22: Love God. Love People. That is the sum total of what we see Jesus doing. And it was hard, and it caused discomfort and struggle and pain for Him. But He was passionate about these very things. And we are called to do the same: "If anyone would come after me, he must deny himself and take up his cross" (Matthew 16:24, Mark 8:34, Luke 9:23). Remember in chapter 22, the words of C. S. Lewis, which said in essence that the Christian life is both harder and easier. Yes, we have to take up our cross, but Jesus also says, "Come to me, all you who are weary and burdened, and I will give you rest. Take my yoke upon you and learn from me, for I am gentle and humble in heart, and you will find rest for your souls. For my yoke is easy and my burden is light" (Matthew 11:28–30).

Participating in missio Dei requires spiritual passion.

Here's the thing: if we want to be passionate about the things Jesus was passionate about, we have to be willing to live as Jesus did. And it is pretty easy, given the complications and situations of the world we live in, to skirt around some of the more radical actions of Christ. But we do so at great cost, as Brennan Manning noted in *The Importance of Being Foolish: How to Think Like Jesus*: "If we wink at the radical demands of the New Testament in our teaching … we make Christianity too easy and take away its meaning" (2005, 27).

In the novel *Chasing Francis* by Ian Morgan Cron, two characters are having a discussion about the biblical concept of peacemaking. During that discussion, one character addresses exactly the point of acting as Jesus did:

> We live in a world full of terrorists, weapons of mass destruction, and war, so we read the Sermon on the Mount and we think, "Jesus couldn't possibly have wanted us to take this stuff literally, it's too idealistic. Let's embrace the spirit of it in our personal lives but not go overboard by trying to apply it in the real world; that would be naïve." But my friends, Jesus intended the Sermon on the Mount to be a very specific, concrete program. Go; talk to your brother or sister; seek to be reconciled with them; go the extra mile; give to anyone who begs; love your enemies; pray for them; seek first God's reign and advance the cause of biblical justice; don't judge others, but take the log out of your own eye and forgive them. These are steps that Jesus literally wants us to follow, not just admire. (2006, 130–31)

So how do we do this? Well, that is what this journey of missio Dei is all about—joining God in what He is doing, and along the way

What Difference Does It Make?

- Do you love God? How do you demonstrate that love to Him? Are obedience and openness to His leading characteristics of your life? Why or why not?

- What kinds of people do you find the most difficult to love? Why? What fears are involved? Do you want to grow in this area? How can you grow in this area?

- Do you think God intends for us to live out the literal example of Jesus that we see in the New Testament? Are we truly supposed to love our enemies, go the extra mile, and give to those who can't or won't return the favor?

letting Him mold us into the people we were made to be. Following in the steps of Jesus is what the last several chapters have been about. Walking the way that Jesus walked—in other words, participating in missio Dei—cannot be done without personal intimacy with God and spiritual passion that springs from that relationship. And that is where the practice comes in. Brennan Manning says, "Authentic, evangelical faith cannot be separated from a readiness to act on the Word of God according to present opportunities. Whenever faith is accepted merely as a closed system of well-defined doctrines, we lose contact with the living God" (2005, 45). Losing contact with the living God means losing our intimacy with Him and thus losing our spiritual passion. And that pretty much means we are not participating—we cannot participate—with Him on His mission. Losing contact with God means we can't love Him. And it means we can't truly love people. Here is the passion of Christ: Love God. Love People. Regardless of cost. Love God. Love People. And participating in missio Dei requires both.

Here is the passion of Christ: Love God. Love People. Regardless of cost.

24

Community Life

We are born to belong, we are created for connection, and whether we admit it to ourselves or not, we spend our whole lives trying to fit in, get in, and stay in. It almost doesn't even matter what "in" is; we just want to belong somewhere. —*Erwin Raphael McManus*

We didn't think we needed community in the modern world. We believed we could make it on our own. But throughout the history of the church, genuine spirituality has always been nurtured in the womb of genuine Christian community. —*Berten Waggoner*

How good and pleasant it is when brothers live together in unity! —*Psalm 133:1*

In the last chapter, we said that spiritual passion boils down to a simple, two-pronged command: love God and love people. Everything about Christian practice, including personal intimacy and spiritual passion, flows from carrying out those two actions. But as you have probably discovered, living out those commands isn't always easy. Loving God may come naturally to you or it may seem like an abstract assignment. Regardless of our success at loving God, however, the loving people part usually trips us up sooner or later. In many ways the hardest thing we are asked to do is to love other people. And yet, it is at the heart of the story of the Bible.

Remember way back in the first unit when we started looking at the one story of the Bible? There we learned that from the absolute beginning—even before there were people—community has been in the heart of God. In ways that our finite minds cannot begin to grasp, God Himself is a community of Father, Son, and Spirit. And the entire story of the Bible is that of God creating for Himself a community of people who will live as one and worship Him as one. We have seen this theme throughout this course. We saw in the Bible Unit the unfolding of a story of God's mission to restore community with us. That community is the kingdom of God, which is both now and not yet revealed. In the Culture Unit, we learned that God doesn't have a single, particular cultural model for Christian life and behavior. He is above culture and works through our many cultural differences to create a tapestry of unity within diversity. Throughout history we have seen that God has been on mission to bring the nations (all peoples) into His kingdom. Through our study of the men and women who have participated with Him on that mission, we have learned that not only is God's mission *about* restored fellowship and community, but it takes place *within* community. This community building started with a man named Abraham, and it will be gloriously fulfilled in the not-yet kingdom of God we see pictured in Revelation 7:9, where people "from every nation, tribe, people and language" will be united in worship around the throne of God. You cannot escape the truth that participating in missio Dei takes place in the context of community.

Participating in missio Dei is lived out in the context of community.

What Difference Does It Make?

- Are you willing to pray the prayer "Help me not to be okay just because everything is okay with me"? Why or why not?

- Who do you naturally include in your life? Who are you inclined to overlook? Are you willing to ask God to show you things through His eyes, even if it means you have to adjust your thinking?

- Do you grasp that you are precious in His sight? Do you believe that others are equally precious in His sight?

This is good news because, as the epigraph to this chapter reminds us, we are created for relationship with others. We are all hardwired with a deep drive for belonging and acceptance. As Leonard I. Sweet writes in *The Gospel According to Starbucks*, "The number one source of stress in life is the feeling of isolation—isolation from God, from yourself, from others, and from creation" (2007, 146). Unfortunately, we are often the last to catch on to our tremendous need for connection. We may have been hurt and burned by others, steeped in a cultural doctrine of self-sufficiency, or have otherwise become numb to our need for connection, relationship, and belonging. We may even believe that since we can find all we need in God, we can go it alone with Him and don't really need anyone else.

It is true that God is our *all in all*, that we will find true satisfaction in no one else. Yet God Himself has set in our hearts the desire for community. He has ordained that kingdom life is community life. Even the seemingly individual pursuits of intimacy with God and a spiritual passion for God that we have been exploring have another dimension, and that is in the way they are carried out and enhanced by participation in community. So, to be truly whole and truly able to participate in missional life as God intends, we must recognize both our own need for, and the role community plays in, living on mission with God.

> Today in a culture that emphasizes self-reliance, being in fellowship with others and coming to depend on them may initially seem scary. It is much easier to trust only ourselves, to hold back from genuine interaction with others, afraid to need others and afraid to lay our souls

bare for fear that we will be rejected or taken advantage of. It is a hard thing to let ourselves become vulnerable. Yet this is just what God asks of us: to be vulnerable not only to him in our prayer life but also to those in our community. To get over our fears, to open our hearts and to trust God to overcome whatever personality conflicts and disagreements and difficulties arise. (Graybeal and Roller 2007, 31)

Make no mistake. Community life is not easy. But it is an expected and critical part of participating with God in missional life. One thing that makes authentic Christian community life challenging is that greatest commandment we looked at in the previous two chapters. We are called not only to love God, but to love other people as we love ourselves. And yet, people are so hard to get along with. We may, by the power of God's Spirit, "like" others. But truly loving people as Christ loved, and living with them in harmony? Well, that is another story. Perhaps that is why so much of the New Testament is devoted to passages that describe how we are to get along with people—in the fellowship of those in the Christian community and those who are not yet Christ-followers. If the ability to love people weren't difficult even for a Christian, Paul and the other New Testament writers probably wouldn't have had as much to write about. Throughout the New Testament we find passages penned to address specific issues of how to live well together, not just with those outside the faith, but with brothers and sisters in Christ also. Take a look at the "Some One Anothers" sidebar to see some of the "one another" verses that New Testament writers related to the practice and importance of community.

God Himself is a community of Father, Son, and Spirit. And the entire story of the Bible is that of God creating for Himself a community of people who will live as one and worship Him as one.

Clearly, just because a person loves God doesn't mean that person is able to live harmoniously with others who also love God—at least that was the case in the first century. Of course, if we are honest, we recognize that the way we relate to our brothers and sisters in Christ really hasn't changed a whole lot since then. Sometimes it is just really challenging to love people—especially those who are different from us, which is, well, pretty much everyone.

Perhaps one of the reasons it is so hard for us to love others is that, in some parts of the world, we are surrounded by a culture that encourages us to be preoccupied with ourselves. Images and slogans declaring that each one of us is the center of the universe bombard us. Imagery of self-importance and self-sufficiency pervades our

Some One Anothers

Throughout the New Testament, we find many words of instruction and encouragement regarding community. Below are some "one another" and "each other" verses that give us a picture of what life in community should look like:

- "Love one another" (John 13:34).
- "Be devoted to one another in brotherly love. Honor one another above yourselves" (Romans 12:10).
- "Live in harmony with one another" (Romans 12:16).
- "Therefore let us stop passing judgment on one another" (Romans 14:13).
- "Accept one another, then, just as Christ accepted you" (Romans 15:7).
- "I appeal to you, brothers, in the name of our Lord Jesus Christ, that all of you agree with one another so that there may be no divisions among you and that you may be perfectly united in mind and thought" (1 Corinthians 1:10).
- "Greet one another with a holy kiss" (2 Corinthians 13:12).
- "Serve one another in love" (Galatians 5:13).
- "Be patient, bearing with one another in love" (Ephesians 4:2).
- "Be kind and compassionate to one another, forgiving each other, just as in Christ God forgave you" (Ephesians 4:32).
- "Speak to one another with psalms, hymns and spiritual songs" (Ephesians 5:19).
- "Submit to one another out of reverence for Christ" (Ephesians 5:21).
- "Bear with each other and forgive whatever grievances you may have against one another" (Colossians 3:13).
- "Let the word of Christ dwell in you richly as you teach and admonish one another with all wisdom" (Colossians 3:16).
- "Therefore encourage one another and build each other up" (1 Thessalonians 5:11).
- "Live in peace with each other" (1 Thessalonians 5:13).
- "But encourage one another daily, as long as it is called Today, so that none of you may be hardened by sin's deceitfulness" (Hebrews 3:13).
- "And let us consider how we may spur one another on toward love and good deeds" (Hebrews 10:24).
- "Keep on loving each other as brothers" (Hebrews 13:1).
- "Brothers, do not slander one another" (James 4:11).
- "Therefore confess your sins to each other and pray for each other so that you may be healed" (James 5:16).
- "Love one another deeply, from the heart" (1 Peter 1:22).
- "Finally, all of you, live in harmony with one another" (1 Peter 3:8).
- "Above all, love each other deeply, because love covers over a multitude of sins" (1 Peter 4:8).
- "Offer hospitality to one another without grumbling" (1 Peter 4:9).
- "All of you, clothe yourselves with humility toward one another, because 'God opposes the proud but gives grace to the humble'" (1 Peter 5:5).
- "This is the message you heard from the beginning: We should love one another" (1 John 3:11).
- "So in everything, do to others what you would have them do to you, for this sums up the Law and the Prophets" (Matthew 7:12).

Here are some biblical warnings against division and disunity:

- "If you keep on biting and devouring each other, watch out or you will be destroyed by each other" (Galatians 5:15).
- "Let us not become conceited, provoking and envying each other" (Galatians 5:26).
- "Do not lie to each other, since you have taken off your old self with its practices" (Colossians 3:9).
- "Make sure that nobody pays back wrong for wrong, but always try to be kind to each other and to everyone else" (1 Thessalonians 5:15).
- "Don't grumble against each other, brothers, or you will be judged. The Judge is standing at the door!" (James 5:9).

culture. We are taught to pull ourselves up by the bootstraps, to stand up for ourselves because no one else will, and to win at all costs. Pop culture glamorizes broken, isolated individuals as superheroes (think of characters like Batman and Spiderman). Reality TV focuses on games in which the object is, no matter what, to be the last person left—integrity has little value, and winning means we end up alone. Career success often is defined in terms of cutthroat competition, so that we can make it to "the top" (where it is expected to be lonely). The phenomenon of megastar athletes has managed to transform even team sports into events that focus on the power of the individual rather than the group. Even our language in Christian circles can be tremendously individualistic. We are challenged to develop our individual spiritual lives, but rarely do we hear someone speaking to the "we" rather than the "I." And yet, as Nancy Ortberg describes in her book *Looking for God*, these pronouns are incredibly important to "getting it" about community:

> A correct understanding of community has *everything* to do with pronouns.
>
> Community is one of the most powerful concepts in the Bible. Genesis begins with it, and Revelation closes with it.
>
> But we don't usually think of *community* as a powerful word. We've diluted its meaning, redefining it so that it's now soft and nondemanding—an unword.
>
> Rightly understood, however, community is very powerful. It is God's people living together with God at their center. It is the way of life out of which evangelism and discipleship emerge. Community is where we learn the truth about ourselves, where we are deeply loved, where walls are broken down, and where people who are usually excluded are included.
>
> When we learn grammar, pronouns seem like such little, inconsequential parts of speech. I know now that it is not true. Much of the language we use to describe spiritual journey today is wrapped around the word *I*. It's a tiresome and small word, much too narrow to be used with something as grand as community.
>
> Community has its own language. And when it comes to community, pronouns are everything. In community, first person singular moves to first person plural: from *I* to *we*. Somewhere my high school English teacher is weeping with joy.
>
> In community, a deep solidarity with others can be found. In community, an identification and collaboration with others occurs. In

community, it really isn't all about us. The kind of sacrificial, others-focused love that Jesus puts within our reach is reflected in the big word *we*. In using that pronoun, we move our focus off of ourselves and onto the bigger picture of others.

One evening, my oldest daughter came home from a Sunday evening worship service. She had been deeply affected by the experience and in response had written on a piece of paper, "Help me not to be okay just because everything is okay with me." I was so moved by what she wrote that I tacked that piece of paper up on our corkboard in the kitchen as a reminder that in community it is always *we*. In community, if someone else is not okay, then to some degree, I am not okay.

The *we* of biblical community points us to a kind of inclusion that is rare for most of us. In the highly stratified and separated social structure of Jesus' day, religious rulers and average folks did not mix. But Jesus demonstrated a radical inclusion that surprised the average person and upset the religious leaders. He spent time with fishermen, rabbis, Roman officials, children, synagogue leaders, farmers, tax collectors, women, and at least a couple of dead people. Jesus had a very big idea about what *we* meant.

In fact, in Luke 14:15–24, we read a story Jesus told that clarifies just how big His idea really was. See, there was a very wealthy man who decided to throw a big party and invite a lot of guests. While he was getting the party ready, he sent some of his hired help to deliver the invitations and bring back the RSVPs. Surprisingly, the assistants came back with forty-two noes and zero yeses. Apparently, everyone they had invited had offered excuses. Some pretty lame ones at that.

The rich guy who was throwing the party was pretty upset. He had expected that all of these people would *want* to be at the party. But since they didn't, and since this party was pretty important, he told his servants to go out and invite everyone they ran into. He told them to invite the homeless guys on the corner, the ladies who worked in the coffee shop, the guys at the bank. He even told them to invite all the people in the hospitals and nursing homes.

When that was done, and it was found that there was *still* room for more at the party, he sent his workers out again and told them to go out on all the roads and keep inviting. Then Jesus used this amazing phrase, "so that my house will be full."

In Jesus' day, the religious rulers would have assumed that God would definitely include them in His Kingdom. But according to this story, these were the people who declined the invitation. And that's when it went from *you* to *them*. Another fabulous pronoun shift.

Part of the surprise is that the Kingdom of God is made up of surprising people. And for our community to accurately reflect the Kingdom of God, we may have to broaden our idea of who to invite. The *we* needs to include *them*. Unsettling at first, but eventually expanding our idea of community to reflect God's.

There is an inclusiveness to the Kingdom of God that is unparalleled. (2008, 36–39)

You may remember from the Culture Unit that God's idea of people is much larger than we generally tend to recognize. God is glorified through unity within diversity, not the uniformity of one particular culture or type of community. We must constantly be aware of our own ethnocentricity, our own cultural assumptions, and our tendencies toward accepting our way of doing things as the "right way" or the "norm." We are naturally given toward excluding those who aren't like us (see the "Being Intentional" sidebar). But God's mission calls us to a higher place, a place where we love God and love people—all of them. God calls us to participate in community that is open to all and that seeks to share the love of Christ

---

Being Intentional

Nancy Ortberg describes a lesson about community that was presented by Jarrett Stevens, a teaching pastor in the Axis ministry at Willow Creek Community Church in Illinois. See if you can identify with the concept that was presented in his example:

One weekend, Jarrett opened his message by asking for ten volunteers to come up onstage. He asked nine of them to stand off to the side and form a close circle facing each other. Then he talked directly to the one remaining.

"Your mission, should you choose to accept it, is to get into the middle of that circle in fifteen seconds. You can do whatever it takes to get in. Pushing, shoving, tickling, even drawing blood is okay." While Jarrett was describing the challenge to the guy, we could see the circle getting tighter. They began to talk among themselves and finally came up with the strategy of locking arms, touching legs, and slowly rotating in a circle to keep this guy from getting in.

During the next fifteen seconds, this twenty-two-year-old guy tried desperately to penetrate the circle. Finally, to the cheers of the crowd, he was able to push apart two bodies and dive in. He did it!

It took a minute or so for the ten volunteers to find their seats and the congregation to settle down. Then Jarrett spoke slowly.

"When I gave the instructions for this exercise, what is the one thing I never said?"

Silence.

"I never told the group to keep him out of the circle."

It's almost instinctive, isn't it? None of us would ever intentionally decide to lock arms and rotate, but with the turn of a shoulder and the averting of an eye, we communicate to someone that he or she is not included. (2008, 43–44)

Can you think of a time when you have in some way or another "kept someone outside the circle" of a community you are a part of? We instinctively tend to separate ourselves from others who for one reason or another don't seem to "fit" with our group. We have to be incredibly intentional about creating community that is community the way Christ would have it be—open to all.

with all. A tendency to exclude others is not, however, something that we have invented here in the twenty-first century, as any casual acquaintance with history will reveal. There has always been thinking that divides the world into "us" and "them." In fact, the Bible is filled with examples of God's people getting this very point wrong. Shane Claiborne and Chris Haw write about how Jesus spoke on this subject: "Jesus reminded Israel that God's plan wasn't for them to be God's favorites or to be more blessed than others. Rather, they were blessed to be a blessing for the whole world" (2008, 91). In fact, Jesus was calling His contemporaries to the same awareness that He calls us to today: that we are to love people, regardless of race, creed, color, wealth, political affiliation, favorite sports team, or any of the numerous other things that we use for grouping and dividing ourselves. We are to love people—all of them.

Obviously, this is a tough assignment. No one said that following Jesus is for the faint of heart. It is so easy to want to exclude those who don't measure up to our standards. We can be so uncomfortable with people who are different from us. It is natural to surround ourselves with people we are comfortable with, those who are more like us than not.

> *"The exclusion of the weak and insignificant, the seemingly useless people, from a Christian community may actually mean the exclusion of Christ; in the poor brother Christ is knocking at the door."*

But we opt out of participating in communities that practice Christlike acceptance at our own peril. Christian martyr Dietrich Bonhoeffer reminds us that there is much more at stake than our own personal comfort when it comes to community and living on mission with God: "The exclusion of the weak and insignificant, the seemingly useless people, from a Christian community may actually mean the exclusion of Christ; in the poor brother Christ is knocking at the door. We must, therefore, be very careful at this point" (1954, 38).

The key to being "very careful at this point" lies in understanding the work of Christ and the fact that He is the foundation of any missional community. We must understand that Christ died on the cross for *all* men. You are His beloved, and *so is anyone else you will ever meet.* We will never meet a person that God doesn't love, that He didn't die to bring life to. As Christopher L. Heuertz writes, "God views every person who has ever lived as worth shedding blood for, worth dying for" (2008, 55). Only when we recognize and fully grasp this truth will we ever be able to joyfully embrace community in the way God intends—kingdom community that is a foreshadowing of the multinational community of worship we see in Revelation 7:9. As a child you may have sung, "Red and yellow, black and white, they are precious in His sight." Do you grasp that you are precious in His sight? Do you believe that others are (equally) precious in His sight? This is such an important foundation to participating in missio Dei. Heuertz continues: "Seeing our own belovedness will give us the eyes to see the belovedness of others. Learning to recognize these truths about ourselves allows us to see these things for and in our community. It creates the space for the miracle of community to happen" (61).

Authentic missional community is a miracle. It can and does happen—though *only through the power of Jesus Christ*. Bonhoeffer writes:

> A Christian comes to others only through Jesus Christ. Among men there is strife. "He is our peace," says Paul of Jesus Christ (Eph. 2:14). Without Christ there is discord between God and man and between man and man.… Without Christ we also would not know our brother, nor could we come to him. The way is blocked by our own ego. Christ opened up the way to God and to our brother. Now Christians can live with one another in peace; they can love and serve one another; they can become one. But they can continue to do so only by way of Jesus Christ. Only in Jesus Christ are we one, only through him are we bound together. (1954, 23–24)

We can't make community happen on our own any more than we can build the kingdom of God. (Remember that from chapter 4?) Community, kingdom, those are things that God handles. As we have said all along about missio Dei, we just join what He is doing. Community, the nexus of kingdom life, is a reality we are invited to step into, to participate in. It is not something we create. The idea of creating an "ideal community" can be a huge pitfall for the Christian. Alongside the joys and solidarity of community life, there can be difficulty and strife. Remember those verses we looked at earlier that were directed at New Testament believers? Everything about community in the Bible and in our own experiences suggests that even Christian community is not devoid of disappointment and difficulty (see "The Difficulty of Community Life" sidebar). Recognizing this reality helps us avoid bailing out of community that we are designed to be a part of just because the going gets tough. Sometimes this strife comes from unrealistic expectations. Missional community is a "vessel" through which God's love is poured into the world. But we cannot mistake the vessel for the one being poured out through it. A danger is that we sometimes allow the community itself to become a substitute for God, who is to be its center. Expecting our community to become our source of life

The Difficulty of Community Life

Christopher Heuertz writes in *Simple Spirituality* on the realities of the difficulty of life in community with others:

> The friends around me have guided me through my darkest days of loneliness, doubt, fear and insecurity. My worst sins have been confessed in community, and the love I've found there has given me the courage to receive real forgiveness.

> As a grace, community has also created some of the deepest wounds in my heart. Unfair or failed expectations, hard words, misunderstandings, betrayal, accusations, disappointments, even loneliness in community—I remember hearing someone say that community is wherever the people you least want to be with always live.

> All of these things have never been very far removed from any of my community experiences. Though I need community more than any other discipline, it has been one of the hardest things for me to find my way in. With as much work that needs to go into community, and as hard and painful as it has been working it out, why in the world would I choose it?

> I choose community because that's where I've found God. Who we are cannot be separated from relationships. We were made for relationships. (2008, 53–54)

and joy is as misguided as expecting a medicine bottle instead of the medicine inside it to heal us. Christian writer and thinker Henri Nouwen, who lived out the last years of his life in a L'Arche community (communities where people with and without disabilities share their lives together) wrote that "no human being can understand us fully, no human being can give us unconditional love, no human being can offer constant affection, no human being can enter into the core of our being and heal our deepest brokenness. When we forget that and expect from others more than they can give, we will be quickly disillusioned; for when we do not receive what we expect, we easily become resentful, bitter, revengeful, and even violent" (1994). We must never forget that the community itself isn't the focus, nor is it in place simply to serve its members' needs. Missional community focuses on God so that it can achieve the purpose for which it was created.

And what is that purpose? That is what we hope to find out in the next chapter.

The Purpose of Community

In Christian community, we can open our lives to God's life by
gathering regularly in little groups of two or more to encourage one
another to discover the footprints of God in our daily existence and
to venture out *with God* into areas where we have previously walked
alone or not at all.   —*Lynda L. Graybeal and Julia L. Roller*

We are one in the Spirit, we are one in the Lord, and we pray that all
unity may one day be restored; and they'll know we are Christians by
our love.   —*Peter Scholtes, lyrics from the song "They'll Know We Are
Christians by Our Love"*

Sorry to leave you hanging at the end of the last chapter. We
stopped just at the edge of taking the plunge into the topic "What
is the purpose of community?"

For the Christian, this is a profound question that has two significant answers: one inwardly focused and one outwardly focused.
They are different sides of the same coin and are therefore both
important. First of all, authentic and healthy Christian community
plays a tremendously significant role in the spiritual development of
its members. As writer Erwin Raphael McManus observes, "When
we live outside of healthy community, we not only lose others, but
we lose ourselves" (2006, Intimacy entry 17). This side of the coin is
primarily inward—toward what the community provides for those
within it. But there is another side to the coin, and that is what
Christian community means to and for those outside it. Missional
community as we see it in the Bible first and foremost declares God
to the world. Missional community reveals the kingdom of God. It
is the "now" foretaste of the "not yet" fully realized kingdom.

But let's start with that inward side of the coin. Being surrounded
by other Christ-followers and living openly with them creates
an opportunity for our own personal spiritual growth. And our
participation will doubtless encourage and challenge others in their

spiritual journeys as well. There is a reciprocal building up of one another as we live together in authentic Christian community. As we hinted at in the last chapter, even our individual pursuit of intimacy with God and spiritual passion are nurtured and encouraged within community. As we bear one another's burdens and openly share our lives with other believers—our successes and failures, hopes and fears—we find in that fellowship new ways to grow in intimacy with God and in our passion for Him. The process of being in close fellowship with others always influences our lives. And because of that fact, it is important to take a look at some of the dynamics of authentic Christian community.

In true Christian community we encounter a place where we can be held accountable for our actions, and we are therefore challenged to become more Christlike. Susan D. Hill describes fellowship as "all important" in developing our relationship with God. She says, "Spiritually mature believers can guide us as we learn to recognize what is God's voice and what isn't. We also discover more about hearing God through others' stories. Most important, in relationship we find accountability" (2008, 201).

But beyond being nurtured and encouraged in our spiritual growth, in Christian community we also get to practice and live out the things God is teaching us, such as bearing one another's burdens or learning to put others' interests ahead of our own. Further, it is a place we can exercise our spiritual gifts, which are given to us for the specific purpose of building up the Body of Christ (Ephesians 4:11–12). Thomas Merton, a Catholic monk who was no stranger to life in a very specific type of Christian community, writes, "God does not give us graces or talents or virtues for ourselves alone. We are members one of another and everything that is given to one member is given for the whole body" (1962, 56). What Merton and the Bible describe is perhaps one of the most distinctive features of Christian community, one that springs from the selfless character of Christ. There are many distinctives to Christian community that may or may not be found in our other interactions. Of course the unique element of Christian community is Christ as its centerpiece. Dietrich Bonhoeffer says, "Christianity means community through Jesus Christ and in Jesus Christ.… Whether it be a brief, single encounter or the daily fellowship of years, Christian community is only this. We belong to one another only through and in Jesus Christ" (1954, 21).

Bonhoeffer hints at the fact that community can be experienced in many venues and for varying lengths of time. Christian community can be thought of in a number of ways—as the larger

What Difference Does It Make?

- Are you a "lone ranger" Christian, interested in individual pursuits and skeptical of community life? What contributes to those feelings if you have them?

- How has community played a role in your spiritual growth and development? Has it been a positive influence or a negative one? How have you been able to love others and minister to them through community? Or does that even play an important role in your life? Why or why not?

- How might God be calling you to proclaim Him to the world through participating in community? What difference does it make for the world to see authentic Christian fellowship?

Body of Christ, the church we attend, the Church universal, our small group, an accountability group, a Bible study group, the fellow Christ-followers you may sit with in the lunchroom. There is not just one "look" to Christian community. Eric Sandras writes, "[Jesus] knows what life-giving community looks like in any culture and for any age group. He knows what his community should look like in your city and mine" (2004, 60). But without Christ as the center of it, community is not Christian. Some community that we engage in can fail to serve the purpose of spiritual development that is one side of the coin of Christian community's purpose, not to mention the other side of the coin—the larger purpose of community, which is mission to the world.

Broadly speaking, there are thousands of different types of community in the world, and they may or may not have the marks of Christian community. Community can be experienced in families, dormitories, neighborhoods, and cities. Community can also be created by shared experiences or interests, and sustained not through geographical proximity but through a shared concern. A lot of attention and time are given to the "virtual community" found in places like social networking sites and online message boards and forums. It may be tempting to think of some of these online communities as a reasonable alternative to traditional, face-to-face community. And cyberspace may be perfectly well-suited to

---

Authentic Community: A Model from Acts

Lots of books have been written about the model of Christian community the early Church in Acts provides for us. And we would do well to think deeply and read widely about how Christian community takes place in different contexts. But a succinct picture of Christian community—one that literally changed the world—can be found in one verse: "They devoted themselves to the apostles' teaching and to the fellowship, to the breaking of bread and to prayer" (Acts 2:42). This verse presents a picture of some of the central elements of missional community life. Graybeal and Roller elaborate on this:

> The first element, teaching, consists of reinforcing for present disciples and instructing new disciples about the ways of Jesus so that we can follow them (Matt. 28:20). The second element, fellowship, involves opening our lives to each other, being together in good times and bad, in leisure and in study. It also means being transparent and open with each other, sharing our dreams and our struggles so that we can receive and give encouragement, support, and help. The third element, breaking of bread, means sharing the Lord's Supper together, but it also means eating regular meals together and sharing in the important events in one another's lives. The fourth element, prayer, means praying together as a community for wisdom and discernment, for boldness to tell the world about Jesus Christ, for guidance and direction in our work in the world, that the sick and infirm may get well, that political and religious leaders may make wise decisions, that those who don't know Christ and those who are hard-hearted may open their hearts to the love of Christ, and much more….
>
> In order to truly engage in the teaching, fellowship, breaking of bread, and prayer that are the hallmarks of Christian community, we must be willing to invest ourselves in relationships with other people, just as Jesus invested himself in relationships with his disciples. (2007, 30–31)

These are the sorts of things that define and distinguish Christian community. At the heart of it is a willingness on our part to dwell openly and lovingly with one another, living out what Christ teaches about how to love and serve.

developing some aspects of community, but there are some limitations. *Simple Spirituality* author Christopher Heuertz muses, "I'm now trying to figure out virtual community and identity as I try to keep up with MySpace and Facebook, where people post anything on public walls—even deeply personal and intimate statements they would never say to the owner of that wall over a cup of coffee. I wonder if this virtual environment is actually damaging the spirit of true community because they're actually more closely related to role-playing games" (2008, 53).

Life online has become so much a part of our culture that it may be hard to recognize its limitations in terms of true community. Heuertz observes that virtual environment is closely related to role-playing games because of the built-in anonymity that comes with "virtual community." You can create and inhabit a persona in online interactions that may or may not be truthful. And there is no assurance of the truthfulness of the identity of others with whom you are interacting. What is significant in a negative way about virtual community is that the vital element of accountability is removed from many encounters. Being responsible to and for one another is a huge part of Christian community life, but that responsibility can be completely erased in the anonymity of an online environment.

> *"To live in the midst of others, sharing nothing with them but the common noise and the general distraction, isolates a man in the worst way."*

This is not to say that places like Facebook and MySpace are not useful in terms of developing and maintaining friendships or communicating about shared interests. And it would be naïve to suggest that Christian witness and fellowship cannot take place within cyberspace. But to think that you are engaging in significant community because you spend all your time in online, virtual community is to miss out on the important dynamics and distinctives of Christian community and its purpose. Nor is simple geographic proximity or shared enthusiasm for a hobby or a sports team enough to serve the specific and special place of Christian community in our lives. It may feel great to be involved and connected in the many ways that our various relationships with neighbors, families, Facebook friends, fellow enthusiasts, and message board partners provide. But as Christians, we are missing something extremely critical to our faith journey if we are not regularly involved in shared life within the Body of Christ for the purpose of intentional pursuit of Christ and His desires.

Even more significant is that often we don't recognize the need for authentic community in our lives. We may substitute "being connected" to others or even deep one-on-one friendships for the very unique role that Christian community is to play in our lives. The worst part is that we can be so surrounded by life in a crowd that we don't realize it's not the same thing as life in community. "There is actually no more dangerous solitude than that of the man who is lost in a crowd, who does not know he is alone and who does not function as a person in a community either," writes Merton (1962, 54). Similar to walking singly or merely anonymously through a large crowd in a shopping center or on a city street, just being with other people, even surrounded by them, doesn't guarantee communion or community. Merton continues: "To live in the midst of others, sharing nothing with them but the common noise and the general distraction, isolates a man in the worst way" (55). It is sometimes easy to confuse a *crowd* and a *community*, to confuse *connecting* with others and *being in community* with others. "Life in a crowd" interactions fall short of the purpose of Christian community.

"We must belong to a community of fellow travelers in order to be spiritually nourished to the fullest extent possible," write the authors of *Living the Mission*. "And this is not just for our own spiritual benefit. It is arranged this way so we can be God's representatives *in* the world to communicate the gospel *to* the world" (Graybeal and Roller 2007, 30). Here we are beginning to see the relationship between the inward and outward sides of the coin. The purpose of community isn't only so that we can grow to be more mature Christians. As we practice spiritual life within community, there is also an outward purpose being served—to proclaim the truth of God to the world around it. As 1 Peter 2:9 says, "You are a chosen people, a royal priesthood, a holy nation, a people belonging to God, *that you may declare the praises* of him who called you out of darkness into his wonderful light" (emphasis added). We are, as the Body of Christ in community, a light shining His truth into the darkness of this world. This is the primary purpose of missional community. The community is a means by which we join God in His mission in the world.

> *As we practice spiritual life within community, there is also an outward purpose being served—to proclaim the truth of God to the world around it.*

So, even though individual spiritual growth and maturity is strengthened in the context of community, there is another larger kingdom purpose for community: "Our participation in community is not only for our own spiritual benefit but for the larger community around us. When we are able to love as Paul describes in 1 Corinthians 13, when we are able to share in a sense of mutual responsibility, belonging, and caring,… then we are able not only to provide an undeniably powerful witness to the way of Christ, but also to accomplish so much more of God's kingdom work in the world around us" (Graybeal and Roller 2007, 33). As Christopher Heuertz writes, "Community is a tangible sign of the kingdom. When communities marked by submission and sacrifice are developed, the fruits naturally follow, often effortlessly" (2008, 77). Notice that Heuertz emphasizes submission and sacrifice. He is talking about the deeper, true hallmarks of community, the things that go beyond simply hanging out with others who share a love of Christ. When we are participating in authentic missional community, we are living in the ways that the "one anothers" of the Bible describe. We are able, through the Holy Spirit, to be knitted together in love with widely diverse people, walking and living in the hard places of getting along. This way of living is a huge testimony to the world because that is not the way the world generally operates. Erwin McManus observes, "There may be no greater proof of God than the power of community" (2006, Intimacy entry 17).

The Fractured Body

One of the facets of Christian life that is getting a whole lot of ink and press in recent years is how Christians are doing on their witness to the world. Books like *unChristian* examine the way young people view the corporate body of Christians in America (and not very positively, by the way). Many Christian voices are calling for a serious examination of our collective portrayal of Christ's message to the world around us. Regardless of your views on the successes or failures of the contemporary Christian church, there is no denying that Christian community bears witness to the world around it—whether for good or ill. Christopher Heuertz offers this meditation:

The apostle Paul reminds us that the church is the body of Christ. In our lack of solidarity and in our fractured communities, that body has become disjointed. It is a tragedy that secondary doctrinal issues have made us unable to embrace fellow Christians as brothers and sisters in Christ. Styles of worship, views on church leadership, varying perspectives on the use of spiritual gifts, and discussions on God's foreknowledge in relationship to humanity's free will often divide the body of Christ. When this happens, it is as if the body of Christ has severed its own members.

Trying to open a peanut shell is a difficult task for any three-year-old, but for Grace, who only has one arm, life provides even greater difficulties. As a three-month-old baby, Grace lost her father, sister, and grandparents in an RUF rebel attack in Sierra Leone. Her left arm was hacked off with a machete. Watching her struggle to open a peanut, I was reminded of the struggle that it is for the dismembered body of Christ to respond to the needs of the world.

As a disjointed body, we find it difficult to perform the tasks that are expected of us. Look around the world today. The world is a place marked by suffering and poverty. Where is the church? In isolated instances, the body of Christ is able to respond effectively; however, most of those who need the embrace of the body of Christ never feel it. The image of little Grace and her amputated arm is as tragic as the reality of a divided church. But unlike the church, Grace didn't choose to sever her arm. Grace and the thousands of others like her need a stronger embrace from us, Christ's body. (2008, 64–65)

As we have discussed, it is notoriously difficult to love God and to love people; we can do it only in the power that God gives us through His Spirit. Knowing and loving God is the absolute key to loving people. We cannot do the second without the first. And doing both is critical to participating with God in a life of mission.

Perhaps this is why there are so many different metaphorical images of community life in the New Testament. Christians are described as a temple (Ephesians 2:21), a flock of sheep (John 10), a family (1 John 3:1), a spiritual house and royal priesthood (1 Peter 2:5, 9), and of course, the familiar description of Christian community as a body (1 Corinthians 12:12–27). It is in this last metaphor that we find the reality of why your participation in community is so important. Not only is community important to you and to your growth as a Christ-follower, but you are important to community. Without you, some portion of the body is missing. Leonard Sweet writes, "Community with God is never a mass, but a body, and in a body every member has a unique role and identity. In a mass there is duplication and replication, but not in a body, where every part is a miracle" (2007, 59). You may sometimes feel as though others have more to offer or as though your gifts are not really that significant. But those feelings are a far cry from what the Bible has to say about you. Ephesians 2:10 says, "For we are God's workmanship, created in Christ Jesus to do good works, which God prepared in advance for us to do" (SE p. 97). You are a work of art created by the Lord to participate in His mission. And that participation is significant, no matter what it is. Each part of the body is needed: "The eye cannot say to the hand, 'I don't need you!' And the head cannot say to the feet, 'I don't need you!' On the contrary, *those parts of the body that seem to be weaker are indispensable*" (1 Corinthians 12:21–22, emphasis added).

> *"Community with God is never a mass, but a body, and in a body every member has a unique role and identity. In a mass there is duplication and replication, but not in a body, where every part is a miracle."*

There is a saying in the theatre world: "There are no small parts, only small actors." In other words, regardless of whether an actor is playing the lead role or playing a role with only a few lines or none at all, every part is important to the telling of the story. A "small actor" is the one who doesn't recognize that each part is needed and who gets discouraged or frustrated by not having a "bigger part." It is the same on the world stage of God's story—each of us has an important part to play in the missional community of God, whether it appears to be significant in our own eyes or not. Just as there are no small parts in theatre, there are no small parts in the Body of Christ. Here are Jesus' words on the subject: "And if anyone gives even a cup of cold water to one of these little ones because he is my disciple, I tell you the truth, he will certainly not lose his reward" (Matthew 10:42). In the journey of missio Dei, you need the community, and the community needs you.

Community life is the only life for a follower of Christ. On one side of the coin, it is where we grow. It provides a place where we can "practice" loving others. On the other side of the coin, it is the vessel through which we demonstrate to the world the grace, mercy, and love of God. Jesus instructed the disciples that loving each other would demonstrate His love to the world: "A new command I give you: Love one another. As I have loved you, so you must love one another. By this all men will know that you are my disciples, if you love one another" (John 13:34–35). If we are serious about participating in the mission of God, we must be serious about participating in community, for it is there that we find God at work to fulfill His purpose.

The purpose of missional community is to enable participation in the life of the kingdom of God, to live and to proclaim the gospel (or good news) of Jesus both for our own growth and for the benefit of those around us. This is missional life that is at the heart of the mission of God. We are invited to participate in something larger than ourselves, something greater than we could accomplish on our own. We journey together, following our Master, knowing that in this way we are walking the same paths of relationship and reconciliation that Jesus walked in the world.

Celebration: The End of the Story

The mission of God is to lead the whole creation and all nations to that universal worship that so fills the final vision of the canon of Scripture.
—*Christopher J. H. Wright*

After this I looked and there before me was a great multitude that no one could count, from every nation, tribe, people and language, standing before the throne and in front of the Lamb. They were wearing white robes and were holding palm branches in their hands. And they cried out in a loud voice: "Salvation belongs to our God, who sits on the throne, and to the Lamb."
—*Revelation 7:9–10*

The opening ceremonies of the 2008 Olympic Games in Beijing, China, demonstrated that, without question, China knows how to host a celebration. The spectacular pageantry of the opening events included a colorful parade of nations as thousands of athletes representing countries from all over the world marched into the National Stadium built specifically for the games. The climactic event of the parade, at least for the host country of China, was the arrival of China's delegation of athletes, more than 1,000 strong, into the stadium. In the position of honor, leading the athletes and presenting the Chinese flag, were Chinese NBA basketball star Yao Ming and a previously unknown nine-year-old boy named Lin Hao. China Daily.com recorded the moment: "Chinese President Hu Jintao and other top leaders of the country seated in the VIP stand all rose to wave to the Chinese team, as the full-packed National Stadium, the Bird's Nest, *was turned into a sea of joy and ecstasy by the enthusiastic home crowd*" (emphasis added).[1]

All we know is that the fulfillment of the mission of God and the full revelation of His kingdom will be more joyous, more uplifting, and more spectacular than any celebration we have ever seen here on earth in our lifetimes.

Lin Hao, a primary school student, is from the quake-affected zone of southwest China's Sichuan Province. "According to media reports, when the May 12 tremor struck, Lin risked his life and suffered multiple injuries for rescuing his schoolmates from the collapsed buildings. He was later awarded the title of 'Teenage Hero in Earthquake Rescue and Relief.' "[2] In other words, this little boy was recognized and celebrated because of his sacrifice. For that sacrifice, he was given a position of honor by a wildly cheering audience that included thousands of people from all around the world—a widely diverse group of people, yet one that was united in celebration of sport and other things human beings have in common. Whether a person likes the Olympics or not, one finds it hard not to be moved by such celebratory displays.

There will be another celebration someday, and it will also involve throngs of people—"from every nation, tribe, people and language." And they, too, will be widely diverse yet unified. But instead of celebrating sports, athletes, or even a little boy who made heroic sacrifices for others, the celebration will be for the one who carried out the ultimate sacrifice, giving His blood for the sins of all people. This celebration and worship of Jesus Christ, the Lamb of God— a joyous occasion of worship and adulation that we cannot begin to fathom—is what we see pictured in Revelation 7:9. All we know is that the fulfillment of the mission of God and the full revelation of His kingdom will be more joyous, more uplifting, and more spectacular than any celebration we have ever seen here on earth in our lifetimes. Something like the opening ceremonies of the Olympics might give us a little taste of what that sort of multinational celebration could entail. But it doesn't come close to the real thing.

This celebration and worship of Jesus Christ, the Lamb of God—a joyous occasion of worship and adulation that we cannot begin to fathom—is what we see pictured in Revelation 7:9.

The book of Revelation gives us pictures of the "not yet" fully revealed kingdom of God. In it we see the culmination of all the threads of God's mission that we have studied throughout this course—the biblical story of mission, unity within diversity, and the fulfillment of mission in history. In the future, the kingdom of God will be fully revealed among all men, and there will be no more conflict, division, or warfare from an enemy who seeks to destroy and discourage Christ's followers. In Revelation 21:1–7, John offers this description:

> Then I saw a new heaven and a new earth, for the first heaven and the first earth had passed away, and there was no longer any sea. I saw the Holy City, the new Jerusalem, coming down out of heaven from

God, prepared as a bride beautifully dressed for her husband. And I heard a loud voice from the throne saying, "Now the dwelling of God is with men, and he will live with them. They will be his people, and God himself will be with them and be their God. He will wipe every tear from their eyes. There will be no more death or mourning or crying or pain, for the old order of things has passed away." He who was seated on the throne said, "I am making everything new!" Then he said, "Write this down, for these words are trustworthy and true." He said to me: "It is done. I am the Alpha and the Omega, the Beginning and the End. To him who is thirsty I will give to drink without cost from the spring of the water of life. He who overcomes will inherit all this, and I will be his God and he will be my son."

At the beginning of this course, we talked about the fact that the Bible tells one story—the story of the tremendous, pursuing love of God and His mission to restore His creation to a redeemed relationship with Him. It is a story, a mission, that spans centuries and centuries, and one that will culminate in a perfected kingdom in eternity future that we see pictured in the passage above. Of course, as a biblical text, Revelation is famous for being challenging to understand. "Though the images are intricate and at times both puzzling and frightening, their general import is clear. God himself is the one who, through his beloved Son, is moving history. God's purposes will be accomplished: his kingdom will come. This is the glorious concluding image of the renewed heaven and earth, shared in Revelation 21 and 22" (Bartholomew and Goheen 2004, 210). There are many details we do not know about that future reality, but we can be sure that our faithful God will end His story, His mission, in victory and in celebration that is glimpsed in Revelation.

<aside>
Signposts for the Future

"All Christian language about the future is a set of signposts pointing into a mist. Signposts don't normally provide you with advance photographs of what you'll find at the end of the road, but that doesn't mean they aren't pointing in the right direction. They are telling you the truth, the particular sort of truth that can be told about the future." (N. T. Wright 2008, 132)
</aside>

Just as in any good story, the story of the Bible has a beginning, a middle, and an end. In this final chapter of *Missio Dei*, the end of the Bible's story is what we are concerned with. The Bible begins with the creation of the world and the pinnacle of that creation, humankind. As we identified in chapter 3, the middle of the Bible's story picks up in Genesis 12, where we see the invitation by God to join His mission extended to a man named Abraham. The story of the Bible continues throughout the books of the Bible until the culminating ending portion of the story, which really gets going in Revelation 5. As Richard Mouw notes in *When the Kings Come Marching In*, "The multinational character of the redeemed community is announced with great fanfare in Revelation 5" (2002, 79). Throughout this course, we have explored the fact that God's healing mission is for the nations, not for just one particular people or culture. This is absolutely the picture we see painted in the end of the story of the Bible. Just as the Bible concludes with a heavenly city, filled with a multinational throng of worshippers living with God in their midst, so too does the mission of God end. Missio Dei culminates in every "tribe, tongue, language and nation" worshipping around the throne of God.

As we have studied, the heart of God for the nations runs through the whole story of the Bible and through the entire history of the mission of God. Way back in chapter 3, we looked at Abraham and at God's promise that "all peoples on earth will be blessed through [him]" (Genesis 12:3). As Christopher Wright notes, "The call of Abram is the beginning of God's answer to the evil of human hearts, the strife of nations and the groaning brokenness of his whole creation" (2006, 199). God's mission is to all peoples, as it always has been. This is the story that runs throughout the whole of the Bible, God's heart for the nations, or what author David Joel Hamilton calls "God's forever dream":

> Though clarified in the New Testament writings, God's forever dream is evident throughout the Scriptures. He tells the patriarch Abraham, "I will bless you … so that you will be a blessing … and in you *all* the families of the earth shall be blessed" [Gen. 12:2–3, NRSV]. King David grasps God's dream when he writes, "*All* the ends of the earth shall remember and turn to the Lord; and *all* the families of the nations shall worship before Him" [Ps. 22:27, NRSV]. The prophets Habakkuk and Isaiah envision the fulfillment of God's global dream, saying "the earth will be full of the knowledge of the Lord as the waters cover the sea" [Isa. 11:9, Hab. 2:14, NRSV]. Similarly, the apostle John sees around the throne of God "a great multitude … from *every* nation, from *all* tribes and peoples and languages" (Rev. 7:9, NRSV). The pages of Scripture reveal a God who wants *every* individual, *every* family, *every* community, *every* town and village, *every* sphere of society, *every* people group and nation to experience the transforming redemption of the gospel. (2008, 49)

As the quotation above reveals, Revelation 7:9, with its image of multinational worship around the throne of God, shows us the fulfillment of God's original promise to Abraham that all peoples on earth would be blessed through him. "God's forever dream" for the nations comes to fruition. God does not exclude people from His invitation because of who their parents are, what political affiliations they may have, where they were born, or any of those ethnocentric labels that are trotted out divisively in the world today. The Revelation 7:9 vision of God's fully revealed kingdom shows us that "people from every nation will be molded into a new 'political' unit, a kingdom. All other patterns of organizing people into national, ethnic, and linguistic groups will have faded away. No longer will human 'blood' have any status in evaluating and organizing people; only the blood of the Lamb is relevant here—thus providing a new basis for human unity. The God who once created all human beings out of one human blood is now reuniting them on the basis of the one Blood of Jesus" (Mouw 2002, 80–81).

Missio Dei culminates in the gathering of every tribe, tongue, language, and nation around the throne of God.

What a picture! And it is reminiscent of another theme we have seen throughout this course: God's vision of *unity* within *diversity*. Only in the redeeming work of Christ can we find the perfect resolution and balance between these two typically opposite concepts. And within this unified diversity is a comforting fact regarding the future. The ultimate fulfillment of unity within diversity does not mean the annihilation of those things that made us diverse or different from one another here in the present day. Some people fear the future kingdom of God because they are unsettled by the idea that in life after death they might cease to exist as distinct individuals with personalities, giftings, and experiences that are unique to them. But this isn't the picture that the Bible paints of what the future holds. To begin with, the very description of "every tongue, tribe, people and language" indicates that there is continuity of diversity from the *now* to the *not yet* kingdom. Markers that distinguish us here on earth—such as tongue, tribe, and nation—have not ceased to exist in the "not yet" kingdom of God. There is continuity between this world and the next. This subject is treated in detail in books like Richard Mouw's *When the Kings Come Marching In* and N. T. Wright's *Surprised by Hope*, and there is not space here to go into the full details of their study. But from Mouw, we have this brief summation:

> As individuals we look forward to the day when we will be transformed, but it is difficult for us to imagine what that will be like: "Beloved, we are God's children now; it does not yet appear what we shall be" (1 John 3:2 [RSV]). We will not be completely annihilated, replaced by some totally different persons, but each of us will be transformed.

> It is difficult, then, for us to know what we will be like as heavenly beings. But we do know that God will work, in each of our cases, with what he originally created. We will be transformed. God will re-create us. A thread of personal identity reaches from the "now" to the "shall be." (2002, 41)

What Difference Does It Make?

How would your day-to-day interactions and choices be different if you lived in constant awareness that in God's kingdom only Jesus matters? that His blood creates equality and forgiveness for all who will receive Him? Is it possible to live a kingdom-of-God life *now*, even though some of it is *not yet*?

In addition to the comfort you may receive in knowing that the Bible teaches that in the future you will continue to be "you"—the originally intended, best, most perfect "you" that is possible—there is another reason it is important to realize the fact of continuity between the "now" and the "not yet." There is purpose to our present participation in God's mission and to our unique role and service to God right now that does somehow carry forward into eternity future. As N. T. Wright says, "The resurrection means that what you do in the present, in working hard for the gospel, is not wasted. It is not in vain. It will be completed, will have its fulfillment, in God's future" (2008, 162). Our work and participation in the mission of God will accomplish its purpose, whether or not we see it at the present time. Speaking of the new Jerusalem, John wrote in Revelation 21:26, "The glory and honor of the nations will be brought into it," thus indicating that there will be a redeeming and continuity of not only our individual selves in the future, but also of our collective lives and service.

Lesslie Newbigin wrote about Revelation in the closing portion of his book *A Walk Through the Bible*, which we read in chapter 1. He says the following regarding the vision of Revelation and the end of the story of the Bible:

> It is a vision that enables us to see the whole human story and each of our lives within that story as meaningful, and which therefore invites us through Jesus Christ to become responsible actors in history, not to seek to run away from the responsibilities and the agonies of human life in its public dimension. Each of us must be ready to take our share in all the struggles and the anguish of human history and yet with the confidence that what is committed to Christ will in the end find its place in his final kingdom. (SE p. 35)

And consider the following description from N. T. Wright:

> Every act of love, gratitude, and kindness; every work of art or music inspired by the love of God and delight in the beauty of his creation; every minute spent teaching a severely handicapped child to read or to walk; every act of care and nurture, of comfort and support …; and of course every prayer, all Spirit-led teaching, every deed that spreads the gospel, builds up the church, embraces and embodies holiness rather than corruption, and makes the name of Jesus honored in the world—all of this will find its way, through the resurrecting power of God, into the new creation that God will one day make. That is the logic of the mission of God. God's recreation of his wonderful world, which began with the resurrection of Jesus and continues mysteriously as God's people live in the risen Christ and in the power of his Spirit, means that what we do in Christ and by the

Spirit in the present is not wasted. It will last all the way into God's new world. In fact, it will be enhanced there....

The work we do in the present, then, gains its full significance from the eventual design in which it is meant to belong. (2008, 208–11)

We are blessed in order to be a blessing. And God will take even our smallest offerings to bless others, offerings that will be enhanced in the future so that "the glory and honor of the nations" will be brought into the new Jerusalem.

We began the journey of this course looking at something we must never forget: the story of the Bible is God's story. God is the main character, and His purpose is the main story of not only the Bible but all of history. It is from this perspective that we must continually remember to view the world, our lives, and our purpose. Otherwise, our perspective gets warped and self-centered, and we lose the opportunity to fulfill that for which we were made—to participate in God's story in the unique role God designed for each of us. One of the themes of this course has been to understand our own

Cathedral

It may be a new idea to you that your participation in God's work here on earth will somehow carry forward and be enhanced in the fully revealed kingdom of God in the future. The writer N. T. Wright elaborates with an analogy in the passage below:

The image I often use in trying to explain this strange but important idea is that of the stonemason working on part of a great cathedral. The architect already drew up the plans and passed on instructions to the team of masons as to which stones need carving in what way. The foreman distributes these tasks among the team. One shapes stones for a particular tower or turret; another carves the delicate pattern that breaks up the otherwise forbidding straight lines; another works on gargoyles or coats of arms; another is making statues of saints, martyrs, kings, or queens. They are vaguely aware that the others are getting on with their tasks, and they know, of course, that many other entire departments are busy about quite different tasks as well. When they're finished with their stones and their statues, they hand them over without necessarily knowing very much about where in the eventual building their work will find its home. They may not have seen the complete architect's drawing of the whole building with their bit identified in its proper place. They may not live, either, to see the completed building with their work at last where it belongs. But they trust the architect that the work they have done in following instructions will not be wasted. They are not, themselves, building the cathedral, but they are building *for* the cathedral, and when the cathedral is complete their work will be enhanced, ennobled, will mean much more than it could have meant as they were chiseling it and shaping it down in the stonemason's yard.

That image, of course, is itself incomplete since actually the cathedral is eventually built by the combination of all the artisans and craftspeople working together, whereas God's eventual kingdom will, as I have said, be a fresh gift of transformation and renewal from the Architect himself. But it is enough to indicate the way in which there is continuity as well as discontinuity between the present life, and the work we do in it, and the ultimate future life in which God has gathered all things together and transformed them, "making all things new" in Christ....

The work we do in the present, then, gains its full significance from the eventual design in which it is meant to belong. (2008, 209–11)

place of participation in the larger story of God's mission. Along the way you likely have quite naturally processed information with reference to yourself and your individual gifting and calling. But as we discussed in the last chapter on community, our individual participation in God's mission is not to be isolated. We are part of a much bigger picture. "We must begin to think of ourselves, not as isolated pools, but as contributing parts of the whole composite of God's will," writes author Bob Sjogren. "Each of our lives can release its potential into the mighty river of God's ultimate plan to reach all nations" (1992, 150).

What we see in the end of the Bible's story is a redeemed community. Revelation shows people who are dwelling in community with others and with God. Here at the end of the story we see a type of restatement of the opening pages of the Bible—life before the fall of man. There in Genesis, in the beginning, we see the creation of community and relationship. God understood the need we have for community and connection, so He made Adam a companion, Eve. And God was fully present with them in community. God and His children were in unbroken fellowship in the Garden of Eden before the Fall. And that same community and relationship are present at the end of the story. In the end, we will be in community. The nations will be there. And God will be there in our midst: "Now the dwelling of God is with men, and he will live with them" (Revelation 21:3). We will live and love in perfection with God at the center of all.

What cause for celebration—the end of all strife, the elimination of all division, and yet, the preservation of distinctiveness, diversity, and creativity—everyone united in worship of the Lamb of God! If you are like some people, the idea of eternal worship of God may not really get you very excited. It may call up pictures of sitting on a cloud with a harp, singing praise songs all day long. But those ideas are full of misconceptions both of what we know about life in the future kingdom of God and what we know about true worship—either in the present or in the future fully revealed kingdom of God. As N. T. Wright says simply, "Worship means, literally, acknowledging the *worth* of something or someone. It means recognizing and saying that something or someone is *worthy* of praise. It means celebrating the worth of someone or something far superior to oneself" (2006, 144).

Our lives here and now on earth should be an expression of worship, just as they will be in the fulfilled kingdom of God in the future. There are many ways for worship to occur, and in truth, all

What Difference Does It Make?

- What difference does it make to you that your participation in the mission of God here and now will accomplish its purpose, whether or not you see it at the present time? Does that inspire you to seek and serve God more? Why or why not?

- Do you view all moments of your life as opportunities to worship God, or do you think of worship as something that happens at certain times of the week in certain corporate settings? Why or why not? How do your views on worship affect your daily life? your enthusiasm for God and His mission?

our moments are opportunities to worship God, whether through participation in His work, fellowship in community, praise and singing, or any of the myriad other ways we can express to God our recognition of who He is. We sometimes make "worship" more complicated than it has to be. It is, quite simply, living our lives in participation with God on His mission, and constantly recognizing and responding to the fact that God is worthy of praise, obedience, and loyalty. It is a thousand ways of living here and now, foreshadowing a time when "a great multitude that no one could count, from every nation, tribe, people and language, standing before the throne and in front of the Lamb … cried out in a loud voice: 'Salvation belongs to our God, who sits on the throne, and to the Lamb' " (Revelation 7:9–10).

The story of the mission of God has a beginning and an end. And the fullness and meaning of the whole story is found in Him. "I am the Alpha and the Omega, the First and the Last, the Beginning and the End" (Revelation 22:13). Author Christopher Wright sums up the Bible's end like this:

> Purged by judgment and the destruction of all wickedness and evil, human and satanic, the nations of the world will join in the praise of God for his salvation (Rev. 7:9–10). They will bring all the wealth of their historical achievements into the city of God, as Isaiah had said they would (Rev. 21:24, 26), the city that now embraces the full extent of the whole new creation. And the river and tree of life, from which humanity had been barred in the earliest chapters of the Bible's grand narrative, will, in its final chapter, provide the healing of the nations … (Rev. 22:2). The curse will be gone from the whole of creation (Rev. 22:3). The earth will be filled with the glory of God and all the nations of humanity will walk in his light (Rev. 21:24).

> Such is the glorious climax of the Bible's grand narrative. Such is the triumph of the mission of God. (2006, 530)

Isn't it wonderful to know that God's mission will be completed, and in such a perfect way? When we participate with God in what He is doing—joining missio Dei—our lives and work have purpose. The question is, What are you waiting for? How will you respond to the invitation God gives to participate in His mission? This course has helped you prepare for journeying more deeply with God by providing different tools in each unit—the compass of the Bible; some binoculars focused on a global cultural view; a travelogue of stories from the history of those who've been down this road before;

How will you respond to the invitation God gives to participate in His mission?

and a study of essential practices that, like a backpack, allows you to take along the things you need for your journey with God. But taking the journey is something that only you can do. May your road be filled with adventure and the presence of God. Bon voyage!

൞

NOTES

1. China Daily.com. 2008. http://www.chinadaily.com.cn/olympics/2008-08/08/content_6918689.htm (accessed December 12, 2008).
2. Ibid.

References

Student Edition Epigraphs

INTRODUCTION

Brownson, James V., Inagrace T. Dietterich, Barry A. Harvey, and Charles C. West. 2003. *StormFront: The good news of God*. The Gospel and Our Culture Series. Grand Rapids, MI: Wm. B. Eerdmans, p. 2.

Sweet, Leonard I. 2007. *The gospel according to Starbucks: Living with a grande passion*. Colorado Springs, CO: WaterBrook Press, p. 21.

CHAPTER 1

Miller, Mark. 2003. *Experiential storytelling: (Re)discovering narrative to communicate God's message*. Grand Rapids, MI: Zondervan, p. 29.

CHAPTER 2

Lewis, C. S. 1996. *Mere Christianity*. New York: Simon & Schuster, p. 176.

CHAPTER 3

Brownson, James V., Inagrace T. Dietterich, Barry A. Harvey, and Charles C. West. 2003. *StormFront: The good news of God*. The Gospel and Our Culture Series. Grand Rapids, MI: Wm. B. Eerdmans, p. 34.

CHAPTER 4

Newbigin, Lesslie. 2005. *A walk through the Bible*. Vancouver, BC: Regent College Publishing, p. 53.

CHAPTER 5

Lewis, C. S. 1996. *Mere Christianity*. New York: Simon & Schuster, p. 51.

CHAPTER 7

Morain, Genelle. n.d. *Toward internationalism*. Quoted in Craig Storti, *Figuring foreigners out: A practical guide* (Boston: Intercultural Press, 1999), p. 10.

CHAPTER 8

Elmer, Duane. 2006. *Cross-cultural servanthood: Serving the world in Christlike humility*. Downers Grove, IL: InterVarsity Press, p. 19.

Manning, Brennan. 1996. *The signature of Jesus: On the pages of our lives*. Sisters, OR: Multnomah, pp. 67–68.

CHAPTER 9

Frost, Michael, and Alan Hirsch. 2003. *The shaping of things to come: Innovation and mission for the 21st-century church.* Peabody, MA: Hendrickson, p. 35.

CHAPTER 10

Russinger, Greg. 2005. A missional unfamiliarity. In *Practitioners: Voices within the emerging church,* ed. Greg Russinger and Alex Field, 23–47. Ventura, CA: Regal Books, p. 39.

CHAPTER 11

Sharman, Scott. Did you happen to mention what line of lubricants Jesus would use? Open conversation blog (posted October 11, 2006). http://www.open conversation.com/.

CHAPTER 12

Kipling, Rudyard. Excerpt from 1926 poem "We and They." http://www .kipling.org.uk/poems_wethey.htm.

CHAPTER 14

Wright, Christopher J. H. 2006. *The mission of God: Unlocking the Bible's grand narrative.* Downers Grove, IL: InterVarsity Press, p. 62.

CHAPTER 15

Irvin, Dale T., and Scott W. Sunquist. 2001. *History of the world Christian movement.* Vol. 1, *Earliest Christianity to 1453.* Maryknoll, NY: Orbis Books, pp. 9, 10, 47.

CHAPTER 16

Bosch, David J. 1991. *Transforming mission: Paradigm shifts in theology of mission.* American Society of Missiology Series, no. 16. Maryknoll, NY: Orbis Books, pp. 190–91.

CHAPTER 17

Bosch, David J. 1991. *Transforming mission: Paradigm shifts in theology of mission.* American Society of Missiology Series, no. 16. Maryknoll, NY: Orbis Books, p. 230.

Newbigin, Lesslie. 1986. *Foolishness to the Greeks: The gospel and Western culture.* Geneva: World Council of Churches, 100. Quoted in Bosch 1991, p. 222.

CHAPTER 18

Thomas, Norman E., ed. 1995. *Classic texts in mission and world Christianity.* American Society of Missiology Series, no. 20. Maryknoll, NY: Orbis Books, p. 32.

CHAPTER 19

Bosch, David J. 1991. *Transforming mission: Paradigm shifts in theology of mission.* American Society of Missiology Series, no. 16. Maryknoll, NY: Orbis Books, p. 268.

Neill, Stephen. 1986. *A history of Christian missions*. 2nd ed. Rev. by Owen Chadwick. New York: Penguin Books, p. 208.

Chapter 20

Walls, Andrew F. 1999. The mission of the church today in the light of global history. In *Mission at the dawn of the 21st century: A vision for the church*, ed. Paul Varo Martinson, 384–88. Minneapolis, MN: Kirk House, p. 385.

Chapter 21

Hill, Susan D. 2008. *Closer than your skin: Unwrapping the mystery of intimacy with God*. Colorado Springs, CO: WaterBrook Press, p. 132.

Chapter 22

McClung, Floyd. 2008. *You see bones, I see an army: Changing the way we do church*. Seattle, WA: YWAM Publishing, p. 191.

McManus, Erwin Raphael. 2005. *The barbarian way: Unleash the untamed faith within*. Nashville, TN: Thomas Nelson, p. 64.

Chapter 23

Sweet, Leonard I. 2007. *The gospel according to Starbucks: Living with a grande passion*. Colorado Springs, CO: WaterBrook Press, p. 20.

Chapter 24

McManus, Erwin Raphael. 2006. *Soul cravings: An exploration of the human spirit*. Nashville, TN: Thomas Nelson, in Intimacy entry 14.

Waggoner, Berten. 2004. Foreword to *Buck-naked faith: A brutally honest look at Christianity* by Eric Sandras. Colorado Springs, CO: NavPress, p. 10.

Chapter 25

Graybeal Lynda L., and Julia L. Roller. 2007. *Living the mission: A spiritual formation guide*. New York: HarperOne, xii. Adapted from an essay in *The Renovaré spiritual formation Bible*, essay ed. Gayle Beebe, Richard J. Foster, Lynda L. Graybeal, Thomas C. Oden, and Dallas Willard. New York: HarperCollins.

Music:

Scholtes, Peter. 1966. They'll know we are Christians by our love. In *Amazing grace: 366 inspiring hymn stories for daily devotions*, by Kenneth W. Osbeck. Grand Rapids, MI: Kregel Publications, p. 62.

Chapter 26

Wright, Christopher J. H. 2006. *The mission of God: Unlocking the Bible's grand narrative*. Downers Grove, IL: InterVarsity Press, p. 478.

Works Cited

Arthur, Kay. 1992. *Lord, I want to know you: A devotional study on the names of God.* Colorado Springs, CO: WaterBrook Press.

Baker, F. Russell. 2004. Roots of our collective sin. Sermon presented at First Congregational United Church of Christ, May 30, in Benton Harbor, MI.

Bartholomew, Craig G., and Michael W. Goheen. 2004. *The drama of Scripture: Finding our place in the biblical story.* Grand Rapids, MI: Baker Academic.

Beaver, R. Pierce. 1999. The history of mission strategy. In Winter and Hawthorne 1999a, 241–52.

Bell, Rob. 2005a. *Nooma: Trees 003.* DVD. Grand Rapids, MI: Zondervan.

———. 2005b. *Velvet Elvis: Repainting the Christian faith.* Grand Rapids, MI: Zondervan.

Blackaby, Henry T., and Richard Blackaby. 2002. *Hearing God's voice.* Nashville, TN: B&H Publishing.

Blackaby, Henry T., and Claude V. King. 1994. *Experiencing God: How to live the full adventure of knowing and doing the will of God.* Nashville, TN: Broadman & Holman.

Blincoe, Robert A. 2003. As the waters cover the sea: His glory expands to the nations. In Crossman 2003, 99–111.

Blue, Ken. 1987. *Authority to heal.* Downers Grove, IL: InterVarsity Press. Quoted in Winter and Hawthorne 1999a, 72.

Bonhoeffer, Dietrich. 1954. *Life together.* Trans. John W. Doberstein. New York: HarperSanFrancisco. Orig. pub. as *Gemeinsames Leben* (Germany).

Bosch, David J. 1991. *Transforming mission: Paradigm shifts in theology of mission.* American Society of Missiology Series, no. 16. Maryknoll, NY: Orbis Books.

Bria, Ion. 1980. *Martyria/mission: The witness of the Orthodox churches today.* Geneva: World Council of Churches, 8–10. Quoted in Bosch 1991, 207–8.

Brownson, James V., Inagrace T. Dietterich, Barry A. Harvey, and Charles C. West. 2003. *StormFront: The good news of God.* The Gospel and Our Culture Series. Grand Rapids, MI: Wm. B. Eerdmans.

Cashin, David. 2007. Perspectives course. Lecture presented at Grace Church, January 23, in Tuscaloosa, AL.

Chaney, Charles L. 1976. *The birth of missions in America.* Pasadena, CA: William Carey Library, 174. Quoted in Bosch 1991, 279.

Claiborne, Shane, and Chris Haw. 2008. *Jesus for president: Politics for ordinary radicals.* Grand Rapids, MI: Zondervan.

Clairmont, Patsy. 1999. *God uses cracked pots.* Wheaton, IL: Tyndale House.

Clark, Chap, and Kara E. Powell. 2007. *Deep justice in a broken world: Helping your kids serve others and right the wrongs around them.* Grand Rapids, MI: Zondervan.

Cornelius, David. 1999. A historical survey of African Americans in world missions. In Winter and Hawthorne 1999a, 287–92.

Cornish, Rick. 2005. *5 minute church historian: Maximum truth in minimum time.* Colorado Springs, CO: NavPress.

Cron, Ian Morgan. 2006. *Chasing Francis: A pilgrim's tale.* Colorado Springs, CO: NavPress.

Crossman, Meg, ed. 2003. *Worldwide perspectives: Biblical, historical, strategic, and cultural dimensions of God's plan for the nations.* Seattle, WA: YWAM Publishing.

David, Simon P. 1987. Food offered to idols. In Hiebert and Hiebert 1987, 38–39.

Dayton, Edward R. 1990. The task at hand: World evangelization. Quoted in Crossman 2003, 161–67.

Durback, Robert, ed. 1997. *Seeds of hope: A Henri Nouwen reader.* 2nd ed. New York: Image Books.

Egeler, Daniel. 2000. Honor your mother and father. Case study presented at the ACSI Pre-Field Orientation, June, Colorado Christian University, in Denver, CO.

Eldredge, John. 2007. *Desire: The journey we must take to find the life God offers.* Nashville, TN: Thomas Nelson.

———. 2008. *Walking with God.* Nashville, TN: Thomas Nelson.

Elmer, Duane. 2002. *Cross-cultural connections: Stepping out and fitting in around the world.* Downers Grove, IL: InterVarsity Press.

———. 2006. *Cross-cultural servanthood: Serving the world in Christlike humility.* Downers Grove, IL: InterVarsity Press.

Erdmann, Carl. 1977. *The origin of the idea of crusade.* Princeton: Princeton University Press, 10. Quoted in Bosch 1991, 224.

Escobar, Samuel. 2003. *The new global mission: The gospel from everywhere to everyone.* Christian Doctrine in Global Perspective series. Downers Grove, IL: InterVarsity Press.

Frost, Michael. 2006. *Exiles: Living missionally in a post-Christian culture.* Peabody, MA: Hendrickson.

Frost, Michael, and Alan Hirsch. 2003. *The shaping of things to come: Innovation and mission for the 21st-century church.* Peabody, MA: Hendrickson.

Funk, Wilfred. 1950. *Word origins and their romantic stories.* New York: Wilfred Funk.

Go, Teg Chin. 1987. To bribe or not to bribe? In Hiebert and Hiebert 1987, 136–37.

Graybeal, Lynda L., and Julia L. Roller. 2007. *Living the mission: A spiritual formation guide.* New York: HarperOne.

Guder, Darrell L., ed. 1998. *Missional church: A vision for the sending of the church in North America,* ed. Darrell L. Guder, 77–109. The Gospel and Our Culture Series. Grand Rapids, MI: Wm. B. Eerdmans.

Hamilton, David Joel. 2008. The New Testament basis for the discipling of nations. In *His kingdom come,* ed. Jim Stier, Richlyn Poor, and Lisa Orvis, 47–76. Seattle, WA: YWAM Publishing.

Hawthorne, Steven C. 1999. The story of his glory. In Winter and Hawthorne 1999a, 34–48.

Henry, Patrick G. 1987. Monastic mission: The monastic tradition as source for unity and renewal today. *The Ecumenical Review* 39:279–80. Quoted in Bosch 1991, 232–33.

Heuertz, Christopher L. 2008. *Simple spirituality: Learning to see God in a broken world*. Downers Grove, IL: IVP Books.

Hiebert, Paul G. 1999. Cultural differences and the communication of the gospel. In Winter and Hawthorne 1999a, 373–83.

Hiebert, Paul G., and Frances R. Hiebert. 1987. *Case studies in missions*. Grand Rapids, MI: Baker Book House.

Hill, Patricia R. 1985. *The world their household: The American woman's foreign mission movement and cultural transformation, 1870–1920*. Ann Arbor: University of Michigan Press, 3. Quoted in Robert 1996, 129.

Hill, Susan D. 2008. *Closer than your skin: Unwrapping the mystery of intimacy with God*. Colorado Springs, CO: WaterBrook Press.

Houweling, Henk, and Jan G. Siccama. 1988. *Studies of war*. With J. Faber and J. B. Kuné. Boston: Martinus Nijhoff.

Howard, David M. 1979. *Student power in world missions*. 2nd ed. Downers Grove, IL: InterVarsity Press. Quoted in Winter and Hawthorne 1999a, 277–86.

Irvin, Dale T., and Scott W. Sunquist. 2001. *History of the world Christian movement*. Vol. 1, *Earliest Christianity to 1453*. Maryknoll, NY: Orbis Books.

Jenkins, Philip. 2002. *The next Christendom: The coming of global Christianity*. New York: Oxford University Press.

Kaiser, Walter C., Jr. 1999. Israel's missionary call. In Winter and Hawthorne 1999a, 10–16.

Kinnaman, David, and Gabe Lyons. 2007. *Unchristian: What a new generation really thinks about Christianity ... and why it matters*. Grand Rapids, MI: Baker Books.

Klingensmith, Leslie A. 2007. Understanding ... against the odds. Sermon presented at St. Matthew Presbyterian Church, May 27, in Silver Spring, MD.

Kraft, Charles H. 1996. *Anthropology for Christian witness*. Maryknoll, NY: Orbis Books.

———. 1998. Culture, worldview and contextualization. In Winter and Hawthorne 1999a, 384–91.

———. 2000. Two kingdoms in conflict. In *Behind enemy lines: An advanced guide to spiritual warfare*, ed. Charles H. Kraft with Mark White, 17–30. Eugene, OR: Wipf and Stock.

Kraft, Marguerite, and Meg Crossman. 1996. Women in mission. In *Worldwide perspectives*, ed. Meg Crossman. Pasadena, CA: William Carey Library. Quoted in Winter and Hawthorne 1999a, 269–73.

Ladd, George Eldon. 1959. *The gospel of the kingdom: Scriptural studies in the kingdom of God*. London, England: Paternoster Press. http://www.gospelpedlar.com/articles/Last%20Things/GK/gospel_of_the_kingdom.html.

Lewis, C. S. 1996. *Mere Christianity*. Rev. ed. New York: Touchstone. (Rev. ed. orig. pub. 1952.)

Lucado, Max. 1987. *God came near: Chronicles of the Christ*. Portland, OR: Multnomah Press.

Manning, Brennan. 1996. *The signature of Jesus: On the pages of our lives*. Sisters, OR: Multnomah.

———. 2005. *The importance of being foolish: How to think like Jesus*. New York: HarperCollins.

Manning, Brennan, and Jim Hancock. 2003. *Posers, fakers, and wannabes: Unmasking the real you*. Colorado Springs, CO: NavPress.

McClung, Floyd. 2008. *You see bones, I see an army: Changing the way we do church*. Seattle, WA: YWAM Publishing.

McKinley, Rick. 2006. *This beautiful mess: Practicing the presence of the kingdom of God*. Sisters, OR: Multnomah.

McLaren, Brian D. 2004. *A generous orthodoxy: Why I am a missional, evangelical, post/Protestant, liberal/conservative, mystical/poetic, biblical, charismatic/contemplative, Fundamentalist/Calvinist, Anabaptist/Anglican, Methodist, Catholic, green, incarnational, depressed-yet-hopeful, emergent, unfinished Christian*. Grand Rapids, MI: Zondervan.

McLaren, Brian D., and Tony Campolo. 2003. *Adventures in missing the point: How the culture-controlled church neutered the gospel*. Grand Rapids, MI: Zondervan.

McManus, Erwin Raphael. 2002. *Chasing daylight: Dare to live a life of adventure*. Nashville, TN: Thomas Nelson.

———. 2005. *The barbarian way: Unleash the untamed faith within*. Nashville, TN: Thomas Nelson.

———. 2006. *Soul cravings: An exploration of the human spirit*. Nashville, TN: Thomas Nelson.

Merton, Thomas. 1962. *New seeds of contemplation*. New York: New Directions Books.

Moffett, Samuel H. 1987. Early Asian Christian approaches to non-Christian cultures. *Missiology* 15:484. Quoted in Bosch 1991, 204.

Mouw, Richard J. 2002. *When the kings come marching in: Isaiah and the new Jerusalem*. Rev. ed. Grand Rapids, MI: Wm. B. Eerdmans.

Neill, Stephen. 1986. *A history of Christian missions*. 2nd ed. Rev. by Owen Chadwick. New York: Penguin Books.

Newbigin, Lesslie. 2005. *A walk through the Bible*. Vancouver, BC: Regent College Publishing.

Nouwen, Henri J. M. 1994. *Here and now: Living in the Spirit*. New York: Crossroad. Quoted in Durback 1997, 47, 90.

Nussbaum, Stan. 2005. *A reader's guide to "Transforming mission."* American Society of Missiology Series, no. 37. Maryknoll, NY: Orbis Books.

Ortberg, John. 2005. *God is closer than you think*. Grand Rapids, MI: Zondervan.

Ortberg, Nancy. 2008. *Looking for God: An unexpected journey through tattoos, tofu, and pronouns.* Carol Stream, IL: Tyndale House.

Paulson, Elliot. 2003. Between a rock and a hard place. *Mission Frontiers* (U.S. Center for World Mission) September–October: 14–16.

Pearcey, Nancy. 2004. *Total truth: Liberating Christianity from its cultural captivity.* Wheaton, IL: Crossway Books.

Pfürtner, Stephan. 1984. Die Paradigmen von Thomas und Luther. Bedeutet Luthers Rechtfertigungsbotschaft einen Paradigmenwechsel? In *Theologie— wohin? Auf dem Weg zu einem neuen Paradigma*, ed. Hans Küng and David Tracy, 181–82. Zürich-Cologne: Benziger Verlag. E. T. 1989. *Paradigm change in theology.* New York: Crossroad. Quoted in Bosch 1991, 242.

Pierson, Paul. 1999. A history of transformation. In Winter and Hawthorne 1999a, 262–68.

Rasmus, Rudy. 2007. *Touch: Pressing against the wounds of a broken world.* Nashville, TN: Thomas Nelson.

Richardson, Don. 1981. *Eternity in their hearts.* Ventura, CA: Regal Books.

Robert, Dana L. 1996. *American women in mission: A social history of their thought and practice.* Macon, GA: Mercer University Press.

Room, Adrian. 1986. *Dictionary of changes in meaning.* New York: Routledge & Kegan Paul.

Rosenkranz, Gerhard. 1977. *Die christliche mission: Geschichte und theologie.* Munich: Chr. Kaiser Verlag, 62–63. Quoted in Bosch 1991, 224.

Ruis, David. 2005. Missionality as relationship with God. In *Practitioners: Voices within the emerging church*, ed. Greg Russinger and Alex Field, 122–45. Ventura, CA: Regal Books.

Sandras, Eric. 2004. *Buck-naked faith: A brutally honest look at Christianity.* Colorado Springs, CO: NavPress.

Shenk, Wilbert R. 1999. *Changing frontiers of mission.* American Society of Missiology Series, no. 28. Maryknoll, NY: Orbis Books.

Sjogren, Bob. 1992. *Unveiled at last.* Seattle, WA: YWAM Publishing.

Smith, David. 1996. What hope after Babel? Diversity and community in Genesis 11:1–9, Exodus 1:1–14, Zephaniah 3:1–13 and Acts 2:1–13. *Horizons in Biblical Theology* 18, no. 2:169–91.

Stanley, Charles. 1985. *How to listen to God.* Nashville, TN: Thomas Nelson.

Stott, John R. W. 1979. The living God is a missionary God. In *You can tell the world*, ed. James E. Berney. Downers Grove, IL: InterVarsity Press. Quoted in Winter and Hawthorne 1999a, 3–9.

Sweet, Leonard I. 2007. *The gospel according to Starbucks: Living with a grande passion.* Colorado Springs, CO: WaterBrook Press.

Tannenbaum, Edward R., ed. 1973. *A history of world civilizations.* New York: John Wiley & Sons.

Thiessen, Henry C. 1979. *Lectures in systematic theology.* Rev. by Vernon D. Doerksen. Grand Rapids, MI: Wm. B. Eerdmans. (Orig. pub. 1949.)

Thomas, Norman E., ed. 1995. *Classic texts in mission and world Christianity*. American Society of Missiology Series, no. 20. Maryknoll, NY: Orbis Books.

Tucker, Ruth A. 2004. *From Jerusalem to Irian Jaya: A biographical history of Christian missions*. 2nd ed. Grand Rapids, MI: Zondervan.

Wachowski, Andy, and Larry Wachowski. 1999. *The matrix*. DVD. Directed by Andy Wachowski and Larry Wachowski. Burbank, CA: Warner Home Video.

Walls, Andrew F. 1996. *The missionary movement in Christian history: Studies in the transmission of faith*. Maryknoll, NY: Orbis Books.

———. 1999. The mission of the church today in the light of global history. In *Mission at the dawn of the 21st century: A vision for the church*, ed. Paul Varo Martinson, 384–88. Minneapolis, MN: Kirk House.

Walsh, Fran, Philippa Boyens, and Peter Jackson. 2001. *The fellowship of the ring*. DVD. Directed by Peter Jackson. New York: New Line Cinemas.

Ward, Roy Bowen. 1958. Ekklesia: A word study. *Restoration Quarterly* 2, no. 4:164–79.

Willard, Dallas. 1998. *The divine conspiracy: Rediscovering our hidden life in God*. New York: HarperCollins.

———. 1999. *Hearing God: Developing a conversational relationship with God*. Downers Grove, IL: InterVarsity Press.

Winter, Ralph D. 1974. The highest priority: Cross-cultural evangelism. Paper sent to congress participants prior to Lausanne 1: The International Congress on World Evangelization in Lausanne, Switzerland. Quoted in Winter and Hawthorne 1999a, 339–53.

———. 1999a. Four men, three eras, two transitions: Modern missions. In Winter and Hawthorne 1999a, 253–61.

———. 1999b. The kingdom strikes back: Ten epochs of redemptive history. In Winter and Hawthorne 1999a, 195–213.

Winter, Ralph D., and David A. Fraser. 1999. World mission survey. In Winter and Hawthorne 1999a, 354–68.

Winter, Ralph D., and Steven C. Hawthorne, eds. 1999a. *Perspectives on the world Christian movement: A reader*. 3rd ed. Pasadena, CA: William Carey Library.

Winter, Ralph D., and Steven C. Hawthorne, eds. 1999b. *Perspectives on the world Christian movement: The notebook*. Pasadena, CA: William Carey Library.

Wright, Christopher J. H. 2006. *The mission of God: Unlocking the Bible's grand narrative*. Downers Grove, IL: InterVarsity Press.

Wright, N. T. 2006. *Simply Christian: Why Christianity makes sense*. New York: HarperCollins.

———. 2008. *Surprised by hope: Rethinking heaven, the resurrection, and the mission of the church*. New York: HarperOne.

Index

locus of, 230
methods of, 189, 193
in Middle Ages, 197–207
military force in, 204–5
modes of, 197–98
by monks, 220, 224
in nineteenth century, 213–18, 219–27
penetration of, 224–25
Protestant, 213–14, 220
during Reformation, 211–14
second-century location of, 190
by slaves, 205
tribal, 229
in twentieth century, 213–18, 227–31
unreached areas, 225, 227, 229
mission of God, xiv, 37–47, 162, 169, 234, 299. *See also*
purpose of God
all-encompassing nature of, 140, 300
answer to evil, 50
barriers to, 205–6
Christ as center of, 239–40
community and, 279–88
continuity throughout history, 205, 236–37
culmination of, 299–302, 305
focus on, 234
God's direction of, 174
for good of world, 99
individual place/role in, 56, 244
invitation to join in, xv, xvi, 3, 50, 63, 171, 224,
236–37, 243
to nations, 54, 60
participation in. *See* participation in mission of God
relationship and, 47
revelation of, 51
use of humans to accomplish, 174, 219, 237
mission societies, 223–24
missional living, 89–90, 95–96, 262. *See also* participation in mission of God
adaptation to other cultures, 111
alignment with God's purpose, 166
basis of, 99
Christ's example for, 131–33, 161, 163
community and, 280–84
cross-cultural relationships, 146–51
cultural differences and, 118
cultural understanding for, 106, 165
focus on God, 124
Holy Spirit and, 173
how to practice, 247
physical proximity and, 146, 163, 166
preparation for, 142–43, 163
sharing blessings in, 93–94
using God's viewpoint, 103
missionaries, 53
cultural imposition by, 124, 242

early, 180–81
Jonah, 55
massacres of, 215
Protestant, 222–23
mistakes, 259
misunderstandings, 120–21, 146, 161, 165
modern, 221
monasticism, 192, 220, 224, 238
Celtic, 194, 200
monastic communities, 22, 192, 237
monastic orders, 202, 215
Protestant Reformation and, 212
witness and, 195, 200–201
Mongolia, 202
Moravians, 214
Moscow, 220
Moses, 12, 14, 85, 172
Mott, John R., 225
Mouw, Richard J., 235, 241–42, 299, 301
murder, 10, 12, 15
Muslims, 147–51. *See also* Islam

N

Naomi, 42
Napoleon, 220
nationalism, 227, 229
nations, 50, 137, 280, 299
heart of God for, 300
holy, 19
ingathering of, 55
of Israel. *See* Israel
kingdom of God and, 66
original, 11
Native Americans, 213
nature, 221, 228
Nazareth Manifesto, 86
Nebuchadnezzar, 55
Nehemiah, 19
Neill, Stephen, 178, 180, 182, 184, 239
on Age of Discovery, 214
on church conflicts, 198
on conversions, 189, 200
on Crusades, 205
on feudal church, 203
on Industrial Revolution, 220–21
on language unity, 202–3
on mission, 211
on mission and Western power, 227
on mission methods, 215
on mission work approaches, 217
on monasticism, 220
on second-century Christianity, 190
on travel, 219
on Xavier, 216
Nestorian Christians, 193

Willard, Dallas, 65, 69–70, 71, 250
Winter, Ralph D., 139, 140, 142, 165, 210, 222
    on European power, 227
    on Taylor, 224, 225
    on twentieth-century mission, 229
    on women in mission, 224
witness, 73, 87, 293–94
    by all believers, 180, 183, 211
    early Christian, 179
    individual, 224
    by martyrs, 195
    by monks, 195, 200–201
    by worshipping community, 192
women, 132, 142, 224
work of God, xvi, 63
    achieving His purpose, 172
    in all circumstances, 198, 227, 239
    human initiative and, 173
    means and methods, 98, 169
    through humans, 98
    throughout history, 233
world, 108, 210
World Missionary Conference (Edinburgh), 225, 230
worldview, 103, 106, 142, 160, 220, 303
    differences in, 107
    Hellenistic, 189
    historical changes in, 228
worship, 18, 46, 171, 263, 304
    according to law, 21–22
    centers of, 193, 195
    communities, 210, 287
    formalized practices, 191, 192
    freedom of, 199
    Jewish, 20, 124
    lives as expression of, 304–5
    misplaced, 59
    multinational, 298–300
    by nations, 54–55
    of Roman emperor, 189
    uniform, 238
    unity in, 202–4, 280
Wright, Christopher J. H., xiv, 50–51, 55, 300, 305
Wright, N. T., 56, 68, 69, 302, 303, 304
Wycliffe, John, 207, 210

X
Xavier, Francis, 216

Y
Yao Ming, 297
Youderian, Roger, 229

Z
Zechariah, 26
Ziegenbalg, Bartholomew, 213

Credits

"Culture, Worldview and Contextualization" by Charles H. Kraft, in *Perspectives on the World Christian Movement: A Reader*, ed. Ralph D. Winter and Steven C. Hawthorne (3rd ed., 1999), William Carey Library, 1605 E. Elizabeth St., Pasadena, CA, 91104, www.missionbooks.org. Used by permission.

"Two Kingdoms in Conflict" by Charles H. Kraft, in *Behind Enemy Lines: An Advanced Guide to Spiritual Warfare.* ©1994 by Charles H. Kraft and Mark White. Reprinted by permission of Wipf and Stock Publishers. www.wipfandstock.com.

God Came Near: Chronicles of the Christ (originally published by Multnomah Press). Reprinted by permission. *God Came Near: Chronicles of the Christ*, Max Lucado, 1987, Thomas Nelson Inc., Nashville, Tennessee. All rights reserved.

"The Parable of the Race" from *Adventures in Missing the Point: How the Culture-Controlled Church Neutered the Gospel* by Brian D. McLaren and Tony Campolo (Grand Rapids, MI: Zondervan, 2003). Used by permission.

A History of Christian Missions by Stephen Neill, revised by Owen Chadwick (New York: Penguin Books, 2nd ed., 1986), pp. 21–22, 24–25, 27, 39, 41, 52–57, 68, 73–74, 81, 93, 95, 98, 120, 127, 133, 143–44, 147–48, 173, 189, 207–10, 336–37, 414, 417, 419. Copyright © Stephen Neill, 1964. Revisions © Owen Chadwick, 1986. Reproduced by permission of Penguin Books Ltd.

A Reader's Guide to "Transforming Mission" by Stan Nussbaum, American Society of Missiology Series, no. 37 (Maryknoll, NY: Orbis Books, 2005). Used by permission.

Taken from *Looking for God: An Unexpected Journey through Tattoos, Tofu, and Pronouns* by Nancy Ortberg. Copyright © by Nancy Ortberg. Used by permission of Tyndale House Publishers, Inc. All rights reserved.

"Between a Rock and a Hard Place" by Elliot Paulson, *Mission Frontiers* (U.S. Center for World Mission) September–October 2003. Used by permission.

"They'll Know We Are Christians" by Peter Scholtes. © 1966 FEL. Assigned 1991 to The Lorenz Corporation. All rights reserved. International copyright secured. Used by permission.

"The New Macedonia: A Revolutionary New Era in Mission Begins" by Ralph D. Winter, in *Perspectives on the World Christian Movement: A Reader*, ed. Ralph D. Winter and Steven C. Hawthorne (3rd ed., 1999), William Carey Library, 1605 E. Elizabeth St., Pasadena, CA, 91104, www.missionbooks.org. Used by permission.